THE NEW CAMBRIDGE SHAKESPEARE

From the publication of the first volumes in 1984 the General Editor of the New Cambridge Shakespeare was Philip Brockbank and the Associate General Editors were Brian Gibbons and Robin Hood. From 1990 to 1994 the General Editor was Brian Gibbons and the Associate General Editors were A. R. Braunmuller and Robin Hood.

KING EDWARD III

Edward III is a major new addition to the Shakespearean canon. Presenting this fully annotated, modern-spelling text of *Edward III*, Giorgio Melchiori does not claim that Shakespeare is the sole author, but author of a significant part of the play, the extent of which is discussed in detail.

The Introduction explores the historical background and the genesis of the play in the context of contemporary theatrical practice and of Shakespeare's own early cycle of history plays. It stresses the original ideological stance and the theatrical qualities of the play as a whole. The Commentary examines in depth the play's linguistic and poetical features, while an extensive appendix on the use of sources explains the stages of its composition.

THE NEW CAMBRIDGE SHAKESPEARE

All's Well That Ends Well, edited by Russell Fraser
Antony and Cleopatra, edited by David Bevington
The Comedy of Errors, edited by T. S. Dorsch
Hamlet, edited by Philip Edwards
Julius Caesar, edited by Marvin Spevack
King Edward III, edited by Giorgio Melchiori
The First Part of King Henry IV, edited by Herbert and Judith Weil
The Second Part of King Henry IV, edited by Giorgio Melchiori
King Henry V, edited by Andrew Gurr
The First Part of King Henry VI, edited by Michael Hattaway
The Second Part of King Henry VI, edited by Michael Hattaway
The Third Part of King Henry VI, edited by Michael Hattaway
King Henry VIII, edited by John Margeson
King John, edited by L. A. Beaurline
King Lear, edited by Jay L. Halio
King Richard II, edited by Andrew Gurr
Macbeth, edited by A. R. Braunmuller
Measure for Measure, edited by Brian Gibbons
The Merchant of Venice, edited by M. M. Mahood
The Merry Wives of Windsor, edited by David Crane
A Midsummer Night's Dream, edited by R. A. Foakes
Much Ado About Nothing, edited by F. H. Mares
Othello, edited by Norman Sanders
Pericles, edited by Doreen DelVecchio and Antony Hammond
The Poems, edited by John Roe
Romeo and Juliet, edited by G. Blakemore Evans
The Sonnets, edited by G. Blakemore Evans
The Taming of the Shrew, edited by Ann Thompson
Titus Andronicus, edited by Alan Hughes
Twelfth Night, edited by Elizabeth Story Donno
The Two Gentlemen of Verona, edited by Kurt Schlueter

THE EARLY QUARTOS

The First Quarto of King Lear, edited by Jay L. Halio
The First Quarto of King Richard III, edited by Peter Davison
The First Quarto of Harnlet, edited by Kathleen O. Irace

KING EDWARD III

Edited by
GIORGIO MELCHIORI
Professor Emeritus of English Literature, Università Roma Tre

PUBLISHED BY THE PRESS SYNDICATE OF THE UNIVERSITY OF CAMBRIDGE
The Pitt Building, Trumpington Street, Cambridge CB2 1RP, United Kingdom

CAMBRIDGE UNIVERSITY PRESS
The Edinburgh Building, Cambridge CB2 2RU, United Kingdom
40 West 20th Street, New York, NY 10011-4211, USA
10 Stamford Road, Oakleigh, Melbourne 3166, Australia

First published 1998

Printed in the United Kingdom at the University Press, Cambridge

Typeset in Ehrhardt 11pt

A catalogue record for this book is available from the British Library

Library of Congress cataloguing in publication data

Shakespeare, William, 1564–1616
King Edward III / edited by Giorgio Melchiori.
p. cm. – (The New Cambridge Shakespeare)
Includes bibliographical references.
ISBN 0 521 43422 X (hardback). – ISBN 0 521 59673 4 (paperback)
1. Edward III, King of England, 1312–77 – Drama. 2. Civilisation, Medieval – 14th century – Drama. 3. Great Britain – Kings and rulers – Drama. I. Melchiori, Giorgio. II. Title. III. Series: Shakespeare, William, 1564–1616. Works. 1984. Cambridge University Press.
PR2859.A2M45 1997
822.3′3–dc21 96-54616 CIP

ISBN 0 521 43422 X hardback
ISBN 0 521 59673 4 paperback

BT

CONTENTS

ILLUSTRATIONS

PREFACE

The Reign of King Edward the third appeared only once in a collected edition of Shakespeare's works: it happened about one hundred and twenty years ago, when F. J. Furnivall included in his *Leopold Shakespeare* (London: Cassell, 1877) the text edited by Nicolaus Delius as the first in his collection of *Pseudo-Shakespere'sche Dramen* (1854). In this edition for the New Cambridge Shakespeare *Edward III* could therefore be presented as '[a]n early play restored to the canon' – a claim appearing on the dust-jacket of a book published when the present volume had already been handed in to Cambridge University Press: *Shakespeare's Edward III*, edited by Eric Sams (New Haven and London: Yale University Press, 1996). I regret that Sams's edition came too late for me to take it into account in my Introduction and Commentary; but his many articles and papers, and especially his *The Real Shakespeare: Retrieving the Early Years (1564–94)* (Yale, 1995) had made me familiar with the substance of his arguments, claiming not only *Edward III*, but also *Edmund Ironside* and the so-called 'bad' quarto versions of the Folio plays as 'Shakespeare's own, unaided work'. Sams implies that the greatness of a writer consists in being the *sole* author of the works assigned to him. In fact the greatness of a man of the theatre like Shakespeare consists in his being able to coordinate and impose his personal imprint onto the work and the language of a number of collaborators in the creation of that everchanging event: a play on the stage.

This is why, when in 1975 I was asked to submit a plan for an Italian edition of Shakespeare's complete plays, I decided that, besides the thirty-six Folio plays, *Pericles*, and *The Two Noble Kinsmen*, accepted in all recent editions of the Collected Works, the last volume of my *Teatro completo di Shakespeare* (comprising the histories that were not part of the traditional tetralogies) should include full texts of two plays in which Shakespeare had surely had a hand: *Sir Thomas More* and *Edward III*. The Shakespearean contributions should be presented in their natural contexts, rather than as mere excerpts (as happens, in the case of *More*, in several modern editions). The volume (*I Drammi Storici, Tomo Terzo*) appeared in 1991, and in the meantime I had edited, with Vittorio Gabrieli, *Sir Thomas More* for the Revels Plays (Manchester University Press, 1990), presenting it as a play by Anthony Munday revised by several other dramatists including Shakespeare. But the work done in preparing my Italian version of *Edward III* convinced me that the extent and the quality of Shakespeare's contribution to the creation of this collaborative play gave it as much right to 'canonical' status as that enjoyed not only by *Pericles* or *The Two Noble Kinsmen*, but also by some of the Folio plays, such as on the one hand the early *1 Henry VI* and on the other the late *Henry VIII*.

My first debt is to the staff of the publishing house Mondadori, particularly to the late Luciano De Maria, who made my undertaking of editing a bilingual version of

Shakespeare's plays possible, and to Richard Proudfoot who, as soon as he heard of my intention of including *Edward III* in it, provided photocopies of both early editions of the play as well as his notes for a collation of the different copies of the 1596 quarto. I feel deeply the loss of my old friends Muriel Bradbrook and John Margeson, to whom I had turned so many times for advice and encouragement, and I shall never forget the indomitable spirit with which the first general editor of the New Cambridge Shakespeare, Philip Brockbank, pursued his task till the end. I am grateful to his successor Brian Gibbons for agreeing to include *Edward III* in the series, and to Albert Braunmuller, who devoted so much time, patience and scholarship to editing my manuscript, correcting my mistakes and making a number of new suggestions. It goes without saying that the remaining faults are all of my own making.

It is with great pleasure that I acknowledge the generosity of many scholars who, upon learning that I was engaged in this edition, not only helped me with suggestions and advice, but let me see in advance (as in the case of Jonathan Hope, Roger Prior, G. Blakemore Evans) the relevant parts of their works in progress or just completed. My only regret is that I saw the proofs of the valuable new edition of *Edward III* for the revised and enlarged *Riverside Shakespeare* too late for me to take it into account. To Miss Maire Jean Steadman I am deeply indebted: she provided, through the kindness of director Raymond Raikes, the original script of his remarkable 1963 radio production of the play. Director Toby Robertson was most helpful in providing photographs of his Theatr Clwyd production which I had had the privilege of seeing in 1983 in the improbable Mediterranean setting of Taormina.

As always, the staff of the University Library and of the English Faculty Library in Cambridge, where I did most of my work, with occasional forays into the British Library, helped me at all stages, and so did Sarah Stanton at the Press; I am also thankful to Margaret Berrill for the last and most delicate stage of all: the final copyediting of the typescript. None of this could have been possible without the generous hospitality of our old friend Doreen Brockbank in Stratford, and the constant welcome, summer after summer, of the President, members and staff of Clare Hall, Cambridge – though on our last visit we sadly missed the companionship of John Garrod, for many years the college Bursar.

At the 1996 Shakespeare Conference in Stratford I was able to tell Kenneth Muir, whose treatment of *Edward III* in his *Shakespeare as Collaborator* (1960) had provided the basic approach to my edition of the play, that I had completed a work to which he repeatedly lent his help. I dedicate it to his memory.

G.M.

ABBREVIATIONS AND CONVENTIONS

1. Shakespeare's works

All quotations from Shakespeare's works in this edition use the lineation but not necessarily the spelling conventions of *The Riverside Shakespeare*, under the general editorship of G. Blakemore Evans. When they reproduce passages from early quartos or from the 1623 Folio, appropriate references to the original signatures are provided. The titles of the plays are abbreviated in a style modified from that used in the *Harvard Concordance to Shakespeare*.

Ado	*Much Ado About Nothing*
Ant.	*Antony and Cleopatra*
AWW	*All's Well That Ends Well*
AYLI	*As You Like It*
Cor.	*Coriolanus*
Cym.	*Cymbeline*
E3	*Edward the Third*
Err.	*The Comedy of Errors*
Ham.	*Hamlet*
1H4	*The First Part of King Henry the Fourth*
2H4	*The Second Part of King Henry the Fourth*
H5	*King Henry the Fifth*
1H6	*The First Part of King Henry the Sixth*
2H6	*The Second Part of King Henry the Sixth*
3H6	*The Third Part of King Henry the Sixth*
H8	*King Henry the Eighth*
JC	*Julius Caesar*
John	*King John*
LLL	*Love's Labour's Lost*
Lear	*King Lear*
Luc.	*The Rape of Lucrece*
Mac.	*Macbeth*
MM	*Measure for Measure*
MND	*A Midsummer Night's Dream*
MV	*The Merchant of Venice*
Oth.	*Othello*
Per.	*Pericles*
PP	*The Passionate Pilgrim*
R2	*King Richard the Second*
R3	*King Richard the Third*
Rom.	*Romeo and Juliet*
Shr.	*The Taming of the Shrew*
Sonn.	*Sonnets*
STM	*Sir Thomas More*
Temp.	*The Tempest*
TGV	*The Two Gentlemen of Verona*

Tim.	*Timon of Athens*
Tit.	*Titus Andronicus*
TN	*Twelfth Night*
TNK	*The Two Noble Kinsmen*
Tro.	*Troilus and Cressida*
Ven.	*Venus and Adonis*
Wiv.	*The Merry Wives of Windsor*
WT	*The Winter's Tale*

2. Editions, other works cited, periodicals, and general references

Works mentioned once in the Commentary appear there with full bibliographical information; all others are cited by the shortened titles listed below.

Abbott	E. A. Abbott, *A Shakespearian Grammar*, 1896 (references are to numbered paragraphs)
anon.	anonymous
apud	adopted or reported by (of a conjecture)
Bandello	Matteo Bandello, *La Seconda Parte delle Novelle* (1554), in *Le quattro parti delle novelle del Bandello*, ed. Gustavo Balsamo-Crivelli, 4 vols., 1911
Bentley	G. E. Bentley, *The Profession of Dramatist in Shakespeare's Time*, 1971
Berry	Philippa Berry, *Of Chastity and Power*, 1989
Bradley	David Bradley, *From Text to Performance in the Elizabethan Theatre*, 1992
Braunmuller	conjecture privately suggested by A. R. Braunmuller
Bullough	Geoffrey Bullough, ed., *Narrative and Dramatic Sources of Shakespeare*, 8 vols., 1957–75
Cairncross	A. C. Cairncross, 'Pembroke's Men and some Shakespearean piracies', *SQ* 9 (1960), 335–49
Capell	Edward Capell, ed., *Prolusions; or, select pieces of Antient Poetry. Part II. Edward the third, an historical Play*. London: Tonson, 1760
Chambers, *Shakespeare*	E. K. Chambers, *William Shakespeare: A Study of Facts and Problems*, 2 vols., 1930
Chambers, *Stage*	E. K. Chambers, *The Elizabethan Stage*, 4 vols., 1923
Champion	Larry S. Champion, ' "Answere in this perillous time": ideological ambivalence in *The Raigne of King Edward III* and the English chronicle plays', *ES* 69 (1988), 117–29
Collier	John Payne Collier, ed., *The Plays and Poems of William Shakespeare* vol. III. Maidenhead: privately printed (58 copies), 1878.
conj.	conjecture
Contention	*The First Part of the Contention betwixt the two famous Houses of Yorke and Lancaster* (1594), ed. William Montgomery, MSR, 1985
Delius	Nicolaus Delius, ed., *Pseudo-Shakespere'sche Dramen*, vol. I. Ebersfeld: 1854. Included in Max Moltke, ed., *Doubtful Plays of William Shakespeare*. Leipzig: Tauchnitz, 1869; and in *The Leopold Shakespeare*, ed. F. J. Furnivall. London: Cassell, 1877

Dent	R. W. Dent, *Shakespeare's Proverbial Language: An Index*, 1981 (references are to numbered proverbs)
Dent, *PLED*	R. W. Dent, *Proverbial Language in English Drama, Exclusive of Shakespeare: An Index*, 1984 (references are to numbered proverbs)
Diehl	Huston Diehl, *An Index of Icons in English Emblem Books 1500–1700*, 1986
ed.	editor, edited by
edn	edition
ES	*English Studies*
Frois.	Froissart (see under 'Ker' for Berners's translation, under 'Frois. 1513' for French original, under 'Luce' for French critical edition)
Frois. 1513	*Le premier volume de Froissart de Croniques de Frances* [etc.], Paris, par Francoys Reynault, 1513 (copy with manuscript notes by Henry Carey, Baron Hunsdon; BL shelfmark 596.h.24, 25)
FV	*The Famous Victories of Henry the fifth . . . Printed by Thomas Creede, 1598.* A facsimile . . . by Charles Praetorius, with an introduction by P. A. Daniel, 1887
George	David George, 'Shakespeare and Pembroke's Men', *SQ* 32 (1981), 305–33
Greg, *BEPD*	W. W. Greg, *A Bibliography of English Printed Drama to the Restoration*, 4 vols., 1939–59
Henslowe	*Henslowe's Diary*, ed. R. A. Foakes and R. T. Rickert, 1961
HLQ	*Huntington Library Quarterly*
Hol.	Holinshed
Holinshed	*The Third Volume of Chronicles . . . First Compiled by Raphael Holinshed, and by him extended to the yeare 1577. Now newlie recognised, augmented, and continued . . . to the yeare 1586*, 1587. References are to the 1807–8 reprint: *The Chronicles of England Scotland and Ireland*, ed. Sir Henry Ellis, 2 vols.
Hope	Jonathan Hope, *The Authorship of Shakespeare's Plays*, 1994
JEGP	*Journal of English and Germanic Philology*
Ker	*The Chronicle of Froissart Translated out of French by Sir John Bourchier Lord Berners, Annis 1523–25*, ed. W. P. Ker, 6 vols., 1901–3 (passages reprinted in Metz, *Sources of Four Plays Ascribed to Shakespeare*, are marked 'Metz')
Lapides	Fred Lapides, ed. *The Raigne of King Edward the Third. A Critical, Old-Spelling Edition*, 1980
L&LC	*Literary and Linguistic Computing*
Le Bel	*Chronique de Jean Le Bel publiée pour la Société de l'Histoire de France par Jules Viard et Eugène Déprez*, vols. I and II, 1904
Luce	*Chroniques de J. Froissart publiées pour la Société de l'Histoire de France par Siméon Luce*, vols. I–V, 1869–74
McMillin, 'Casting'	Scott McMillin, 'Casting for Pembroke's Men: the *Henry VI* quartos and *The Taming of A Shrew*', *SQ* 23 (1976), 141–59
Matthews & Merriam I	Robert A. J. Matthews and Thomas V. N. Merriam, 'Neural computation in stylometry I: an application to the works of Shakespeare and Fletcher', *L&LC* 8 (1993), 203–9

Matthews & Merriam II	Robert A. J. Matthews and Thomas V. N. Merriam, 'Neural computation in stylometry II: an application to the works of Shakespeare and Marlowe', *L&LC* 9 (1994), 1–6
Melchiori	Giorgio Melchiori, ed. *Teatro Completo di William Shakespeare*, IX. *I drammi storici*, vol. III, 1991
Melchiori, *Garter Plays*	G. Melchiori, *Shakespeare's Garter Plays. 'Edward III' to 'Merry Wives of Windsor'*, 1994
Melchiori, 'Hand D'	G. Melchiori, 'Hand D in *Sir Thomas More*', *S. Sur.* 38 (1985), 101–14
Melchiori, *Meditations*	G. Melchiori, *Shakespeare's Dramatic Meditations: An Experiment in Criticism*, 1976
Merriam, 'Marlowe'	T. V. N. Merriam, 'Marlowe's hand in *Edward III*', *L&LC* 8 (1993), 59–72
Metz	G. Harold Metz, *Sources of Four Plays Ascribed to Shakespeare*, 1989
MLR	*Modern Language Review*
mod. edns	consensus of modern editions
Moltke	variant introduced by Max Moltke in *Edward III* edited by Nicolaus Delius (see under Delius)
MSR	Malone Society Reprints
Muir	Kenneth Muir, *Shakespeare as Collaborator*, 1960
Nashe	Thomas Nashe, *Pierce Pennilesse his Supplication to the Diuell* (1592), facsimile edn, 1969
N&Q	*Notes and Queries*
NM	*Neuphilologische Mitteilungen*
ODEP	*The Oxford Dictionary of English Proverbs*, 3rd edn, revised by F. P. Wilson, 1970 (references are to page and column (a/b))
OED	*The Oxford English Dictionary*, 2nd edn, 1989
Ormrod	W. M. Ormrod, *The Reign of Edward III*, 1990
Østerberg	V. Østerberg, 'The "Countess scenes" of *Edward III*', *Shakespeare Jahrbuch* 65 (1929), 49–91
Packe	Michael Packe, *King Edward III*, ed. L. C. B. Seaman, 1983
Painter	'The Forty-sixth Nouell' in *The Palace of Pleasure* (1575) by William Painter (references are to the reprint from Joseph Jacobs's 1890 edn in Metz, *Sources of Four Plays Ascribed to Shakespeare*, pp. 107–29)
PBA	*Proceedings of the British Academy*
Peele	D. H. Horne, ed., *The Life and Minor Works of George Peele*, 2 vols., 1952
Prestwich	Michael Prestwich, *The Three Edwards*, 1980
Prior, 'Compliment'	Roger Prior, 'Was *The Raigne of King Edward III* a compliment to Lord Hunsdon?', *Connotations* 3 (1993/94), 243–64
Proudfoot	Richard Proudfoot, '*The Reign of King Edward the third* (1596) and Shakespeare', *PBA* 71 (1985), 169–85
punct.	punctuation
Q1	*The Raigne of King Edvvard the third:* . . . London, Printed for Cuthbert Burby, 1596 (first quarto)
Q2	*The Raigne of King Edward the Third.* . . . Imprinted at London by Simon Stafford for Cuthbert Burby . . . 1599 (second quarto)

Qq	Agreement between the two quartos 1596 and 1599
ref., refs	reference, references
RES	*Review of English Studies*
Riverside	*The Riverside Shakespeare*, ed. G. Blakemore Evans, 1974
RLA	R. L. Armstrong, ed., *Edward III*, in *Six Early Plays Related to the Shakespeare Canon*, ed. E. B. Everitt (*Anglistica*, 14), 1965
Sams	Eric Sams, *The Real Shakespeare. Retrieving the Early Years, 1564–1594*, 1995
SD	stage direction
SH	speech heading
Slater	Eliot Slater, *The Problem of 'The Reign of King Edward III': A Statistical Approach*, 1988
Smith	G. C. Moore Smith, ed., *Edward III* (Temple Dramatists). London: Dent, 1897
Smith, 'Authorship'	M. W. A. Smith, 'The authorship of *The Raigne of King Edward the Third*' *L&LC* 6 (1991), 166–75
R. M. Smith	Robert Metcalf Smith, 'Edward III (a study of the authorship of the drama in the light of a new source)', *JEGP* 10 (1911), 90–104
SQ	*Shakespeare Quarterly*
S. Sur.	*Shakespeare Survey*
STM	*Sir Thomas More. A Play by Anthony Munday and Others*, ed. Vittorio Gabrieli and Giorgio Melchiori (Revels Plays), 1990
subs.	subsequent
subst.	substantively
SV	sub verbo
TB	C. F. Tucker Brooke, ed., *The Shakespeare Apocrypha*, 1908 (frequently reprinted)
Teetgen	Alexander Teetgen, *Shakespeare's 'King Edward the Third'*, 1875
Textual Companion	Stanley Wells and Gary Taylor, with William Montgomery and John Jowett, *William Shakespeare: A Textual Companion*, 1987
Tilley	Morris Palmer Tilley, *A Dictionary of the Proverbs in England in the Sixteenth and Seventeenth Centuries*, 1950 (references are to numbered proverbs)
TLN	through line numbering
TLS	*The Times Literary Supplement*
TRI	*Theatre Research International*
Tyrrell	Henry Tyrrell, ed., *The Doubtful Plays of Shakespeare*. London and New York: Tallis, 1851
Vale	Juliet Vale, *Edward III and Chivalry: Chivalric Society and its Context, 1270–1350*, 1982
P. Vergil	Polydore Vergil, *Historia Anglica* (1555), facsimile edn, 1970
WAA	William A. Armstrong, ed., *Elizabethan History Plays*, 1965
Wentersdorf, 'Authorship'	Karl P. Wentersdorf, 'The Authorship of *Edward III*' (unpublished PhD dissertation, Cincinnati, 1960)
Wentersdorf, 'Date'	Karl P. Wentersdorf, 'The date of *Edward III*' *SQ* 16 (1965), 227–31

Whiting	Bartlett J. Whiting, *Proverbs, Sentences, and Proverbial Phrases in English Writings Mainly before 1500*, 1968 (references are to numbered proverbs)
Whitney	Geoffrey Whitney, *A Choice of Emblemes, and other devises* (1586). Facsimile reprint, Introduction by John Manning, 1989
WP	Karl Warnke and Ludwig Proescholdt, eds. *Pseudo-Shakespearian Plays*, 5 vols., vol. III: *Edward III*, revised and edited with Introduction and Notes. Halle: Niemeyer, 1886
Yates	Frances A. Yates, *Astraea: The Imperial Theme in the Sixteenth Century*, 1975

The usual abbreviations are used for the books of the Bible (including the Apocrypha). All biblical quotations are from the Geneva version.

INTRODUCTION

The suppression into the Kingdoms of Darkness of this Masterpiece, King Edward III, for more than two centuries, is simply in its way a *national* scandal, blot, and reproach. I repeat, another of the Incredible Facts! one of the most ridiculous, futile, humiliating things in literary history. But, O Shakespeare! even in thy death thou teachest us lessons. What is Fame? – and Merit?[1]

These are the words of the worthy German scholar Alexander Teetgen, in a booklet published in London in 1875 under the impressive title: *Shakespeare's 'King Edward the Third,' absurdly called, and scandalously treated as, a 'DOUBTFUL PLAY:' An Indignation Pamphlet*. He had come across it in Max Moltke's Tauchnitz edition of *Six Doubtful Plays of William Shakespeare* (1869), and in his enthusiasm for the discovery sent a copy to the Poet Laureate, Alfred Lord Tennyson, who was kind enough to reply: 'I have no doubt a good deal of it is Shakespeare's. You have given me a great treat.'[2] The suggestion that the anonymous play on *The Reign of King Edward the Third*, never reprinted since 1599, might have been Shakespeare's, was first advanced by Edward Capell when he provided a modern-spelling edition in 1760, but in the next hundred years or so it found support only in Germany, with the translations of the play included by Ludwig Tieck in his *Vier Schauspiele von Shakespeare* (Stuttgart and Tübingen, 1836) and by Ernst Ortlepp in *Nachträge zu Shakespeare's Werken* (vol. II, Stuttgart, 1840), while in England Henry Tyrrell reprinted it in the cautiously entitled collection *The Doubtful Plays of Shakespeare* (London, 1851). The attribution was firmly contested by another authoritative German scholar, Nicolaus Delius, when he re-edited Capell's text as the first of his *Pseudo-Shakesperesche Dramen* (Elberfeld, 1854), on which the Tauchnitz edition, known to Teetgen – and Tennyson – was based. But in 1874 John Payne Collier privately published 'King Edward III: a historical play by William Shakespeare. An essay in vindication of Shakespeare's authorship of the play', in which he confessed: 'I take shame to myself that I could omit, in both my editions of Shakespeare, such a grand contribution to the series of our English dramas as King Edward III.' And he made amends by including Capell's text in the third volume of *The Plays and Poems of William Shakespeare*, privately printed in 1878.

Both Collier's vindication, and Teetgen's extravagant and peremptory claim of the whole 'Masterpiece' for Shakespeare, seemed to raise more misgivings than approval in the most serious scholars and editors of the play. F. J. Furnivall denied Shakespeare's authorship when he reprinted Delius's edition in the Leopold Shakespeare (London, 1877), and, more seriously, Karl Warnke and Ludwig Proescholdt, in pro-

[1] Alexander Teetgen, *Shakespeare's 'King Edward the Third'* (1875), p. 17.
[2] Teetgen, p. 20.

viding the first critical old-spelling edition of *King Edward III* as volume III of their *Pseudo-Shakespearian Plays* (Halle, 1886), after discussing at length F. G. Fleay's theory (which was to find ample credit in later times) of double authorship, attributing to Shakespeare only the first two acts of the play,[1] came to the conclusion that 'Neither is it established that two authors have been at work in the composition of our play, nor is there any reason for supposing Shakespeare to have written part of the play.'

The ban of *Edward III* from the Shakespeare canon was confirmed by C. F. Tucker Brooke's denial that any part of *Edward III* could be by Shakespeare (suggesting instead George Peele as its sole author), when he reprinted it as the third of the fourteen plays included in his collection *The Shakespeare Apocrypha* (1908), destined to remain for a long time the most authoritative pronouncement on the 'doubtful' or 'disputed' plays. By now Brooke's attribution of the play to Peele is as much discredited as his contention that *The Two Noble Kinsmen* is the result of a collaboration not between Shakespeare and Fletcher but between Fletcher and Massinger, and since then a growing body of critics, scholars, and editors has recognised the presence in varying measure of Shakespeare's hand in the play.[2] The ban on *Edward III* has not been lifted, however, while from 1966 onwards *Kinsmen* has been included in all editions of Shakespeare's Complete Plays,[3] albeit it is acknowledged that it is by no means all his own work.

Edward III has appeared separately (ed. G. C. Moore Smith for the *Temple Dramatists*, 1897, J. S. Farmer for the Tudor Facsimile Texts, 1910, F. Lapides for the Garland Renaissance Drama Series, 1980, G. Parfitt for the Nottingham Drama Series, 1986), or in variously named collections: *Shakespeare's Doubtful Plays* (A. F. Hopkinson, 1891), *English History Plays* (Thomas Donovan, 1896 and 1911), *Three Elizabethan Plays* (J. Winny, 1959), *Six Early Plays Related to the Shakespeare Canon* (R. L. Armstrong for E. B. Everitt, 1965), *Elizabethan History Plays* (W. A. Armstrong, 1965), *Disputed Plays of William Shakespeare* (W. Kozlenko, 1974). The 'apocryphal' label is hard to remove, and the caution of the most recent Oxford editors is emblematic – as Gary Taylor puts it,[4] 'if we had attempted a thorough reinvestigation of candidates for inclusion in the early dramatic canon, it would have begun with *Edward III*'.

[1] Fleay had put forward the hypothesis of double authorship at first in *The Academy*, 25 April 1874, 461 ff., and then in his *Shakespeare Manual* (1878), pp. 303 ff.

[2] The most recent scholarly works providing convincing evidence in support of this attitude are those of Fred Lapides (Introduction to his critical, old-spelling edition of the play, 1980, pp. 3–31), Richard Proudfoot ('*The Reign of King Edward the third* (1596) and Shakespeare', *PBA*, 71 (1985), 169–85), Eliot Slater (*The Problem of 'The Reign of King Edward III': A Statistical Approach*, 1988), G. Harold Metz (*Sources of Four Plays Ascribed to Shakespeare*, 1989, pp. 7–20), M. W. A. Smith ('The authorship of *The Raigne of King Edward the Third*', *L&LC* 6 (1991), 166–75), and Jonathan Hope (*The Authorship of Shakespeare's Plays*, 1994, pp. 133–7).

[3] See *The Two Noble Kinsmen*, ed. Clifford Leech (Signet Shakespeare, 1966); ed. G. Blakemore Evans (*Riverside*, 1974); ed. N. W. Bawcutt (New Penguin Shakespeare, 1977); ed. W. Montgomery *et al.* (Oxford *Complete Works*, 1986); ed. E. M. Waith (Oxford Shakespeare, 1989).

[4] Stanley Wells and Gary Taylor, with William Montgomery and John Jowett, *William Shakespeare: A Textual Companion*, 1987, p. 137. According to Eric Sams, *The Real Shakespeare. Retrieving the Early Years 1564–1594*, 1995, pp. 101, 111, 117 etc., in an interview reported in *Shakespeare Newsletter*, 2 (1990), 28, Wells and Taylor seem now to accept *Edward III* as 'Shakespeare's work in its entirety'.

The inclusion of *Edward III* in the New Cambridge Shakespeare – its first appearance in a multi-volume edition of Shakespeare's works – is not a recognition of Teetgen's or Collier's sweeping claims. The play is perhaps no 'Masterpiece', though no worse than many history plays of the time, and probably Shakespeare is not its sole author. But several of the plays in the Folio, both early and late, from *1 Henry VI* to *Henry VIII*, are also the result of more or less openly acknowledged collaboration. The omission of *Edward III*, though the play had been in print since 1596, from Francis Meres's list of twelve of Shakespeare's plays compiled in 1598, does not by itself confine it to the 'apocrypha': Meres ignored also the three parts of *Henry VI* – plays written and performed before 1594 with which *Edward III* has the closest formal affinities. On the strength of their inclusion in the 1623 Folio, they are received in the canon, though Shakespeare's sole authorship of at least the first of them is more than questionable. The reasons for the omission of *Edward III* from the Folio will be discussed in the section of this Introduction on 'Authorship'. The fact is that *Edward III* is the natural prelude to the second Shakespearean historical cycle, from *Richard II* to *Henry V*. Since, in Richard Proudfoot's words,[1] it is also 'the sole remaining doubtful play which continues, on substantial grounds, to win the support of serious investigators as arguably the work of Shakespeare', *Edward III* has as much right to 'canonic rank' as the earliest Folio Histories.

Date and destination

Cuthbert Burby entered (1 December 1595) on the Stationers' Register 'A book Intitled Edward the Third and the blacke prince their warres wth kinge Iohn of Fraunce'. The title-page of the first quarto, 'printed for Cuthbert Burby' in 1596, reads: THE RAIGNE OF KING EDVVARD the third: *As it hath bin sundrie times plaied about the Citie of London*. The only information conveyed by the registration and the title-page is that the play existed and had been performed before the end of 1595. When and by whom? The vagueness of the expression 'sundrie times plaied about the Citie of London',[2] used by Burby also in the case of *A Knack to Know an Honest Man*, entered in the Register only five days before *Edward III*, suggests one of two things: either the publication of the plays was not authorised by the company owning them;[3] or they were at the time temporarily derelict, i.e. the company which had performed them was no longer in existence, and no other claim had as yet been put forward for them. This is the most likely explanation in view of the date, 1595, not long after the

[1] Proudfoot, p. 185.

[2] Proudfoot (p. 162) remarks on the ambiguity of the preposition 'about'. It probably means not 'within' the City limits, but outside, where the three public playhouses (Theatre, Curtain, and Rose) used by the main acting companies were located. On the other hand, the fact that it had been performed 'sundrie times' seems to rule out the possibility that the play had been presented only privately.

[3] This may well be the case with *A Knack*, known to have been performed by the Admiral's Men on 22 October 1594. Burby was probably equivocating on the confusion with the title of its predecessor, *A Knack to Know a Knave*, performed on 10 June 1592, a day or two before the closing of the theatres because of the plague, which was published in 1594 as 'sundry times played by Ed. Allen [Alleyn] and his Companie', that is, Lord Strange's Men, a company no longer active in 1595.

1 A battle at sea, illustration in a manuscript copy (now in the British Library) of Jean de Wavrin's *Cronique d'Angleterre*, made at Bruges for Edward IV (1461–83)

end of the plague that had repeatedly caused the closure of playhouses between June 1592 and the middle of 1594, the consequent disruption of most theatre companies, and the dispersal of their play-books.[1] It can safely be assumed therefore that *Edward III*, derelict in 1595, had been performed by one of the disbanded companies before

[1] Two other plays, registered in this period (14 May 1594) though performed in earlier times, carried when published evasive formulas on their title-pages, with no indication of acting company: Greene's *James IV* (1598, 'sundry times publikely plaied'), and Peele's *David and Bethsabe* (1599, 'divers times plaied on the stage'). *Mucedorus*, not entered in the Stationers' Register, was published in 1598 as acted 'in the honorable Cittie of London'.

1594. On the other hand, the epic description in 3.1 of the English naval victory off Sluys in 1340 deliberately evokes the recent defeat of the Spanish Armada in 1588. The author or authors relied for several details on the celebrative literature of the event published in the following years,[1] and this probably places the composition of the play after 1590, when the most impressive reports of the Armada appeared in print.

1590 and 1594 are the unquestionable limits of composition. Any attempt at narrowing them must rely on internal evidence. The parallels with the Sonnets particularly evident in 2.1 and the mention of Roman Lucrece at 2.2.192–5, which suggested to Chambers 'a date in 1594–1595',[2] and to Kenneth Muir 'after 1593',[3] are inconclusive: the Lucrece theme runs through the whole of Shakespeare's work,[4] and the allusion is in the most surely Shakespearean part of the play. It is to the same part that Østerberg refers in giving on stylistic grounds 1592–4 as the date.[5] The closing of the theatres caused by the plague in June 1592 cannot be assumed as a terminus, since performances took place in or 'about' London for short periods during the epidemics. MacDonald Jackson, finding echoes of *Edward III* in the two parts of the *Contention between the two Famous Houses of York and Lancaster*, which are considered reported texts of *2* and *3 Henry VI*, 'constructed by some of Pembroke's Men upon the collapse of that company in the summer of 1593',[6] argues for an early date, and tends to agree with Wentersdorf who, on the basis of the topical allusions to the Armada, thinks that '*Edward III* was written . . . about 1589–90'.[7] Here is a double fallacy: the reports of the Armada, dating from 1590, were not necessarily echoed in the play in the year of their publication, and, as Jackson himself acknowledges, the reported texts of the two plays, published in 1594 and 1595 respectively, cannot have been compiled before 1593 (and more likely, shortly before their publication). This makes 1592 or early 1593 as possible a date as any for the performance of *The Raigne of King Edward the third* 'about the Citie of London'.[8]

[1] See the section 'From sources to structure'.

[2] E. K. Chambers, *William Shakespeare: A Study of Facts and Problems*, 1930, I, 517.

[3] K. Muir, *Shakespeare as Collaborator*, 1960, p. 39.

[4] G. Melchiori, *Shakespeare's Garter Plays. 'Edward III' to 'Merry Wives of Windsor'*, 1994, pp. 131–2.

[5] V. Østerberg, 'The "Countess scenes" of *Edward III*', *Shakespeare Jahrbuch* 65 (1929), 49–91.

[6] MacD. P. Jackson, '*Edward III*, Shakespeare, and Pembroke's Men', *N&Q* 210 (1965), 329–31.

[7] Karl P. Wentersdorf, 'The date of *Edward III*', *SQ* 16 (1965), 227–31. Jackson does not refer to this paper, published after his note, but to Wentersdorf's unpublished thesis on 'The authorship of "Edward III"' presented at the University of Cincinnati in 1960, from which the paper was extracted.

[8] A later date not only for the performance but also for the writing of the play is proposed by Roger Prior, who some time ago ('The date of *Edward III*', *N&Q* 235 (1990), 178–80), in view of some topical allusions, had argued that 'the play was written after June 1593', or rather, since the theatres were closed at the time and reopened only from 28 December 1593 till 5 February 1594, and then from 4 June 1594 on, either 'in the six weeks at the beginning of the year [1594]' or after June of the same year. The discovery of marginal annotations in the hand of Henry Carey Lord Hunsdon, the Lord Chamberlain from 1585, in his copy of the 1513 French edition of Froissart, has induced Prior, in a new closely argued paper ('Was *The Raigne of King Edward III* a compliment to Lord Hunsdon?', *Connotations* 3 (1993–4) 242–64) to suggest that '*Edward III* was written as a deliberate compliment to Henry Carey, Lord Hunsdon . . . and that it was performed before him and his family in 1594 by the actors whom he took into his service in that year, the company commonly known as the Lord Chamberlain's Men.' The suggestion is attractive, but I find it hard to believe that a play which went through more than one stage of elaboration (see the section 'The genesis of *Edward III*') could have been written in so short a time.

The most interesting aspect of Jackson's contribution is his claim, recently strongly supported by Proudfoot,[1] that *Edward III* must be added to the scanty repertory of the Earl of Pembroke's Men. Little is known of this company, first heard of as active in Leicester in 1592, when the London playhouses were shut. Surprisingly, Pembroke's Men presented two plays at court in the Christmas season 1592–3, but by September 1593, upon returning from another provincial tour, they were so impoverished that they had to pawn their playing apparel,[2] and they are heard of no more,[3] except for the appearance of their name on the title-pages of: Marlowe's *Edward II*, registered 6 July 1593, published 1594; *Titus Andronicus*, registered 6 February 1594, published 1594; *The Taming of A Shrew*, registered 2 May 1594, published 1594; *The True Tragedy of Richard Duke of York*, published 1595, but not registered separately because it was the sequel of *The First Part of the Contention between the two Famous Houses of York and Lancaster*, which had been entered on 12 March 1594 and published the same year with no indication of acting company. The dates of registration and publication of the five plays are a sure sign that in 1593 the company was disbanded and had variously disposed of its playscripts. The two parts of the *Contention* and *A Shrew* are now considered memorial reconstructions of perhaps reduced versions of *2* and *3 Henry VI* and of an earlier version of *The Taming of the Shrew* respectively.[4] Taking them together with *Titus*, the association of Shakespeare, at some stage, with Pembroke's Men is undeniable.

Other unassigned plays were thought to have been acted by Pembroke's: at first, on stylistic grounds, *Arden of Feversham*, *Soliman and Perseda*, *Massacre at Paris*,[5] then, in view of the state of the early quartos, *Spanish Tragedy*, *Richard III*, *Romeo and Juliet*, as well as *1 Henry VI*, though the last is known only in the Folio version.[6] Twelve plays seem too large a repertory for so short-lived a company. In an attempt to antedate its origin, A. C. Cairncross wrote:

> Pembroke's, *under whatever name or with whatever organization*, existed before 1592, probably as early as 1589, and . . . it was then Shakespeare's company, as it was, for a time at least, Kyd's and Marlowe's [my italics].[7]

[1] Proudfoot, pp. 181–3.

[2] *Henslowe's Diary*, ed. R. A. Foakes and R. T. Rickert, 1961, p. 280.

[3] As Chambers suggests (*The Elizabethan, Stage*, 1923, II, 131), the Earl of Pembroke's Men who had an engagement at the Swan in 1597 must have been a temporary offshoot of the Chamberlain's Men.

[4] For the two histories see Madeleine Doran, 'Henry VI, Parts II and III', *University of Iowa Humanistic Studies*, 4.4 (1928), and Peter Alexander, *Shakespeare's Henry VI and Richard III*, 1929. For *A Shrew* Peter Alexander in *TLS*, 16 September 1926, and Richard Hosley, 'Sources and analogues of *The Taming of the Shrew*', *HLQ* 27 (1964), 289–308; but compare G. I. Duthie, '*The Taming of a Shrew* and *The Taming of the Shrew*', *RES* 19 (1942), 337–56. Recently, though, the idea of 'bad' quartos and 'memorial reconstructions' has been hotly contested: for instance *A Shrew* has been published by G. Holderness and B. Loughrey (1993) as an early Shakespearean version of the play, and Eric Sams has devoted several chapters of his book (1995) to providing 'evidence' that *A Shrew* and *Contention* are Shakespeare's original works (Sams, pp. 136–45 and 154–62), and to demolishing the very notion of memorial reconstruction (ch. 31, pp. 173–9).

[5] Hart, *Stolne and Surreptitious Copies*, 1942, pp. 389–90.

[6] A. C. Cairncross, 'Pembroke's Men and some Shakespearean piracies', *SQ* 9 (1960) 335–49.

[7] Cairncross, p. 344.

There is no evidence for the existence of Pembroke's Men under that or another name before 1592. The largest acting companies equipped to stage full-scale history plays in the late eighties and early nineties were the Admiral's, the Queen's, and Lord Strange's Men. Leaving aside the Admiral's Men, who one way or another managed to weather the plague years and to survive into the next century, the June 1592 crisis played havoc not only with the Queen's own players, replaced at court in the 1592–3 Christmas season by Pembroke's Men, but also with Lord Strange's, who had petitioned the Privy Council in July to be allowed to play in town to avoid 'division and separation' inside the company.[1] It has been suggested that Pembroke's Men emerged as a result of a split that took place some time earlier in the Queen's company,[2] but Scott McMillin, examining casting and doubling patterns in the *Contention* plays and *A Shrew*, as well as the names of actors appearing in them, compared with those that figure in the plot of *2 The Seven Deadly Sins* (performed by Lord Strange's Men about 1590), demonstrated that Pembroke's Men were the result of a split during the plague years in Lord Strange's Men,[3] the very 'division and separation' Strange's Men feared in July. It must have been a reduced company that was finally allowed to play at the Rose during the intermission of the plague between 29 December 1592 and 1 February 1593, when they revived *1 Henry VI*, which they had first presented in the same theatre on 3 March 1592, performing it no less than thirteen times before the closing of the playhouses in mid-June.[4] It can be concluded that *2* and *3 Henry VI* as well as the other three plays bearing the name of the Pembroke's Men on their title-pages had been staged in previous years by Lord Strange's Men, and were taken over by the new formation when the plague caused a division of the company. This is made obvious by the title-page of *Titus Andronicus* (Q1, 1594), 'As it was Plaide by the Right Honourable the Earle of Darbie, Earle of Pembrooke, and Earle of Sussex their Seruants': the play was first performed by Strange's (in 1593 Ferdinando Lord Strange had acquired the title of Earl of Derby) and then by Pembroke's Men; when both companies collapsed and the plays became temporarily derelict, a minor company, Sussex's Men, were able to play 'Titus & ondronicus' in a Henslowe playhouse on 24 January 1594. Signifi-

[1] Chambers, *Stage*, II, 311–12.

[2] G. M. Pinciss, 'Shakespeare, Her Majesty's Players and Pembroke's Men', *S.Sur.* 27 (1974), 129–36, placing the split around 1590–1. The opinion that Pembroke's were an offshoot of the Queen's Men is shared by Karl P. Wentersdorf, 'The origin and personnel of the Pembroke Company', *TRI* 5 (1989–90), 45–68.

[3] Scott McMillin, 'Casting for Pembroke's Men: the *Henry VI* quartos and *The Taming of a Shrew*', *SQ* 23 (1976), 141–59. See p. 158: 'It very much appears that the *Sins* plot represents a large company from about 1590 which a year or two later divided into two groups: one group carried Strange's name and included such established members of the large company as Alleyn, Brian, Phillips, Pope, and Cowley; the other group, gaining new patronage from the Earl of Pembroke, included the younger elements of the large company – the nine actors whose names are shared between the Pembroke plays and the plot.' Also Mary Edmond ('Pembroke's Men', *RES* 25 (1974), 129–36), in the wake of Chambers, *Shakespeare*, I, 49, had seen Pembroke's Men as a splinter of Strange's Men. This opinion is shared by David George, 'Shakespeare and Pembroke's Men', *SQ* 32 (1981), 305–23, who goes on to argue that, after the dissolution of the company in 1593, some Pembroke actors joined Derby's Men, others Sussex's Men, and possibly for a time, in 1594, the three companies counted as one.

[4] See Michael Hattaway, ed., *The First Part of King Henry VI* (New Cambridge Shakespeare, 1990), pp. 36–8.

cantly, these Pembroke plays entered the repertory of the Chamberlain's/King's Men, who were joined at the same time by most of the actors who are known to have belonged either to Pembroke's or to Lord Strange's Men – or to both.[1]

What is the connection of *Edward III* with either or both companies, apart from the unquestionable fact that Shakespeare had been associated with them, and the more questionable one that he was at least part-author of the play? And how would such a connection, if it exists, affect the dating of the play? That all the 'Pembroke plays' are pre-plague plays, originally destined for performance in regular London playhouses, is proved by their large cast and staging requirements, with particular attention to the use of extended platforms for crowd, court, and battle scenes, of at least two 'doors' and of an upper stage – the first act of *Titus*, for instance, loses all meaning unless it is played on two levels. Original stage directions repeatedly stipulate these theatrical needs.

Not so in *Edward III*. The last scene (5.1.187–end) demands a maximum of ten adult actors and a boy, plus possibly a few mute extras ('soldiers').[2] In the rest of the play no more than seven actors are ever present at the same time on the stage, except for 3.3.46–178, when ten (plus 'soldiers') are required. In all cases ample scope is given for doubling, and there is an unusual restraint in the presentation of battle scenes: no fighting on stage, apart from the brief 'crossing of the stage' at the beginning of 3.4;[3] a variety of sound effects must serve to suggest battles described by outside observers. A. R. Braunmuller remarks[4] that a famous earlier play, *Tamburlaine*, also 'relies on sound effects for its battles, which are never represented before us'. The authors of *Edward III* may have learnt their technique from it, when uncertain of the availability of regular playhouses for their play.

Still more surprising, in *Edward III* there is a siege (Calais, 4.2) with no mention of walls or gates, and no use of the upper stage, a regular feature of numberless similar scenes in other history plays for the public stage. The 'six poor Frenchmen' enter apparently unnoticed from the side (see 6 SD n.), and even the Captain of Calais

[1] McMillin, 'Casting', p. 159. Like the Oxford editors (*Textual Companion*, p. 113) I am 'unpersuaded' by David George's argument (George, pp. 315–23) that the title-page of *Titus* does not refer to three companies acting the play in succession, but to a single company which, in 1594, included actors from all three (see p. 7, n. 3) – an argument on which Jonathan Bate, in the Introduction to his edition of *Titus Andronicus* (Arden 3, 1995, pp. 74–9), bases his view that *Titus* 'was written in late 1593', but which does not substantially affect the question of the original destination of *Edward III*, a play not mentioned by George.

[2] They are King Edward, Queen Philippa (a boy-actor), and Derby, present from the beginning, Copland and King David of Scotland, entering at 63, Salisbury, entering at 96, Prince Edward, King John of France, his son Philip, Audley, and Artois (the last three do not speak), entering at 186. The exit for the six citizens of Calais, who entered at 7, is clearly marked at 59, and, though no exit is marked in the text, the Herald entering at 175 is no longer needed on stage after 186. The figures of '21+' adults and 4/5 boys suggested by David Bradley (*From Text to Performance in the Elizabethan Theatre*, 1992, p. 232) for the cast of *Edward III* are overestimated. Proudfoot (pp. 162–3), though maintaining that the play was meant for a large company requiring 'a properly equipped playhouse', remarks that the absence from the last scene, where he should have appeared, of Prince Charles of France is due to the actor doubling for King David.

[3] *Alarum. Enter a many French men flying. After them Prince Edward running. Then enter King Iohn and Duke of Loraine.* (Q1, sig. F3v).

[4] Private communication.

negotiating the surrender does not speak from the wall or enter through a town-gate, but slips in quietly from an unstated direction. The same is true of the scene of the surrender (5.1.1–59), where, in the 1596 quarto, the entrance of *sixe Citizens in their Shirts, bare foote, with halters about their necks* is placed at the beginning, before that of Edward, his queen, Derby, and soldiers.

In one case, nonetheless, the use of the upper stage seems inescapable – when, at 1.2, the Countess of Salisbury, from the battlements or windows of her castle, overhears the talk of the besieging Scots, welcomes her 'cousin' Montague (who exclaims: 'we are not Scots, / Why do you shut your gates against your friends?') and finally descends to 'show her duty' at the arrival of King Edward who has come to her rescue. Neither quarto indicates in stage directions that she is 'above', or on the walls or at the window. And when at 87 Montague invites her to 'descend and gratulate his highness' who is about to arrive, there is no direction for her exit from above; instead, a few lines later (93), the direction 'Enter Countess', with which the scene had begun, is repeated. It looks as if the author of this passage is particularly wary of providing directions indicating specific stage requirements. This is consistent with the idea, developed in a later section of this Introduction, that the 'Countess scenes' replace an earlier treatment of the episode which perhaps did not present such requirements.[1]

In conclusion: the devisers of the play for Pembroke's or Lord Strange's Men were not sure that its performance could enjoy the stage facilities offered by the Rose or the other regular theatres, which had been instead freely exploited, for instance, in *Titus Andronicus* and in the *Henry VI* plays. *Edward III* is the only major history written while keeping in mind that it might have to be played outside the London playhouses. Its date cannot be other than late 1592–early 1593.[2]

Authorship

The main argument against the inclusion of *The Reign of Edward the Third, King of England* in what has become known as the Shakespeare canon is its absence from all the seventeenth-century Folio editions. Justifications have been found for the omission of

[1] Roger Prior ('Compliment', p. 260) takes a different view. Arguing for May or June 1594 as the date of composition of *Edward III* Prior concludes: 'Its first performance would presumably have been a private one, given before an audience composed of Hunsdon, his family and friends. Yet it was clearly also designed to be acted in a public theater, and, according to the title-page, was so acted.' Uncertainty about the destination of the play, rather than the fact that it had 'to be written quickly' for a specific occasion, seems a better reason for the lack of staging directions. Besides, when Prior remarks 'hasty writing may be one explanation for the play's uneven quality', he ignores the question of multiple authorship and of the belated replacement of the Countess scenes (see especially 'The final version of the Countess scenes' below).

[2] It is perhaps no mere coincidence that the other play of multiple authorship to which Shakespeare contributed at least one very remarkable 'addition', was most probably written exactly at this time. As Scott McMillin remarks (*The Elizabethan Theatre and 'The Book of Sir Thomas More'*, 1987, p. 72), 'I would say that *Sir Thomas More* was originally written for Strange's Men between the summer of 1592 and the summer of 1593.' Further evidence for a date 'before 1593' has been recently provided by W. Godshalk ('Dating Edward III', *N&Q* 240 (1995), 299–300), who noted that Thomas Deloney's ballad 'Of King *Edward* the third, and the faire Countesse of *Salisbury*', largely based on the play, was included in *The Garland of good Will*, entered in the Stationers' Register on 5 March 1593.

the two other plays which generally figure in the most recent editions of the collected plays, though they had been overlooked by Heminges and Condell when in 1623 they offered to 'the great variety of readers' the writings of their friend and fellow. Of *Pericles*, already in print in a form obviously 'maimed and deformed by the frauds and stealths of injurious impostors', they could not secure a text answering their intention of presenting the plays 'cured and perfect of their limbs'; *The Two Noble Kinsmen*, on the other hand, could be claimed by John Fletcher, the surviving co-author. Neither argument holds for *Edward III*. The anonymous printings of 1596 and 1599 were reasonably correct by current standards, and no other dramatist laid claim to the play.

What is surprising about *Edward III* is the total lack of any mention or reference to it from its second publication in 1599 until nearly sixty years later,[1] in 1656, when the booksellers Richard Rogers and William Ley, in 'An exact and perfect Catalogue of all the Playes that are Printed' appended to their edition of Thomas Goff's *The Careless Shepherdess*, listed *Edward II*, *Edward III*, and *Edward IV*, as works of William Shakespeare. The arbitrariness of the attribution is self-evident not only because the other two Edward plays are by Marlowe and Heywood respectively, but also because a similar catalogue of plays in stock published the same year by the more reliable bookseller Edward Archer contains the title of the play with no mention of the author, and the same happens with the lists of plays in print compiled by Francis Kirkman in 1661 and 1671.

Edward Capell first associated the play with the name of Shakespeare more than a century and a half later. In his *Prolusions; or, select pieces of Antient Poetry* (1760) he, though acknowledging that the external evidence for an attribution to Shakespeare was less than slight, provided the first modern edition of the text so as to enable readers to confirm or reject his attribution on stylistic and other grounds.[2] The arguments in favour or against it put forward by a large number of scholars in the following centuries are carefully examined by Harold Metz, and his conclusions deserve attention:

> The evidence adduced by such leading critics as Chambers, Muir, and Proudfoot makes clear that Shakespeare is the playwright of at least scenes 1.2, 2.1, 2.2, and 4.4, and the convincing arguments set forth by these and other sound scholars concerning Shakespearean structural, lexical, and imagistic elements elsewhere in the play establish the likelihood that his hand is present in scenes other than those four. The hypothesis that he wrote the entire play may be questionable, but it cannot be completely ruled out . . . On balance, though, it would appear that the traces of his work in the second half of the play, except for 4.4, which fired his imagination, are not quite sufficient as a basis for the claim that he is the sole author of *Edward III*.[3]

[1] In 1610 it was included by Sir John Harington in the catalogue of the plays in his collection, where only titles are given, with no indication of authors. The catalogue and the booksellers' lists mentioned here are reproduced in Greg, *A Bibliography of English Printed Drama to the Restoration*, III.1306–62.

[2] Capell, *Prolusions; or, select pieces of Antient Poetry. Part II. Edward the third, an historical Play* (1760), x: 'But after all, it must be confess'd that it's being his [Shakespeare's] work is conjecture only, and matter of opinion; and the reader must form one of his own, guided by what is now before him, and by what he shall meet with in perusal of the piece itself.'

[3] Metz, pp. 6–20.

Side by side with this we should place the conclusions of the extremely detailed statistical study of the play conducted in 1981 by Eliot Slater, but published posthumously in 1988:

The suggestion arises that not only part A [1.2, 2.1, 2.2, 4.4] but also part B [the rest of the play] could well be the work of Shakespeare. If so, it might be that the two parts were written not quite at the same time, and that part B dates from an earlier stage in his career.

And again:

Both part A and part B are regarded as his work, though probably written at different times.[1]

Both scholars seem inclined to accept the possibility of Shakespearean authorship of the play, though Metz is not prepared to claim *sole* authorship for him, while Slater postulates two separate stages of composition. M. W. A. Smith, though maintaining that Slater's method has 'merit for the resolution of problems of chronology' but 'unfortunately . . . has been demonstrated to fail when applied to questions of authorship',[2] is more peremptory in attributing the whole play to Shakespeare:

From the results obtained in this paper, stylometric evidence that *Edward III* is Shakespearian in its entirety is undoubtedly stronger than the equivalent evidence for the authentic *Richard II* . . . In view of the strong subjective impression that *Edward III* is Shakespearian, perhaps the independence and objectivity of the stylometric argument could tilt the balance in favour of the immense step of increasing the Shakespeare canon to thirty-eight plays.[3]

More recently Jonathan Hope, by applying to all Shakespeare's collaborative and so-called apocryphal works an elaborate socio-historical linguistic approach, entailing comparison with samples from Fletcher, Marlowe, Dekker, Middleton, and Massinger (but not Munday), found no clear-cut evidence for the presence of two hands in the play, one responsible for Acts 1 and 2 and the other for 3 to 5. His conclusion coincides with Smith's:

Nothing in the findings of this study offers a serious challenge to the status of *Edward III* as the best candidate from the apocryphal plays for inclusion in the canon.[4]

I propose to approach the problem from a different, more traditional, angle, by emphasising two points: (1) The lack of any credible mention of Shakespeare as author or co-author of the play from the moment it was published till 1760. (2) The current practice in the supply of 'books' for use in public (as contrasted with private) theatres in Elizabethan times.

The preliminary question is: why was a play of undoubted merit – whoever its author – so totally ignored for over two and a half centuries? The reason must be external to the play, connected with the history of the Elizabethan stage at large. It should be noted that the real 'villains' in the play, boastful and cowardly, lacking all

[1] Slater, pp. 133–5.
[2] Smith, 'Authorship', p. 166.
[3] *Ibid.*, p. 171. Evidently Smith does not yet accept *The Two Noble Kinsmen* as a canonical work.
[4] Hope (1994), pp. 133–7. I am grateful to Dr Hope for letting me see the section of his book concerned with *Edward III* and the relevant tables well in advance of publication.

sense of honour, are not the French, but the Scots. Of their king Edward says (1.1.136–7):

> Ignoble David, hast thou none to grieve
> But silly ladies with thy threatening arms?

And their greed, their 'rough insulting barbarism', and finally their cowardice is exposed in 1.2.1–93, while the last scene of the play presents King David led prisoner on the stage. On the attitude towards the Scots in the last years of Elizabeth's reign Chambers quotes a letter sent on 15 April 1598 by George Nicolson, Queen Elizabeth's agent in Edinburgh, to Lord Burghley in London, informing him of the strong feeling of resentment of King James VI's court for the abuse of the Scottish nation on the English stage:

> It is regrated [= regretted] to me in quiet sort that the comedians of London should in their play scorn the King and people of this land and wished that it may be speedily amended and stayed, lest the worst sort getting understanding thereof should stir the King and country to anger thereat.[1]

Critics have looked for some satirical comedy of the period as the occasion for the Scottish protest, but no certain identification has been made. Is it not more likely that the offence was caused by a revival on the London stage of the recently printed *Edward III*, where scorn is poured on the King and people of Scotland? The fact that this was not a comedy, but a history, and that the appearance of the Scots in 1.2 provided the only comical episode in a humourless play, was liable to stir the anger of the people so mercilessly satirised. The only solution was to have the play 'speedily amended and stayed', i.e. withdrawn from public performance. If such is the case, the 1599 reprint can be taken as an attempt by the publisher to get some profit from a play that was no longer to be seen on the stage, though its subject-matter had acquired a new topicality, thanks to the references to Edward in *Henry V*, triumphantly presented at the Globe in the same year.[2] It should be noted that the new edition reproduces verbatim the noncommittal statement in the title-page of the 1596 quarto: 'As it hath been Sundry times played about the Citie of London'. This formula runs counter to the practice of mentioning the company owning the play at the time of publication, especially if it was revived in 1598 by a different company from that for which it was written, as may well be the case with *Edward III*, first performed presumably before the radical changes of 1594 in the London theatre world. It suggests that no company was then eager to claim the play.

[1] Chambers, *Stage*, I, 323, provides a shortened version of the passage. The text reproduced here has been traced by A. R. Braunmuller to J. D. Machie, *Calendar of State Papers Relating to Scotland . . . in the Public Record Office* (1969), vol. XIII (1597–1603), Part 1, p. 188.

[2] Richard Proudfoot (Proudfoot, pp. 182–3) suggests that the performance of a play 'on so closely related a subject . . . may explain the reprinting of *Edward III* in 1599, the year of Shakespeare's *Henry V*'. He also hints at the possibility that the original registration on 1 December 1595 and publication in 1596 of *Edward III* might have been prompted by the fact that between 28 November 1595 and 15 July 1596 the Admiral's Men performed thirteen times at the Rose a play recorded in Henslowe's Diary as 'harey the v', which can hardly have been a revival of the Queen's Men's *Famous Victories*.

There was of course no question of lifting the ban (if one existed) on the play after the accession in 1603 to the throne of England of King James of Scotland, who may have originated the veto five years before. So after a time, although some booksellers still had copies in stock, the play would have been completely forgotten. Under such circumstances, even if Shakespeare had had a hand in the writing of *Edward III*, by the time Heminges and Condell prepared the 1623 Folio they would hardly have remembered or thought of including, alongside the early histories and comedies which were still alive on the stage, a play which had totally disappeared from it a quarter of a century before. This speculative account of the most likely reason for the disappearance of the play from circulation for such a long time[1] leaves the question of authorship wide open: Shakespeare may or may not have been involved to a greater or lesser extent in the writing of *Edward III*.

More relevant is an understanding of how professional players secured texts for public performance. While authors' names figured from an early time on title-pages of academic and other plays intended for private presentation or offered for performance by travelling players, until about 1597 the vast majority of plays presented on the public stage were published with no indication of authorship, but only of the companies that owned them.[2] Up to the same date Henslowe's Diary entered only receipts from performances, with no mention of the plays' authors; from then on it began to record payments to playwrights, but in most cases they were to teams of three or more working on single plays, or to odd writers for 'additions' to existing play-books. There could be no better evidence that play-writing for public playhouses was originally conceived as a collective endeavour, in which no doubt the actors themselves had the last word. This applies to the early work of the actor William Shakespeare, so that Gary Taylor's remark that 'Shakespeare only wrote about 20 per cent' of *The First Part of Henry VI*[3] is far from unfounded, an implicit acknowledgement that some of the early canonical works of Shakespeare consecrated by inclusion in the First Folio bear evidence of multiple authorship.

Collaboration in the writing of a 'book' for the stage took different forms, comparable to what happens now in script-writing for film and television. The starting point must be in all cases what at the time was called the 'plot', setting down the general outlines of the play (an essential 'scenario') to which the different collaborators were

[1] The only allusion to the play during this period, as Proudfoot points out (Proudfoot, p. 163), is in Thomas Heywood's *Apology for Actors* (1612), where the Countess of Salisbury, and 'the true portraiture of that famous King *Edward* the third, foraging France, taking so great a King captiue in his owne country, quartering the English Lyons with the French Flower-delyce' (compare 3.1.73–9 and 3.2.41–3) are quoted as examples of the positive influence of the theatre on spectators. Heywood, a young actor and budding playwright in the early nineties, may have remembered playing in it or even contributing to its writing.

[2] Apart from his poems, Shakespeare's name made its first appearance on title-pages of plays in 1598 (*Love's Labour's Lost*, the second quarto of *Richard III*, and the second and third quartos of *Richard II*), but the early quartos of *Titus Andronicus* (1594, 1600, 1611), *Romeo and Juliet* (1597, 1599, 1609), *Richard III* (1597), *Richard II* (1597), *1 Henry IV* (1598), and even *Henry V* (1600, 1602), as well as the two parts of the *Contention* (*2–3 Henry VI*, 1594–5, 1600), and *The Taming of a Shrew* (1594), appeared anonymously.

[3] 'The canon and chronology of Shakespeare's Plays', *Textual Companion*, p. 137.

asked to contribute.[1] The 'plotter' then assembled the various contributions, providing a first treatment, or at times indeed a 'book', that is, a complete script, for submission to the players. They in turn would impose adjustments and changes in the text, answering further theatrical requirements, or even more substantial modifications (at times of a censorial nature). These 'additions' could be entrusted either to some of the original contributors, or to others, including the actors themselves to whom the play had been offered. Though the manuscript *Book of Sir Thomas More* (1592–3) may be considered a special case, in view of the heavy censorial interference which prevented its acting and of the doubts as to the date of its many additions, it remains the best available evidence of the process of composition of play-texts for the public theatre. The original book was planned and transcribed in a fair copy by the man who enjoyed the reputation of being the 'best plotter' of the age, Anthony Munday,[2] with the help of one or two others (probably Henry Chettle and possibly Thomas Heywood, a beginner at the time). When this first treatment was submitted to a company of actors, a number of substantial changes were required, both for theatrical and censorial reasons, entailing the intervention, at different times, not only of Chettle and Heywood, but also of other young actor–playwrights connected with the company, namely Thomas Dekker and William Shakespeare, while a professional book-keeper was put in charge of inserting the new material in the book as well as of correcting and transcribing the additions.[3]

Edward III belongs to the same period and probably involves Shakespeare at least as collaborator. If we accept that this procedure – a 'plotter' laying down the general outlines of the play and providing, possibly with the help of others, its first complete treatment, followed in turn by further interventions by the same or other writers intended to improve the stage-worthiness of the whole – was the current practice at the time, there is no reason to disbelieve that *Edward III*, or for that matter *1 Henry VI*, the two Parts of *The Contention between the two Famous Houses of York and Lancaster* (later known as *2* and *3 Henry VI*), and a number of other plays, especially histories, produced in the late eighties and early nineties of the sixteenth century, underwent a similar process. The 'plotter' fulfilled a key function, since he had to select, conflate, and manipulate the historical sources for dramatic effect, but he could hardly be considered the author of the play in the modern sense of the word, because the guidelines he provided were not necessarily developed by him. In a way, the later revisers of the books, responsible for substantial additions and changes that gave the texts their final shape, have a stronger claim to authorship than the devisers of the original treatment.

1 On the work of 'plotters' see Bradley, pp. 75–94 and *passim*.

2 Francis Meres, *Palladis Tamia, Wits Treasury* (1598): 'the best for Comedy amongst vs bee, *Edward* Earle of Oxforde, Doctor *Gager* of Oxforde, Maister *Rowley* once a rare Scholler of learned Pembrooke Hall in Cambridge, Maister *Edwardes* one of her Maiesties Chappell, eloquent and wittie *Iohn Lilly*, *Lodge*, *Gascoyne*, *Greene*, *Shakespeare*, *Thomas Nash*, *Thomas Heywood*, *Anthony Mundye* our best plotter, *Chapman*, *Porter*, *Wilson*, *Hathway*, and *Henry Chettle* . . .' Reproduced in *Riverside*, p. 1844.

3 See Introduction to *Sir Thomas More. A play by Anthony Munday and Others*, edited by Vittorio Gabrieli and Giorgio Melchiori (Revels Plays, 1990), pp. 3–29, and for a more detailed study of the sequence of Additions, Melchiori, '*The Booke of Sir Thomas Moore*: a chronology of revision', *SQ*, 37 (1986), 291–308.

Composition as well as performance were communal activities in the Elizabethan public theatre. We should not, therefore, think of *Edward III* in terms of sole authorship, whether Shakespeare's or one of the other numerous playwrights variously suggested as authors,[1] or of collaborations between only two authors, carefully apportioning different scenes to the one or the other, or even of revision or rewriting by one author of a pre-existing work by somebody else.[2] Let us consider in the first place the original 'plotting' of *Edward III*, in order to clear the ground from some persistent misconceptions. The Appendix on the use of sources makes it clear that the 'plotter' drew the outlines of the play at first from Holinshed's chronicles of the reign of Edward III, soon integrated with those of Froissart, but there was a third distinct stage in the elaboration which took into account a novel of Painter's. This stratification in the plotting cannot be ignored. There are no firm grounds for supposing that the original plotter was Shakespeare himself. The evidence is inconclusive; the manipulation of historical facts and chronology in the play closely resembles that practised in most histories of the period, including Shakespeare's, but by no means only his. The claim that Shakespeare never based his histories on Froissart is deceptive. As I have pointed out elsewhere,[3] the mention of Froissart in *1 Henry VI*, 1.2.29–31, reveals a man who had an exceptionally thorough knowledge of the French historian, but it should be kept in mind that *1 Henry VI* is the least Shakespearean of the histories: he may have given it its final form, but presumably he neither plotted nor rewrote it completely, and the passage mentioning Froissart may well be another author's.

As for the stratification in the plotting, there is ample evidence that the most undoubtedly Shakespearean scenes of *Edward III*, those concerned with the episode of the Countess of Salisbury, though presumably included in a different form in the second stage of the original plot, were developed only during the third stage, when the author(s) became familiar with William Painter's novel 46 in his *Palace of Pleasure*, which gave a new twist to the marginal episode related by Froissart but not by

[1] Apart from Tucker Brooke (1908) who, as already stated, thought of George Peele as the author, J. M. Robertson (1924) assigned it to Christopher Marlowe with contributions from Greene, Peele, and Kyd; E. A. Gerrard (1928) and H. W. Crundell (1939) to Michael Drayton; S. R. Golding (1929) to Robert Wilson; W. Wells (1940) and G. Lambrechts (1963) to Thomas Kyd; R. G. Howarth (1964) to Robert Greene. For a discussion of these attributions see Metz, pp. 11–17. Sole Shakespearean authorship is favoured by recent scholarship using sophisticated statistical and linguistic techniques: Slater (1988), Smith, 'Authorship' (1991), and Hope (1994). Finally Robert A. J. Matthews and Thomas V. N. Merriam, by applying a new variant of the stylometric method ('Neural computation in stylometry II: an application to the works of Shakespeare and Marlowe', *L&LC* 9 (1994), 1–6) find (p. 4) that *Edward III* 'has the lowest SCM [Shakespearean Characteristics Measure] of any play classified as Shakespearian . . . This lends support to Robertson's (1924) view that Marlowe had a considerable influence on the play, a view also partly supported by the findings of Merriam ['Marlowe's hand in *Edward III*', *L&LC* 8 (1993), 59–72], who gives stylometric arguments for Marlowe's authorship of scenes III.i and ii in this play.' They conclude (p. 6) that *Edward III*'s 'relatively weak Shakespearian character may well provide reason for pondering whether the argument for collaborative authorship can be dismissed'. On the question of the Marlowean echoes see the section 'From sources to structure' below.

[2] A distinction should be made between 'rewriting' and 'remaking': *1* and *2 Henry IV*, *Henry V*, *Hamlet*, *Troilus and Cressida*, *King Lear*, and possibly even the two Richard plays, are remakes and not just revisions of earlier works by other hands. See my 'The corridors of history: Shakespeare the re-maker', *PBA* 76 (1987), 67–85.

[3] Melchiori, *Garter Plays*, p. 120.

Holinshed. The evidence for considering the Countess's scenes (1.2, 2.1, 2.2) in the nature of an 'addition' integrated in the play in the third stage of plotting is provided by the character of the Earl of Warwick, presented by Painter, but not by Froissart, as the Countess's father. The plotter or reviser of the play did insert Warwick, though very marginally, in 1.1, from which he was originally absent,[1] but (in spite of the fact that the historical Warwick, according to both Holinshed and Froissart, had a fairly prominent part in events dramatised in the last three acts) he never appears after the second act. This suggests that his presence in the play had not been planned in the original plot.

The risk of overstressing the genetic affinities between *Edward III* and *Sir Thomas More*, limiting Shakespeare's role to that of author of a belated addition to somebody else's play, can be avoided by remembering that recent, and not so recent, critical opinion attributes the taunting of Prince Edward by the messengers of King John of France and his two sons (4.4) exclusively to Shakespeare. Verbal and structural affinities with Shakespeare's work are inevitable in a scene which sounds like an anticipation of the taunting of Henry by the ambassador of the French Dauphin in *Henry V*, 1.2. But (a) the latter episode had already been dramatised in *The Famous Victories of Henry the Fifth* (before 1588), though the garbled and reduced version of it published in 1598 does not permit a comparison with *Edward III*, and (b) there are more numerous verbal and iconic analogies with *earlier* Shakespearean plays and poems scattered throughout the rest of the play than appear in 4.4, where such analogies are with later works. In other words: (a) the analogies between 4.4 and *Henry V* 1.2 may be due mainly to their having a common source of inspiration in an earlier play, but at the same time (b) the diffused echoes of and analogies with other early Shakespearean works both in words and imagery suggest Shakespeare as collaborator if not in the original plotting of the play, at least in some early phases of its treatment, before providing the substantial 'addition' (1.2, 2.1, 2.2, replacing a shorter and different account of the Countess affair), which represents by itself about a third of the total length of the play.

The genesis, growth, and structure of *Edward III* are discussed in later sections, but some conclusions on the vital question of authorship may be drawn. The play originated as a collaborative work destined to one of the companies active before the complete reorganisation of the London theatres in 1594. The plotter was not necessarily Shakespeare, and successive stages can be detected both in the devising of the general outlines of the play and in the writing of the book. Internal evidence suggests that Shakespeare contributed in some measure, in conjunction with other more or less experienced script-writers, to the first stages of this process, and that he took over completely in the last stage, when it appeared that Painter's *Palace of Pleasure* offered a new and dramatically more effective version of a peripheral episode reported by Froissart and already incorporated in the play. Shakespeare alone was responsible for the replacement of the relevant scenes in the early acts.

The participation of Shakespeare at first as one of the collaborators in a multiple-

[1] See Appendix, pp. 179 and 184–5.

authorship play, and then as the sole author of an 'addition' (meaning a substitute scene, like Addition IID in *Sir Thomas More*) explains why the most careful explorers of the play's linguistic features[1] or of its themes, imagery and structure,[2] either tentatively accepted Shakespeare's authorship of the whole, or saw the play as the work of others revised by Shakespeare. His hand as collaborator can be detected in many scenes of the play, but his sole authorship of at least Act 2 is undeniable. Slater, in advocating Shakespeare's authorship, says that 'part B [most of the play] dates from an earlier stage' than the Countess scenes [part A]. The difference is not so much one of dates as of stylistic consistency. Michael Hattaway asked the essential question *à propos 1 Henry VI*: 'even if it could be proved that the play was in whole or in part not by Shakespeare, should that affect the way in which we read or direct it?'[3]

The genesis of *Edward III*: a Garter Play

The success of history plays on the public stage in the late sixteenth century was undoubtedly due to the nationalistic spirit promoted by Elizabeth in the country at large, which reached its peak just after the defeat of the Armada in 1588. The attention of playwrights focused on the Hundred Years War for the French succession (1337–1453), when the English repeatedly conquered large parts of France and for a time the crowns of England and France were united. The claim to the French succession was first advanced on dynastic grounds by Edward III in 1337, and its achievement seemed consolidated in 1356, when the Black Prince captured the French King himself at the battle of Poitiers. But by Edward's death in 1377 only Calais remained in English hands, and after the troubled reigns of Richard II, deposed in 1399, and of the Lancastrian Henry IV, it was the latter's son Henry V who, shortly after his accession in 1413, renewed the claim, and his new conquest of France resulted in the recognition of Henry as the heir to the French crown at Troyes in 1420. The triumph was short-lived, and after Henry's death two years later, the protracted French campaigns of the following thirty years registered the loss of most of the territories conquered by the English, engaged from 1455 at home in the Wars of the Roses. The pages of the chronicles that lent themselves to the celebration of a renewal of the conquering spirit of the English nation were those concerned with the years 1337–56, and 1415–20.

We know for certain that by 1588 the Queen's Men had very successfully presented a play, possibly in two parts, covering the second of these periods, *The Famous Victories of Henry the fifth*,[4] whose text was printed ten years later in an extremely

[1] Hart, ('The vocabulary of *Edward III*', in *Shakespeare and the Homilies*, 1934, pp. 219–41); Everitt ('The young Shakespeare', *Anglistica* 2 (1954), 219–41); Lapides (1966, pub. 1980); Slater (1981, pub. 1988); Smith, 'Authorship' (1991); Hope (1994).

[2] Østerberg (1929), pp. 49–91; Muir (1960), pp. 10–55; Wentersdorf, 'Authorship' (1960); Inna Koskenniemi, 'Themes and imagery in *Edward III*', *NM* 65 (1964), 146–80. Compare Lapides (1966, pub. 1980).

[3] *The First Part of King Henry VI*, ed. Michael Hattaway (New Cambridge Shakespeare, 1990), p. 43.

[4] The *terminus ad quem* for the performance of the play is established by an anecdote (reported in *Tarltons Iests*, 1638) according to which the famous clown of the Queen's Men, Richard Tarlton, who died in 1588, had lent himself on one occasion to play in it the role of a judge, 'besides his owne part of the clowne'.

2 The coronation of King Edward III. From the Coronation Order of a King in a manuscript of c. 1330, intended rather as a ceremonial 'Glory of Regality' than as a realistic representation

garbled and reduced version. *Famous Victories* was meant as a tribute to the English fighting spirit at a time when Elizabethan England was under threat of a Spanish invasion. After the defeat of the Armada, *The Reign of King Edward the third* was conceived in a similar vein, as a celebration of the achievements of the earlier English conqueror of France. In fact, *The Famous Victories of Henry the fifth* and *The Reign of King Edward the third* present an identical pattern, showing at first the weak sides of their respective heroes, and then their reformation and triumph.

The original deviser of the play turned at first to the chronicles of Holinshed, in the edition printed the year before the Armada, in order to cull from them the most glorious events of the reign, as the basis on which to construct his history. They were:[1]

II.611–12: Edward's claim to France (see the marginal title on 612, 'King Edward signifieth his right to the crowne of France').
II.614–15: The naval battle off Sluys, 1340 ('The victorie of the Englishmen at the battell of Sluise'), suggesting a parallel with the defeat of the Armada.
II.628–9: The founding of the Order of the Garter, 1344[2] ('The order of the garter founded', 'The occasion that mooued K. Edward to institute the order of the garter').
II.634–40: The landing in Normandy and the victory at Crécy, 1346.
II.640–8: The siege and conquest of Calais, 1346–7 (the narrative is interrupted – pp. 644–5 – by the relation of the Scottish campaign of 1346, when King David was captured while Edward was at the siege of Calais).
II.662–9: Edward the Black Prince's victory at Poitiers and the capture of John, King of France, 1356.

These were the salient episodes on which the original plotter and his collaborators were to construct the new history, with the usual compressions and transpositions of historical time, conflations and multiplications of characters, and other devices familiar to all men of the theatre. But the text as we have it now lacks one of the episodes, that of the founding of the Order of the Garter, which would have offered ample scope for impressive stage pageantry. This lack is the more surprising in view of the time when the play was first conceived. In 1591 the values represented by the Garter had been solemnly celebrated on the London stage in the memorable speech of John Talbot, another national hero, in a play, *1 Henry VI*, that, according to Thomas Nashe, had attracted to the theatre 'ten thousand spectators at least (at seuerall times)':

> When first this Order was ordain'd my Lords,
> Knights of the Garter were of Noble birth;
> Valiant, and Vertuous, full of haughtie Courage,
> Such as were growne to credit by the warres:
> Not fearing Death, nor shrinking for Distresse,
> But alwayes resolute in most extreames.[3]

From the beginning of her reign, Queen Elizabeth had revived, in the splendid Accession Day Tilts, those rites of chivalry that Edward III had founded, making of

[1] References are to volume and pages of the 1807–8 reprint of the 1587 edition of Holinshed's *Chronicles*.

[2] Actually this date, suggested by Froissart, refers to Edward's earlier unfulfilled intention of reviving in Windsor King Arthur's Round Table. Both Juliet Vale (*Edward III and Chivalry: Chivalric Society and its Context, 1270–1350*, 1982, pp. 76–91) and D'A. J. Dacre Boulton (*The Knights of the Crown: The Monarchical Orders of Knighthood in Later Medieval Europe 1325–1520*, 1987, pp. 101–17) place the foundation of the Garter Order around 1348, after Edward's return in late 1347 from his victorious campaign in France. As Vale remarks (p. 81), 'Participation at Crécy is the most immediately striking common factor among the first knights of the Garter.'

[3] *1H6* 4.1.33–8; 1623 Folio, sig. L3v. Thomas Nashe's well-known remark comes from *Pierce Pennilesse his Supplication to the Diuell* (1592), facsimile edn, 1969, fol. 26r, sig. H2.

3 King Edward III as the founder of the Order of the Garter, showing the insignia of the Order and the arms of England and its dominions. From an early fifteenth-century manuscript in the British Library

them an essential part of the Elizabethan myth of Astraea.[1] That in the 1590s particular stress was placed on the Order of the Garter is attested by George Peele's poem, *The Honour of the Garter*,[2] which, in more than four hundred lines of blank verse, recounts in dream form the story of the Order and its foundation ('the manner how this matter grew at first'). He tells how

> The King disposed on a time
> To reuell, after he had shaken Fraunce . . .
> Found on the ground by Fortune as he went
> A Ladies Garter: And the Queenes I troe
> Lost in a daunce, and tooke it vp himselfe.

Noticing the ironical smiles of the courtiers at his gesture,

> Honi Soit Qui mal y pense, quoth he,
> Wherewith vpon advizement, though the cause
> Were small, his pleasure and his purpose was
> T'aduance that Garter, and to institute
> A noble order sacred to S. George.

Peele was merely versifying a page of Holinshed, which in turn translated with some omissions a passage from Polydore Vergil's Latin *Historia Anglica* (1555).[3] According to Holinshed, the Order of the Garter was 'devised' by Edward III at the conclusion of a series of 'martiall feasts, and iousts, tornaments, and diuerse other the like warlike pastimes', held at Windsor Castle 'betwixt Candlemasse and Lent' at the beginning of the eighteenth year of his reign (1344):

The cause and first originall of instituting this order is vncerteine. But there goeth a tale amongst the people, that it rose by this means. It chanced that K. Edward finding either the garter of the queene, or of some* ladie with whom he was in loue, being fallen from hir leg, stooped downe and tooke it vp, whereat diuerse of his nobles found matter to iest, and to talke their fansies merilie, touching the kings affection towards the woman, vnto whome he said, that if he liued, it should come to passe, that most high honor should be giuen vnto them for the garters sake: and there vpon shortlie after, he deuised and ordeined this order of the garter, with such a posie, wherby he signified, that his nobles iudged otherwise of him than the truth was. Though some may thinke, that so noble an order had but a meane beginning, if this tale be true,

[1] See Frances A. Yates, *Astraea: The Imperial Theme in the Sixteenth Century*, 1975, especially pp. 108–12 on the Garter and Elizabethan chivalry.

[2] The poem was published in 1593, on the occasion of the installation of the Earl of Northumberland as a Knight of the Garter. See D. H. Horne, ed., *The Life and Minor Works of George Peele* 1952, I, 173–7; text pp. 245–59. I quote lines 108–9, 113–15, 127–31.

[3] *Historia Anglica*, facsimile edn, 1970, lib. XIX, pp. 378–9. The book had been published first in Basle (1534), but the episode of the fallen garter as the occasion for the founding of the Order had been related long before by the Valencian writer Joanot Martorell in his chivalric romance *Tirant Lo Blanch*, written in 1460, published in 1490, translated into Castilian in 1511 and into Italian in 1538. In that romance (mentioned in *Don Quixote* as 'the best book in the world') the garter picked up at the court dance and worn by Edward III did not belong to a noble lady, but to a 'damsel' named Madresilva. I am grateful to Jesús Tronch of the Instituto Shakespeare of Valencia for providing this information. Compare Boulton, p. 155.

yet manie honorable degrees of estates haue had their beginnings of more base and meane things, than of loue, which being orderlie vsed, is most noble and commendable, sith nobility it selfe is couered vnder loue, as the poet *Ouid* aptlie saith,

Nobilitas sub amore iacet.[1]

Holinshed not only omitted some of Polydore's classical references in the passage, but also made an unobtrusive addition to his faithfully reported text: next to the words 'some ladie with whom he was in loue' he placed the marginal note 'The countes of Salisburie', to which attention is drawn in the 1587 edition by an asterisk in the text. The hint is not developed, and the countess does not figure elsewhere in the chronicles. The lady is not even mentioned by Polydore Vergil, though he says that the fallen garter must have been *reginae seu amicae*, 'of the queen or of a lady-friend'.

If it is true that the 1587 edition of Holinshed was the starting point for the original plotter of the play, the tantalising marginal note in his account of the origin of 'this most Honourable Order', a note which suggested further possibilities for dramatising the episode, but left unexplained Edward's involvement with the Countess of Salisbury, must have been the decisive factor in inducing the plotter to turn from Holinshed to the earlier chronicler of Edward's reign, Jean Froissart.[2] The chapter 'Of the order of saynt George that kyng Edwarde stablysshed in the castell of Wyndsore', in Froissart's *Cronycle* translated into English at the command of King Henry VIII by John Bourchier Lord Berners (1523–5),[3] is disappointing. It does not even hint at the reason for the name given to the Order:

There [in Windsor castle, rebuilt by Edward on the site where King Arthur had founded the Round Table] kyng Edwarde determyned to make an order and a brotherhode of a certayne nombre of knyghtes, and to be called knyghtes of the blewe garter; and a feest to be kept yerely at Wynsore on saynt Georges day.

But though the Countess is not mentioned in connection with the founding of the Order, she appears in an earlier chapter, 77, 'Howe the kyng of Englande was in amours with the Countesse of Salisbury'.[4] Most of the first book of Froissart's chronicles is closely based on Jean Le Bel's *Vrayes Chroniques*, covering the years 1326–61,

[1] Holinshed, II, 628–9.

[2] That Froissart was the main source for the play was first pointed out by Robert Metcalf Smith, 'Edward III (A study of the authorship of the drama in the light of a new source)', *JEGP*, 10 (1911), 90–104. Finding in Froissart the episode of the Countess of Salisbury, Smith deplored the 'many critics' who maintained that 'the episode was thrust into an earlier version [of the play] by Shakspere [*sic*]', judged 'untenable' the theory of double authorship or the attribution of the play to Marlowe, Greene, Peele, or Lodge, and concluded by quoting Capell's invitation to the reader to 'form an opinion of his own' about the author. Recently Roger Prior ('Compliment', 1994) maintained that the author of *Edward III* had direct access to the copy of the French 1513 edition of Froissart owned by Henry Carey Lord Hunsdon (in which he recorded the births of his children as in a family Bible), where Carey had entered marginal comments in English on episodes related in the first three acts of the play. Prior concludes that the whole play was conceived as a compliment to Carey, Lord Chamberlain and from 1594 patron of Shakespeare's company (see p. 5, n. 8).

[3] Froissart, ch. 100 (Ker, I, 232–3). As already stated (p. 19, n. 2), Froissart – followed by Holinshed – confused the founding of the Order of the Garter with Edward's idea, entertained in 1344, of creating a body of three hundred knights on the model of Arthur's Round Table. See Vale, p. 77.

[4] In Metz, pp. 65–7. See Appendix, pp. 184–9.

and the episode of the Countess of Salisbury reproduces Le Bel's chapter 50, 'Comment le roy Edowart vint au chastel de Salebry . . . et comment il s'enamoura de la belle contesse de Salbry'.[1] The plotter of the play, then, learnt from Berners's translation of Froissart that Edward had fallen in love with the Countess during a visit to her castle in the North which had been besieged by the Scots; and that when she rejected his advances, 'the kyng departed all abasshed'.[2] But he did not know that Le Bel concluded instead his chapter on an ominous note of warning. Speaking of the King's passion for the lady, he added:

et au derrain, le poingny si fort l'aguillon d'amours que il en fit telle chose dont il fut amerement blasmé et repris, car quant il ne peut faire sa volenté de la noble dame par amours ne par priere, il l'eut à force, ainsy que vous orrez cy apres.[3]

'Cy apres' is actually Le Bel's chapter 65 of his work, 'Comment le roy Edowart forfist grandement quant il efforcha le contesse de Salbry',[4] a chapter known to Froissart who, in a passage not included in the final version of his chronicle, deplores and denies its contents.[5] According to Le Bel, at first Edward arranged great festivities in London in August 1342 in honour of the Countess, without obtaining her love,[6] but two years later, while the Earl of Salisbury was on a mission in France, he visited her in her castle, and raped her:

l'enforcha à telle doulour et à tel martire qu'onques femme ne fut ainsy villainement traittiée; et la laissa comme gisant toute pasmée, sanant par nez et par bouche et aultre part . . . Puis s'en parti l'endemain sans dire mot.[7]

The passage sounds like a crude anticipation of the narrative of the rape in Shakespeare's *Lucrece*, when, after the event, Tarquin (lines 736–42)

> like a thievish dog creeps sadly thence,
> She like a wearied lamb lies panting there;
> He scowls and hates himself for his offence,
> She desperate with her nails her flesh doth tear;
> He faintly flies, sweating with guilty fear,
> She stays, exclaimimg on the direful night.
> He runs, and chides his vanished loath'd delight.

Froissart's version is a far cry from this. He simply relates that

[1] *Chronique de Jean Le Bel publiée pour la Société de l'Histoire de France par Jules Viard et Eugène Déprez* (1904), I, 290–4.
[2] Metz, p. 67 (bk I, ch. 77).
[3] Le Bel, I, 293–4. 'And in the end the shaft of love pierced him so sharply that he did something for which he was bitterly blamed and reproved; for when he could not have his way with the noble lady either by love or by prayer, he had it by force, as you will hear hereafter' (trans. in Michael Packe, *King Edward III*, ed. L. C. B. Seaman, 1983, p. 103).
[4] 'How King Edward gravely sinned when he ravished the Countess of Salisbury'; Le Bel, II, 30–4.
[5] See Melchiori, *Garter Plays*, pp. 128–9.
[6] Le Bel, II, 1–2, ch. 61.
[7] *Ibid.*, II, 31: 'he raped her so savagely that never was a woman so badly treated; and he left her lying there all battered about, bleeding from the nose and the mouth and elsewhere . . . Then he left the next day without saying a word' (trans. in Packe, p. 120).

for the loue of this lady, and for the great desyre that the king had to se her, he caused a great feest to be cryed, and a justyng to be holden in the cyti of London in the myddes of August [1342?].[1]

But the king's aim was defeated:

All ladyes and damoselles were fresshely besene accordyng to their degrees, except Alys countesse of Salisbury, for she went as simply as she myght, to the intent that the kyng shulde nat sette his regarde on her, for she was fully determyned to do no maner of thynge that shulde tourne to her dyshonour nor to her husbandes.[2]

After this the Countess disappears altogether from Froissart's *Cronycle*. Even if the play's plotter had heard of Le Bel's lurid account, he conformed to Froissart's report, according to which no violence was offered to the Countess: her virtuous behaviour was an object lesson for the king, who turned his attention to state matters, upon hearing that the Scots were once again up in arms, and that the French 'made great preparacions for the warre'.[3]

Though the devisers of the play originally intended to include a treatment of the circumstances in which the honourable Order of the Garter was founded, Froissart's failure to connect the king's 'amours with the countesse of Salisbury' with the legend of the lost garter induced a change of mind. The Garter values were to be celebrated implicitly, by presenting the ceremonial arming of the Black Prince before Crécy (3.3.172–218) and his knighting after the battle (3.4.101–6) – both unhistorical events – and by developing to an exceptional extent two minor episodes reported by Froissart (but not by Holinshed) apt to illustrate the aims of the Order of the Garter,[4] by introducing the theme of the education of princes, which Tillyard recognised as the unifying structural element of the play.[5]

One of the episodes was that of King Edward's curbing his unruly passion for the Countess of Salisbury, initially introduced in the play as told in Froissart's chapters 77 and 89, with no threats of suicide or murder and no indication of the pressure put on her father Warwick – a character who, as I indicated (p. 16), did not figure at all in the play as originally written.[6] The other episode, interwoven in the plot and considerably developed in 4.1, 4.3.1–56 and 4.5.56–126, was that, related in Froissart's chapter

[1] Metz, p. 67 (bk I, ch. 89).

[2] *Ibid.*, p. 68.

[3] *Ibid.*

[4] They are described in the reformed statutes of Henry VI: 'To aduance to honor and glory good, godly, valiant, well couraged, wise and noble men for their notable desertes, and to nourishe a certaine amytie, fellowship, and agrement in all honest thinges among all men, but specially among equalles in degre.' See Richard C. McCoy, *The Rites of Knighthood: The Literature and Politics of Elizabethan Knighthood*, 1989, p. 20.

[5] E. M. W. Tillyard *Shakespeare's History Plays*, 1944, pp. 113–14.

[6] The existence, after completion of the play, of an earlier version of 1.2, 2.1, and 2.2, is supported not only by the absence of Warwick in it, but also by those two allusions to the episode in later scenes, by King John at 3.3.155–7 and by Edward himself at 3.4.112–14, which have been taken as evidence of single authorship for the whole play (see the nn. to the passages). If the writer had been referring to the final version of the episode, he would have imputed to the king much more grievous offences than a temporary lapse into wantonness and love-sickness.

135,[1] of the safe-conduct through France granted to Sir Walter de Manny, an example of honourable behaviour by all concerned, English and French. The treatment of the Black Prince in 3.3 and 3.4 and of the two episodes from Froissart confirms that *Edward III* was conceived in the spirit of what Peter Erickson, with reference to such histories as *1 Henry VI* and *Henry V*, called 'Garter Plays'.[2]

From sources to structure

From an initial plot based on Holinshed, the author, or rather the collaborators in the communal enterprise of playwriting, devised a play-book comprising, reordering, and manipulating the ample material provided by Froissart. Writing a history play required in the first place a process of simplification. The two countries in conflict should be incarnated by two contrasting dominant figures from beginning to end. The fact that Edward had to face in history not one but two successive Kings of France, Philip VI at Sluys and Crécy, his son John at Poitiers, would create confusion. So Philip was eliminated from the start, and this omission entailed not only a revision of the Capetian genealogy,[3] but also substantial alterations in the chronology of events and in the ages and actions of their relatives and followers, beyond the compression of time which was an accepted convention in the presentation of history on the stage. The most striking example of this procedure is found in *1 Henry VI* where the author, having decided to personify the virtues of England in the noble Talbot and the vices of France in Joan of Arc, did not scruple to keep Joan, executed in 1431, alive till after Talbot's death in 1453, and to have, among many such anachronisms, the loss of Bordeaux in 1453 precede the armistice with France in 1444. Less drastically, in *Edward III* only Artois and Mountford are kept alive to the end (they both died before Crécy) as emblematic of the French who recognised Edward as their king. These and many other such cases of manipulation of the sources are illustrated and discussed in the Appendix. From the structural point of view the case of the Earl of Salisbury is more significant. After being mentioned in the first two acts as the absent husband of the Countess, doing good service in France for King Edward (a fact variously confirmed by the chronicles), Salisbury suddenly appears on stage in Acts 4 and 5, when the historical earl had been dead several years. He is actually cast in the role of the protagonist of the episode of the safe-conduct, replacing in it the valiant knight indicated by Froissart, Sir Walter de Manny. The relevance of the episode to what I should call the 'Garter theme' has already been noted, and it is exactly there that we must look for the reason for this resuscitation and substitution. It was not a matter of avoiding the confusion caused by the belated introduction of yet another character, but

[1] Metz, pp. 84–5. See Appendix and nn. to the relevant scenes.

[2] Peter Erickson, 'The Order of the Garter, the cult of Elizabeth, and class–gender tension in *The Merry Wives of Windsor*', in *Shakespeare Reproduced. The Text in History and Ideology*, ed. Jean E. Howard and Marion F. O'Connor, 1987, pp. 116–40. For a book-length treatment of the subject see Melchiori, *Garter Plays*.

[3] See 1.1.21 n. and the discussion in the Appendix, pp. 180 and 199, of the changes caused by the 'suppression' of the first Valois to ascend the throne of France.

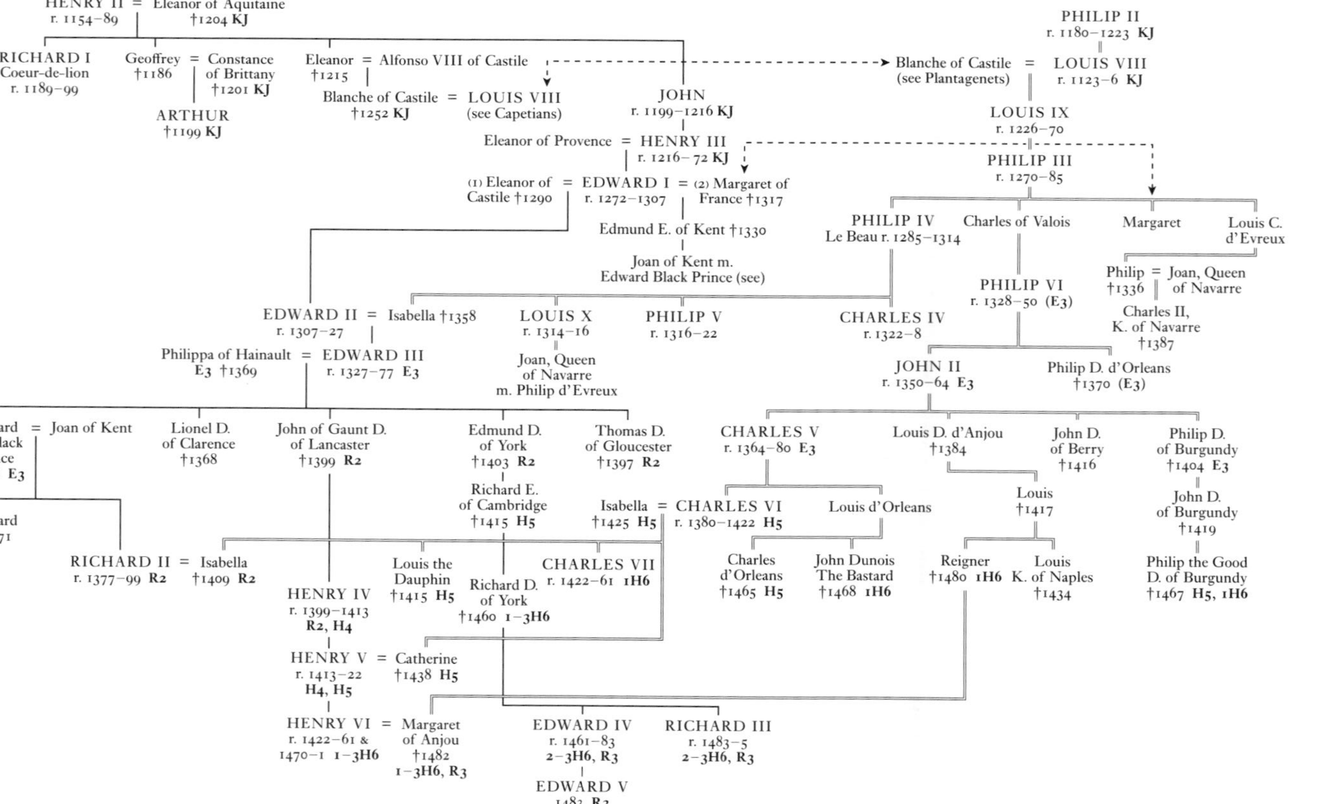

4 Intermarriages between the Houses of England (single line) and France (double line), showing characters appearing in Shakespeare's history plays (KJ = *King John*, E3 = *Edward III*, R2 = *Richard II*, 1-2H4 = *1, 2 Henry IV*, H5 = *Henry V*, 1-3H6 = *1, 2, 3 Henry VI*)

a way of creating a structural link with the early scenes in which that theme first emerged. A symmetry is established: the Earl of Salisbury incarnates in Acts 4 and 5 the same values as the Countess of Salisbury in Acts 1 and 2. And together they enclose as in a frame the emblematic presentation of the rites of chivalry through the arming and knighting of the Black Prince in Act 3.

This is clear evidence of the professional skill with which the play was planned and structured both at the narrative and at the ideological level. Richard Proudfoot has warned that 'the division of the play's eighteen scenes[1] into five acts, introduced by Capell, is misleading. The true structure is tripartite.'[2] And he identifies what he calls the three phases of the play with Acts 1 and 2, Act 3, and Acts 4 and 5 respectively. The placing of the ideologically relevant scenes which I have just described confirms the correctness of his division. A subtler and probably unconscious link between the first appearances on stage of the Countess and of the Earl of Salisbury at 1.2 and 4.1 respectively can be detected. As shown in the Appendix (pp. 187–8), the brave behaviour of the Countess besieged by the Scots was modelled on another chapter of Froissart, describing the heroic resistance of the Countess of Mountford, while her husband was absent, to the siege of her castle in Brittany by the French, until she was liberated by the English led by Sir Walter de Manny. Unhistorically, 4.1 presents Lord Mountford liberated and restored to the earldom of Brittany by the Earl of Salisbury, in preparation for an episode which Froissart reports *not* of Salisbury, but of Sir Walter de Manny. The Mountfords and the Salisburys out of the pages of Froissart seem inextricably interconnected in the author's mind with the ghostly presence of Manny, whose role is played by King Edward in 1.2 and by the Earl of Salisbury himself in 4.1. Such are the suggestions prompted by the sources to the creation of new dramatic structures.

It is rewarding to examine other displacements of source material required by the tripartite structure. The first dramatic phase, or rather block, is concerned with giving the reasons for the English claim to France and with showing – along the pattern provided by *The Famous Victories of Henry the fifth* – how the hero was able to curb his sensual impulses and embrace the ideals of patriotic conquest. This imposed the initial transposition: the episode of the King's 'amours' must precede the first famous victory, the naval battle off Sluys, in spite of the fact that Froissart reported the two events in the reverse order. The frame for this part of the play is represented by the claim to and declaration of war on France in 1.1, and the orders for the invasion of the country at the end of Act 2. Chronological compression – a constant feature of all history plays, where events distant many years in time are presented as following each other in a matter of a few days or even hours – affects the ages of all characters

[1] Sixteen scenes in the present edition. Proudfoot, in his forthcoming edition of the plays for the *Shakespeare Apocrypha*, has no act but only scene divisions. He considers 1.2 and 2.1 as a single scene, assuming that Lodowick had entered as one of the *others* at 1.2.89 SD 2 and was left alone on the stage after the general *Exeunt* at 1.2.162, so that there was no break before his soliloquy at the beginning of 2.1 (see 2.1.0 SD n.). He accepts instead Capell's division of 3.4 at line 13, and Werner and Proescholdt's breaks at lines 17 and 52 of 4.6. The reasons for rejecting these divisions in the present edition are given in the Note on the Text.

[2] Proudfoot, p. 166. The same tripartite structure characterises each of the three parts of *Henry VI*.

throughout the play, beginning with Prince Edward, who remains the same valiant boy from the declaration of war, when he was seven, to the time of Poitiers, when he was twenty-six. Only five characters are present in all three blocks of the play. Besides the King and the Prince, Artois represents the French who recognise Edward's right, Derby the true nobility of England, and Audley is cast in the role of the wise old Nestor, or rather Mentor, controlling the youthful enthusiasm of the Black Prince. Since the first two acts concentrate on the motives inspiring the English side, the appearance of the French monarch is delayed till Act 3. King David of Scotland, who figures in the Countess episode, replaces King John of France in the role of antagonist (although on a much reduced scale) to the dominant figure of the first block, King Edward, and the only other character to have a considerable weight at this stage is the Countess herself, destined to disappear from the rest of the play, but indispensable to the theme of the King's mastering his human passions.

The second dramatic block (Act 3), running together two famous battles by sea and by land, required only one major manipulation of the material provided by the sources, apart from the abolition of the six-year time-gap between them: in order to provide a frame for the whole action, the French preparations for the land encounter at Crécy (1346) are presented (3.1.1–61) before the description of the naval battle off Sluys (1340). This manipulation provides the opportunity for opening the act by at last introducing on stage the real antagonists of Edward, the French King and his sons.[1] The other advantage of presenting in 3.1 the famous English victory off Sluys through French eyes was that the narrative could assume the epic tone not so much of Holinshed's and Froissart's reports (though they were not ignored), as of the triumphal descriptions of a much more recent event, the defeat of the Spanish Armada. Such details as the havoc caused by the use of naval artillery (hardly employed at the time of Sluys), the mention of *Nonpareille* (*Nom per illa* in both quartos) as the name of a ship, and above all the description of the English half-moon battle formation are strong evidence that the playwright was treating Sluys in terms of the Armada, relying in particular, as Karl Wentersdorf has shown,[2] on Petruccio Ubaldino's well-known *Discourse Concerning the Spanish Fleet Invading England, in the Year 1588* (published in 1590). Ubaldino mentions repeatedly the English vessel *Non Pariglia*, and states that the Spanish fleet in the English Channel 'was placed in battle array after the manner of the moon crescent . . . her horns being extended in wideness about the distance of eight miles', a passage echoed not only in the description of the English ships before Sluys at 3.1.71–2, 'Majestical the order of their course, / Figuring the hornèd circle of the moon', but also in Audley's speech giving an imaginary picture of the French army deployed on the hills before Poitiers at 4.4.31–2: 'like a half moon opening but one way, / It rounds us in.'

Connecting the battle off Sluys and the recent defeat of the Armada is one way of

[1] See Appendix, pp. 199–200, for the manipulation of the French royal family: at the time of Crécy Philip VI of Valois was King of France and his son John was Duke of Normandy. In the play John is already king, and only the eldest and youngest of his four sons are presented; in fact in 1346 Prince Charles was nine and Philip five years old.

[2] Wentersdorf, 'Date', pp. 227–31.

5 English troops embarking for France, with flags and pennons bearing the arms of England quartered with those of France. From a contemporary manuscript in the British Library

celebrating the noble achievements of the English nation. The other is the behaviour of Edward at the next famous battle, Crécy, the baptism of fire for the sixteen-year-old Black Prince, when, as all chroniclers report, the Prince was beset by overwhelming French forces but the King refused to send any help because he wanted his son to win his spurs once and for all. The presentation of this episode at 3.4.14–73 balances the description of the naval battle at 3.1.142–84. What matters is the skill with which the two events are connected through a series of bridging scenes drawn from or inspired by Holinshed and Froissart. The confrontation between the two nations is presented first at the level of the common people – the townsmen flying before the invading army (3.2) and the historical anecdote of the French soldier showing the English the way to cross the Somme (3.3.1–45) – and then through the imaginary meeting of the two kings themselves (3.3.46–167). The dramatic masterstroke, though, is the way in which the core of the battle scene – seen through the eyes of King Edward standing, as the chroniclers report, on a 'windmill hill' while one messenger after another asks for help for the beleaguered Prince (3.4.1–73) – is framed by two imaginary scenes visually figuring the solemn rites of chivalry: the arming of Prince Edward (3.3.169–228) and his knighting (3.4.74–121), an implicit statement of the Garter theme. The fact that the central block of the play stages the open conflict between France and

6 The gold noble commemorating the naval battle of Sluys, first minted in 1344. See Appendix, p. 201

England is reflected in the distribution of lines between the main speakers: nearly 25 per cent to King John and nearly 23 per cent to King Edward. Significantly, immediately after them come Prince Edward, the hero of Crécy and the incarnation of the virtues of knighthood (over 13 per cent), and the French Mariner, the reporter of the battle off Sluys (more than 10.5 per cent).

A comparison between these percentages for Act 3 and those for the next dramatic block, Acts 4 and 5, centring on the English victory at Poitiers, is revealing of the technique used in manipulating the historical sources for both theatrical and ideological purposes. Also in this case, of the total number of lines in the block, only four characters speak more than 10 per cent each. But this time Prince Edward comes first (over 20 per cent), followed by the two warring kings, Edward of England (nearly 16 per cent) and John of France (more than 13 per cent), and by a new character, the Earl of Salisbury, with 10.5 per cent (the same proportion as the French Mariner in the second block). The predominance of the Black Prince was inevitable: historically Poitiers and the capture of the King of France were his personal triumph, at a time when his father King Edward was in London. Dramaturgical expediency, though, imposed the abolition of the ten-year time gap between the battle of Crécy in 1346,

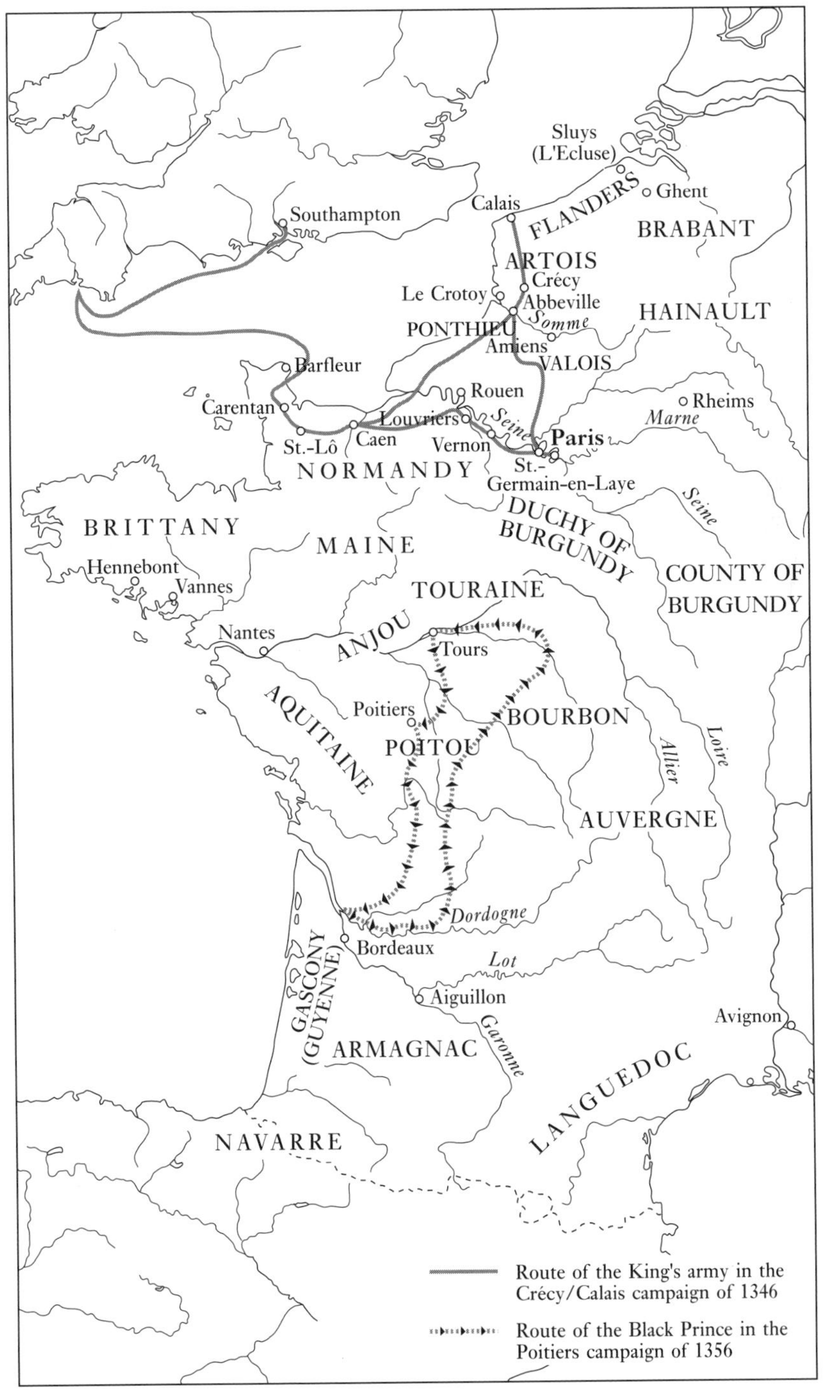

7 The English campaigns in France: Edward III in 1346 (——), and Prince Edward in 1356 (▸▸▸).
See Appendix, pp. 199–215

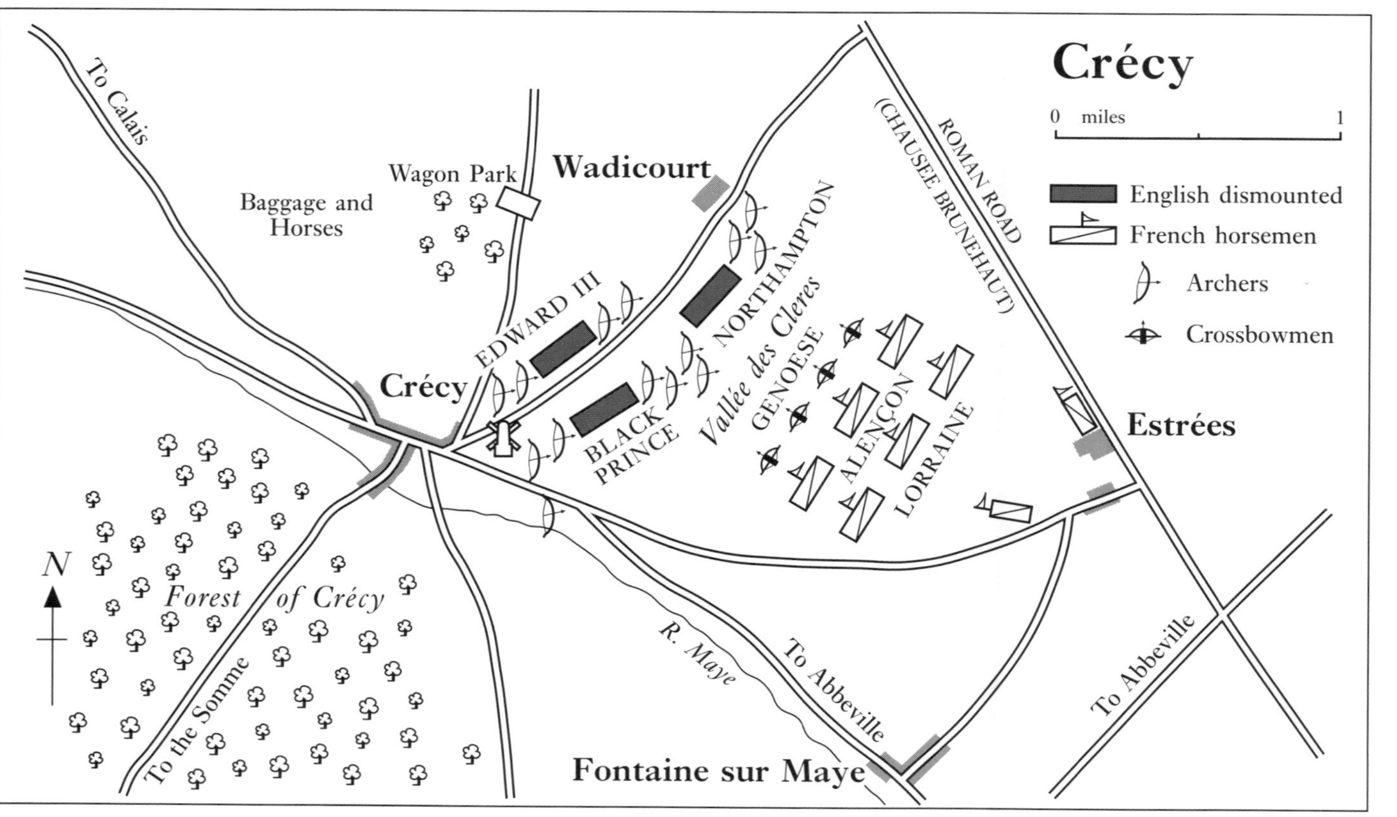

8 Map of the battle of Crécy, from John Laffin, *Brassey's Battles*. The initial onslaught by the Genoese crossbowmen was successfully countered by the English archers armed with longbows, who routed them and decided the day. See Appendix, pp. 205–7

which was followed immediately by the siege of Calais, and the battle of Poitiers in 1356. The playwright solved the time problem by building on Holinshed's and Froissart's reports of the town's resistance, of the self-sacrifice of the rich burghers of Calais and of King Edward's magnanimity, two scenes (4.2 and 5.1.1–62) that served as a frame for the scenes devoted to the battle of Poitiers (4.4 to 4.7). The events at Calais justified the absence of the King from the battlefield. At the same time, the chroniclers' accounts of the battle, underlining the constant tactical supremacy of the English in spite of their numerical inferiority, did not offer scope for dramatic suspense. The play therefore reverses the situation, taking from the chronicles only some relevant details such as the heroic behaviour of Lord Audley, his reward and generosity (4.6.53–62 and 4.7.18–55), but ignoring the rest and reverting to the situation at Crécy ten years before, where Prince Edward was surrounded by overwhelming French forces (see 4.3.57–62, 4.4.1–65 and 124–62, 4.5.109–26, 4.6.1–17). The backward look from Poitiers to Crécy suggests also the episode of the flight of ravens frightening the French army (4.5.1–55), which is drawn directly from Holinshed's and Froissart's reports of the earlier battle. Another episode, the taunting of Prince Edward by the French heralds (4.4.66–123), is modelled on the ironical offer by the French Dauphin of a tun of tennis balls to Henry V in *Famous Victories*. The main historical event of the battle, the capture of King John of France and his son Philip, is not presented on stage but given as a *fait accompli* at the beginning of 4.7 (1–17), with an addition: Prince Charles, Duke of Normandy, who in fact had escaped from the battle, figures among the captive French royalty.

There is a reason for this unwarranted inclusion, which is forgotten in the next act, where, true to history, the herald announces the arrival (5.1.182–3) of 'King John of France together with his son [Philip] / In captive bonds', and Charles Duke of Normandy is not listed in the entrance stage direction at line 186. The reason is more of an ideological than of a theatrical nature. Next to the report of the early stages of the siege of Calais in 1346, Froissart (but not Holinshed) places the episode, already amply discussed in this Introduction (pp. 24–5 and 27), of the safe-conduct to Calais obtained by Sir Walter de Manny, identified in the play with the Earl of Salisbury. I need not rehearse the significance of the episode – developed in 4.1, 4.3.1–56, 4.5.56–126, and concluded with the arrival of the earl at Calais (5.1.97–175) – which constitutes the ideological frame of the third dramatic block of the play. What is worth noticing is the key role played by the Duke of Normandy, who grants the safe-conduct and, against the will of his father, prevents the detention of Salisbury. Now, the Duke of Normandy referred to by Froissart was John, the son of King Philip VI. In the play King Philip is suppressed, and the episode is made contemporary with the battle of Poitiers. This entails that the Duke of Normandy cannot be John, by now King of France, but his son Charles – and Charles must figure prominently in the events, more imaginary than historical, connected with the battle. Hence his capture together with his father is taken for granted.

To ensure a firm dramatic structure, the third part of the play presents a more drastic manipulation of the sources and of historical chronology than the other two. The central event is placed in an inner dramatic frame represented by the siege and

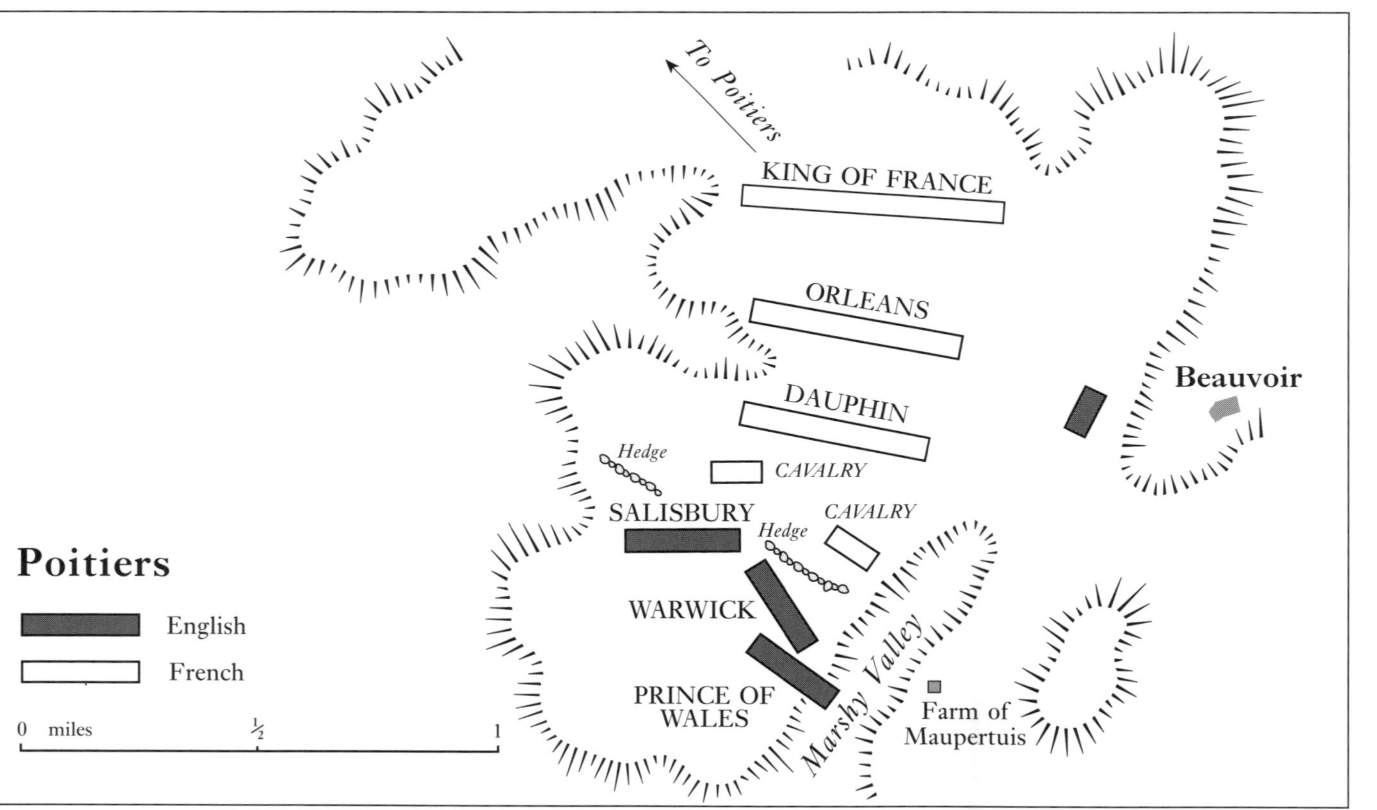

9 Map of the battle of Poitiers, from John Laffin, *Brassey's Battles*. See Appendix, pp. 210–14

surrender of Calais (4.2 and 5.1.1–62), which in turn is enclosed in a wider ideological context, the safe-conduct episode (4.1, 4.3.1–56, 4.5.56–126, 5.1.97–175), an object lesson in chivalric honour. Links are established between this double concentric structure and that of the first dramatic block through the reappearance at Calais of King David of Scotland (5.1.63–96), who had figured only in 1.2, and through the parallel ideological function of the Earl of Salisbury in Acts 4 and 5 and of the Countess of Salisbury in Acts 1 and 2. The freedom taken with the source material to achieve these ends suggested further significant variations on the stylistic level. The invention of the taunting of Prince Edward at 4.4, modelled on an episode in the reign of King Henry V which had already been presented on the stage in *Famous Victories*, but was to become well known in Shakespeare's version in *Henry V*, 1.2, has induced many scholars to assign 4.4 to Shakespeare's hand, but the striking stylistic analogies, as noted in the section on 'Authorship', p. 16 above, may be due to a common source.

More interesting are the obvious echoes of Marlowe's *Tamburlaine*, especially in King Edward's tirade at 5.1.167–75, when he thinks that his son the Prince has been killed. It should be noted that only the characters on stage believe the Black Prince has died, whereas the audience knows (4.7), after the dramatic suspense of the previous scenes, of the Prince's famous victory and the capture of the French King. The audience listens in expectation of the triumphal entrance of the Prince with his prisoner, which punctually happens at lines 176–243, as the fit conclusion to the play. The general awareness that the King's speech is somewhat supererogatory accounts for its highly rhetorical form. The best-known model for such an occasion was undoubtedly Tamburlaine's magnificent furious outburst over dead Zenocrate in the popular current success, *2 Tamburlaine*, 3.2. There is no need to suspect Marlowe's hand in *Edward III*.[1] The King's speech was conceived and written as a deliberate imitation or near quotation of another speech, Tamburlaine's, highly suited to the dramatic circumstances presented, already familiar and recognisable to the audience.

It appears that the author or authors of *Edward III* expertly manipulated the source materials to devise an elaborate, balanced dramatic structure which fused together patriotic celebration with more subtle themes such as the education of the prince. But the most serious criticism of the play has been levelled exactly at its structural consistency. In the words of an early critic:

> The plan pursued in the *Edward III* is, to say the least, exceedingly inartificial. If the writer of this play had possessed more dramatic skill, he might have made the severance of the action less abrupt. As it is, the link is snapped short. In the first two acts we have the Edward of Romance – a puling lover, a heartless seducer, a despot, and then a penitent. In the last three acts we have

[1] The presence of Marlowe's hand in *Edward III* was maintained most recently (1993) by Thomas Merriam (Merriam, 'Marlowe', pp. 60–72), though he did not apply his stylometric analysis to this scene (5.1) of the play, but to 3.1 and 2; in a later paper written in collaboration with Robert Matthews (Matthews & Merriam II) he seems to have modified to a certain extent his view. See p. 15, n. 1, and compare Sams, p. 191, stating that in the later paper the two authors suggest 'that *Edward III* was written by Shakespeare under considerable influence from Marlowe' – a sentence not to be found in the paper itself.

the Edward of history – the ambitious hero, the stern conqueror, the affectionate husband, the confiding father.[1]

The imputation of being a split play comes from the space given, in the final version of *Edward III*, to Edward's 'amours'. The so-called Countess scenes on the other hand are the most celebrated as attesting Shakespeare's authorship of the play. The contradiction can be reconciled if we accept that those scenes are an 'addition' replacing a section of an already complete book, an alteration suggested by the emergence of a new source for the episode related by Froissart in a story of Painter's *Palace of Pleasure*, and that the writing of the addition was entrusted to Shakespeare. The pros and cons for this last-minute decision must be discussed separately.

The final version of the Countess scenes: ideological ambiguity

What moved the devisers of a well-planned play to disturb its structural and ideological symmetries by replacing Froissart's narrative of Edward's exemplary 'amours' with an amplified version containing obvious historical distortions? William Painter's collection of 'Novels', *The Palace of Pleasure*, first published in 1567 and frequently reprinted, had become the most accessible repertory of fictional 'plots' for comedies and tragedies, in the same way as Holinshed had for histories. But authors only rarely drew on both. In fact, the origin of Painter's forty-sixth novel dealing with 'a King of England' and the Countess of Salisbury[2] is highly ambiguous. Matteo Bandello, a Roman Catholic prelate, had originally written it in 1547 upon hearing of the death of Rome's arch-enemy, Henry VIII, who 'spilled so much blood that it can be said that, compared with him, any prince or cruel tyrant in our age, whether a Christian or a barbarian, may be reputed merciful'. And he had started his story on a note of deliberate denigration: 'It seems to me right to say of these monarchs of England, whether of the white or of the red rose, that, as they all sprang from the same roots, nearly all of them coveted their neighbours' wives, and all thirsted after human blood more than Crassus after gold.'[3] It appears that Bandello was stimulated at first by an oral account that must have been close to Le Bel's story of the Countess's rape,[4] but when he looked for written testimony on which to base his narrative, he found only the

[1] Charles Knight, *Studies in Shakespeare* (1849), p. 279; quoted in Metz, p. 8.

[2] The full title of Painter's 'Forty-sixth Nouell' is: 'A King of England loued the daughter of one of his noble men, which was Countesse of Salesburie, who after great sute to atchieue that he could not winne, for the entire loue he bare her, and her greate constancie, hee made her his queene and wife.' References are to the reprint of the complete text in Metz, pp. 107–29.

[3] Matteo Bandello, *La Seconda Parte delle Novelle* (1554), Novella 37, 'Odoardo III re d'Inghilterra ama la figliuola d'un suo soggetto, e la piglia per moglie'. Quotations from *Le quattro parti delle novelle del Bandello*, a cura di Gustavo Balsamo-Crivelli, 1911, III, 94. My translations.

[4] In the dedicatory epistle of the novella to 'Monsignor Giorgio cardinale d'Armignacco [Armagnac]', Bandello tells how, in discussing the reign of King Henry VIII upon receiving the news of his death, the heinous crimes, vices, and iniquities of all the English monarchs were rehearsed, with particularly gruesome details from the lives of Henry II, John, Edward II, Richard III, and even Henry VII. Finally 'messer Giulio Basso' contributed the story which Bandello immediately after wrote out (Bandello, III, 91–4).

version in Froissart's French chronicles. So he transformed what should have been an *exemplum horrendum* of the English King's disregard for the Commandments into a fictional example of female virtue rewarded. Being a master story-teller, he manipulated and enriched Froissart's plain narrative by introducing new characters and circumstances: Edward's secretary unwillingly acting as a go-between, the pressure put by the King on the Countess's parents, alternating appeals to their loyalty, promises and threats in order to achieve his end, and the Countess's determination to commit suicide rather than sin. If tragedy had to be avoided, the only possible happy ending to the story must be lawful marriage: in the teeth of historical evidence, Bandello makes the King a bachelor and the Lady a widow, so that the Countess of Salisbury can become Edward's queen.

This is the story that Painter, apologising for the historical 'errours' it contains,[1] translated and included in *The Palace of Pleasure* as 'describing the perfect figure of womanhode, the naturall qualitie of loue incensinge the hartes indifferently of all nature's children, the liuely image of a good condicioned Prince, and zealous loue of parentes and the glorious reward that chastitie conduceth to her imbracers.'[2] The relevance of Edward's infatuation with the Countess of Salisbury to the theme of the 'education of princes' accounts for the inclusion in the play of such a peripheral episode out of Froissart. Bandello/Painter's version, by stressing in particular the values of womanhood and chastity, presented a further appeal in Elizabeth's time.[3] It is perhaps no mere coincidence that George Peele, a court poet ready to second and even anticipate his sovereign's wishes,[4] in the very same year 1593 when he published his poem *The Honour of the Garter*, should have contributed to the collection *The Phoenix Nest* a poem under the title 'The Praise of Chastity'.[5] Such considerations were a powerful inducement to replace in the play the Countess episode as told by Froissart with Painter's more elaborate version. And it was expedient to entrust the task of rewriting the relevant scenes to a young playwright who had apparently some experience in the job of remaking or adding to pre-existing plays. Shakespeare's addition to *Sir Thomas More*, whether written shortly before or after this, bears witness to his skill on such occasions.

The evidence for considering the Countess scenes as an 'addition' like that in *Sir Thomas More*, replacing, extending, and re-elaborating one or two scenes in an earlier version now lost, is of a double nature. At the textual level, there is marked carelessness, amply illustrated in the Textual Analysis, in the treatment of stage directions and speech headings, especially in Act 2, a feature shared with the pages in Hand D in

[1] 'Although the auctour . . . perchaunce hath not rightly touched the proper names of the aucthours of this tragedie, by perfecte appellations . . .' (Metz, p. 109). See Appendix, pp. 184–6.

[2] Metz, p. 107.

[3] Philippa Berry, *Of Chastity and Power*, 1989, misses the relevance to the main argument of her book of the Countess of Salisbury episode in *Edward III*.

[4] Yates, pp. 60–2, points out the importance of Peele's 1591 City pageant *Descensus Astraeae* in shaping the myth of the virgin queen as Astraea.

[5] Berry does not mention Peele's poem but elaborates (p. 143) on Shakespeare's allusion to the virgin queen in *A Midsummer Night's Dream*, 2.1.155–64, a play that must have been written not long after.

More.[1] The abrupt transition from the general *exeunt* at the end of Act 1 to Lodowick's soliloquy (misattributed to *Lor.* in the speech heading)[2] at the beginning of Act 2 suggests the insertion at that point of leaves written in a different hand from the rest of the manuscript. The numerous misreadings in this part of the text indicate that the compositor of the first quarto was confronted with copy in a hand less familiar than that of the rest, witness the muddle caused possibly by the omission of a line at 2.1.106, and the extraordinary misreading 'I will throng a hellie spout of bloud'[3] (for 'I will through a Hellespont of blood') in the allusion to the Hero and Leander story at 2.2.154. As pointed out in the Textual Analysis, pp. 174–6, the evidence that the hand responsible for the inserted leaves was Shakespeare's does not consist so much in the allusion to the rape of Lucrece at 2.2.192–5, as in the survival in quarto of the obviously authorial spelling 'emured' for 'immured' at 2.1.178 and of a capital for a lower case 'C' for a mid-line 'Cannot' at 2.2.148, both reflecting exclusively Shakespearean writing habits.

If the decision to replace Froissart's narrative of the Countess episode as an example of the education of princes with the version in Painter's novel was motivated by the intention of adding the celebration of the female virtue of chastity to that theme, Shakespeare's dramatisation of the story went well beyond this simple aim. Whether or not he had already written *Lucrece*, the allusion to the Roman lady at the end of Act 2 introduces a significant ideological ambiguity, which Larry Champion has brought to light by placing *Edward III* and the English chronicle plays in their historical context.[4] It renders explicit Shakespeare's ambivalent treatment of two themes that run through the whole of his work, from *Titus Andronicus* to the final romances, including *Two Noble Kinsmen*. One is the question of allegiance to a ruler, the other, hardly separable from it, that of the interplay of sexual passion and power.

A feature of Painter's novel, not mentioned by Froissart, is the pressure placed by the King on the Countess's parents to obtain her love. But while in Painter the pressure was exercised through promises of advancement alternating with threats of violence, in the play it is stated in political terms: the King extracts from the Earl of Warwick, the Countess's father, an oath of absolute allegiance, and in the name of this he tries to force him to become a pandar to his daughter. It is a problem of divided allegiance, to God's anointed sovereign or to individual conscience – a problem which was uppermost in the consciousness of an age uncertain of its values. Tudor jurists had tried to solve it by postulating the doctrine of the King's double body (echoed in *Richard II*),[5] but its presence is no less felt in a play like *Sir Thomas More*, written at about the same time as *Edward III*. Its contradictory nature is explored in Sonnet 94,

[1] See especially Melchiori, 'Hand D in *Sir Thomas More*', *S.Sur.* 38 (1985), 101–14.

[2] A mistaken amplification of a speech heading indicated only by an initial in the copy. The point is discussed in the Textual Analysis, pp. 172–3.

[3] Quoted by Charles Algernon Swinburne as evidence of the author's 'life-long and irremediable impotence', which led him to conclude that the author was not Shakespeare but 'a devout student and a humble follower of Christopher Marlowe' (*A Study of Shakespeare* (1879, rep. 1918), pp. 231–75).

[4] Larry S. Champion, '"Answere in this perillous time": ideological ambivalence in *The Raigne of King Edward III* and the English chronicle plays', *English Studies*, 69 (1988), 117–29.

[5] See E. H. Kantorowicz, *The King's Two Bodies: A Study in Medieval Political Theology*, 1957.

Shakespeare's meditation on the ethics of power, which shares its last line – 'Lilies that fester smell far worse than weeds' – with Warwick's speech at 2.1.452,[1] and it finally merges with the more general theme of the uses of policy, creating the ideological ambiguities of both parts of *Henry IV* and of *Henry V*. The last of them, as Stephen Greenblatt put it, 'deftly registers every nuance of royal hypocrisy, ruthlessness, and bad faith, but it does so in the context of a celebration, a collective panegyric to "This star of England", the charismatic leader who purges the commonwealth of its incorrigibles and forges the martial national State.'[2]

In *Edward III* the playwright insists on the theme of allegiance by making the Countess in her turn bind the King to an oath: that of killing both her husband and his queen. The deceitful nature of oath-taking (and oath-breaking) is in fact, as Champion noted,[3] a pervasive feature not only of these scenes but of the whole play, suggesting, together with the representation of the sharp contrast between the glory and the misery of war and invasion, an ambivalent attitude towards those patriotic and chivalric values that the play is supposed to celebrate. Was this the reason in the first place for omitting any direct mention of the founding of the Order of the Garter, but hinting at it deviously by recalling the episode of Edward's 'amours' for the lady whose dropped garter seems to have been 'the occasion that moved King Edward to institute the order'?[4]

Shakespeare, for his part, found an extraordinary way of suggesting this ironical and ambivalent approach to such sensitive subject-matter. He did it by calling into question his own profession, his skill in poetry as well as drama. Taking advantage of the presence in Painter's novel of the king's secretary, an unwilling bearer of Edward's love messages to the Countess, he created the figure of the courtier–confidant Lodowick, 'well read in poetry', whom Edward asks to write a love poem for the lady. The scene (2.1.1–184) is a radical criticism of current literary conventions, an indictment of the instrumental use of poetry, and at the same time a statement of Shakespeare's poetics as a sonnet-writer, which he certainly was at the time. The self-irony with which the author treats his own art enhances the ambivalence that presides over the approach to history in the rest of the play, as well as in the two parts of *Henry IV* and, more subtly, in *Henry V*.

The play in the context of the histories

Whatever the dramatic merits of *Edward III*, its importance, and what entitles it to enter the Shakespeare canon, resides in its being the natural prelude to Shakespeare's second historical cycle, not just because it deals with the reign of the immediate

[1] The parallelism between this sonnet and the Countess scenes in *Edward III*, as well as *Richard II*, is discussed in Melchiori, *Shakespeare's Dramatic Meditations: An Experiment in Criticism*, 1976, pp. 35–68. See also Appendix, p. 190.

[2] Stephen Greenblatt, 'Invisible bullets: Renaissance authority and its subversion, *Henry IV* and *Henry V*', in *Political Shakespeare: New Essays in Cultural Materialism*, ed. John Dollimore and Alan Sinfeld, 1985, pp. 18–47, later included in his *Shakespearean Negotiations*, 1987.

[3] Champion, pp. 121–3.

[4] The wording of the marginal heading in Holinshed, II, 629.

10 The burghers of Calais surrender to Edward III. From a manuscript of *Brut* in the Lambeth Palace Library

predecessor of Richard II and, as Muriel Bradbrook pointed out,[1] bears striking structural similarities with *Henry V*. In fact it prefigures all three Henry plays: its first two acts correspond to Prince Hal's dissipation and reformation in *1 Henry IV*; the lesson imparted to the Black Prince at Crécy and his knighting in Act 3 parallel the lesson to Prince Hal at his father's death-bed and his coronation in *2 Henry IV*; and the obvious analogies between Acts 4 and 5 and the famous victories celebrated in *Henry V* are emphasised by the acts of magnanimity and reunion at the conclusion of the plays: Edward, finally reunited with Queen Philippa, pardons at her request the burghers of Calais; Henry atones for the ruin caused to France by marrying Princess Katherine. Much more relevantly, *Edward III* introduces and develops the basic themes that sustain the whole historical cycle in exactly that mode of ideological ambiguity that transforms them from mere chronicles into explorations of policy confronted with human passion.

A. P. Rossiter was among the first to underline the ambivalence of such plays,[2] and Norman Rabkin, speaking of *Henry V*, found that its 'ultimate power is precisely the fact that it points in two opposite directions' at once; 'for a unique moment in

[1] M. C. Bradbrook, *The Living Monument*, 1976, pp. 230–32.

[2] Rossiter, *Angel with Horns and Other Shakespearian Lectures*, 1961, p. 51. By ambivalence he meant that 'two opposed value-judgements are subsumed, and that both are valid'.

Shakespeare's work ambiguity is the heart of the matter'.[1] More recently Wolfgang Isar, endeavouring to account for the lasting impact of Shakespeare's histories in our time, did not confine himself to the Lancastrian plays, but took *Richard III* as his starting point 'to establish a perspective from which to view' the second tetralogy, and found in Richard's monologue before Bosworth, 'What do I fear? Myself?' (5.3.183–204) the proof that 'Power always entails ambivalence'.[2] None of these critics mentions *Edward III*, a play whose central theme is exactly the ambivalence of power. And a play, whoever its author, apparently written and performed in the same years as *1 Henry VI* (if the Oxford editors are correct in dating Part 1 *after* Parts 2 and 3[3]) and *Richard III*; as such, it occupies an intermediate position between the two tetralogies.

In respect of plays like *The Famous Victories of Henry the fifth*, Peele's *Edward I*, or *Edmund Ironside*, conceived in the climate of the Elizabethan revival of chivalric values, David Riggs wrote,[4]

> *Edward III* represents a far more sophisticated attempt to present a version of heroic honour based on feudal custom and medieval chivalry. Like *1 Henry VI* and *Henry V*, the play is largely occupied with an exposition of two approaches to the conduct of war. [Unlike the French] the English observe a solemn chivalric ideal . . . [Edward's] participation in a traditional fellowship of arms is fully articulated through the recurrent public ceremonies of the play, most notably the investiture of his son, the Black Prince (3.3) . . . In *Edward III*, then, the requisites of chivalric worth are enlarged beyond the narrow confines of current patriotism to include the hero's responsibility to a public tradition of spiritual values.

What Riggs failed to emphasise is the fact that, of all the plays produced in the Elizabethan age, including Shakespeare's, *Edward III* is the one in which the external aspects of chivalry are most fully presented. The play opens with a ceremonial occasion: Artois is created Earl of Richmond (1.1.1–4); and in the second part, the on-stage investiture of Prince Edward (3.3.172–205) and his knighting (3.4.99–104), Mountford's presentation of his ducal coronet in sign of allegiance to the King of England (4.1.1–9), the Prince's life grant to Audley (4.7.48–57), and the knighting of Copland (5.1.94–6) are other examples of chivalric ritual. Apart from these episodes, the whole play has a heraldic quality. Four (mute) Heralds bring the coat of armour, helmet, lance, and shield to the investiture of Prince Edward, when the King announces: 'To dub thee with the type of chivalry, / In solemn manner we will give thee arms' (3.3.175–8); three French Heralds, from King John, Prince Charles, and Prince Philip respectively, bring ironical greetings to the Black Prince (4.4.66–123); finally an English Herald announces the Prince's victory at Poitiers (5.1.176–84) before the triumphant entrance of the Prince himself with his captive king.

Heraldry, in fact, is the most striking feature in the description of battles by sea and by land. Edward's 'proud armado' off Sluys flaunts 'streaming ensigns wrought of

[1] Rabkin, *Shakespeare and the Problem of Meaning*, 1981, pp. 34, 62.
[2] Isar, *Staging Politics*, 1993, pp. 45, 65–6.
[3] *Textual Companion*, pp. 136–7.
[4] Riggs, *Shakespeare's Heroical Histories: 'Henry VI' and its Literary Tradition*, 1971, pp. 81–2.

11 The arms of England quartered with those of France by Edward III from c. 1337: quarterly, 1st and 4th azure, semée of fleurs de lys or; 2nd and 3rd gules, three lions passant gardant or

coloured silk', while '. . . on the top gallant of the admiral . . . / The arms of England and of France unite / Are quartered equally by herald's art' (3.1.68, 73–6), which causes King John's 'Dare he already crop the fleur-de-lis?' (79). Edward's decision to quarter the Plantagenet arms (three lions passant gardant) with the Capetian (the fleur-de-lis) is next presented in the form of popular prophecy by a French woman (3.2.38–43):

> . . . there goes a prophecy abroad,
> Published by one that was a friar once . . .
> . . . he says, the time will shortly come
> Whenas a lion rousèd in the West
> Shall carry hence the fleur-de-lis of France.

This anticipates the other emblematic prophecies of 'an aged hermit' at 4.3.68–73: the flight of ravens (fulfilled at 4.5.1–55), and the flying stones (fulfilled at 4.6.4–52). But before them there is the enigmatic (and presumably misplaced) presentation of the heraldic emblem of the 'vulning pelican in his piety' (see 3.4.122–6n. and Appendix, p. 207), with its tantalising motto '*Sic et vos*: And so should you', unknown to all handbooks of heraldry. It must refer, beyond the usual implication of self-sacrifice in the pelican emblem, to what Riggs called 'the hero's responsibility to a public tradition of spiritual values'. The most splendid heraldic picture is Audley's imaginary description of the battlefield at Poitiers (4.4.18–29):

12 The arms of the Pelham family, augmented by quartering the pelican device with one representing military buckled belts, to commemorate the supposed capture of King John of France by Sir William Pelham at Poitiers: gules two demi-belts polewise in fess, their buckles in chief, argent; quartered in 2nd and 3rd with azure, three pelicans argent, vulning themselves proper. See note to 3.4.122–6

an orb
Aloft the which the banners, bannerets,
And new replenished pendants cuff the air
And beat the winds, that for their gaudiness
Struggles to kiss them . . .
. . . all his gilded upright pikes do seem
Straight trees of gold, the pendants, leaves,
And their device of antique heraldry,
Quartered in colours seeming sundry fruits,
Makes it the orchard of the Hesperides.

Heraldry is the distinguishing feature of *Edward III* in respect of the other histories of the period. But its heraldic quality does not make it an unconditional celebration of the values of chivalry: the counterpart of the 'streaming ensigns wrought of coloured silk' (3.1.68) before the naval battle off Sluys is 'the streaming gore that from the maimèd fell' (3.1.162) after the battle; and though the verb 'quarter' is found twice in its heraldic meaning, it is used on two other occasions (3.2.5 and 5.1.37) in a much grimmer acceptation, alluding to the 'quartering' not of convicted felons, but of the innocent inhabitants of conquered towns.

Here, on the verbal level, is another aspect of the play's ideological ambiguity or ambivalence. One of the main arguments used against Shakespeare's authorship of *Edward III* is the lack of comedy in it.[1] There is no clowning in any of the early

[1] See, e.g., R. M. Smith (1911), p. 103: 'The whole drama is by no means up to Shakspere's level. There is an absence of comedy, and a general want of characterization.'

13 The emblem of the 'vulning' pelican, with the motto 'Give utterance to what is within you', in Geoffrey Whitney's *A Choice of Emblemes and other Deuises* (Leyden 1586), p. 87. See Appendix, p. 207

histories; but how do we define, in *2 Henry VI*, the mock miracle of St Albans (2.1), the mock duel between the armourer and his man (2.3), and the scenes of the Jack Cade rebellion (4.2–8),[1] the cruel taunting and mock coronation of the Duke of York by Queen Margaret in *3 Henry VI*, 2.4, the Pucelle and the Dauphin flying from Orléans 'leaving their clothes behind' in *1 Henry VI*, 2.1? Black humour has been recognised as a major component of the character of Richard III, from his first appearance as Richard Crookback in *2 Henry VI*, 5.1. Leo Salingar concludes his reconsideration of the 'grand design' of the first tetralogy[2] by observing that Shakespeare makes Richard

> a conscious and consummate actor; in *Richard III* he equates himself with the Vice in a morality play.[3] This side of him lends a buoyant humour to his crimes . . . Throughout the tetralogy a

[1] In the 1594 quarto version, *The First Part of the Contention betwixt the two Famous Houses of York and Lancaster*, there is, in the scene corresponding to 4.2, parody of the knighting ceremony, when Cade confers the honour first upon himself and then upon Dick Butcher. The quarto contains farcical elements not present in the Folio.

[2] Salingar, 'The "grand design" of Shakespeare's first History plays'. *Surprised by Scenes. Essays in Honour of Professor Yasunari Takahashi*, ed. by Yasunari Takada, 1994, pp. 41–53.

[3] Salingar's direct reference is to *R3* 3.1.62–3: 'Thus, like the formal Vice, Iniquity, / I moralize two meanings in one word.' Once again the stress is placed on political ambiguity.

thread of sardonic humour has followed the tragic postures of the leading characters. In *Richard III* it rises to the surface, as if bringing a tragic phase of history on the stage to an end.

It is exactly this kind of sardonic humour rising to the surface in *Richard III* that informs the treatment of heraldry in *Edward III*, with its hidden references to the founding of the Order of the Garter (see 'The genesis of *Edward III*' above). In the undoubtedly Shakespearean scene between the King and Lodowick (2.1.1–184) the sardonic mood is expressed in a subtler form, acquiring, by its transposition onto the level of current literary fashions (see p. 39 above), a tinge of ironical self-deprecation, perfectly in tune with the theme of political ambiguity. The heraldic play of *Edward III* bridges the apparent ideological gap between *Richard III* and *Richard II*, between the first and the second tetralogy. In the histories that followed, the ambivalence of approach to politics, policy, and power was fully revealed in the creation of Falstaff, and the final comic twist came with his exposure during the Garter masque in *The Merry Wives of Windsor*.

The play on the stage

The statement on the title-pages of both quarto editions of *Edward III*, that 'it hath been sundry times played about the city of London' is the only evidence that the play was performed in the Elizabethan age, and more precisely, in view of the entry in the Stationers' Register, before the end of 1595. The conclusions reached in the discussion of its 'Date and destination' (pp. 5–9 above), that it may have been acted just before or during the plague years – June 1592–June 1594 – by Pembroke's Men, are no more than conjectural, unsupported by external evidence. The only fact that emerges from an analysis of the dramatic techniques employed by the author(s) is that they envisaged the possibility that the play could not be performed in a regular London theatre; also cast requirements were contained within reasonable limits, by having only five characters present in all three parts of the play and no more than ten speaking actors (plus a few mute extras) present at any time on the stage, so that, by careful doubling, a maximum of sixteen actors including two boys would be required. It would add piquancy to the story for the audience to recognise in Queen Philippa in Act 5 the same boy who had filled the exacting part of the Countess of Salisbury in Acts 1 and 2, while in 3.2, as a poor French woman, he had prophesied the triumph of the English 'lion'. To give some further examples, Warwick in Acts 1 and 2 could turn into Salisbury in 4 and 5, after having put in brief appearances in Act 3, as the eloquent Mariner who reports the battle off Sluys, and as Gobin de Grace who shows the English how to cross the Somme. And David King of Scotland in 1.2 could double for Prince Charles of Normandy in Acts 3 and 4, before resuming his Scottish role as a mute in Act 5, from which Charles is unaccountably (but significantly) absent.

What is for us a guessing-game on doubling can go on indefinitely, but it must be kept in mind that Shakespeare and his fellows were past masters in the game, or practice, or art, of doubling.[1] The reduced stage and casting requirements leave the

[1] Compare Melchiori, 'Peter, Balthazar, and Shakespeare's art of doubling', *MLR* 78 (1983), 777–92.

possibility open that the 'sundry' performances 'about the city of London' before 1595 (there is no mention of 'great applause', as for other plays of the time) either were undertaken by Pembroke's Men, or, as Roger Prior believes,[1] were meant for a private occasion to be followed by public presentations. What seems certain is that, after these, *Edward III* was forgotten by the theatrical profession for more than three centuries.

The first modern attempt at testing the theatrical value of the play on the stage came from the great pioneer of the Elizabethan revival, the actor–director William Poel, founder of the Elizabethan Stage Society.[2] With his limited means, at a time when the fortunes of the Society seemed to be declining, he did not dare to produce the whole play but, as a reviewer put it, 'gave as Shakespeare's what he considered to be the master's share in the work',[3] i.e. Act 2. It was presented at a single matinée performance at the Little Theatre in London on 6 March 1911 under the title *The King and the Countess*, attributed to Shakespeare, as part of a double bill with the mid-sixteenth-century interlude *Jacob and Esau*. The play was directed by Gertrude Kingston and William Poel, with Arthur Wontner and Helen Haye in the title roles, and five supporting parts – Lodwick, Warwick, Derby, Audley, and the Prince of Wales (the young Prince was played by a woman, Irene Greenleaf). *Jacob and Esau* captured the attention of most reviewers, who hardly took any notice of the Shakespearean appendage to the longer biblical interlude. Such is the case of *The Sketch*,[4] which, after remarking that 'Mr William Poel's "Elizabethan Stage Society" is by no means dead. It has reappeared after an interval with two interesting relics of the past', devoted most of the review to the 'secular morality', adding at the end, as an afterthought: 'The supposed Shakespearean extract certainly seemed like Shakespeare . . . it was very ably played by Mr Arthur Wontner and Miss Helen Haye.' *The Athenaeum* was more generous with space:

> It was well set on in the Society's manner, though there was not sufficient manliness in the King's part as rendered by Mr Arthur Wontner. Mr Kenyon Musgrove was fine as Warwick, and Miss Helen Haye rose admirably to the part of the Countess of Salisbury, his daughter. The character of Lodwick the poet was played effectively by Mr Reginald Williams.

But it concluded: 'it would have been better to play the Interlude [*Jacob and Esau*] alone'.

Fifty more years passed before the play, in a fuller version, was revived, not on the stage but for the BBC Third Programme, on 28 November 1963, adapted and produced by Raymond Raikes, with a twenty-one-strong cast headed by Stephen Murray as the King and Googie Withers as the Countess.[5] In order to contain the action time

[1] Prior, 'Compliment', p. 260. Compare p. 5, n. 8 and p. 9, n. 1.

[2] See Marion O'Connor, *William Poel and the Elizabethan Stage Society*, 1987.

[3] *The Athenaeum*, 11 March 1911, p. 288. The reviewer writes that 'the Elizabethan Stage Society had previously presented the play as a whole', but I found no record of such a performance, unlisted in J. P. Wearing, *The London Stage 1900–1909*, and *The London Stage 1910–1919*, 1982.

[4] 'A new Morality play', *The Sketch*, 15 March 1911, p. 308.

[5] Other major roles were entrusted to Philip Morant (Artois), Norman Shelley (Audley), John Westbrook (Prince Edward), Carleton Hobbs (Warwick). The incidental music was composed by Thomas Eastwood, and the other parts were played by members of the BBC Repertory Company. I am deeply indebted to

14 Edward gives free rein to his passion: Ian McCulloch as the king and Annabel Leventon as the Countess of Salisbury. Act 2, Scene 2 in the 1987 Theatr Clwyd production directed by Toby Robertson

in the 102 minutes allotted to the broadcast, Raikes, who prefaced it with Capell's remark that 'it must be confessed that it's being Shakespeare's is conjecture only, and matter of opinion, and the [listener] must form one for himself', made judicious cuts in the script, introducing a narrator to link together the drastically reduced historical

Miss Maire Jean Steadman for informing me of the production, and procuring from Mr Raikes – to whom I must also express my gratitude – a photocopy of the complete script used in rehearsal.

scenes. By dispensing with the character of the Earl of Salisbury (entailing the elimination of the scenes connected with the safe-conduct episode – 4.1, 4.3.1–56, 4.5.56–126 – and the artificial suspense created by his arrival before the entrance of the Black Prince in the last act), he tightened and speeded up most effectively the action in the second part of the play. On the other hand, the preservation of such scenes as those presenting the French citizens escaping the English invasion (3.2), the ceremonial arming and knighting of the Black Prince (3.3 and 3.4), the prophecies (4.3.68–73), the dire plight of the Prince at Poitiers (4.4), Audley's courage (4.7), places the Countess episode in a human rather than heroic context.

In the 1980s Thad Taylor and Jay Uhley undertook to produce for the Shakespeare Society of America at the Globe Playhouse of Los Angeles all fourteen plays included in Tucker Brooke's *Shakespeare's Apocrypha* (with the addition of *Edmund Ironside* and *Cardenio*), starting with *The Two Noble Kinsmen* and *Sir Thomas More*. The fifth production, in July 1986, was *Edward III*, directed by Dick Dotterer.[1] It was once again an event hardly noticed outside academic circles.

The first professional performance of an acting text of the whole play, prepared by director Toby Robertson with Richard Proudfoot and Jeremy Brooks, was that staged by Theatr Clwyd at Mold in June 1987, and taken to Cambridge in July and to a Shakespearean Symposium in Taormina in August. 'Nobody before Toby Robertson had set about showing how the work shapes on the stage', wrote Jeremy Kingston;[2] his verdict is: 'not badly at all'. Ian Williams[3] agreed that the play was 'well worth staging, and director Toby Robertson has done us a big favour by rescuing it from the obscurity of the Shakespearean apocrypha'. Though expressing doubts about authorship ('There are indeed moments when "Edward III" seems to have been worked over by S. J. Simon and Caryl Brahms in wicked "No Bed for Bacon" vein') Michael Ratcliffe[4] concludes: 'The question is open, the play entirely worth doing, and very well done indeed at Mold.'[5] Robert Hewison[6] has greater reservations: 'While *Edward III* is well worth doing, if it is by Shakespeare he was quite right to keep quiet about it, once he had better work to his name.' He finds that 'The real justification for reviving *Edward III* is the close parallels it has with Shakespeare's *Henry V*, which Theatr Clwyd are adding to their repertory. In the collaborative world of Elizabethan play-writing, we can see the one was father to the other.'

The political implications of the play are emphasised by Ratcliffe:[7] 'The solemn and moving investiture of [Prince Edward] was well calculated to thrill the subjects of a

[1] Reviewed, with *Arden of Faversham* and *The Puritan*, by Joseph H. Stodder, 'Three apocryphal plays in Los Angeles', *SQ* 38 (1987), 243–8.

[2] *The Times*, 1 July 1987.

[3] *Independent*, 2 July 1987, p. 12.

[4] *Observer*, 5 July 1987, p. 17.

[5] When the play was presented in Taormina it received long and favourable notices in the Italian press; but authorship was the most debated point, as the translations of the titles of three representative reviews may indicate: 'All agree: the King is Shakespeare's' (Aggeo Savioli, *L'Unità*, 5 August 1987, p. 19); 'Is it true Shakespeare?' (Rodolfo di Giammarco, *La Repubblica*, 6 August 1987, p. 20); 'Shakespeare or not: Edward did not convince' (Franco Cicero, *La Gazzetta del Sud*, 5 August 1987, p.16).

[6] *The Sunday Times*, 12 July 1987, p. 49.

[7] *Observer*; see n. 4 above.

15 Prince Edward (Colin Hurley, centre) triumphs over King John of France (Jonathan Burn) and Prince Philip (Sam Howard) at Poitiers. Act 4, Scene 7, in the 1987 Theatr Clwyd production

16 Queen Philippa (Zoë Hicks) at Calais, fearing for the life of the Black Prince in the battle of Poitiers, is comforted by the king (Ian McCulloch). Act 5 in the Theatr Clwyd production

childless monarch who would be ruled by a remote and unknown Scot as soon as she died. It is an unquestioningly patriotic and briskly xenophobic piece, in which the Scots are rated even lower than the French.' He appreciates that 'there are no star parts, and the company makes up a consistent ensemble that speaks clearly and moves well'. Praise of individual actors in the thirteen-strong cast singles out Ian McCulloch as the King ('physically and vocally dominant, a man of honour but little detachment, perplexed by his own passions of lust and rage' – Proudfoot[1]), and Annabel Leventon ('stands out as the virtuous Countess' – Hewison), while the interpretation of Prince Edward is more controversial: for Kingston[2] it is 'played by Colin Hurdley with a street fighter stance and grin, but has little of Prince Hal's subtlety'; for Proudfoot 'Hurdley charts with precision the Black Prince's metamorphosis from bookish sixth-former to blood-spattered football captain.'

Some perplexity is created by the sets and costumes; the fairest account is the *Observer*'s:

> Sean Cavanagh sets the action within blackened stone walls and all over a movable timbered tower, which is flexible, silent and fast. A huge mask stares down on the action from the back, martially Japanese, but in the half light almost a distortion of Shakespeare's himself. Judith Dolan's black, red, silver and gold combat-gear suggests Samurai, Hell's Angels and all the timeless peacock-ambiguities of the fighting life.[3]

The most fitting conclusion is Proudfoot's: 'Shakespeare or not Shakespeare, *Edward III* is revealed . . . a gripping play'. It is to be hoped that it will take its place on the stage side by side with Shakespeare's other histories.

[1] Richard Proudfoot, 'The rituals of war', *TLS*, 17 July 1987, p. 770.
[2] *The Times*; see p. 48, n. 2.
[3] For the *Times* critic, costumes 'are part samurai, part motor-bike gang, reminding us that the battle of Poitiers was fought between the Kings of Yamaha and Kawasaki'; the *Independent*'s speaks of 'ominously black padded uniforms with swelling priapic codpieces'.

NOTE ON THE TEXT

This edition is necessarily based on the first (1596) quarto of the play, the only one to carry some authority, in spite of its being derived from a manuscript presumably of an intermediate nature, neither prompt-book nor authorial foul papers, set by not very expert compositors. Some peculiar features, discussed in the Textual Analysis, of the part of the play generally attributed to Shakespeare suggest that, in putting together contributions from different hands, the assembler of the script did not always transcribe them, but at times inserted the original leaves as they had come to him. Apart from more or less obvious printing errors and misreadings of the text, the punctuation is slovenly throughout, and there are serious confusions especially in the treatment of speech headings.

The only other early edition of the play, the second quarto of 1599, is printed from the first, but shows signs that a reviser had carefully gone over the earlier printed text in an attempt at correcting what he thought to be misprints, compensating for occasional omissions of stage directions, regularising punctuation and speech headings as well as spelling. These matters are discussed at greater length in the Textual Analysis. The present edition treats the second quarto variants with discrimination, being aware both of their non-authorial origin and of the fact that the reviser is liable at times to over- or miscorrect as well as to misinterpret the first quarto text. Q2 variants, whether adopted or rejected, are recorded in the Collation and, when necessary, discussed in the Commentary, except for insignificant orthographic differences and punctuation variants in obvious cases, as when, as it frequently happens, a speech in Q1 ends with a comma instead of the full stop or other appropriate mark (e.g. the question mark, 1.1.41) used in Q2; but dubious instances are discussed (see, for instance, 1.1.28–9n. and 1.2.37–45n.).

In this edition the erratic and abbreviated speech headings of the quartos are normalised and given in full form, and the same applies to characters' names in stage directions; such changes are collated when appropriate. Stage directions are standardised in accordance with New Cambridge Shakespeare practice: they are in italics without terminal punctuation, but Roman capitals are used for speaking characters named in entrance directions, where descriptive names such as 'soldiers', 'citizens', etc. are in italics with capitalised initials; but when one such character has a speaking role Roman capitals are used. Punctuation is modernised, avoiding as far as possible the introduction of extra punctuation in addition to that present in the quartos. Spelling is silently modernised, sounded -ed terminations are marked by a grave accent (-èd), but old colloquial forms such as 'a' for 'he' and 'and' for 'if' are retained, and all ambiguous cases are collated and discussed in the Commentary. Original spellings are modernised in lemmas, but retained in the section of the Collation following the square bracket, including the use of 'i' for 'j' and of 'u' for medial 'v'.

This rule is generally observed in quotations from source-books in the Commentary, but quotations from Shakespeare and his contemporaries are given in modern spelling, except when the form of the original is relevant to the point under discussion. Place-names, both English and French, are given whenever possible in their modern forms, and the quartos' spellings are collated; the French 'Bretagne' has been preferred to English 'Brittany', as reflecting the bisyllabic form 'Brittayne' (1.1.133 and 2.2.93) or 'Brittaine' (4.1.4 and 5.1.97) used in Q1 (Q2 has 'Brittayne', 'Britany', 'Brytane', and 'Britaine'). When the two quartos agree in everything except insignificant variants, the Collation records 'Qq' followed by the Q1 version.

The Collation records also all the relevant variants and emendations suggested by modern editors, whether adopted or not in the present edition, noting their first appearance. The most significant of them are discussed in the Commentary. Stage directions have been kept to a minimum; additions to those in the original are enclosed in square brackets. Additional stage directions introduced by modern editors are recorded in the Collation and, where appropriate, discussed in the Commentary.

The original editions have no act or scene divisions. The present edition adopts those suggested by Capell in 1760, except for 3.4, divided by Capell into two scenes at line 13, where there is a general exit, though no break in location or time sequence. The same circumstances (exits with no time breaks) occur twice in 4.6, at lines 17 and 52, which induced Werner and Proescholdt and subsequent editors to introduce further divisions, so that in their texts Act 4 comprises nine instead of seven scenes. This fragmentation has been avoided here, though it is noted in the Collation.

King Edward III

LIST OF CHARACTERS

The English

KING EDWARD III
QUEEN *Philippa, his wife*
Edward PRINCE *of Wales, their son*
Earl of SALISBURY
COUNTESS *of Salisbury, his wife*
Earl of WARWICK, *her father*
Sir William MONTAGUE, *Salisbury's nephew*
Earl of DERBY
Lord AUDLEY
Lord PERCY
John COPLAND, *an esquire, later Sir John Copland*
LODOWICK, *King Edward's secretary*
Two ESQUIRES
A HERALD

Supporters of the English

Robert, Count of ARTOIS, *and Earl of Richmond*
Lord MOUNTFORD, *Duke of Brittany*
GOBIN *de Grace, a French prisoner*

The French

KING JOHN II
Prince CHARLES, *Duke of Normandy, his oldest son*
Prince PHILIP, *his youngest son*
Duke of LORRAINE
VILLIERS, *a Norman Lord*
The CAPTAIN *of Calais*
Another CAPTAIN
A MARINER
Three HERALDS
Two CITIZENS *from Crécy*
Three other FRENCHMEN
A WOMAN *with two children*
Six wealthy CITIZENS } *of Calais*
Six POOR *Frenchmen* } *of Calais*

Supporters of the French
King of BOHEMIA
A POLONIAN CAPTAIN
Danish troops

The Scots
KING DAVID *Bruce of Scotland*
Sir William DOUGLAS
Two MESSENGERS

Lords, Attendants, Officers, Soldiers, Citizens, Servants, etc.

Notes

The list of characters, not in Qq, was first introduced by Capell. The present version reproduces substantially that in Melchiori.

KING EDWARD Edward III (1312–77), firstborn of Edward II and Isabel, daughter of Philip IV (le Beau) of France. King of England from 1327.

QUEEN Philippa, daughter of William Earl of Hainault, married Edward III in 1328. Died 1369. She gave birth to seven sons and five daughters.

PRINCE Edward (1330–76), firstborn of Edward III, Prince of Wales from 1343, became known as the Black Prince from the colour of his armour in his military exploits in France.

SALISBURY Sir William Montague (Montacute) was created first Earl of Salisbury in 1337 (1333 according to others) in recognition of his service against the Scots (see Appendix, pp. 182–3 and notes). He died in 1344, but in the play he is made to survive and attributed the role filled in history by Sir Walter de Manny (actually Walter Mauny, like the historian Froissart a native of Hainault, who was one of the first Knights of the Garter and died in 1372 – see Appendix, pp. 208–9). The Salisbury title was transferred to the Neville family a century later, when Alice Montague married Richard Neville; their son Richard, by marrying Anne Beauchamp, secured the title of Earl of Warwick, and appears as 'king-maker' in *2* and *3H6*.

COUNTESS The Earl of Salisbury's wife was Catherine Grandisson, neither 'Alice' as in Froissart, nor the daughter of the Earl of Warwick, as in Bandello/Painter and in the play. See Introduction and 'The Countess's identity' in Appendix, p. 186.

WARWICK Thomas de Beauchamp was Earl of Warwick in Edward III's time, and one of the Knights Founders of the Order of the Garter. He did not father the Countess of Salisbury. For the later connections between the Beauchamp, Montague, and Neville families see n. to SALISBURY, above.

MONTAGUE Son of the sister of his namesake, the first Earl of Salisbury (see above), Sir William Montague was the captain of the castle of Roxborough (Wark according to others) besieged by the Scots in 1341, when the Earl was in France. See Appendix, pp. 182–3 and p. 186.

DERBY Henry of Lancaster, great-grandson of Henry III, was created Earl of Derby in 1337 and first Duke of Lancaster in 1351, and was one of the Knights Founders of the Order of the Garter. His daughter Blanche married the third son of Edward III, John of Gaunt, who inherited the title of Lancaster at the death of the first Duke in 1361.

AUDLEY Sir James Audley (or Audeley) was a 'knight bachelor' who went to Normandy in 1346, was a Knight Founder of the Order of the Garter, and distinguished himself at the battle of Poitiers (1356). He was not old (as in the play) but a near contemporary of the Black Prince.

PERCY A forebear of the first Earl of Northumberland who figures prominently in *R2* and *1* and *2H4*, Henry Lord Percy was appointed in 1346, together with Ralph Neville, Warden of the Realm of England while Edward III was engaged in the war in France.

COPLAND John Copland (or Copeland), an esquire who captured King David of Scotland at the battle of Neville's Cross (1346), was rewarded with a knighthood and a yearly pension of 500 pounds. See Appendix, pp. 210, 214.

ARTOIS Robert de Beaumont-le-Roger (1287–1343) claimed the earldom of Artois, which had been assigned to a collateral branch of the family at the death of his grandfather, the second Earl. In 1334 he took refuge in England, and obtained from Edward III the title of Earl of Richmond. He died of the wounds received during the expedition he led in Brittany in 1342 in aid of the Countess of Mountford (see n. on MOUNTFORD), but in the play he is made to survive till after the battle of Poitiers, filling the role played in the Crécy campaign by another rebellious Frenchman, Godefroy d'Harcourt, a Norman baron deprived by the Valois of his dominions, see Appendix, p. 202.

MOUNTFORD Jean IV de Montfort (1293–1345) in 1341 claimed the dukedom of Brittany (assigned to Charles de Blois, nephew to the King of France) and paid homage for it to the King of England. He was captured in the same year and ended his life as a prisoner in the Louvre. Thanks to the heroic resistance of his wife, Jeanne of Flanders, and to repeated English interventions, Brittany remained in the hands of his descendants. In the play he is made to survive and is restored to the dukedom; see nn. to 4.1, and Appendix, pp. 185–7, 209.

GOBIN Gobin de Grace, a French commoner who reportedly revealed to the English the tidal ford in the River Somme at Blanchetaque. For his name see 3.3.0 SD n. and Appendix, p. 203.

KING JOHN Jean II *le bon* de Valois (1319–84), Duke of Normandy till 1350, when he succeeded his father Philip VI as King of France. In the first three acts of the play John is attributed actions which occurred during the reign of Philip; see Introduction and Appendix, *passim*.

CHARLES The firstborn of King John, Prince Charles (1337–80) became Duke of Normandy in 1350, and King of France, as Charles V, in 1364. Chronological confusions connected with his person and title are discussed in the Appendix, see especially pp. 199–200, 210.

PHILIP Prince Philip (1341–1404), fourth son of John II, was created Duke of Burgundy in 1363, and became known as Philip the Bold. For the confusion with his homonymous uncle, Philip Duke of Orléans, see Appendix, p. 200.

LORRAINE The Duke of Lorraine, Raoul (or Rudolph), a powerful ally of King Philip VI of France, was killed in the battle of Crécy.

VILLIERS A name assigned by the playwright to an unnamed 'knight of Normandy' mentioned by Froissart, see 4.1.18 n.

BOHEMIA John the Blind (1296–1346), Earl of Luxembourg, became King of Bohemia in 1311 when he married Elizabeth, daughter of the previous King Venceslaus IV. He died at Crécy, see Appendix, pp. 200 and 201, n. 1.

KING DAVID David II (1318[?]–71) succeeded his father Robert Bruce on the throne of Scotland in 1329, and in the same year married Joan, sister of Edward III. He was defeated and captured in the battle of Neville's Cross (1346) and remained a prisoner in London till he was ransomed in 1356.

DOUGLAS Sir William Douglas, a valiant Scottish military commander who conquered Edinburgh castle in 1340, but was taken prisoner with King David II at the battle of Neville's Cross.

THE REIGN OF KING EDWARD THE THIRD

1.1. *Enter* KING EDWARD, DERBY, PRINCE *Edward*, AUDLEY, *and* ARTOIS [*with* WARWICK *and others*]

KING EDWARD Robert of Artois, banished though thou be
From France thy native country, yet with us
Thou shalt retain as great a seigniory;
For we create thee Earl of Richmond here.
And now go forward with our pedigree:
Who next succeeded Philip le Beau?
ARTOIS Three sons of his, which all successively
Did sit upon their father's regal throne,
Yet died and left no issue of their loins.
KING EDWARD But was my mother sister unto those?
ARTOIS She was, my lord, and only Isabel
Was all the daughters that this Philip had,
Whom afterward your father took to wife;
And from the fragrant garden of her womb

Act 1, Scene 1 1.1] *Capell (ACT* I. *SCENE* I. London. *A Room of State in the Palace. Flourish); no act or scene divisions in* Qq 0 SD.1 AUDLEY] *Capell; Audely/* Qq *(subsequently /Audeley/ Awdley/)* 0 SD.2 *with . . . others*] *Capell, subst.; not in* Qq 1 SH KING EDWARD] Q2 *(King Edward./ centred); King. (centred)* Q1 4 here.] Q2 *(*here:*);* heere, Q1 6 succeeded] Qq*;* succeeded to *conj. Capell* 6 le Beau?] *Capell, subst.;* of Bew? Q2*;* of Bew, Q1 7 successively] *Capell;* successefully, Q1*;* successefully Q2 10 those?] Q2*;* those: Q1 11 Isabel] Q2*;* Issabel, Q1 12 Philip] Q2*;* Phillip Q1 *(throughout)*

Act 1, Scene 1

1.1 The location is Westminster and the historical events referred to took place between 1337 (the beginning of the Hundred Years War) and 1341 (the third Scottish campaign). In constructing the plot, the authors draw on both Holinshed and Froissart, telescoping events that took place at different times. See Appendix on the use of sources.

0 SD.2 WARWICK The absence of Warwick in Qq entrance SD indicates that his inclusion in the scene came as an afterthought (his first speech is at 98–100), suggested by his unhistorical involvement in the Countess of Salisbury episode, first broached at 121 ff.

1–4 On the role of Robert of Artois as instigator of the war against France see Hol., II, 605, quoted in the Appendix, p. 180.

3 **seigniory** feudal domain and title.

5–27 The discussion of Edward's right to the crown of France, denied on the strength of the Salic law that excluded women from the line of succession, anticipates the more extended ironical treatment of the same subject in *H5* 1.2.

6 **Philip le Beau** Philip IV (the Fair) reigned in France 1285–1314. The name is correctly spelt in Hol. Qq's 'of Bew' misunderstands the title in Frois., ch. 5 (Metz, p. 43), 'Philyp la Beawe'.

7 **Three sons** Louis X (r. 1314–16), Philip V (r. 1316–22), Charles IV (r. 1322–8).

9 **no . . . loins** See Frois., ch. 5 (Metz, p. 43): 'without hauyng any issue male of theyr bodies laufully begoten'.

12 **all the daughters** Hol. correctly states that Philip had another daughter who died in infancy. Isabel married Edward II of England in 1308, Edward III was born in 1313.

Your gracious self, the flower of Europe's hope,
Derivèd is inheritor to France.
But note the rancour of rebellious minds:
When thus the lineage of le Beau was out,
The French obscured your mother's privilege,
And though she were the next of blood, proclaimed
John of the house of Valois now their king.
The reason was, they say the realm of France,
Replete with princes of great parentage,
Ought not admit a governor to rule,
Except he be descended of the male;
And that's the special ground of their contempt,
Wherewith they study to exclude your grace.

KING EDWARD But they shall find that forgèd ground of theirs
To be but dusty heaps of brittle sand.

ARTOIS Perhaps it will be thought a heinous thing
That I, a Frenchman, should discover this;
But heaven I call to record of my vows:
It is not hate nor any private wrong,
But love unto my country and the right
Provokes my tongue thus lavish in report.
You are the lineal watchman of our peace,
And John of Valois indirectly climbs.
What then should subjects but embrace their king?

17 note] Q2; not Q1 18 le Beau] *Capell, subst.;* Bew Qq 22 say] Qq; said, *conj. Melchiori* 28 SH] *This edn; not in* Qq 30 SH] Q1; *not in* Q2 *and mod. edns* 36 watchman] *Capell;* watch men Q1; watchmen Q2 37 indirectly climbs.] Q2; in directly climbes, Q1 38 king?] Q2 (King?); King, Q1

18 le Beau In Qq 'Bew'. Here, as at 6, the line lacks one syllable: 'Bew' is considered a dissyllable.

21 Not John but Philip of Valois, a cousin of the dead monarch, succeeded him in 1328 and reigned as Philip VI till 1350. John II (r. 1350–64) was his son. The existence of Philip VI is deliberately ignored in order to present a single royal French counterpart to Edward in the campaign that lasted from 1337 till 1356.

22–5 See Frois., ch. 5 (Metz, p. 43): 'They sayd and mayntayned, and yet do, that the realme of Fraunce is so noble that it ought nat to go to a woman.'

26 special (1) specific, (2) specious, deceptively plausible.

28–9 In Qq these lines are a continuation of Artois's speech. The presence in Q1 of the SH *Art.* at 30 suggests that his speech had been previously interrupted by what RLA (240) calls 'a passionate interjection by the king', a dramatically effective break in a long recitation. The accidental loss of the SH at 28 caused the reviser to omit that at 30 in Q2; see Textual Analysis, pp. 175–6. For the colon instead of full stop at the end of 27 in Q1 see 1.2.37–45n.

30 heinous hateful, wicked.

32 to record As witness.

35 induces me to be so insistent. An awkward construction: 'to be' is implied after 'tongue'.

36 lineal in the direct line of descent, hence 'rightful'.

37 indirectly (1) not as a direct descendant, (2) in a devious way; compare *2H4* 4.5.184: 'by what by-paths and indirect crooked ways I met this crown'.

38 'do' is implied before 'but', an omission frequent in Shakespeare especially before 'not' (Abbott 305).

Ah, wherein may our duty more be seen
Than striving to rebate a tyrant's pride,
And place the true shepherd of our commonwealth?

KING EDWARD This counsel, Artois, like to fruitful showers,
Hath added growth unto my dignity,
And by the fiery vigour of thy words
Hot courage is engendered in my breast,
Which heretofore was racked in ignorance,
But now doth mount with golden wings of fame,
And will approve fair Isabel's descent,
Able to yoke their stubborn necks with steel
That spurn against my sovereignty in France.

Sound a horn

A messenger. – Lord Audley, know from whence.

Enter, as messenger, LORRAINE

AUDLEY The Duke of Lorraine, having crossed the seas,
Entreats he may have conference with your highness.

KING EDWARD Admit him, lords, that we may hear the news. –

39 Ah,] Q2*;* Ah Q1*;* And *Delius, conj. Capell* 40–1] Qq (comonwealth, Q1)*;* Than, striving . . . pride, / Place *Capell* 50 SD] Q1 (*sound a horne/opposite 50*) 51 messenger.] Q2*;* messenger, Q1*;* messenger? *Capell, WP, TB* 51 SD] *This edn; Enter a messenger Lorragne,* Qq (Lorraigne Q2); *Exit* Audley, *and returns / Capell, WP, TB; Enter a Messenger, Lorraine / Smith, WAA, RLA* 54 news. –] Qq *subst.;* news. *Exeunt Lords. King takes his State. Re-enter Lords; with* Lorrain, *attended. / Capell, TB;* news. *Enter* LORRAYNE *WP*

39–41 Capell's suggestion to replace 'Ah,' with 'And', to consider 'striving . . . pride' as a parenthetic clause, and to omit 'And' at 41, creates a new construction that avoids the hypermetric last line and is grammatically more correct, but dramatically less effective.

40 rebate repress, stop (obsolete, see *OED* sv *v*[1] 3c)

41 place 'establish in office', as in Shakespeare, e.g. *Per.* 4.6.193, 'if I can place thee, I will'. Compare 'plant' at 134. '[To] place', like 'to rebate', depends on 'striving' at 40.

46 racked in ignorance tormented by ignorance (WP, Lapides), but possibly also 'ridden or driven by ignorance as a cloud in the wind'; see *OED* Rack *v* 2, and 2.1.3–4: 'like inconstant clouds / That rack upon the carriage of the winds'.

48 approve prove right, make proof of (*OED* sv *v* 2,3).

49 yoke . . . steel yoke with steel the stubborn necks of those.

50 spurn against kick (*OED* Kick *v*[1] 2), oppose with scorn (*OED* Spurn *v* 3). Compare *Luc.* 1026: 'In vain I spurn at my confirmed despite.'

51 SD The placing of this SD has been questioned. Capell and others moved it after 54, introducing more SDs: Audley exits at the king's request at 51 to interview the new arrival offstage, re-enters with his message (52–3), and at 54 he or some other lord admits Lorraine. A simpler solution on the Elizabethan stage would be for Lorraine to enter at 51, wait in view of the audience in the discovery place while Audley interviews him, and advance on the main stage when Edward grants him permission at 54. Compare Braunmuller's discussion of the entrance of 'a sheriff' in *John*, 1.1.43.1, in his edition of the play (Oxford, 1989), 122.

52 Duke of Lorraine The Duke of Lorraine is mentioned by Frois. among those who received young Edward in France when paying homage for the duchy of Guienne in 1329, and later sided with the French King in military actions in 1339, 1341, and 1346, but never acted as ambassador. The French envoys who asked for the Guienne homage in 1329 were two bishops and four other noblemen.

Say, Duke of Lorraine, wherefore art thou come.
LORRAINE The most renownèd prince King John of France
Doth greet thee, Edward, and by me commands
That, for so much as by his liberal gift
The Guienne dukedom is entailed to thee,
Thou do him lowly homage for the same.
And for that purpose here I summon thee,
Repair to France within these forty days,
That there, according as the custom is,
Thou mayst be sworn true liegeman to our king;
Or else thy title in that province dies,
And he himself will repossess the place.
KING EDWARD See how occasion laughs me in the face:
No sooner minded to prepare for France,
But straight I am invited – nay, with threats,
Upon a penalty enjoined to come!
'Twere but a childish part to say him nay.
Lorraine, return this answer to thy lord:
I mean to visit him as he requests –
But how? Not servilely disposed to bend,
But like a conqueror to make him bow:
His lame unpolished shifts are come to light,
And truth hath pulled the vizard from his face,
That set a gloss upon his arrogance.
Dare he command a fealty in me?
Tell him the crown that he usurps is mine,

56 King] Q2; K. Q1 **59** Guienne] *RLA;* Guyen Qq **64** our] Q1; the Q2 **71** childish] Q1; foolish Q2 **78** gloss] glosse Q2; glasse Q1 **79** me?] Q2; mee, Q1

56–60 Frois. devotes the whole of ch. 24 (Metz, pp. 44–8) to the informal homage paid in 1329 by Edward III (sixteen years old) to the new King of France, Philip VI of Valois, for the duchy of Guienne (to which Henry II had become entitled in 1152, when he married Eleanor, heiress of the last Duke of Guienne), and to his subsequent undertaking to renew it in a more solemn form.

61–6 There is no mention of a refusal of the homage as a *casus belli* with France, though Frois. remarks (Metz, p. 46): 'There were many as than in Englande that murmured and sayd, how the kyng theyr lorde was ne[a]rer by true succession of herytage to the crowne of Fraunce than Phylippe of Valoys, who was as than Kyng of Fraunce.'

63 custom The 'custom', i.e. the order of the ceremony with which the King of England, as Duke of Guienne, professed himself liegeman to the King of France, is set out at length in letters patent sent in 1330 by Edward to Philip, reproduced by Frois. (Metz, pp. 47–8).

65 dies expires.

67 Compare *Ham.* 4.4.32–3: 'How all occasions do inform against me, / And spur my dull revenge.'

76 lame . . . shifts imperfect rude expedients.

78 gloss deceptive appearance. Q1's 'glasse' is an alternative form of 'gloss' in this meaning (*OED* Glass *sb* 13).

79 fealty The feudal obligation of obedience of a vassal to his lord.

And where he sets his foot he ought to kneel:
'Tis not a petty dukedom that I claim,
But all the whole dominions of the realm,
Which if with grudging he refuse to yield,
I'll take away those borrowed plumes of his
And send him naked to the wilderness.

LORRAINE Then, Edward, here in spite of all thy lords
I do pronounce defiance to thy face.

PRINCE Defiance, Frenchman? We rebound it back,
Even to the bottom of thy master's throat;
And – be it spoke with reverence of the king
My gracious father and these other lords –
I hold thy message but as scurrilous,
And him that sent thee like the lazy drone
Crept up by stealth unto the eagle's nest,
From whence we'll shake him with so rough a storm,
As others shall be warnèd by his harm.

WARWICK Bid him leave off the lion's case he wears
Lest, meeting with the lion in the field,
He chance to tear him piecemeal for his pride.

ARTOIS The soundest counsel I can give his grace

87 spite] Q2; spight Q1; sight *Delius, conj. Capell* 89 Defiance, Frenchman?] Q2; *no punct. in* Q1 91–2 And – be . . . lords –] *Capell, subst.*; And be . . . lords, Qq (*subst.*)

81 where . . . kneel Compare *STM* 2.3.118–19 (a passage in Hand D, attributed to Shakespeare): 'your unreverent knees / Make them your feet'.

83 dominions provinces, territories.

85 I'll . . . plumes A figurative expression unrecorded by Tilley. See Dent, *PLED*, P441.1, and *1H6* 3.3.7: 'We'll pull his plumes.'

87 spite Capell's conjecture (see Collation) may well be correct.

89–97 Edward the Black Prince, oldest son of Edward III, born 1330, would have been only seven when this scene is supposed to take place.

90 'To lie in one's throat' is proverbial (Tilley T268). Dent, *PLED* (T268.11) quotes the present variant, and compare *Tit.* 2.1.53–5, 'till I have . . . Thrust those reproachful speeches down his throat'.

93 but as merely.

93 scurrilous offensive like a coarse jest.

94–5 like . . . nest The idea of the parasitical drone in the eagle's nest, ultimately derived from Virgil, *Georgics*, IV, was known through John Lyly (*Euphues*, *Endymion*), and suggested to Shakespeare the recurrent image-cluster 'eagle/weasel/drone', studied by E. A. Armstrong, *Shakespeare's Imagination*, 1946, pp. 25–34. See *2H6* 4.1.109, 'Drones suck not eagles' blood, but rob beehives', and especially *H5* 1.2 (the scene on the English claim to the French crown, 5–27 n. above), where, after identifying England with the eagle (169), Canterbury, in a lengthy comparison between the state of man and the beehive, speaks (203–4) of 'Delivering o'er to executors pale / The lazy yawning drone'.

98 case skin (*OED* sv *sb* 4). The reference is to Aesop's fable, which became proverbial (Tilley A351), of the 'ass in a lion's skin', betrayed by his braying. The variant offered here, at 99–100, where the real lion kills the ass, may have suggested *H5* 4.3.93–4: 'The man who once did sell the lion's skin / While the beast lived, was killed with hunting him.' The Bastard in *John* repeatedly plays upon it (2.1.137–44, and 3.1.128–33) and on the parallel proverb, 'hares may pull dead lions by the beard' (Tilley H165), see A. R. Braunmuller, ed., *King John*, 1989, Introduction, pp. 13–14.

Is to surrender ere he be constrained.
A voluntary mischief hath less scorn
Than when reproach with violence is borne.

LORRAINE Regenerate traitor, viper to the place
Where thou wast fostered in thine infancy!
Bearest thou a part in this conspiracy?
He draws his sword

KING EDWARD [*Drawing his sword*] Lorraine, behold the sharpness of this steel:
Fervent desire that sits against my heart
Is far more thorny-pricking than this blade;
That, with the nightingale, I shall be scarred
As oft as I dispose myself to rest
Until my colours be displayed in France.
This is thy final answer; so, be gone.

LORRAINE It is not that, nor any English brave,
Afflicts me so, as doth his poisoned view:
That is most false, should most of all be true. [*Exit*]

KING EDWARD Now, Lord, our fleeting bark is under sail:
Our gage is thrown, and war is soon begun,
But not so quickly brought unto an end.

105 Regenerate] Qq; Degenerate *Tyrrell, Delius and mod. edns* **106** wast] Q2; was Q1 **107** SD] Qq; *The King draws his sword / RLA, Lapides* **108** SD] *Capell (drawing his); not in* Qq, *RLA, Lapides* **110** blade;] Q2; blade. Q1 **117** SD] *Capell, subst.; not in* Qq **118** Lord] Qq; lords *Capell*

103–4 The rhyme underlines the gnomic nature of this couplet: a disgraceful action ['mischief'] (such as surrender) done voluntarily, carries less blame ['scorn'], than reacting violently to the just accusation ['reproach'] (of being a usurper). The metrical irregularity of 104 is only apparent: 'ví/o/léncе' is a doubly stressed trisyllable.

105 Regenerate Unnatural (*OED* sv *adj* 3), possibly confused with 'renegade'. Most modern eds. adopt Tyrrell's emendation 'Degenerate', with the same meaning.

105 viper Allusion to the proverbial viper reared in a person's bosom, killing its benefactor, quoted by Erasmus (*Adagia*, 999[B]) as an emblem of ingratitude (Tilley v68). Artois was born and bred in France.

107 SD Since there is only one SD in Qq, '*He*' was taken, in view of 108–10, to refer to the king drawing his sword. But no king would draw first against an ambassador. The action envisaged is: Lorraine threatens Artois with his sword, and the king intervenes, drawing his.

110 thorny-pricking pricking like a thorn, see 111n.

111 nightingale Proverbial (Tilley N183), referring to the common belief that the song of the nightingale was produced by her pressing her breast against a thorn. Compare *Luc.* 1128–48.

113 colours the army banners and the royal arms of England.

115 brave boast.

117 the fact that a man (Artois) who should have been most sincere and faithful is instead most false.

118 Lord Edward invokes God's protection, but many modern eds. emend to 'lords', as if he were addressing his followers. The vocative 'Lord' for 'God' is frequent in Shakespeare, e.g. *2H4* 3.2.177, 179, *H5* 4.1.292.

118 fleeting moving swiftly (*OED* sv *ppl.a* 4).

119 gage a glove thrown on the ground as a challenge to battle.

119–20 war . . . end Proverbial; see Dent, *PLED*, W39.11, and *ODEP*, 866a.

Enter MONTAGUE

But wherefore comes Sir William Montague?
How stands the league between the Scot and us?
MONTAGUE Cracked and dissevered, my renownèd lord:
The treacherous king no sooner was informed
Of your withdrawing of your army back,
But straight, forgetting of his former oath,
He made invasion of the bordering towns:
Berwick is won, Newcastle spoiled and lost,
And now the tyrant hath begirt with siege
The castle of Roxborough, where enclosed
The Countess of Salisbury is like to perish.
KING EDWARD That is thy daughter, Warwick, is it not?
Whose husband hath in Bretagne served so long
About the planting of Lord Mountford there?
WARWICK It is, my lord.
KING EDWARD Ignoble David, hast thou none to grieve
But silly ladies with thy threatening arms?

121 But] Q2; *Moun.* But Q1 **125** your army] Q1; our army Q2 **133** Bretagne] Brittayne Qq **134** Mountford] *Tyrrell;* Mouneford Qq; *Montfort / Capell*

121 Sir . . . Montague Frois., ch. 76 (Metz, pp. 63–5), relates that, during the 1341 Scottish campaign, Sir William Montague, 'son to the earl of Salisbury's sister', being captain of a castle of that earl besieged by King David II of Scotland, managed to reach York and ask King Edward for help. These events, not mentioned in Hol., took place after the battle off Sluys (1340), presented later in the play (3.1).

122 league The chronology of historical events is deliberately confused. Not a league but a truce with the Scots was concluded some ten years before the siege mentioned in 121 n., but was broken by King David in 1332 when he took the border town of Berwick (see 128), causing the English reaction. It was during this campaign that Sir William Montague (not his younger homonymous nephew mentioned at 121) was created Earl of Salisbury and 'married nobly' for his bravery. See Appendix, p. 183.

128 Berwick See 122 n. But here the reference is to the 1341 war with Scotland, as reported in Frois., chs. 74–5, see Appendix, p. 183.

130 Roxborough The castle is unnamed in Frois., ch. 76 (Metz, pp. 63–5), though it is said that 'There was within present the noble countesse of Salysbury', and 'Rousburge' is mentioned elsewhere in the *Cronycle*. Qq's spelling 'Rocksborough' suggests that the author is following Painter, novel 46 (Metz, p. 110), where 'Roxborough' appears.

132 daughter Frois. does not specify the Countess's parentage; only Painter, following Bandello, states (Metz, p. 114) that, after the death of her husband, she 'returned to her father's house, who was Earle of Warwike'.

133–4 Mountford (Montfort in French) declared his allegiance to the King of England for the dukedom of Brittany, claimed by Charles of Blois, with the support of the French King (Frois., chs. 66–72, compare 4.1 below). When in 1341 Mountford was taken prisoner, his wife valiantly resisted the French forces besieging her castle, and was rescued by an English army sent by Edward under the conduct of Walter of Manny (Frois., chs. 79–80; see Appendix, p. 185, for the dovetailing of the stories of the Countesses of Mountford and of Salisbury). The Earl of Salisbury, according to Frois. (ch. 76, Metz, p. 64) and Painter, was taken prisoner in Flanders and was released (Frois., ch. 78) only after the siege of Roxborough.

134 planting installing.

137 silly helpless, defenceless (*OED* sv *adj* 1b).

But I will make you shrink your snaily horns!
First therefore, Audley, this shall be thy charge:
Go levy footmen for our wars in France;
And, Ned, take muster of our men at arms,
In every shire elect a several band,
Let them be soldiers of a lusty spirit
Such as dread nothing but dishonour's blot;
Be wary therefore, since we do commence
A famous war, and with so mighty a nation.
Derby, be thou ambassador for us
Unto our father-in-law, the Earl of Hainault:
Make him acquainted with our enterprise,
And likewise will him, with our own allies
That are in Flanders, to solicit too
The Emperor of Almagne in our name.
Myself, whilst you are jointly thus employed,
Will, with these forces that I have at hand,
March, and once more repulse the traitorous Scot.
But, sirs, be resolute: we shall have wars
On every side; and, Ned, thou must begin
Now to forget thy study and thy books,
And ure thy shoulders to an armour's weight.

PRINCE As cheerful sounding to my youthful spleen
This tumult is of war's increasing broils,
As at the coronation of a king
The joyful clamours of the people are,
When *Ave Caesar* they pronounce aloud.
Within this school of honour I shall learn

148 Hainault] Henalt Qq 151 too] Q1 (to) 152 Almagne] Qq (Almaigne) 155 Scot] Qq; Scots *Capell*

138 **shrink . . . horns** The phrase 'to draw (shrink) in one's horns' was current since c. 1300 (Whiting H491); the examples quoted by Tilley (H620) have 'pull' or 'pluck', except *Ven.* 1033–4: 'Or like the snail, whose tender horns being hit, / Shrinks backward in his shelly cave with pain'.

141 **Ned** Familiar for Edward, the Black Prince, a boy at the time.

142 **a several band** a separate (*OED* Several *adj* 1b) body of armed men.

146 **famous** (1) memorable, (2) that will bring fame.

148 **father-in-law** Edward III had married (1328) Philippa, daughter of William Earl of Hainault, in Flanders.

150 **allies** See Frois., ch. 32, 'How kyng Edwarde of England made great alyances in the empyre'.

152 **Almagne** French (Allemagne) for Germany. See Frois., ch. 34, 'How kyng Edwarde of England was made vycare generall of thempyre of Almaygne'.

155 **Scot** Capell's emendation, 'Scots', is unnecessary, since the singular refers to King David as representative of the whole nation.

159 **ure** inure, accustom.

160 **spleen** high spirit, eagerness (*OED* sv *sb* 5).

164 ***Ave Caesar*** 'Hail Caesar', the formal salute to newly elected Roman emperors.

Either to sacrifice my foes to death,
Or in a rightful quarrel spend my breath.
Then cheerfully forward, each a several way;
In great affairs 'tis naught to use delay.

Exeunt

1.2. *Enter the* COUNTESS [*of Salisbury, above*]

COUNTESS Alas, how much in vain my poor eyes gaze
For succour that my sovereign should send!
Ah, cousin Montague, I fear thou want'st
The lively spirit sharply to solicit
With vehement suit the king in my behalf.
Thou dost not tell him what a grief it is
To be the scornful captive to a Scot,
Either to be wooed with broad untunèd oaths,
Or forced by rough insulting barbarism;
Thou dost not tell him, if he here prevail,
How much they will deride us in the North,
And, in their vile uncivil skipping jigs,
Bray forth their conquest and our overthrow,
Even in the barren, bleak, and fruitless air.

169 SD *Exeunt*] Q2; *Exunt* Q1   Act 1, Scene 2   **1.2**] *Capell; no scene division in* Qq   **0** SD] *This edn after Capell* (Roxborough. *Before the Castle. Enter Countess of* Salisbury, *and certain of her People, upon the Walls*); *Enter the Countesse* Qq   **1** SH] Q2 (*Countesse*); *not in* Q1   **3** Ah,] Q2; A Q1   **3** want'st] Q2; wants Q1   **14** SD *below*] *RLA; not in* Qq

168 several separate, see 142 above.

169 naught wrong, hurtful (*OED* Naught *adj* 3).

Act 1, Scene 2

1.2 The scene is based on Frois., chs. 76–7, and on Painter, novel 46, but the defiance of the Scots by the Countess (1–80) recalls the valiant behaviour of the Countess of Mountford besieged by the French in Frois., ch. 80 (see 1.1.133–4n. and Appendix, p. 185).

0 SD The following speeches make it clear that the Countess stands on the upper stage, representing the battlements of her castle, while the Scots enter at 14 on the lower stage, in front of the castle. She descends at the arrival of King Edward (89).

1 SH The name of the Countess is never mentioned in the play, though Frois., ch. 89, gives it as Alice (see Appendix, p. 186).

3 cousin Used of any relative except parents and brothers, as well as of social equals on familiar terms. Montague is a nephew of the Countess, see 'aunt' at 82 below, and 1.1.121n.

3 want'st lack. Q1's 'wants' is an alternative form of the second person singular in verbs ending with -t (Abbott 340).

7 scornful scorned (*OED* sv *adj* 2, quoting *Luc.* 519–20: 'thy surviving husband shall remain / The scornful mark of every open eye').

8 untunèd rude, distressing. Compare *Err.* 5.1.311: 'untuned cares'.

9 barbarism rudeness in language and behaviour.

12 skipping jigs Jigs were lively grotesque dances to the tune of scurrilous ballads, typical of Scotland (*OED* Jig *sb* 3); 'skipping' is (1) leaping (of the dance), (2) wanton (of the ballads).

14 fruitless barren. Compare the same association of 'barren' and 'fruitless' at 151.

Enter [*below* KING] DAVID *and* DOUGLAS [*meeting*] LORRAINE

I must withdraw: the everlasting foe
Comes to the wall; I'll closely step aside,
And list their babble, blunt and full of pride.

KING DAVID My lord of Lorraine, to our brother of France
Commend us, as the man in Christendom
That we most reverence and entirely love.
Touching your embassage, return and say
That we with England will not enter parley,
Nor never make fair weather, or take truce,
But burn their neighbour towns, and so persist
With eager rods beyond their city, York;
And never shall our bonny riders rest,
Nor rusting canker have the time to eat
Their light-borne snaffles, nor their nimble spurs,
Nor lay aside their jacks of gimmaled mail,
Nor hang their staves of grainèd Scottish ash
In peaceful wise upon their city walls,
Nor from their buttoned tawny leathern belts
Dismiss their biting whinyards, till your king
Cry out: 'Enough, spare England now for pity!'

14 SD DAVID . . . LORRAINE] *This edn, after* Q1 (*Dauid and Douglas, Lorraine.*); *Dauid, Douglas and Lorraine.* Q2 **17** babble] Q1*;* rabble Q2 **20** most] Q2*;* must Q1 **25** rods] Rods Qq*;* roads *Capell etc.* **27** rusting] *Capell;* rust in Qq **28** spurs] Q2 (spurres)*;* spurre Q1 **29** gimmaled] *This edn;* Gymould Qq*;* gymold *Capell.* **34** out: 'Enough . . . pity'] Q2 (out, Enough)*; Capell* (*subst.*)*;* out enough, Q1

14 SD Q1's punctuation, as Braunmuller notes, suggests that King David and Douglas enter at one door and Lorraine at another.

16 closely hidden from view.

17 list listen to.

17 babble . . . pride stupid and arrogant chatter.

18–34 See Frois., ch. 33 (Metz, pp. 58–9) 'Howe kyng Dauyd of Scotlande made alyance with kyng Phylippe of Fraunce'. The condition imposed by the French was that the Scots 'wolde take no peace, nor truse, with the kyng of Englande, without it were by his [the French king's] agrement'.

20 most Q2's reading seems more appropriate than Q1's 'must', which implies a forced reverence rather than a free disposition to respect and love the French King above all others.

23 make . . . weather pretend good will, a common proverbial phrase (Tilley W221).

25 rods inroads, forays. So repeatedly in Frois. (*OED*, Road *sb* 2).

26 bonny Scottish for 'comely'. Compare the ironical use of the word by the Countess at 70 with reference to King David's horse.

27 rusting canker Rust is the canker of metal. Lapides (p. 217) explains Qq's 'rust in canker' as 'rust as the result of canker'; but Capell's emendation is palaeographically sound and in line with current usage, as in *Ven.* 767: 'Foul cank'ring rust the hidden treasure frets.'

28 snaffles horse bits.

29 jacks . . . mail tunics (*OED* Jack *sb* 1b) of chain mail. Qq's 'Gymould' is an old spelling of the participial form from 'gimmal', meaning 'joint, link' (*OED* Gimmal *sb* 2 and 6). Compare *H5* 4.2.49–50: 'the gimmal'd [Folio: 'Iymold'] bit / Lies foul with chaw'd-grass'. In New Cambridge Shakespeare *H5*, 1992, Andrew Gurr prefers 'gemeled', from 'gemel', a double ring. The implied subject in this line shifts from 'rusting canker' to 'our . . . riders'.

32 buttoned adorned with metal bosses.

33 whinyards short swords (*OED* Whinyard *sb* a), used by the Scots.

34 Cry . . . Enough 'Enough' capitalised in Q2

Farewell, and tell him that you leave us here
Before this castle; say you came from us
Even when we had that yielded to our hands.
LORRAINE I take my leave, and fairly will return
Your acceptable greeting to my king. *Exit*
KING DAVID Now, Douglas, to our former task again,
For the division of this certain spoil.
DOUGLAS My liege, I crave the lady, and no more.
KING DAVID Nay, soft ye, sir; first I must make my choice,
And first I do bespeak her for myself.
DOUGLAS Why then, my liege, let me enjoy her jewels.
KING DAVID Those are her own, still liable to her,
And who inherits her hath those with all.

Enter a Scot [*as* MESSENGER] *in haste*

MESSENGER My liege, as we were pricking on the hills
To fetch in booty, marching hitherward,
We might descry a mighty host of men.
The sun reflecting on the armour showed
A field of plate, a wood of picks advanced.
Bethink your highness speedily herein:
An easy march within four hours will bring
The hindmost rank unto this place, my liege.
KING DAVID Dislodge, dislodge: it is the King of England.
DOUGLAS Jemmy my man, saddle my bonny black.

38 I] Q2; *not in* Q1 **39 SD**] *This edn; Exit Lor.* Q1; *Exit Lorraine.* Q2 **43 ye**] Q1; *not in* Q2 **45 SH**] Q2 (*Douglas.*); *Da.* Q1 **47 SD** *as* MESSENGER] *This edn after Capell(a Messenger/ omitting /a Scot); not in* Qq **52 picks**] pickes Q1; pikes Q2

suggests this as the beginning of reported speech, but the punctuation in Q1 allows for the reading: Cry: 'Out, enough, spare. . .' (Braunmuller).

37–45 The implication of Q1 ending 37, 42, 44, 45 with commas (instead of Q2's full stops) would be that in each case the next speaker interrupts the previous one preventing him from completing his sentence. This could perhaps apply to 42 (King David interrupting Douglas), but not in all other instances.

39 acceptable welcome.

45 jewels The reference to Scottish greed for jewels could only have been suggested by Froissart's report of William Montague's daring sortie from the castle to attack a passing Scottish convoy, when he 'toke mo than sixscore horses charged with pillage' (ch. 76; Metz, p. 63), if the author knew the French text (Frois. 1513, fol. LIIIv), 'bien six vingtz cheuaulx chargez de ioyaulx et devoir', with Lord Hunsdon's marginal comment: 'Wyllyam montague and xl wythe hym ouerthreu iic skots and tooke vixx horsys laden wt iuels and uthar stufe.'

46 liable legally bound, inseparable from.

48 pricking riding fast (*OED* Prick *v* 11).

52 picks pikes, a 'chiefly Scottish' usage according to *OED* (Pick *sb* 2). Q2's 'pikes' (generally preferred by eds.) spoils the Scottish linguistic flavour of the passage (see 26, 33, 57, 70).

52 advanced advancing: an active use of the past participle (Abbott 374).

55 hindmost rank rearguard (of the advancing army).

56 Dislodge Withdraw.

57 Jemmy Another Scottishism (so *OED*), noted by Braunmuller; see 26, 33, 52.

57 bonny black favourite black horse. For 'bonny' referring to a horse see *2H6* 5.2.11–12, and 70n. below.

KING DAVID Meanst thou to fight, Douglas? We are too weak.
DOUGLAS I know it well, my liege, and therefore fly.
COUNTESS My lords of Scotland, will ye stay and drink?
KING DAVID She mocks at us, Douglas; I cannot endure it.
COUNTESS Say, good my lord, which is he must have the lady,
And which her jewels? I am sure, my lords,
Ye will not hence till you have shared the spoils.
KING DAVID She heard the messenger, and heard our talk,
And now that comfort makes her scorn at us.

[Enter] another MESSENGER

SECOND MESSENGER Arm, my good lord! O, we are all surprised.
COUNTESS After the French ambassador, my liege,
And tell him that you dare not ride to York,
Excuse it that your bonny horse is lame.
KING DAVID She heard that too, intolerable grief!
Woman, farewell. Although I do not stay –

Exeunt Scots

COUNTESS 'Tis not for fear, and yet you run away. –
O happy comfort, welcome to our house!
The confident and boist'rous boasting Scot,
That swore before my walls they would not back
For all the armèd power of this land,
With faceless fear that ever turns his back,
Turned hence again the blasting north-east wind,
Upon the bare report and name of arms.

Enter MONTAGUE

O summer's day: see where my cousin comes!

59 fly] Q1 (flie); flee Q2 **66** SD *Enter*] Q2; *not in* Q1 **67** SH SECOND] *This edn; not in* Qq **68** SH] *Capell; not in* Qq **71** She] *Capell;* He Qq **72** stay –] *Capell;* stay. Qq **76** they] Qq; he *Delius, conj. Capell* **79** again] Qq; against *Delius, conj. Capell* **80** name] Q1; names Q2 **81** O] *Capell; Mo.* O Q1; *Mounta.* O Q2

66 comfort The news brought by the Messenger of the arrival of the English army.

69 York Compare 25 above.

70 bonny horse Compare 57; see also 2.1.98n. below and *H5* 3.7.1–81, ridiculing the excesses of horse-lovers.

73 The Countess completes ironically the sentence left unfinished by King David.

78 his Referring to 'faceless [cowardly, *OED* sv *adj* a] fear' personified. The identification of 'fear' with the 'Scot' (75), taken collectively, makes it/them the implicit subject of 79.

79 again facing (*OED* Again *prep* 1). The fearful Scots fled from here ('turned hence'), facing the wind blowing from Scotland in the North. Delius's emendation is unnecessary.

81 summer's day lucky circumstance; proverbial (Tilley S967).

81, 84 cousin nephew, see 3n.

MONTAGUE How fares my aunt? – We are not Scots,
Why do you shut your gates against your friends?
COUNTESS Well may I give a welcome, cousin, to thee,
For thou com'st well to chase my foes from hence.
MONTAGUE The king himself is come in person hither:
Dear aunt, descend and gratulate his highness.
COUNTESS How may I entertain his majesty,
To show my duty and his dignity? [*Exit from above*]

Enter KING EDWARD, WARWICK, ARTOIS, *with others*

KING EDWARD What, are the stealing foxes fled and gone
Before we could uncouple at their heels?
WARWICK They are, my liege, but with a cheerful cry
Hot hounds and hardy chase them at the heels.

Enter COUNTESS

KING EDWARD This is the countess, Warwick, is it not?
WARWICK Even she, liege, whose beauty tyrants' fear,
As a May blossom with pernicious winds,
Hath sullied, withered, overcast, and done.
KING EDWARD Hath she been fairer, Warwick, than she is?
WARWICK My gracious king, fair is she not at all,

82 SH] *Capell; not in* Qq 82 We] we Qq; Why, aunt, we *Capell* 89 SD] *Capell, subst.; not in* Qq 95 liege] Q1; my liege Q2 95 tyrants'] Qq (tyrants); tyrant *Delius* 96 with . . . winds,] Q1; which . . . windes Q2, *Collier* 97 Hath] Qq; Have *Collier*

82 SH Misplaced in Qq before 81, a common error due to the fact that SHs were usually added in MSS. after the speeches had been copied out.

82 Capell inserts two words (see Collation) to regularise the line, not taking into account the pause between Montague's question and the rest of his speech.

87 gratulate greet (*OED* sv *v* 1).

89 SD.1 The SD, not in Qq, is suggested by 'descend' at 87 and by the new entrance of the Countess at 93.

89 SD.2 ***with others*** The 'others' presumably include Lodowick, Edward's confidant, though mute in this scene, but see 2.1.0 SD n.

91 uncouple . . . heels Hunting imagery: before we had time to release (our hounds, see 93) in pursuit of them.

94–166 This section of the scene draws both upon Frois., ch. 77 (first part, Metz, pp. 65–6) and upon Painter, novel 46 (Metz, pp. 110–11).

94 Recalling Edward's question to Warwick at 1.1.132.

95 tyrants' The absence of the article suggests a plural genitive, 'the fear of tyrants [= the Scot]'; Delius's emendation makes 'tyrant' an attribute of 'fear'.

96–7 A difficult construction: 96 is a parenthetic clause implying the passive forms of the verbs in 97: 'Fear has sullied, withered, overcast and destroyed ['done'] her beauty in the same way as a May blossom *is* sullied, withered etc. with ill winds.' Compare *Sonn.* 18.3: 'Rough winds do shake the darling buds of May.' Collier adopts Q2's reading 'which' for 'with' (assuming a misreading of 'w^{th}' for 'w^{ch}'), but the resulting relative clause leaves the main sentence unfinished.

99–101 Another tortuous construction. Lapides (p. 219) renders: 'So great would be the contrast between her former beauty and her present beauty that her present self would appear stained (defective) if both "selves" could be present for comparison.'

If that her self were by to stain herself,
As I have seen her when she was her self.

KING EDWARD What strange enchantment lurked in those her eyes,
When they excelled this excellence they have,
That now her dim decline hath power to draw
My subject eyes from piercing majesty
To gaze on her with doting admiration?

COUNTESS In duty lower than the ground I kneel,
And for my dull knees bow my feeling heart
To witness my obedience to your highness
With many millions of a subject's thanks,
For this your royal presence whose approach
Hath driven war and danger from my gate.

KING EDWARD Lady, stand up; I come to bring thee peace,
However thereby I have purchased war.

COUNTESS No war to you, my liege; the Scots are gone,
And gallop home toward Scotland with their hate.

KING EDWARD Lest, yielding here, I pine in shameful love,
Come, we'll pursue the Scots. – Artois, away.

COUNTESS A little while, my gracious sovereign, stay,
And let the power of a mighty king
Honour our roof; my husband in the wars,
When he shall hear it, will triumph for joy.
Then, dear my liege, now niggard not thy state:

100 her self . . . herself] Q1; her selfe . . . her selfe Q2; herself . . . herself *Capell and mod. edns* **101** her self] her selfe Qq; herself *Capell and mod. edns* **102** lurked . . . eyes,] lurkt . . . eies, Q2; lurke . . . eyes? Q1 **104** her] Qq; their *Delius, conj. Capell* **116** hate] Qq; haste *Capell* **117** SH] Q2; *not in* Q1

102 The common d/e misreading ('lurke' for 'lurkd') induced the compositor of Q1 to treat this line as an independent interrogative sentence in the present tense. Q2 moves the question mark to 106.

104 That . . . decline Since even now, when her beauty is dimmed by her loss of vitality (*OED* Decline *sb* 1). Delius's emendation (see Collation) is unjustified: not her eyes, but the beauty of her person has suffered a 'dim decline'.

104–6 to draw . . . admiration WP (p. 86) explain: 'to take piercing majesty from my eyes and to make them gaze on her with doting admiration'. The play is on the contrast 'subject/majesty': the king's eyes should be 'piercing' (penetrating like the eagle's, that can look at the sun), but the lady's beauty has turned the king into a 'subject'.

107–12 See Frois., ch. 77 (Metz, p. 65): 'Whan she came to the kyng, she knelyd downe to the yerth, thankyng hym of his socours.'

108 for in the place of (Abbott 148): the homage paid by the insensitive knees must be taken as coming from the heart.

114 I . . . war A deliberate equivocation on Edward's part: he alludes to his new love passion in terms that are applicable also to the military campaign he has undertaken ('purchased').

116 hate frustrated hostility. The emendation to 'haste' (Capell) impoverishes the meaning.

117–18 Lest . . . Scots A partial aside, clarifying the meaning of 114; only the last five words should be heard by the characters on stage.

123–4 The first in a sequence of twenty-one rhymed couplets, suggesting a transition to the conventions of love poetry.

123 niggard begrudge (*OED* sv *v* 2). Used as verb only by Shakespeare.

123 state royal presence.

Being at the wall, enter our homely gate.
KING EDWARD Pardon me, countess, I will come no nea'r;
I dreamed tonight of treason, and I fear.
COUNTESS Far from this place let ugly treason lie.
KING EDWARD [*Aside*] No farther off than her conspiring eye,
Which shoots infected poison in my heart,
Beyond repulse of wit, or cure of art.
Now in the sun alone it doth not lie
With light to take light from a mortal eye;
For here two day-stars that mine eyes would see
More than the sun steals mine own light from me.
Contemplative desire, desire to be
In contemplation that may master thee. –
Warwick, Artois, to horse and let's away.
COUNTESS What might I speak to make my sovereign stay?
KING EDWARD [*Aside*] What needs a tongue to such a speaking eye,
That more persuades than winning oratory?
COUNTESS Let not thy presence, like the April sun,
Flatter our earth, and suddenly be done;
More happy do not make our outward wall
Than thou wilt grace our inner house withal.
Our house, my liege, is like a country swain,
Whose habit rude and manners blunt and plain
Presageth nought, yet inly beautified

125 nea'r] *This edn;* neare Qq **128** SD] *Capell, subst.; not in* Qq **133** two day-stars] two day starres Q2; to day stars Q1 **139** SD] *Capell, subst.; not in* Qq **144** inner] Q1; inward Q2

125 nea'r nearer. Qq's 'neare' was the current monosyllabic form of the comparative.

126 tonight last night.

128 conspiring acting as part of a conspiracy against the king.

131–4 The power to blind ('take light from') a mortal eye with its light no longer belongs ('doth not lie') only to the sun, because now there are two diurnal stars (the lady's eyes) in my sight capable of depriving my eyes of light. Compare *LLL* 1.1.77, 'Light, seeking light, doth light of light beguile', and 5.2.374–6, 'When we greet, / With eyes best seeing, heaven's fiery eye, / By light we lose light.'

134 steals The third person plural in -s (or -th) is extremely common in Shakespeare (Abbott 333).

135–6 Edward reacts to his passion by invoking the Platonic doctrine: the soul must master desire in order to reach, through the contemplation of earthly beauty, the absolute beauty of the world of ideas.

139 speaking eye A common phrase typical of courtly poetry (Dent, *PLED*, SS16.1).

142 be done end, finish, referring to the proverbial inconstancy of the April weather (To be like the April sun, Dent, *PLED*, A310.11). Here the sun is a figure of the king's majesty.

144 inner Q2 substitutes 'inward', with the same meaning, presumably for the sake of symmetry by contrast with 'outward' at 143.

145–8 The first of the two parallel extended similes ('all too long compare', 156) on which the speech is built. The castle is like the country swain, outwardly poor but inwardly rich, in the same way as the ground above a gold-mine is barren but hides a treasure (149–55).

147 Presageth nought Create no expectations (of riches). 'Presageth' is a singular form for the plural, see 134n.

147 inly beautified is inwardly adorned.

With bounty's riches, and fair hidden pride.
For where the golden ore doth buried lie,
The ground, undecked with nature's tapestry,
Seems barren, sere, unfertile, fruitless, dry;
And where the upper turf of earth doth boast
His pride, perfumes, and parti-coloured cost,
Delve there and find this issue and their pride
To spring from ordure and corruption's side.
But, to make up my all too long compare,
These ragged walls no testimony are
What is within, but like a cloak doth hide
From weather's waste the undergarnished pride.
More gracious than my terms can, let thee be:
Entreat thyself to stay a while with me.

KING EDWARD [*Aside*] As wise as fair: what fond fit can be heard
When wisdom keeps the gate as beauty's guard? –
Countess, albeit my business urgeth me,
It shall attend while I attend on thee. –

148 bounty's] Qq (bounties) **153** pride, perfumes] *Smith, WAA after* Q1 (pride perfumes); pride presumes Q2; proud perfumes *Capell;* pide (= *pied*) perfumes *Delius (conj. Capell), WP, TB, RLA* **153** cost] Q1; coast Q2, *RLA* **157** testimony] Q2 (testimonie); testomie Q1 **159** waste] *WP, conj. Delius, Collier;* West Qq **160** can, let . . . be:] *This edn;* can let . . . be, Qq **162** SD] *This edn; not in* Qq

148 bounty's riches the wealth ('riches' is singular) of a generous nature.

148 pride splendour (*OED* sv *sb* 6).

149–51 A rhyming tercet instead of a couplet, beginning the second 'long compare'.

150 undecked . . . tapestry unadorned by colourful vegetation.

151 Compare 14n.

153 The splendid appearance ('pride', see 148), perfumes, and variegated ('parti-coloured') richness ('cost') of the earth personified ('His'). The omission of a comma in Q1 misled the reviser to replace in Q2 'perfumes' with 'presumes' (e/r transposition and long s/f confusion) and suggested to modern editors that 'pride' is a misprint for 'pide', i.e. 'pied', a synaesthetic description of sweet-smelling flowers, rendered supererogatory by 'parti-coloured' in the same line.

153 cost costly appearance, richness (compare *Sonn.* 64.2: 'The rich proud cost of outworn buried age'). The Q2 reading 'coast' could mean 'bank' (colourful with flowers), see 'flow'ring bank' (*2H6* 3.1.228).

154 this . . . pride The 'issue' of the earth is the rich vegetation; as a collective noun it requires the plural possessive adjective ('their') to describe its splendid appearance ('pride', see 148n.).

155 corruption's side (growing out of) the side of decaying carcases (buried in the ground).

156 make up conclude. For 'compare' see 145–8n., but 158–9 provide a further subsidiary simile.

157 ragged rough and decaying. Compare *2H4* Ind.35, 'this worm-eaten hold of ragged stone', and *R2* 5.5.21, 'my ragged prison walls'.

158 doth A singular form for the plural (see 134n.) depending on 'walls', but allowing for the construction 'a cloak [that] doth hide'.

159 undergarnished pride The splendidly ornate (*OED* Garnish *v* 4) garments ('pride', see 148n., 153n.) under the cloak.

160 Be you more gracious than my words can be.

162–3 The Countess's speech shows such wisdom that, together with her beauty, it can strike the hearer ('can be heard') with a passionate fit ('fond fit').

165 attend . . . thee Playing on the two meanings of 'attend': (1) wait, tarry; (2) act as a gentleman-in-waiting (*OED* Attend *v* 8b).

Come on, my lords, here will I host tonight.

Exeunt

2.1. [*Enter* LODOWICK]

LODOWICK I might perceive his eye in her eye lost,
His ear to drink her sweet tongue's utterance,
And changing passions, like inconstant clouds
That rack upon the carriage of the winds,
Increase and die in his disturbèd cheeks.
Lo, when she blushed, even then did he look pale,
As if her cheeks by some enchanted power
Attracted had the cherry blood from his;
Anon, with reverent fear when she grew pale,

Act 2, Scene 1 2.1] *Capell; no act or scene division in* Qq 0 SD] *Capell (The same. Gardens of the Castle. Enter* LODOWICK*); not in* Qq 1 SH] Q2 *(also /Lodowicke/ or /Lodo./ throughout); Lor:* Q1 *(also at 80, 95, 99 (Lor,), 194, /Lo:/ in all other cases)* 3 passions,] *This edn;* passion Qq; passion, *Capell;* passion – *WP* 3 clouds] *WP;* clouds: Qq; clouds, – *Capell* 4 rack] Q1 (racke); rackt Q2, *Capell, Delius, WP* 5 die] Q1; die, Q2; die, – *Capell, Delius;* die – *WP* 8 cherry] Q1 (cherie), *Capell;* cheerie Q2 9 Anon] Q2; A none Q1

166 host lodge (*OED* sv v^2 2). Compare *Err* 1.2.9: 'the Centaur, where we host'.

Act 2, Scene 1

2.1 Based on Painter, novel 46, with repeated echoes in the first part also from Frois., ch. 77, this scene is located, like 1.2, in Roxborough Castle. The mention of a 'summer arbour' at 61 suggests the castle garden or orchard, see 61 n.

0 SD The absence of the entrance direction in Qq indicates that the new act followed 1.2 without intermission. Originally the author must have considered Lodowick as one of the anonymous 'others' entering as mutes with King Edward at 1.2.89; failing to join the general exit at the end of the scene, he was left alone on the stage at the beginning of Act 2. An identical situation is that of Aaron in *Tit.*, who enters with Tamora and others at 1.1.295, is a mute for the rest of the act, but remains alone on stage at the end of it to deliver the opening speech of Act 2.

1 SH In Q2's dialogue, the name is consistently spelt 'Lodowicke', and treated indifferently as a tri- or a disyllable, while in Q1 'Lodowike' is found only at 59 – otherwise it is 'Lodwicke' (twice), 'Lodwike' (twice) or 'Lodwick' (twice). The confusion in speech headings in Q1 is discussed in the Textual Analysis, pp. 172–3. The character of the king's confidant was suggested by the figure of the secretary who, in Painter's novel, acts as a messenger for the king, though being critical of his behaviour (Metz, pp. 114–15, 124–5, 128, see Appendix, pp. 189–90), but the task imposed on him of composing a love sonnet is the playwright's invention.

2 to drink drinking, parallel with 'lost' (= being lost) in 1 and 'Increase and die' in 5; the variation in the use of verbal modes and tenses in a series of clauses depending on a single verb ('perceive') is common in Shakespeare (Abbott 351).

3 passions Probably the compositor of Q1 misread the final *s* (a plural agreeing with the verbs in 5) for a comma, and then omitted it in arbitrarily repunctuating the passage.

4 rack drive before the wind (*OED* sv v^1, but see 1.1.46n.). Q1's mispunctuation (see 3n.) induced the reviser to change a present to a past participle, making 'racked upon the carriage of the winds' an apposition to 'That' as part of a relative clause depending on 'clouds'. Capell and others adopted this reading.

5 Increase and die Wax and wane, referring to the 'passions' colouring the king's cheeks, not (as Capell and others thought) to the movement of clouds in the wind.

9 Anon By and by.

His cheeks put on their scarlet ornaments,
But no more like her oriental red
Than brick to coral, or live things to dead.
Why did he then thus counterfeit her looks?
If she did blush, 'twas tender modest shame,
Being in the sacred presence of a king.
If he did blush, 'twas red immodest shame,
To vail his eyes amiss, being a king.
If she looked pale, 'twas silly woman's fear,
To bear herself in presence of a king.
If he looked pale, it was with guilty fear,
To dote amiss, being a mighty king.
Then, Scottish wars, farewell; I fear 'twill prove
A lingering English siege of peevish love.
Here comes his highness, walking all alone.

Enter KING EDWARD

KING EDWARD She is grown more fairer far since I came hither,
Her voice more silver every word than other,
Her wit more fluent – what a strange discourse
Unfolded she, of David and his Scots?
'Even thus', quoth she, 'he spake' – and then spoke broad,
With epithets and accents of the Scot,
But somewhat better than the Scot could speak.
'And thus quoth she' – and answered then herself –

10 cheeks] *Capell;* cheeke Qq 11 oriental] Q2 (orientall)*;* oryent all Q1 15 presence] Q2*;* present Q1 17 vail] *Capell;* waile Qq 25 hither] Q2*;* thither Q1 29 spoke] Q1*;* spake Q2 31 Scot] Qq*;* Scots *Delius* 32 thus . . . she' –] *This edn after* Q1*;* thus, quoth she, Q2, *Capell*

10 put . . . ornaments blushed. The expression 'scarlet ornaments' is found in *Sonn.* 142.6 with reference to the unfaithful mistress's lips, where 'scarlet' implies sinfulness. If Qq's singular form 'cheeke' in this line is accepted, 'their' refers to 'her cheeks' (7), meaning: 'the king's face blushed like the lady's cheeks had done'.

11 oriental orient, i.e. resplendent, shining like the dawn (*OED* Orient B *a* 2b).

12 coral Proverbially a paragon of shining redness (Dent, *PLED*, C648.1).

17 vail lower in sign of submission (*OED* sv v^2 1c). A king should not submit to a subject.

17, 21 amiss wrongly, improperly.

18 silly weak, compare 1.1.137.

19 To . . . herself About how to behave.

23 peevish capricious (*OED* sv *a* 4).

25–47 The king's soliloquy implies that, at his sight (24), Lodowick has retired, presumably to the 'summer arbour' mentioned at 61, sheltered from part of the stage but not from the audience.

25 more fairer The use of 'more' with comparatives for greater emphasis is common (Abbott 11).

29 spake . . . spoke The use of two distinct forms both current at the time emphasises the difference between direct and reported speech.

29 broad Used adverbially.

30 epithets typical expressions (*OED* sv *sb* 3).

32 And . . . she In her humorous report of the verbal skirmish with the Scots the Countess speaks of herself in the third person.

For who could speak like her? – But she herself
Breathes from the wall an angel's note from heaven
Of sweet defiance to her barbarous foes.
When she would talk of peace, methinks her tongue
Commanded war to prison; when of war,
It wakened Caesar from his Roman grave
To hear war beautified by her discourse;
Wisdom is foolishness but in her tongue,
Beauty a slander but in her fair face,
There is no summer but in her cheerful looks,
Nor frosty winter but in her disdain.
I cannot blame the Scots that did besiege her,
For she is all the treasure of our land,
But call them cowards that they ran away,
Having so rich and fair a cause to stay. –
Art thou there, Lodowick? Give me ink and paper.

LODOWICK I will, my liege.

KING EDWARD And bid the lords hold on their play at chess,
For we will walk and meditate alone.

LODOWICK I will, my sovereign. [*Exit*]

KING EDWARD This fellow is well read in poetry,
And hath a lusty and persuasive spirit;
I will acquaint him with my passion,
Which he shall shadow with a veil of lawn,
Through which the queen of beauty's queen shall see
Herself the ground of my infirmity.

Enter LODOWICK

Hast thou pen, ink, and paper ready, Lodowick?

33 her? – . . . herself] Q2; her . . . herselfe: Q1 34 heaven] Q2; Heauen: Q1 48 Lodowick? . . . paper.] Q2; Lodwicke, . . . paper? Q1 49 liege] Q1; soueraigne Q2 52 sovereign] Q1; liege Q2 52 SD] Q2; *not in* Q1 53 well] Q1; *not in* Q2 57 beauty's queen] Qq (beauties Queene); beauties Queenes *WP after Delius* 59 Hast . . . Lodowick?] *all mod. edns; Ki*: Hast . . . Lodowike. Q1; *King Ed.* Hast . . . Lodow. Q2

50 hold on go on with.

52–3 The change in Q2 from 'sovereign' to 'liege' at 52 (which entailed a reverse exchange at 49) and the omission of 'well' at 53 may be due to a reviser's attempt at regularising the metre, by transformimg Lodowick's one-line speech and the first line of the king's reply into a single pentameter: 'I will, my liege. / This fellow is read in poetry.'

56 shadow . . . lawn depict transparently (*OED* Shadow *v* 8). 'Lawn' was a linen fabric so fine as to be compared to a spider's web (*OED* sv *sb*[1] 1).

57 queen . . . queen Venus, queen of beauty, is a mere subject of the Countess, the real sovereign. WP, accepting Delius's emendation to 'beauty's queens', consider 'queen of queens' as a form of superlative, like 'song of songs', and interpret: 'the supreme queen of beauty'.

58 ground cause.

LODOWICK Ready, my liege.
KING EDWARD Then in the summer arbour sit by me,
Make it our council house or cabinet:
Since green our thoughts, green be the conventicle
Where we will ease us by disburd'ning them.
Now, Lod'wick, invocate some golden Muse
To bring thee hither an enchanted pen
That may for sighs set down true sighs indeed,
Talking of grief, to make thee ready groan,
And when thou writest of tears, encouch the word
Before and after with such sweet laments,
That it may raise drops in a Tartar's eye,
And make a flint-heart Scythian pitiful –
For so much moving hath a poet's pen.
Then, if thou be a poet, move thou so,
And be enrichèd by thy sovereign's love.
For if the touch of sweet concordant strings
Could force attendance in the ears of hell,
How much more shall the strains of poets' wit
Beguile and ravish soft and human minds?
LODOWICK To whom, my lord, shall I direct my style?
KING EDWARD To one that shames the fair and sots the wise,
Whose body is an abstract or a brief,
Contains each general virtue in the world.

62 council] *Capell;* counsel Q1; counsell Q2 **65** Lod'wick] Q1 (Lodwike); Lodowicke Q2 **68** ready] Qq; really *Collier* **71** Tartar's] *Capell and mod. edns;* Torters Qq **75** sovereign's] Q2 (soueraignes); soueraigne Q1 **77** attendance] Qq; attention *Collier* **78** strains] Q1 (straines); straine Q2 **78** poets'] *This edn, after* Qq (poets); poet's *Capell* **79** Beguile] Q2; Beguild Q1 **82** body is] Qq (bodie is); body, as *Capell*

61 summer arbour tree bower. Possibly envisaging a piece of property like the one in the vignette on the title-page of the 1615 quarto of Kyd's *Spanish Tragedy*.

62 cabinet private room or treasure-chamber (*OED* sv 3,6).

63 green . . . thoughts new, lively reflections.

63 conventicle place of meeting (*OED* sv *sb* 6).

68 ready Used adverbially: promptly. Collier's emendation ('really') is unjustified.

69 encouch embed.

71–2 The inhabitants of both Tartary, in central Asia, and Scythia, in eastern Europe and western Asia, are frequently mentioned in Elizabethan plays for their reputation for ruthlessness and cruelty.

73 moving power to move.

76–7 Referring to the myth of Orpheus' descent to Hades: through the charm of his lyre he was allowed to rescue Eurydice from the dead.

77 attendance sympathy (an obsolete form of 'attention').

78 poets' Qq fail to clarify whether this is a singular or plural genitive. The reference seems to be to poets in general; see 1.2.95n.

79 human (1) of man, (2) humane, tender.

80 style possibly 'stylus' (= pen), as well as literary style (Lapides).

81 sots besots, renders foolish.

82 abstract . . . brief Both terms mean 'summary, epitome'.

83 Either the line is a relative clause where 'which' is understood before 'Contains' (TB), or both 'is' at 82 and 'Contains' depend on the single subject 'body' (Lapides). By emending 'is' to 'as' in 82 Capell construes: 'her body contains, as in a summary, all virtues'.

'Better than beautiful', thou must begin;
Devise for fair a fairer word than fair,
And every ornament that thou wouldst praise
Fly it a pitch above the soar of praise.
For flattery fear thou not to be convicted,
For, were thy admiration ten times more,
Ten times ten thousand more the worth exceeds
Of that thou art to praise, thy praise's worth.
Begin; I will to contemplate the while.
Forget not to set down how passionate,
How heart-sick, and how full of languishment
Her beauty makes me.

LODOWICK Write I to a woman?

KING EDWARD What beauty else could triumph on me?
Or who but women do our love-lays greet?
What, thinkst thou I did bid thee praise a horse?

LODOWICK Of what condition or estate she is
'Twere requisite that I should know, my lord.

KING EDWARD Of such estate, that hers is as a throne,
And my estate the footstool where she treads;
Then mayst thou judge what her condition is
By the proportion of her mightiness.
Write on, while I peruse her in my thoughts.
[. . .]
Her voice to music or the nightingale:
To music every summer-leaping swain

90 the] Q2; thy Q1 **91** thy] *Capell;* their Qq **92** Begin; I] *WP after* Q2 (Begin, I); Beginne I Q1 **95** Write] Q2; Writ Q1 **95** a] Q1; *not in* Q2 **96** on] Q1; ouer Q2 **106** *missing line*] *conj. Smith, TB* **108** summer-leaping] *Capell;* sommer leaping Q1; summer leaping Q2

86 ornament Intellectual as well as physical quality; see 10 above.

87 A common metaphor from falconry, see e.g *R2* 1.1.109: 'How high a pitch his resolution soars'. 'Pitch' is the highest point to which a falcon can fly (*OED* sv *sb*[2] 18).

89–91 were . . . worth A hyperbole: even if your praises (admiration) were ten times more, the Countess's merit ('that thou art to praise') exceeds a hundred thousand times your praises' worth.

97 love-lays love songs.

98 This irony may have suggested the exchange between the Dauphin (Bourbon in Q) and Orleans in *H5* 3.7.39–42: 'I once writ a sonnet in his [my horse's] praise and began thus: "Wonder of nature" — *Orl.* I have heard a sonnet begin so to one's mistress.'

101–2 hers . . . treads Edward plays on the meaning of 'estate' as the outward display of royal pomp (*OED* Estate *sb* 4): the Countess is the throne itself, the seat of majesty, while he is the stool at the foot of the throne.

104 proportion measure, extent (*OED* sv *sb* 5).

106 As Moore Smith and Tucker Brooke surmised, the king's tirade on the rhetoric of love poetry must have begun with a line or lines now lost, introducing the conventional catalogue of the mistress's beauties.

108 summer-leaping eager for the summer (*OED* Leap *v* 2e, see 2.2.13n.). For this type of compounds WP compare *TGV* 2.4.162 ('summer-swelling flower'), and Braunmuller, *Mac.* 4.3.86 ('summer-seeming lust').

Compares his sun-burnt lover when she speaks –
And why should I speak of the nightingale?
The nightingale sings of adulterate wrong,
And that, compared, is too satirical,
For sin, though sin, would not be so esteemed,
But rather virtue sin, sin virtue deemed.
Her hair, far softer than the silkworm's twist,
Like to a flattering glass, doth make more fair
The yellow amber – 'like a flattering glass'
Comes in too soon; for, writing of her eyes,
I'll say that like a glass they catch the sun,
And thence the hot reflection doth rebound
Against my breast, and burns my heart within.
Ah, what a world of descant makes my soul
Upon this voluntary ground of love!
Come, Lod'wick, hast thou turned thy ink to gold?
If not, write but in letters capital
My mistress' name, and it will gild thy paper.
Read, lord, read,
Fill thou the empty hollows of mine ears
With the sweet hearing of thy poetry.

112 that, compared,] *Capell; no punct.* Qq; that compare *conj. this edn (see Commentary)* **116** to] Q1; as Q2 **123** love!] Q2 (loue?); loue, Q1 **124** Lod'wick] Q1 (Lodwick); Lodowicke Q2 **125–7**] *So divided WP; as two lines divided at* name, Qq; *as three lines divided at* capital / name, / read, *Capell* **125** write but] Qq; but write *Collier* **127** lord,] Qq (Lorde,); lad, /*or*/ Lord! *conj. Collier;* Lodwick, *conj. WP*

109 sun-burnt A dark complexion was the mark of a low condition.

111 Alluding to the myth of Philomel, transformed into a nightingale after being raped by Tereus, see *Luc.* 1128, 'Philomel, that sing'st of ravishment', and the frequent references in *Tit.*

112 compared Possibly a misreading of 'compare' as a noun (= comparison): a comparison between the mistress and ravished Philomel would be a piece of cruel irony ('satirical'). Qq's reading, as punctuated by Capell, is more awkward but does not alter the meaning.

115 softer . . . twist Proverbial, 'as soft as silk' (Tilley S449).

116 flattering glass Another poetical commonplace (Dent, *PLED*, G132.1).

117 yellow amber Fair hair was commonly compared to amber: *LLL* 4.3.85, 'her amber hairs'.

119 like a glass The image is from the concave mirrors (burning glasses) used to destroy the wooden ships of approaching enemies.

122–3 A musical metaphor: 'descant' designates the melodic variations composed over a constant rhythmic 'ground' (bass or base).

123 voluntary spontaneous. RLA finds the expression paradoxical in that 'love [the 'ground'] comes to the lover from an external source, yet it seems in a way his own creation, and his whole heart wills it'.

126 gild thy paper Gold leaf was used to decorate the initial capital letters (see 125) in illuminated manuscripts.

127 lord The form of address to Lodowick is perhaps meant jocularly, since he is not a nobleman. Capell sees it as an exclamation of impatience ('Lord!') or a misreading of 'lad'. WP suggest a misreading of 'Lod.', a graphic abbreviation of 'Lodowick'.

128 hollows . . . ears Compare *Rom.* 3.5.3: 'the fearful hollow of thine ear'.

LODOWICK I have not to a period brought her praise.
KING EDWARD Her praise is as my love, both infinite,
Which apprehend such violent extremes
That they disdain an ending period.
Her beauty hath no match but my affection;
Hers more than most, mine most and more than more;
Hers more to praise than tell the sea by drops,
Nay, more than drop, the massy earth by sands,
And sand by sand print them in memory.
Then wherefore talkst thou of a period
To that which craves unended admiration?
Read, let us hear.
LODOWICK 'More fair and chaste than is the queen of shades' –
KING EDWARD That line hath two faults, gross and palpable.
Comparest thou her to the pale queen of night
Who, being set in dark, seems therefore light?
What, is she, when the sun lifts up his head,
But like a fading taper, dim and dead?
My love shall brave the eye of heaven at noon
And, being unmasked, outshine the golden sun.
LODOWICK What is the other fault, my sovereign lord?
KING EDWARD Read o'er the line again.
LODOWICK 'More fair and chaste' –
KING EDWARD I did not bid thee talk of chastity,
To ransack so the treasure of her mind,

138 sand by sand] *Capell;* said, by said, Qq 143 line] Q2; loue Q1 153 treasure] *Capell;* treason Qq

130 period end, full stop (see 133 and 139).

134 affection passion, infatuation (*OED* Affection *sb* 3).

135 Hers . . . mine 'Hers' (also at 136) refers to 'Her beauty', which is superior to most beauties, and 'mine' to 'my affection', which is even greater.

136–8 The poetic hyperbole is based on two common proverbial expressions indicating numberlessness: to tell the praises of her beauty is like counting ('tell', 136) the drops in the sea (see Dent, *PLED*, D615.11), or rather numbering sands (Tilley S91), both ultimately from Rev. 20.8: 'The number of whom is as the sand of the sea'. Capell was surely right in emending the meaningless 'said, by said' at 138 in Qq.

142 queen of shades Diana, goddess of the moon and of chastity.

143 palpable obvious; compare *1H4* 2.4.226: 'gross as a mountain, open, palpable'.

144–9 The sequence of three rhymed couplets presents this as a typical poetic conceit. The same, though in a less elaborate form, is found in *Rom.* 2.2.4–6, where Juliet as the sun makes the moon 'sick and pale' with envy (WP).

145 The moon (queen of night, 144) seems bright only because it is surrounded by darkness.

148 brave . . . heaven challenge the sun.

149 being unmasked when she shows her face.

153 treasure Qq's 'treason' is an obvious compositorial misreading: 'sure' and 'son' are hardly distinguishable in Elizabethan handwriting.

For I had rather have her chased than chaste.
Out with the moon line, I will none of it,
And let me have her likened to the sun.
Say she hath thrice more splendour than the sun,
That her perfections emulates the sun,
That she breeds sweets as plenteous as the sun,
That she doth thaw cold winter like the sun,
That she doth cheer fresh summer like the sun,
That she doth dazzle gazers like the sun,
And in this application to the sun,
Bid her be free and general as the sun,
Who smiles upon the basest weed that grows
As lovingly as on the fragrant rose. –
Let's see what follows that same moonlight line.

LODOWICK 'More fair and chaste than is the queen of shades,
More bold in constancy' –

KING EDWARD In constancy than who?

LODOWICK 'than Judith was' –

KING EDWARD O monstrous line: put in the next a sword
And I shall woo her to cut off my head!
Blot, blot, good Lod'wick. Let us hear the next.

LODOWICK There's all that yet is done.

KING EDWARD I thank thee then: thou hast done little ill –

154 had] Qq; would *Collier* **158** perfections] Qq; perfection *Capell* **163** to] Qq; of *Collier* **168** queen] *Capell;* louer Qq **173** Lod'wick] Q1 (Lodwicke); Lodowicke Q2

154 chased pursued and caught, possibly playing on the meaning 'embossed, engraved in relief' (*OED* sv *ppl a*[2]), used figuratively for 'portrayed (in the poem)'. The aural pun 'chased'/'chaste' is given a solemn ring in Brutus' speech at the close of *Luc.*, depicting Tarquin 'forth [Rome's] fair streets chased' (1834) in revenge for Lucrece's 'chaste blood so unjustly stained' (1836).

157–66 Another example of the rhetoric of love-poetry: eight lines with identical rhymes closed by a couplet.

158 emulates A third person plural in -s; compare 1.2.134n.

159 plenteous Used adverbially.

163 application reference, recourse.

164 general affable to all (*OED* sv *adj* 6b).

165–6 The conventional expressions 'basest weed' and 'fragrant rose' are found only once in Shakespeare, in two consecutive Sonnets: 94.12 and 95.2 respectively. Their significance in this context is discussed in Melchiori, *Meditations*, 44–5.

167 moonlight line the line mentioning the moon: ironical, moonlight being associated with lunacy.

168 queen Surprisingly, Qq have 'louer' for 'queen' in a line that should reproduce verbatim 142. Is it Lodowick's attempt at meeting the king's criticism of the moon line, or simply a printer's confusion? At 143 Q1 printed 'loue' for 'line', an obvious misreading corrected in Q2.

171–2 'Then [Judith] . . . took down [Holofernes's] fauchion . . . and she smote twice upon his neck with all her might, and she took away his head from him'. Judith (Apocrypha) 13.6–8.

172 woo plead with.

But what is done is passing passing ill.
No, let the captain talk of boist'rous war,
The prisoner of immurèd dark constraint,
The sick man best sets down the pangs of death,
The man that starves the sweetness of a feast,
The frozen soul the benefit of fire,
And every grief his happy opposite:
Love cannot sound well but in lovers' tongues.
Give me the pen and paper, I will write.

Enter COUNTESS

But soft, here comes the treasurer of my spirit –
Lod'wick, thou knowst not how to draw a battle:
These wings, these flankers, and these squadrons
Argue in thee defective discipline;
Thou shouldst have placed this here, this other here –
COUNTESS Pardon my boldness, my thrice gracious lords;
Let my intrusion here be called my duty,
That comes to see my sovereign, how he fares.
KING EDWARD Go, draw the same, I tell thee in what form.
LODOWICK I go. [*Exit*]

178 immurèd] *Capell;* emured QQ 184 SD *Enter*] Q1*; Enter the* Q2 185 treasurer] Q1*;* treasure Q2 186 Lod'wick] Q1 (Lodwick)*;* Lodowicke Q2 187 squadrons] QQ*;* squadrons here *Capell* 190 lords] QQ*;* lord *Capell* 194 SD] Q2*; not in* Q1

176 is passing . . . ill exceeds the worst (you have written ['what is done'] so far); 'is passing' is a verbal form (= exceeds), the second 'passing' is an adjective (= exceedingly [bad as a poetic expression of feeling]).

178 immurèd walled up. On the significance of the spelling 'emured' in QQ see Textual Analysis, p. 174.

180–2 WP observe that 'these lines are not in conformity' with 177–9 or 183, which maintain that a 'passion' is best expressed by those who profess or suffer it.

182 happy opposite the happy condition opposite (to the particular grief). See 'by the opposite' (454).

183 Compare *Rom.* 2.2.165: 'How silver-sweet sound lovers' tongues.'

185 treasurer . . . spirit In Painter (Metz, p. 112, see Appendix, p. 191) 'you . . . onely treasurer of my hart'. Q2 substituted 'treasure' for the sake of metre (WP).

186–93 Edward pretends to be discussing military matters with Lodowick: 'battle' (186) = array, deployment of troops (*OED* sv *sb* 8); 'flankers' (187) = forces deployed so as to flank the enemy assailants; 'discipline' (188) = skill in the art of war (*OED* sv *sb* 3b). Capell adds 'here' to 187 to regularise the metre, but 'squadrons' can be treated as trisyllablic.

189 Apparently instructions on how to draw a battle plan, but also on how to rewrite a love poem, see 155–66.

190 lords Perhaps 'lord' (Capell), since Lodowick is no lord and 'thrice gracious' is proper for a king (see 'Thrice gentle', 202, 'thrice dread', 218); but the Countess is addressing both persons on stage.

192 my . . . fares how my sovereign fares. A common construction (Abbott 414).

193 draw . . . form draw the battle plan according to my instructions (in the form I have been explaining to you), but also 'write the sonnet the way I told you'; see 189n.

COUNTESS Sorry I am to see my liege so sad;
What may thy subject do to draw from thee
Thy gloomy consort, sullen melancholy?
KING EDWARD Ah, lady, I am blunt, and cannot strew
The flowers of solace in a ground of shame;
Since I came hither, countess, I am wronged.
COUNTESS Now God forbid that any in my house
Should think my sovereign wrong! Thrice gentle king,
Acquaint me with your cause of discontent.
KING EDWARD How near then shall I be to remedy?
COUNTESS As near, my liege, as all my woman's power
Can pawn itself to buy thy remedy.
KING EDWARD If thou speakst true, then have I my redress:
Engage thy power to redeem my joys,
And I am joyful, countess; else I die.
COUNTESS I will, my liege.
KING EDWARD Swear, countess, that thou wilt.
COUNTESS By heaven, I will.
KING EDWARD Then take thyself a little way aside,
And tell thyself a king doth dote on thee;
Say that within thy power doth lie
To make him happy, and that thou hast sworn
To give him all the joy within thy power.
Do this, and tell me when I shall be happy.
COUNTESS All this is done, my thrice dread sovereign.

197 Thy] Q1; This Q2 **197** sullen] *Capell;* sullome Qq **202** wrong! . . . king,] *Capell;* wrong, . . . king: Qq **203** Acquaint . . . your] Q2; *King*: Acquant . . . theyr Q1 **204** SH] Q2; *not in* Q1 **210** countess] Q2 (Countesse); Counties Q1 **214** doth] Qq; it doth *Capell and mod. edns* **215** that] Q1; *not in* Q2 **216** him] Qq; me *Capell* **218**] *As one line,* Q1; *as two lines divided at* done, Q2

195–204 Modelled on Frois. (Metz, p. 66) as well as Painter, see Appendix, p. 190.

197 Thy . . . consort thy sad companion.

197 sullen Lapides (p. 226) considers Qq's spelling 'sullome' 'a combination of the words solemn and sullen'.

198–9 cannot . . . shame Compare *Luc.* 1074–5: 'My sable ground of sin I will not paint, / To hide the truth of this false night's abuses.'

202 think . . . wrong think of doing wrong to – with unconscious irony: it would be right to think that the king's behaviour is wrong. 'Thrice gentle king' (where 'gentle' = noble) according to Qq's punctuation is a vocative attached to the previous clause instead of beginning a new sentence.

203 Q1 assigns this line to King Edward.

209 else I die From Frois. (Metz, p. 66): 'without your love I am but deed'. Painter obscures the meaning through over-elaboration, see Appendix, p. 191.

214 doth Capell inserts 'it' before 'doth', which is grammatically and metrically more correct. He suggests similar metrical adjustments at 250, 258, and elsewhere but they are by no means indispensable.

218 thrice dread The Countess's forms of address become progressively more detached: she had called the king 'gracious' (endowed with divine grace and benevolent) at 190, 'gentle' (noble) at 202, and now 'dread' (held in awe). Compare 'most dradde soueraigne Lord' in Painter (Metz, p. 113, reported in the Appendix, p. 192).

That power of love that I have power to give,
Thou hast with all devout obedience:
Employ me how thou wilt in proof thereof.
KING EDWARD Thou hearst me say that I do dote on thee.
COUNTESS If on my beauty, take it if thou canst:
Though little, I do prize it ten times less.
If on my virtue, take it if thou canst,
For virtue's store by giving doth augment.
Be it on what it will that I can give,
And thou canst take away, inherit it.
KING EDWARD It is thy beauty that I would enjoy.
COUNTESS O, were it painted I would wipe it off
And dispossess myself to give it thee.
But, sovereign, it is soldered to my life:
Take one and both, for, like an humble shadow,
It haunts the sunshine of my summer's life.
KING EDWARD But thou mayst lend it me to sport withal.
COUNTESS As easy may my intellectual soul
Be lent away, and yet my body live,
As lend my body, palace to my soul,
Away from her, and yet retain my soul.
My body is her bower, her court, her abbey,
And she an angel pure, divine, unspotted:
If I should lend her house, my lord, to thee,
I kill my poor soul, and my poor soul me.
KING EDWARD Didst thou not swear to give me what I would?
COUNTESS I did, my liege, so what you would, I could.

231 dispossess] Q2; disposse Q1 **235** SH] Q2; *not in* Q1 **235** lend] Q2; leue Q1 **242** lend] Q2; leaue Q1 **245** liege] Qq; lord *Collier*

221 in . . . thereof to test the truth of my statement.

227–8 have ('inherit') whatever you dote on, provided it is something which is in my power to give and in yours to take.

233–4 like . . . life A paradoxical comparison: life being summer sunshine, beauty is the shadow caused by that sunshine.

235, 242 lend Q2's 'lend' for Q1's 'leue' at 235, 'leaue' at 242, is perhaps a reviser's attempt to clarify the use of 'leave' in the sense of 'put at the disposal of'. See 'Be lent', 237, and 'lend', 238.

236 intellectual soul The soul was considered the seat of intellect. WP compare *Err.* 2.1.20–2, 'Man, more divine, the master of all these, . . . Indued with intellectual sense and souls'.

238–43 The comparison develops the current concept of the body as the house or palace of the soul (ultimately from 2 Cor. 5.1–2). Shakespeare based on it *Sonn.* 146, where the body is the 'fading mansion' (6) of the 'poor soul'. Compare the Countess in Painter (Metz, p. 113): 'I intend to keepe the same [my faith] vnspotted [see 241] so long as my soule shalbe caried in the Chariot of this mortall body'.

245 so . . . could provided I had the power to give the thing you want. See 227–8n.

KING EDWARD I wish no more of thee than thou mayst give,
Nor beg I do not, but I rather buy –
That is, thy love; and for that love of thine
In rich exchange I tender to thee mine.
COUNTESS But that your lips were sacred, my lord,
You would profane the holy name of love.
That love you offer me, you cannot give,
For Caesar owes that tribute to his queen.
That love you beg of me, I cannot give,
For Sarah owes that duty to her lord.
He that doth clip or counterfeit your stamp
Shall die, my lord; and will your sacred self
Commit high treason against the king of heaven,
To stamp his image in forbidden metal,
Forgetting your allegiance and your oath?
In violating marriage' sacred law
You break a greater honour than yourself.
To be a king is of a younger house
Than to be married: your progenitor,
Sole reigning Adam on the universe,
By God was honoured for a married man,
But not by him anointed for a king.
It is a penalty to break your statutes,
Though not enacted with your highness' hand;
How much more to infringe the holy act
Made by the mouth of God, sealed with His hand?
I know my sovereign, in my husband's love –

250 my] Qq; o my *Capell* **258** against] Qq; 'gainst *Capell* **269** with] Qq; by *Capell* **270** How] Qq; But how *Collier*

253 Caesar . . . queen even a monarch is bound by the marriage vow. Contrary to Painter, who speaks of the king's liberty, 'which of long time I haue so happily preserued' (Metz, p. 112), the playwright is aware that Edward was married.

255 Sarah Sarah, Abraham's wife, is quoted as an example of submission to her husband in 1 Pet. 3.6: 'Even as Sara obeyed Abraham, calling him lord'.

256–60 The metaphor of adultery as counterfeiting coins is echoed in *MM*. 2.4.45–6, 'Their saucy sweetness that do coin heaven's image / In stamps that are forbid'.

256 clip mutilate current coin by fraudulently paring the edges (*OED* sv v^2 4), a practice, like counterfeiting, punished with death.

256 stamp the image of the king on coins.

262 you commit treason against a power higher than that (of king) implicit in your title ('honour').

263–7 The sacrament of marriage (treated as an honour conferred upon man, 266) preceded the creation of the title of king.

263 of . . . house a title of more recent date.

267 for as.

268 penalty penal offence (*OED* sv *sb* 4 gives this as the only example).

269 even those enforced before you became king.

272–5 The Countess pretends to believe that the king's words are meant only to test her fidelity to her husband. This is hinted at in Frois. (Metz, p. 66): 'A, ryght noble prince, for Goddes sake mocke nor tempt me nat: I can nat byleve that it is true that ye say. . .' (see Appendix, p. 191).

Who now doth loyal service in his wars –,
Doth but so try the wife of Salisbury,
Whether she will hear a wanton's tale or no.
Lest being therein guilty by my stay,
From that, not from my liege, I turn away. *Exit*

KING EDWARD Whether is her beauty by her words divine,
Or are her words sweet chaplains to her beauty?
Like as the wind doth beautify a sail
And as a sail becomes the unseen wind,
So do her words her beauty, beauty, words.
O, that I were a honey-gathering bee,
To bear the comb of virtue from this flower,
And not a poison-sucking envious spider,
To turn the juice I take to deadly venom!
Religion is austere, and beauty gentle –
Too strict a guardian for so fair a ward.
O, that she were as is the air to me!
Why, so she is; for when I would embrace her,
This do I, and catch nothing but myself.
I must enjoy her, for I cannot beat

274 so] *TB;* to Qq **275** Whether] Q2*;* Whither Q1 **278** divine,] Q1*;* diuine? Q2 **279** beauty?] Q2*;* bewtie, Q1 **282** beauty, beauty, words] *Capell, subst;* bewties, bewtie wordes Q1*;* beauties, beautie words Q2*;* bewties, bewties words *Collier* **284** this] *Capell;* his Qq **286** juice] *Collier* (iuce)*;* vice Qq **286** take] Qq*;* talk *conj. Braunmuller* **288** Too strict] Q2*;* To stricke Q1 **288** ward] *Capell;* weed Qq

273 Compare Frois. (Metz, p. 66): 'my husbande, who is so valyant a knight, and hath done your grace so gode servyce, and as yet lyethe in prison for your quarell'.

274 but so Qq's 'to' instead of 'so' is acceptable only if 'so' is inserted after 'Doth' ('Doth so but to try').

275 hear . . . tale listen to the words of a libertine.

277 From that from the 'wanton's tale'.

278 divine made divine.

279 chaplains religious ministers (of 'divine' beauty).

281 becomes (1) befits, see 396, (2) comes to be, gives existence to.

282 her words become her beauty as her beauty becomes her words. Qq's 'beauties, beauty' must be emended to conform to 278–9.

283–6 Proverbial, 'where the bee sucks honey the spider sucks poison' (Tilley B208).

284 comb The nectar gathered from the flowers to make the honeycomb.

284 this The misreading 'his' for 'this' and vice versa is common. Qq's 'his', though, could refer to 'bee'.

286 juice 'iuce', the current spelling of 'juice', could easily be misread 'vice'. Braunmuller suggests a different fairly common misreading, 'take' for 'talk': 'To turn the vice I talk to deadly venom'.

288 ward A minor under the control of a guardian (*OED* sv *sb*[2] 6). Capell's emendation of Qq's 'weed' is rejected by RLA and Lapides, and see the paradox in *Oth.* 4.2.67–8 (Folio TLN 2762–3): 'Oh thou weed: / That are so louely faire, and smell'st so sweete'. But 'ward' as a metaphor for beauty under the strict guardianship of religion is more appropriate.

289 as . . . air as free as air. Proverbial, Tilley A88.

291 This do I An action pointer, indicating Edward's gesture with his arms.

With reason and reproof fond love away.

Enter WARWICK

Here comes her father: I will work with him
To bear my colours in this field of love.

WARWICK How is it that my sovereign is so sad?
May I, with pardon, know your highness' grief,
And that my old endeavour will remove it,
It shall not cumber long your majesty.

KING EDWARD A kind and voluntary gift thou proferest,
That I was forward to have begged of thee.
But O thou world, great nurse of flattery,
Why dost thou tip men's tongues with golden words,
And peise their deeds with weight of heavy lead,
That fair performance cannot follow promise?
O, that a man might hold the heart's close book
And choke the lavish tongue when it doth utter
The breath of falsehood not charactered there!

WARWICK Far be it from the honour of my age
That I should owe bright gold and render lead:
Age is a cynic, not a flatterer.
I say again, that if I knew your grief,
And that by me it may be lessenèd,
My proper harm should buy your highness' good.

KING EDWARD These are the vulgar tenders of false men,

299 It] QQ; I *RLA* **300** proferest] Q1; offerest Q2 **312** if I] Q2; I if Q1 **315** SH] *Capell; not in* QQ

293 fond (1) cherished, (2) foolish, doting.

294–460 This part of the scene is based exclusively on Painter's novel, see Appendix, pp. 193–6.

295 bear my colours fight under my banners (on my side). Military metaphors are frequent in love poetry.

298 that . . . it A rare construction, explained by WP (quoting a parallel from *Sonn.* 39.10–13) as depending on 'May I' (= if I may) at 297, so that 'that' = 'if': if my endeavours as an old man are able to remove it. RLA, by changing 'It' at 299 into 'I', suggests 'I shall not importune you long, if my efforts manage to remove your grief.'

300 proferest utter (*OED* Profer *v* 3); Q2's 'offerest' is weaker.

301 was forward was going.

302–8 The king's false sermonising on the contrast between words and deeds replaces his moral discourse on the conflict between reason and passion in Painter. See Appendix, pp. 192–3.

304 peise weigh down (*OED* sv *v* 4).

306 hold . . . book keep his heart closed (refrain from undertakings prompted by the heart rather than the brain).

307 lavish overgenerous, too ready to make promises.

308 not . . . there which is not deeply seated in it; 'charactered' = engraved, compare *Sonn.* 122.1–2: 'my brain / Full charactered with lasting memory'.

310 owe . . . lead give lead in return for gold.

311 cynic disposed to rail or find fault (*OED* sv *sb* 2).

315 tenders promises of payment.

That never pay the duty of their words.
Thou wilt not stick to swear what thou hast said,
But, when thou knowest my grief's condition,
This rash disgorgèd vomit of thy word
Thou wilt eat up again, and leave me helpless.
WARWICK By heaven, I will not, though your majesty
Did bid me run upon your sword and die.
KING EDWARD Say that my grief is no way medicinable
But by the loss and bruising of thine honour.
WARWICK If nothing but that loss may vantage you,
I would account that loss my vantage too.
KING EDWARD Thinkst that thou canst unswear thy oath again?
WARWICK I cannot, nor I would not if I could.
KING EDWARD But if thou dost, what shall I say to thee?
WARWICK What may be said to any perjured villain,
That breaks the sacred warrant of an oath.
KING EDWARD What wilt thou say to one that breaks an oath?
WARWICK That he hath broke his faith with God and man,
And from them both stands excommunicate.
KING EDWARD What office were it to suggest a man
To break a lawful and religious vow?
WARWICK An office for the devil, not for man.
KING EDWARD That devil's office must thou do for me,
Or break thy oath or cancel all the bonds
Of love and duty 'twixt thyself and me.
And therefore Warwick, if thou art thyself,
The lord and master of thy word and oath,
Go to thy daughter, and in my behalf

317 Thou] *Capell; Kin*: Thou QQ **323** SH] Q2; *not in* Q1 **326** account] Q2; accomplish Q1; accompt *TB* **327** unswear] *Capell;* answere QQ **330** to] QQ; of *Collier* **331** breaks] Q2; breake Q1 **339** or cancel] QQ; and cancell *WP* **342** thy] QQ; the *Collier*

316 duty what is due, debt (*OED* sv 2).

317 stick . . . swear keep to your word as far as to swear (*OED* Stick *v*[1] 26d).

319–20 This . . . again Alluding to the proverbial dog returning to his vomit (Tilley D455), from Prov. 26.11.

323–6 In Painter (Metz, p. 117) Warwick himself spontaneously swears, 'if it were for your sake, to transgresse and exceede the bondes of mine honour' (see Appendix, p. 194).

327 unswear retract (compare *John* 3.1.245, and *Oth.* 4.1.31). Capell's emendation is not accepted by Lapides, who reads QQ's 'answere' as 'be equal to, fulfil'. But 'unswear' is supported by the following speeches about breaking oaths.

329, 330, 332 to In all cases 'to' stands for 'of', as frequently at the time.

334 excommunicate excommunicated, banned from the community of religion and mankind.

335 suggest induce, prompt to evil-doing (*OED* sv *v* 2).

342 Compare *Sonn.* 94.7, 'the lords and owners of their faces', and Melchiori, *Meditations*, pp. 45–6.

Command her, woo her, win her any ways
To be my mistress and my secret love.
I will not stand to hear thee make reply:
Thy oath break hers, or let thy sovereign die. *Exit*

WARWICK O doting king, O detestable office!
Well may I tempt myself to wrong myself,
When he hath sworn me by the name of God
To break a vow made by the name of God.
What if I swear by this right hand of mine
To cut this right hand off? The better way
Were to profane the idol than confound it.
But neither will I do: I'll keep mine oath,
And to my daughter make a recantation
Of all the virtue I have preached to her.
I'll say she must forget her husband Salisbury,
If she remember to embrace the king;
I'll say an oath can easily be broken,
But not so easily pardoned, being broken;
I'll say it is true charity to love,
But not true love to be so charitable;
I'll say his greatness may bear out the shame,
But not his kingdom can buy out the sin;
I'll say it is my duty to persuade,
But not her honesty to give consent.

Enter COUNTESS

See where she comes; was never father had
Against his child an embassage so bad.

COUNTESS My lord and father, I have sought for you.

347 break] Q1; breakes Q2 348 SH] Q2 *(War.)*; *King*: Q1 348 O detestable] *Capell*; or detestable Qq 351 by] Qq; in *Collier* 354 idol than] Idoll then Q1; idole, then Q2 355 mine] Q1; my Q2

347 **Thy . . . hers** Warwick's oath requires that his daughter should break her marriage vow. An imperative: 'thy oath *must* break hers . . .'.

347 **or . . . die** Compare Painter (Metz, p. 118): '[it] resteth in you, either by death to ende my life, or by force to obtayne my desire'.

348 **O detestable** Qq's reading 'or' weakens the exclamation.

351 **a vow** his daughter's marriage vow.

353–4 **The . . . it** It is better to commit sacrilege ('profane the idol') by breaking an oath, than to overthrow ('confound', *OED* sv *v* 1) the 'idol' itself, meaning the authority under which the oath was made. Oaths are sworn by one's right hand, see 352–3.

358–67 A typical rhetorical construction: five symmetrical unrhymed couplets based on the contrast duty/honesty expressed in the last.

364 **bear out** endure, suffer without succumbing (*OED* Bear v^1 15b), contrasted with 'buy out' (compensate for) at 365.

My mother and the peers importune you
To keep in presence of his majesty,
And do your best to make his highness merry.
WARWICK [*Aside*] How shall I enter in this graceless errand?
I must not call her child, for where's the father
That will in such a suit seduce his child?
Then 'wife of Salisbury' – shall I so begin?
No, he's my friend – and where is found the friend
That will do friendship such endamagement? –
Neither my daughter, nor my dear friend's wife,
I am not Warwick as thou thinkst I am,
But an attorney from the court of hell,
That thus have housed my spirit in his form,
To do a message to thee from the king.
The mighty King of England dotes on thee:
He that hath power to take away thy life
Hath power to take thine honour; then consent
To pawn thine honour rather than thy life;
Honour is often lost and got again,
But life, once gone, hath no recovery.
The sun that withers hay doth nourish grass:
The king that would distain thee will advance thee.
The poets write that great Achilles' spear

372 presence] Q2; promise Q1 **374** SD] *WP; not in* Qq **387** thine] Q2; thy Q1 **391** hay doth] Q2 (haye, doth); heye goth Q1

372 keep . . . of attend upon. Q1's 'promise' for 'presence' is another misreading due to Elizabethan handwriting.

374 graceless errand Qq's 'arrant' was an alternative spelling of 'errand', common in Shakespeare and elsewhere; 'graceless' = wicked.

379 endamagement harm, see *John* 2.1.209.

383 have . . . form Warwick speaks in the person of the devil's advocate (382, 'attorney from the court of hell'), referring to himself in the third person ('his' = Warwick's).

385 In Painter (Metz, pp. 121–2): 'He . . . told me, that the torment which he indured, proceded no where els but of the feruent loue he bare vnto you.'

386–409 A sequence of pithy sayings or maxims – called *sententiae* in rhetoric – in support of an argument (*OED* Sentence *sb* 4). Their deceptive nature is pointed out by Warwick himself when he calls them 'virtuous sentences' (411), and later when he pronounces an even longer series of aphorisms (433–54) contradicting the previous ones (432, 'mark how I unsay my words again').

386–7 He . . . honour Compare *Sonn.* 94.1, 'They that have power to hurt', and the discussion in Melchiori, *Meditations*, pp. 42–8.

391 Compare the saying on the corruption of carrion in the summer (439–40), and Edward likening the Countess to the sun at 157–66.

392 would distain wants to corrupt (*OED* Distain *v* 2).

392 advance In Painter (Metz, p. 117) Edward tells Warwick: 'You haue also foure sonnes, whom you cannot honourably aduaunce with out my fauour.'

393–4 The . . . made Alluding to Telephus, cured by the rust scraped from Achilles' spear that had wounded him (Ovid, *Metamorphoses*, xii. 122). See *2H6* 5.1.99–101: 'these brows of mine, / Whose smile and frown, like to Achilles' spear, / Is able with the change to kill and cure'.

Could heal the wound it made: the moral is,
What mighty men misdo, they can amend.
The lion doth become his bloody jaws,
And grace his foragement by being mild
When vassal fear lies trembling at his feet.
The king will in his glory hide thy shame,
And those that gaze on him to find out thee
Will lose their eyesight looking in the sun.
What can one drop of poison harm the sea,
Whose hugy vastures can digest the ill
And make it lose his operation?
The king's great name will temper thy misdeeds
And give the bitter potion of reproach
A sugared, sweet, and most delicious taste.
Besides, it is no harm to do the thing
Which without shame could not be left undone.
Thus have I, in his majesty's behalf,
Apparelled sin in virtuous sentences,
And dwell upon thy answer in his suit.

COUNTESS Unnatural besiege! Woe me unhappy,
To have escaped the danger of my foes

403 vastures] Qq; vastness *Collier* **405** thy] *Capell;* their Qq **406** potion] Q2; portion Q1 **407** sugared, sweet] *TB, subst;* sugred sweete Qq; sugar'd-sweet *Capell*

396 become befit, see 281 above.

397–8 It was commonly believed that the lion spared a prey ready to submit to him. WP compare *LLL* 4.1.90–1: 'Submissive fall his [the lion's] princely feet before, / And he from forage will incline to play.'

397 grace reprieve, remit (a capital sentence); unrecorded in this meaning as verb in *OED*, but see Grace *sb* 15.

397 foragement prospective prey (the lion's forage). A nonce-word, glossed in *OED* as 'the act of foraging'.

398 vassal submissive, compare *LLL* quoted at 397–8n.

399 glory royal splendour. The sun was a figure of kingship (400–1).

402 What How, to what extent (*OED* sv B II 4 *adv*).

403 vastures vastness. Another nonce usage (*OED*).

404 his operation its effect.

405 A conceit parallel to that of 389, but Qq have 'their' for 'thy', acceptable only if taken to mean 'anybody's indiscretions'.

406 reproach blame, public disapproval.

408–9 it . . . undone To refuse (leave undone) a king's request is a 'shame', therefore doing the thing requested is no harm. Compare *Sonn.* 94.2, 'That do not do the thing, they most do show', and see 386–7n.

411 Apparelled Dressed up.

411 virtuous sentences wise sayings; ironical, see 386–409n.

412 dwell . . . suit wait for your answer to his request.

413 Unnatural Compare Painter (Metz, p. 122) 'I do perceiue that not onely al nature's lawes be cancelled and mortified in you, but which is worse, you doe exceede therin the crueltie of beastes, who for all their brutishenesse be not so vnnatural to do wrong to their owne yong.'

413 besiege siege, a verbal form used as noun.

And to be ten times worse envired by friends!
Hath he no means to stain my honest blood,
But to corrupt the author of my blood
To be his scandalous and vile solicitor?
No marvel though the branches be then infected,
When poison hath encompassèd the root;
No marvel though the leprous infant die,
When the stern dame envenometh the dug.
Why then, give sin a passport to offend
And youth the dangerous rein of liberty;
Blot out the strict forbidding of the law,
And cancel every canon that prescribes
A shame for shame, or penance for offence.
No, let me die, if his too boist'rous will
Will have it so, before I will consent
To be an actor in his graceless lust.

WARWICK Why, now thou speakst as I would have thee speak,
And mark how I unsay my words again:
An honourable grave is more esteemed
Than the polluted closet of a king;

415 envired] Qq (inuierd), *Capell;* inwir'd *Delius;* environ'd *Moltke;* iniured *WP, TB* **419** though] Q1, *Capell;* then though Q2, *Tyrrell* **419** branches] Qq; branch *Collier* **419** be then] Qq; be *Capell, Tyrrell, Delius* **427** shame . . . shame] Qq; shame for sin *conj. Smith*

415 envired environed, beset (*OED* Envire *v*). WP think this meaning too weak, and emend Qq's 'inuierd' to 'iniured' (injured).

417 author . . . blood In Painter (Metz, p. 122): 'I . . . which am deriued of your owne fleshe'.

418 scandalous bringing discredit to your position (*OED* sv *a* 1).

418 solicitor (1) instigator, pandar, see Painter (Metz, p. 123): 'your selfe is the shameless post of an act so dishonest', (2) advocate, compare 'attorney from the court of hell' at 382 and 383 n.

421 leprous leproused, meaning 'tainted' (by the poisoned dug, 422).

422 Infants were weaned by anointing the nipples of the nurse ('dame') with bitter substances. See *Rom.* 1.3.30–1: 'When it did taste the wormwood on the nipple / Of my dug, and felt it bitter'.

423 passport permission.

424 rein . . . liberty Depending on 'give' (423): leave (young people) free to act irresponsibly ('liberty' = licence).

426 canon rule of law.

427 shame for shame shameful punishment for a shameful action. No need to emend to 'shame for sin' (Smith).

428–30 In Painter (Metz, p. 123): 'if so be he doe continue obstinate in his olde folly, I am determined rather to die, than to doe the thing that shall hurt me and pleasure him . . . I had rather lose my life after the moste cruell and shameful maner that may be deuised, then to consent to a thing so dishonest.'

428 boist'rous violent, savage (*OED* sv *a* 9).

430 graceless wicked, see 374.

432 unsay retract, abjure. Compare 'unswear' at 327.

433–54 Warwick's speech is constructed as two sequences of proverbial sayings. The first sequence (433–47) is meant to counterbalance the 'virtuous sentences' in his previous speech (391–409) by contradicting (see 'unsay', 432) them; the second sequence (450–4) is a sample of the 'spacious field of reasons' (448) on the contrast between power and honour.

434 closet private bedroom.

The greater man, the greater is the thing,
Be it good or bad, that he shall undertake;
An unreputed mote, flying in the sun,
Presents a greater substance than it is;
The freshest summer's day doth soonest taint
The loathèd carrion that it seems to kiss;
Deep are the blows made with a mighty axe;
That sin doth ten times aggravate itself,
That is committed in a holy place;
An evil deed, done by authority,
Is sin and subornation; deck an ape
In tissue, and the beauty of the robe
Adds but the greater scorn unto the beast.
A spacious field of reasons could I urge
Between his glory, daughter, and thy shame:
That poison shows worst in a golden cup;
Dark night seems darker by the lightning flash;
Lilies that fester smell far worse than weeds;
And every glory that inclines to sin,
The shame is treble by the opposite.

439 freshest] QQ; fiercest *Delius, conj. Capell* 449 glory, daughter] *Capell;* gloomie (gloomy Q2) daughter QQ

435–6 Proverbial, 'the greater the man the greater the crime' (Tilley M153). *ODEP* gives this as the earliest example. Compare *Sonn.* 94.1–8 discussed in Melchiori, *Meditations*, pp. 42–56.

437 unreputed unnoted, insubstantial (*OED* gives this as the only example). Motes can be 'noted' only in sunlight.

439–40 Recalling the sun comparison at 164–6, and see *Ham.* 2.2.181–2: 'if the sun breed maggots in a dead dog, being a good kissing carrion'.

439 freshest brightest (*OED* Fresh *a* 9); Capell's conjecture, 'fiercest', is unnecessary.

442 doth . . . itself is ten times more heinous (*OED* Aggravate *v* 6b).

444 by authority taking advantage of a position of power. Compare *Sonn.* 66.9, 'art made tongue-tied by authority', and the treatment of the abuses of authority in *MM*.

445 subornation Inducement to commit an evil action (*OED* sv *sb* 1), frequent in Shakespeare, where, for instance, in a similar situation, Lucrece accuses Opportunity of 'perjury and subornation' (*Luc.* 919).

445–7 deck . . . beast Proverbial, Erasmus, *Adagia* 264, commonly rendered as 'An ape is an ape though clad in scarlet (gold, purple)' (Tilley A263).

446 tissue cloth interwoven with gold or silver (*OED* sv *sb* 1a).

448 A . . . reasons Many arguments, or 'sentences', see 433–54n.

449 to show the connection between splendid appearance (the king's) and shameful reality (the Countess's condition).

449 glory royal splendour. Capell's emendation of QQ's 'gloomie' is surely right, in view of 'glory' at 399.

450 Proverbial, 'Poison is hidden in golden cups' (Tilley P458).

451 A recurrent image in *Rom.*, for instance, 2.2.118–20.

452 This line (proverbial, 'The lily is fair in show but foul in smell' Tilley L297) is identical with the last line of Sonnet 94.

453 glory A metonymy: the attributes of power (see 'glory' at 399 and 449) are used to indicate the person endowed with that power.

454 by . . . opposite by contrast (between the 'glory' of majesty and the sin committed in its name), compare 'happy opposite' at 182.

So leave I, with my blessing in thy bosom,
Which then convert to a most heavy curse
When thou convert'st from honour's golden name
To the black faction of bed-blotting shame.
COUNTESS I'll follow thee, and when my mind turns so,
My body sink my soul in endless woe.
Exeunt

2.2. *Enter at one door* DERBY *from France, at another door* AUDLEY *with a drum*

DERBY Thrice noble Audley, well encountered here.
How is it with our sovereign and his peers?
AUDLEY 'Tis full a fortnight since I saw his highness,
What time he sent me forth to muster men,
Which I accordingly have done, and bring them hither
In fair array before his majesty.
What news, my lord of Derby, from the emperor?
DERBY As good as we desire: the emperor
Hath yielded to his highness friendly aid,
And makes our king lieutenant-general
In all his lands and large dominions.

458 bed-blotting] *Capell after* Q2 (bed blotting)*;* bed blotting, Q1 **458** shame.] Qq*;* shame! *Exit.* / *Capell* **459** I'll] Q2 (Ile)*;* Ils Q1 **460** SD *Exeunt*] Qq; Exit./ Capell Act 2, Scene 2 **2.2**] *Capell; no scene division in* Qq **0** SD] Qq*; The same. A room in the Castle. Enter* DERBY, *and* AUDLEY, *meeting.* / *Capell* **5** hither] Qq*; not in Capell, Tyrrell* **7** What] Q2*; King*: What Q1

456 convert 'I shall' is understood before 'convert'.

458 black . . . shame Adulterers (defiling the marriage bed) are seen as a hellish (black is the colour of hell) sect ('faction').

Act 2, Scene 2

2.2 The location is the same as 2.1 and the time 'after dinner' (15–21) the same day. As indicated at 3, a fortnight has elapsed since 1.1.

0 SD ***with a drum*** ushered in by a drummer – indicating that Audley is leading a body of soldiers. In the case of Derby, 'from France' suggests that he must be dressed for travel; actually his mission had been to Hainault, on the French border of Flanders.

4 What time When (on the occasion when).

4 he . . . men See 1.1.139–40.

5 hither Omitted by Capell as hypermetrical, but lines with two extra syllables are frequent in Shakespeare (Abbott 458).

6 In . . . array Well fitted for combat (*OED* Array *sb* 8).

7 Q1 assigns this line to '*King*' (not on stage yet), a mistake due to the habit of adding headings only after transcribing the text of all speeches on the page (see Textual Analysis, pp. 173–4).

7–9 At 1.1.147–52 Derby was sent as ambassador to the Earl of Hainault to ask him 'to solicit . . . The Emperor of Almagne in our name'.

10–11 makes . . . dominions Frois. devotes the whole of ch. 34 (Ker, I, 103–5) to the fact that in 1338 'Kyng Edwarde of Englande was made vycare generall of thempyre of Almaygne' (see Appendix, p. 196).

Then *via* for the spacious bounds of France!
AUDLEY What, doth his highness leap to hear these news?
DERBY I have not yet found time to open them.
The king is in his closet, malcontent
For what I know not, but he gave in charge
Till after dinner none should interrupt him.
The Countess Salisbury and her father Warwick,
Artois, and all, look underneath the brows.
AUDLEY Undoubtedly then something is amiss.
[*Trumpet within*]
DERBY The trumpets sound, the king is now abroad.

Enter the KING

AUDLEY Here comes his highness.
DERBY Befall my sovereign all my sovereign's wish.
KING EDWARD Ah, that thou wert a witch to make it so!
DERBY The emperor greeteth you –
KING EDWARD Would it were the countess.
DERBY And hath accorded to your highness' suit –
KING EDWARD Thou liest, she hath not, but I would she had.
AUDLEY All love and duty to my lord the king.
KING EDWARD Well, all but one is none. – What news with you?
AUDLEY I have, my liege, levied those horse and foot
According as your charge, and brought them hither.
KING EDWARD Then let those foot trudge hence upon those horse,
According to our discharge, and be gone.

13 these] Q1; this Q2 **20 SD**] *Capell; not in* Qq **21 SD**] *As in Capell; after 20* Qq **22 SH**] Q2 *(Awd.); Ar.* Q1 **25** you –] Qq (you.); you: [*presenting Letters./ Capell* **25** Would . . . countess.] *As half-line this edn; New line* Qq; *(Aside.)* Would . . . Countesse! *WP* **26** suit –] *RLA, after* Q1 (suite,); sute. Q2 **27** Thou] Qq; *(Aside)* Thou *WP* **31** as] Q1; to Q2

12 *via* away, come on! (Italian), pronounced as a disyllable.

13 leap . . . hear (1) rejoice in hearing, compare 'summer-leaping' at 2.1.108; (2) show eagerness to be informed of (*OED* Leap *v* 2e).

14 open them communicate the news. 'News' is treated as plural; compare 'these' at 13.

15 closet private room, see 2.1.434.

16 gave in charge ordered.

19 underneath . . . brows downcast.

21 abroad about, out of his room. In Qq the king enters after 20.

22 SH The wrong heading *Ar.* (Artois) in Q1 is discussed in the Textual Analysis, p. 172 and n. 3.

24–9 The king's speeches at 24, 25, 27, and 29 ('Well . . . none') are not real asides but muttered sentences to convey to the characters on stage as well as to the audience that he, in Painter's words (Metz, p. 124), 'was like to haue runne out of his wittes'; see Appendix, p. 196.

24 witch Playing on 'wish' at 23.

26 accorded to granted.

29 all . . . none Proverbial, 'one and none is all one' (Tilley O52). If all except the Countess love him, their loves are no good to him.

30 horse and foot cavalry and infantry.

32 trudge hence go away, depart (*OED* sv *v* 1c).

33 discharge dismissal, playing on 'charge' at 31.

Derby, I'll look upon the countess' mind anon.
DERBY The countess' mind, my liege?
KING EDWARD I mean the emperor. – Leave me alone.
AUDLEY What's in his mind?
DERBY Let's leave him to his humour.
Exeunt [*Derby and Audley*]
KING EDWARD Thus from the heart's abundance speaks the tongue:
'Countess' for 'emperor' – and indeed, why not?
She is as imperator over me, and I to her
Am as a kneeling vassal, that observes
The pleasure or displeasure of her eye.

Enter LODOWICK

What says the more than Cleopatra's match
To Caesar now?
LODOWICK That yet, my liege, ere night
She will resolve your majesty.
[*Drum within*]
KING EDWARD What drum is this that thunders forth this march
To start the tender Cupid in my bosom?
Poor sheepskin, how it brawls with him that beateth it!
Go, break the thund'ring parchment-bottom out,
And I will teach it to conduct sweet lines
Unto the bosom of a heavenly nymph;
For I will use it as my writing paper,
And so reduce him from a scolding drum

34] *As one line* Qq*; as two lines divided at* mind *Capell; divided at* Derby, *WP* 36 emperor] Qq*;* Emperor's *Collier* 37 What's in] *Capell, after* Q2 (What is in)*;* What is Q1 37 SD] *Capell, subst; Exunt* Q1*; Exeunt* Q2 38 abundance] *Delius, Collier, WP subst;* aboundant Qq 40] Qq*; as two lines divided at* me, *Capell* 42 eye.] Q2*;* cye Q1 43 What] *Capell etc.; Ki:* What Q1*; Kin.* What Q2 44–5 That . . . majesty] *So divided* Qq*; lines divided at* liege, *Collier* 45 SD] *Capell; not in* Qq 48 sheepskin] Q2*;* shipskin Q1 49 parchment-bottom] *This edn; no hyphen* Qq

34 **Derby** A hypermetrical vocative, a frequent feature of verse plays, see Abbott 512.

38 A biblical quotation, 'Of the abundance of the heart the mouth speaks' (Matt. 12.34), which had become proverbial (Tilley A13). Qq's 'aboundant' is an obvious misreading of the copy.

40–2 The same conceit expressed by the king at 2.1.101–4. The lack of punctuation after 'eye' in Q1 may indicate that the king is interrupted by the entrance of Lodowick (Lapides).

43–4 **What . . . now** Caesar designates a king: Edward, referring to Roman history, suggests that he has better reason than Caesar for being in love since the Countess's beauty is superior ('more than match') to Cleopatra's. Compare 2.1.252–3.

44 **ere** before.

45 **resolve** give an answer to, see 166–7.

46–7 The drumbeats offstage emphasise ('start' = startle) the king's heartbeats, quickened for love of the Countess ('the tender Cupid in my bosom').

48 **sheepskin** Parchment, used both in drums ('parchment-bottom', 49) and as 'writing paper' (52), is made out of sheepskin.

48 **it . . . it** The noise of the drum is like that of a quarrel (brawl) between the drum itself and the drummer beating it ('beateth' is a monosyllable).

50 **conduct** (1) compose, (2) convey.

53 **him** The drum personified.

To be the herald and dear counsel-bearer
Betwixt a goddess and a mighty king.
Go, bid the drummer learn to touch the lute,
Or hang him in the braces of his drum,
For now we think it an uncivil thing
To trouble heaven with such harsh resounds.
Away.

Exit Lodowick

The quarrel that I have requires no arms
But these of mine, and these shall meet my foe
In a deep march of penetrable groans;
My eyes shall be my arrows, and my sighs
Shall serve me as the vantage of the wind,
To whirl away my sweetest artillery.
Ah, but alas, she wins the sun of me,
For that is she herself, and thence it comes
That poets term the wanton warrior blind.
But love hath eyes as judgement to his steps,
Till too much lovèd glory dazzles them. –
How now?

59–60] *So divided Capell; as one line* Qq **60** SD] Q2 *(Exit Lodo.); Exit.* Q1 **65** vantage] Qq*;* ventage *Delius* **66** sweetest] Qq*;* swift'st *Swinburne apud TB* **71** too] Q2*;* two Q1

54 counsel-bearer bearer of private messages (*OED* Counsel *sb* 5, compare 'counsel-keeper', *2H4* 2.4.267).

57 hang . . . drum 'Brace' is the thong sliding on the drum cord to regulate the tension of the skin, but here the cord itself, playing with the proverb 'he may go hang himself in his own garters' (Tilley G42). Compare *TN* 1.3.12: 'let them hang themselves in their own straps'.

59 resounds echoing sounds (*OED* Resound *sb*).

61–9 The king's monologue develops the common conceit of love as a battle, beginning with the obvious pun on 'arms' (61) as (1) weapons, (2) human limbs.

63 a . . . groans The sexual encounter is presented in terms of single hand-to-hand combat: 'penetrable' = piercing, referring to the aural quality of the 'groans', with obvious sexual implications, present also in 'deep', applied to the tone of the sequence ('march') of sounds coming from those engaged in the combat.

65 vantage favour.

66 sweetest artillery In the convention of love poetry, the lover's passionate looks are the 'artillery' (see 'arrows' at 64) used to overcome his mistress's resistance. Hence 'sweetest' (pronounced as monosyllable); Swinburne's suggested emendation, 'swift'st', is inappropriate.

67 wins . . . me has the sun in her favour. Proverbial 'to get the sun of one' (Tilley S987); compare, for a very similar metaphorical context, *LLL* 4.3.363–6: 'Saint Cupid, then! . . . but be first advised, / In conflict that you get the sun of them', with a further quibble on 'sun/son'.

68 that . . . herself The Countess had already been identified with the sun at 2.1.119–21, 148–9, 157–66.

69 wanton warrior Cupid was always represented as armed with bow and arrows, and frequently blindfolded.

70 hath . . . steps is guided by sight.

71 too . . . glory the excessive splendour (see 'glory' at 2.1.399, 449) of the loved object.

72 How now An exclamation caused not by Lodowick's entrance (unnecessarily moved by most modern eds. to 71) but by hearing again the drum (73) which the king had ordered silent at 56–9.

Enter LODOWICK

LODOWICK My liege, the drum that stroke the lusty march
Stands with Prince Edward, your thrice valiant son. [*Exit*]

Enter PRINCE *Edward*

KING EDWARD [*Aside*] I see the boy. Oh, how his mother's face,
Modelled in his, corrects my strayed desire,
And rates my heart, and chides my thievish eye,
Who, being rich enough in seeing her,
Yet seeks elsewhere; and basest theft is that
Which cannot cloak itself on poverty. –
Now, boy, what news?

PRINCE I have assembled, my dear lord and father,
The choicest buds of all our English blood
For our affairs to France, and here we come
To take direction from your majesty.

KING EDWARD [*Aside*] Still do I see in him delineate
His mother's visage: those his eyes are hers,
Who looking wistly on me make me blush,
For faults against themselves give evidence.
Lust is a fire, and men, like lanthorns, show
Light lust within themselves, even through themselves.
Away, loose silks of wavering vanity!

72 SD] *As in* QQ; *after 71 / Capell, Delius, WP* **74** SD.1 *Exit*] *WAA; not in* QQ; LODOWICK *retires to the Door. / Capell (after / Enter* Prince.*)* **74** SD.2 *Enter . . . Edward*] QQ; *after 80 / Melchiori* **75** SD] *This edn; not in* QQ **76** Modelled] Q1 (modeld), *RLA;* Molded Q2, *Capell* **80** cloak] QQ (cloke); check *Capell* **84** to] Q1; in Q2 **86** SD] *This edn; not in* QQ **88** make] Q1; made Q2 **90**] *Capell, and mod. edns;* Lust as a fire, and me like lanthorne show, QQ (shew Q2) **92** of] Q2; or Q1

73 stroke . . . march has been playing a lively march.

74 Stands with Accompanies.

75–80 The king's lengthy aside in the presence of the Prince is awkward. Perhaps the latter's entrance should be moved to 80, and this be taken as a short soliloquy in which the king visualises the features of his son; or, in view of the absence of Lodowick's 'exit' at 74 in QQ, as a confidence of the king to his secretary. But see the even longer aside at 86–99.

76 Modelled Both readings, Q1's 'modeled' or Q2's 'molded', have the same meaning, 'reproduced as by a sculptor in clay'.

77 rates berates, reproaches.

80 cannot . . . poverty has not even the pretext (*OED* Cloak *v* 2b) of poverty (to justify the theft).

82–5 See the orders given to the Prince at 1.1.141–6.

86 delineate Treated as a participle, 'delineated', 'pictured'.

88 wistly intently (*OED* sv *adv*).

90 A badly garbled line in QQ. Capell's emendations are universally accepted, but Lapides objects to the change from 'as' to 'is'.

91 Light (1) wanton, (2) alight (like fire). Compare a similar quibble on the lanthorn image in *2H4* 1.2.46–8 (Q1, TLN 293–6): 'for he hath the horne of aboundance, and the lightnesse of his wife shines through it . . . & yet can not he see though he haue his owne lanthorne to light him'.

92 wavering inconstant.

Shall the large limit of fair Bretagne
By me be overthrown, and shall I not
Master this little mansion of myself?
Give me an armour of eternal steel,
I go to conquer kings; and shall I not then
Subdue myself, and be my enemies' friend?
It must not be. – Come, boy, forward, advance!
Let's with our colours sweet the air of France.

Enter LODOWICK

LODOWICK My liege, the countess with a smiling cheer
Desires access unto your majesty.
KING EDWARD [*Aside*] Why, there it goes: that very smile of hers
Hath ransomed captive France, and set the king,
The Dauphin, and the peers at liberty. –
Go, leave me, Ned, and revel with thy friends.
Exit Prince
– Thy mother is but black, and thou, like her,
Dost put it in my mind how foul she is. –
Go, fetch the countess hither in thy hand,
Exit Lodowick
And let her chase away these winter clouds,
For she gives beauty both to heaven and earth.
The sin is more to hack and hew poor men,
Than to embrace in an unlawful bed

93 limit] Qq; limits *Collier* 93 Bretagne] Brittayne Q1; Britany Q2 97 I not] Qq; I *Capell* 98 enemies'] Qq (enimies); enemy's *Capell and mod. edns* 100 sweet] Qq (sweete), *WP*; sweep *Capell, Tyrrell;* beat *Delius;* sweat *Collier* 100 SD] Qq; *advancing from the Door and whispering him / Capell (after 102)* 103 SD] *This edn; not in* Qq 108 it in] Qq; into *Capell* 109 SD] *As in* Qq, *RLA; after 111 / Capell and all other mod. edns* 110 these] Q1; those Q2

93–8 Echoing part of the first speech of the king to Warwick in Painter (Metz, p. 116), see Appendix, p. 197.

95 mansion For the body as the mansion of the soul, see 2.1.238–43n.

97–8 shall . . . friend Two separate questions depending on the same auxiliary: shall I not be able to control my passion? and shall I by this disability become the ally of my enemies?

100 sweet sweeten (*OED* sv v^1 2b). Compare *Rom.* 2.6.36–7: 'sweeten with thy breath / This neighbour air'. None of the suggested emendations is pertinent.

101 cheer countenance. See Appendix, p. 197, for Painter's account of the meeting.

107 black A colour associated with physical and moral ugliness, compare 'sun-burnt', 2.1.109n.

109 in thy hand under your escort.

112 it is a greater sin to wage war.

The register of all rarieties
Since leathern Adam till this youngest hour.

Enter [LODOWICK *with the*] COUNTESS

Go, Lod'wick, put thy hand into thy purse,
Play, spend, give, riot, waste, do what thou wilt,
So thou wilt hence a while, and leave me here.
[*Exit Lodowick*]
Now, my soul's playfellow, art thou come
To speak the more than heavenly word of yea
To my objection in thy beauteous love?

COUNTESS My father on his blessing hath commanded –

KING EDWARD That thou shalt yield to me.

COUNTESS Ay, dear my liege, your due.

KING EDWARD And that, my dearest love, can be no less
Than right for right, and render love for love.

COUNTESS Than wrong for wrong, and endless hate for hate.
But sith I see your majesty so bent,
That my unwillingness, my husband's love,
Your high estate, nor no respect respected,
Can be my help, but that your mightiness
Will overbear and awe these dear regards,
I bind my discontent to my content,
And what I would not I'll compel I will,

114 rarieties] Qq; varieties *Delius, Collier;* fair rarities *Moltke* **115** till] Qq; to *Collier* **115** SD] *Capell, subst; Enter Countesse.* Qq **116** Go] *Capell; King.* Goe Qq **116** Lod'wick] Q1 (Lodwike); Lodowicke Q2 **116** thy purse] Qq; my purse *Capell, Delius, WP, TB* **118** SD] *Capell and all mod. edns; not in* Qq **119** art] Qq; and art *Capell, Tyrrell* **121** objection] Qq; subjection *Delius;* abjection *Collier* **122** commanded –] *Capell and mod. edns;* commanded. Qq **126** render] Qq; tender *Capell* **133** bind] Qq (bynd Q1, binde Q2); bend *Collier* **133** my content] Qq; thy content *Collier*

114 register record; compare 'abstract' at 2.1.82.

114 rarieties exceptional gifts (*OED* Rariety *sb*).

115 leathern clothed in skins; Gen. 3.21: 'Unto Adam also and to his wife did the Lord God make coats of skin and clothed them.'

116 put . . . purse Capell's emendation (followed by others) of 'thy' into 'my' is unnecessary, especially in view of the parallel with Iago's repeated advice to Roderigo, 'put money in thy purse' (*Oth.* 1.3.340–52).

119 soul's playfellow Compare Painter (Metz, p. 126): 'Welcome, my life and soul'.

121 objection claim (with a view to securing an object). *OED* sv *sb* 4 gives this example for the meaning 'representation'.

124 your due what is due to you. Compare 2.1.219, 227–8.

126 render exchange, see 2.1.310.

127 wrong for wrong Compare 'shame for shame', 2.1.427.

128 sith since.

130 nor . . . respected no regard for any other consideration ('neither' is understood before the three previous clauses at 129–30).

132 awe control through reverential fear (*OED* sv *v* 2).

132 regards considerations, see 'respect' at 130.

133 I render my discontent subject to my submission (WP).

134 what . . . will I'll force myself to do ('will') what I do not wish.

Provided that yourself remove those lets
That stand between your highness' love and mine.
KING EDWARD Name them, fair countess, and by heaven I will.
COUNTESS It is their lives that stand between our love
That I would have choked up, my sovereign.
KING EDWARD Whose lives, my lady?
COUNTESS My thrice loving liege,
Your queen, and Salisbury my wedded husband,
Who, living, have that title in our love
That we cannot bestow but by their death.
KING EDWARD Thy opposition is beyond our law.
COUNTESS So is your desire. If the law
Can hinder you to execute the one,
Let it forbid you to attempt the other.
I cannot think you love me as you say,
Unless you do make good what you have sworn.
KING EDWARD No more: thy husband and the queen shall die.
Fairer thou art by far than Hero was,
Beardless Leander not so strong as I:
He swum an easy current for his love,
But I will through a Hellespont of blood
To arrive at Sestos, where my Hero lies.
COUNTESS Nay, you'll do more: you'll make the river too
With their heart bloods that keep our love asunder,

137 them] *Capell;* then Qq 138 love] *This edn;* loue. Qq 145 So] Qq*;* And so *Capell* 148 I cannot] Q2*;* I Cannot Q1 *(see Commentary)* 150 SH] Q2 *(Kin.); not in* Q1 150 more: thy] Q2*;* mor, ethy Q1 150 the queen] Qq*;* my queen *Collier* 154 through] Q2*;* throng Q1 154 Hellespont] *conj. Tyrrell, Collier;* hellie spout Q1*;* helly spoute Q2 155 To . . . Sestos] Qq (To . . . Cestus)*;* Arrive that *Sestos / Capell* 157 heart bloods] Qq*;* heart's blood *Collier*

135 lets hindrances.

138 their . . . that the lives of those who. A common construction (Abbott 218).

140 thrice loving thrice beloved, see the appellations of the King at 2.1.190, 202, and 218. The use of the present for the past participle was common (Abbott 372), but here possibly intentional, ironising on the King's show of passion.

142 title in right to.

143 bestow give away.

144 opposition counter-proposition (*OED* sv *sb* 4b).

148 cannot Printed with a capital C in Q1, its significance is discussed in the Textual Analysis, pp. 174–5.

151–5 Alluding to the familiar story of Leander, the youth of Abydos who died while swimming across the Hellespont in an attempt to reach his beautiful lover Hero, a priestess in the temple of Aphrodite at Sestos. Marlowe's poem 'Hero and Leander', left unfinished at his death in 1593, but already well known in manuscript at that date, was completed by George Chapman and published in 1598.

154 I will I will swim (understood from 153). The confusions in the rest of the line both in Q1 and Q2 are discussed in the Textual Analysis, p. 176.

156–7 you'll . . . that you will make a stream with the blood from the hearts of those who (for a similar construction see 138). The Hellespont is not a river but the Dardanelles straits joining the Sea of Marmara to the Aegean.

Of which my husband and your wife are twain.
KING EDWARD Thy beauty makes them guilty of their death
And gives in evidence that they shall die,
Upon which verdict I, their judge, condemn them.
COUNTESS O perjured beauty, more corrupted judge!
When to the great Star-chamber o'er our heads
The universal sessions calls to 'count
This packing evil, we both shall tremble for it.
KING EDWARD What says my fair love? Is she resolved?
COUNTESS Resolved to be dissolved, and therefore this:
Keep but thy word, great king, and I am thine.
Stand where thou dost – I'll part a little from thee –
And see how I will yield me to thy hands.
Here by my side doth hang my wedding knives:
Take thou the one, and with it kill thy queen,
And learn by me to find her where she lies;
And with this other I'll dispatch my love,
Which now lies fast asleep within my heart.
When they are gone, then I'll consent to love. –
Stir not, lascivious king, to hinder me:
My resolution is more nimbler far
Than thy prevention can be in my rescue;

162 O] Qq; *(aside)* O *WP* **164** sessions] Qq; session *conj. Capell* **165** evil] Qq; ill *conj. Capell* **166** resolved] *This edn, after WP (*resolude*)*; resolute Qq **167** Resolved] *Delius, conj. Capell (*Resolv'd*)*; Resolute Qq **167** dissolved] dissolu'de Q2; dissolude Q1 **170** hands.] Qq (hands:); hands. [*turning suddenly upon him, and shewing two Daggers* / *Capell, WP, TB*; hands. *Shows daggers* / *RLA* **171** doth] Qq; do *Capell* **174** this] Q1; the Q2, *Capell*

158 Of . . . twain two Of which are my husband and your wife.

160 gives . . . die provides evidence for their death sentences.

163 Star-chamber . . . heads A frequent metaphor for God's justice. The Star-chamber was the supreme court of justice under the direct control of the sovereign. It was established in the fifteenth century, so its mention at the time of Edward III is anachronistic.

164 the Final Judgement calls to reckoning ('count = account).

165 packing secret, underhand (*OED* Pack v^2 1).

166–7 resolved . . . dissolved See 45, 'She will resolve your majesty'. Qq's 'resolute' at both 166 and 167 is a variant spelling of 'resolude', i.e. 'resolved'; that the latter was meant is supported also by the metre and by the quibble with 'dissolved' (spelt 'dissolude' in Q1) in the sense of 'destroyed, annulled'.

169 Compare Edward's words to the Countess at 2.1.212.

171–5 The double suicide pact is the dramatist's variation on Painter's novel, where, since Edward is unmarried and the Countess a widow, the alternative given the king is between killing her with his own hand or letting her stab herself. See 180–7n. and Appendix, p. 198.

171 wedding knives A pair of knives in one sheath worn at the girdle by brides at weddings (Lapides).

173 where . . . lies i.e. in his bosom, see 175.

178 more nimbler faster, an emphatic comparative, see 2.1.25n.

179 prevention intervention.

And if thou stir, I strike – therefore stand still
And hear the choice that I will put thee to:
Either swear to leave thy most unholy suit
And never henceforth to solicit me,
Or else, by heaven, this sharp-pointed knife
Shall stain thy earth with that which thou wouldst stain,
My poor chaste blood. Swear, Edward, swear,
Or I will strike, and die before thee here.

KING EDWARD Even by that power I swear, that gives me now
The power to be ashamèd of myself,
I never mean to part my lips again
In any words that tends to such a suit.
Arise, true English lady, whom our isle
May better boast of than ever Roman might
Of her, whose ransacked treasury hath tasked
The vain endeavour of so many pens.
Arise, and be my fault thy honour's fame,
Which after ages shall enrich thee with.
I am awakèd from this idle dream. –
Warwick, my son, Derby, Artois, and Audley,
Brave warriors all, where are you all this while?

Enter all

Warwick, I make thee Warden of the North;
Thou, Prince of Wales, and Audley, straight to sea,

184 sharp-pointed] *Capell;* sharpe poynted Qq **185** wouldst] Q2*;* would Q1 **186** blood.] Qq*;* blood. *(kneeling) / WP (after* heaven, *at 184 / Capell)* **191** words] Qq*;* word *Capell* **193** ever] Qq*;* e'er *Capell* **194** tasked] Q1 (taskt)*;* taske Q2 **200** SD] Qq*; Enter Prince, and Lords / Capell* **202** Thou] Qq*;* You *Capell*

180–7 In Painter, in spite of the different situation pointed out at 171–5n., the wording of the corresponding passage is very similar to the play's, see Appendix, p. 198.

185 thy earth the earth of thy kingdom.

188 that power God's power.

191 tends A singular form for the plural, see 1.2.134n.

192–5 Roman Lucrece, who killed herself after being raped by Tarquin, was celebrated as a paragon of married chastity in histories, plays, and poems (compare 194–5); the best known of them, Shakespeare's *Rape of Lucrece*, was published in 1594. In Painter the reformed king, after exclaiming, 'Rise vp Lady, and liue from henceforth assured', praises the Countess's 'inexpugnable chastitie' (Metz, p. 128, see Appendix, p. 198).

194 ransacked treasury violated chastity.

197 after ages future times. Compare *Sonn.* 101.11–12: 'To make him much outlive a gilded tomb, / And to be praised of ages yet to be'.

199–200 In Painter (Metz, p. 128) the king at this point 'opened the doore . . . and same time hee called also the Courtiers and Piers of the Realme'. See Appendix, pp. 198–9.

201 Warden . . . North in charge of the defence of the Scottish border (unhistorical).

Scour to Newhaven: some there stay for me.
Myself, Artois, and Derby will through Flanders
To greet our friends there and to crave their aid.
This night will scarce suffice me to discover
My folly's siege against a faithful lover,
For ere the sun shall gild the eastern sky
We'll wake him with our martial harmony.

Exeunt

3.1. *Enter* KING JOHN *of France, his two sons,* CHARLES [*Duke*] *of Normandy and* PHILIP, *and the Duke of* LORRAINE

KING JOHN Here, till our navy of a thousand sail
Have made a breakfast to our foe by sea,
Let us encamp, to wait their happy speed.
Lorraine, what readiness is Edward in?
How hast thou heard that he provided is
Of martial furniture for this exploit?
LORRAINE To lay aside unnecessary soothing,

208 gild] *Capell;* guide Qq Act 3, Scene 1 **3.1**] *Capell; no act or scene division in* Qq **0 SD.1** *Enter*] Qq*;* Flanders. *The* French *Camp. Enter / Capell* **0 SD.1** *Duke*] *Capell; not in* Qq **0 SD.2** *and the . . .* LORRAINE] Qq*; Duke of* LORRAIN, *and Others / Capell* **2** by] Qq*;* at *Collier*

203 Scour to Newhaven sail quickly to Newhaven (a port in Sussex for journeys to Flanders). Audley is not mentioned by the historians in this connection, and the Prince of Wales was a young boy at the time.

203 some . . . me Either (1) there are forces there waiting for me, or (2) some of you wait for me there (imperative).

204–5 Frois. (ch. 50, Metz, p. 61) lists Derby and Artois among the many lords and knights taking part in the naval battle of Sluys in 1340 together with King Edward, described as 'a noble knight of his owne hande, he was in the flouer of his yongth'. 'Go' is understood after 'will' at 204.

206 discover relate. In Painter (Metz, p. 128) the king 'recited particulerly the discourse of his loue' to the Archbishop of York (see Appendix, p. 199).

208 gild Qq's 'guide' is surely a misreading of 'guilde'. Compare *TGV* 5.1.1: 'The sun begins to gild the western sky.'

Act 3, Scene 1

3.1 Located somewhere near the coast in Flanders, the scene is based on Holinshed's and Froissart's accounts of the naval battle of Sluys (L'Ecluse), 'fought (as some write) on midsummer daie, in the yeare aforesaid', i.e. 1340 (Hol. II, 615), well before the Scottish episode presented in the earlier acts. See Appendix, p. 201.

0 SD Philip, not John, of Valois was King of France at the time. See 1.1.21 n. and Appendix, p. 199.

1 thousand sail According to Frois. (Metz, p. 60) 'mo than sixscore great vessels, besyde other'; for Hol. (II, 614) the French at Sluys had 'foure hundred ships', and the English 'had in all about three hundred saile, or (as other saie) three hundred and three score'.

2 made . . . to devoured, destroyed.

3 their . . . speed for news of their success.

6 martial furniture military equipment.

7 soothing reassurance.

And not to spend the time in circumstance,
'Tis bruited for a certainty, my lord,
That he's exceeding strongly fortified:
His subjects flock as willingly to war
As if unto a triumph they were led.

CHARLES England was wont to harbour malcontents,
Bloodthirsty and seditious Catilines,
Spendthrifts, and such that gape for nothing else
But changing and alteration of the state;
And is it possible that they are now
So loyal in themselves?

LORRAINE All but the Scot, who solemnly protests,
As heretofore I have informed his grace,
Never to sheathe his sword or take a truce.

KING JOHN Ah, that's the anch'rage of some better hope.
But on the other side, to think what friends
King Edward hath retained in Netherland,
Among those ever-bibbing epicures –
Those frothy Dutchmen puffed with double beer,
That drink and swill in every place they come –
Doth not a little aggravate mine ire.
Besides, we hear the emperor conjoins
And stalls him in his own authority.
But all the mightier that the number is,
The greater glory reaps the victory.

16 changing] Qq; change *Capell* **17–18**] *As two lines so divided / Capell; lines divided at* possible, Q1; *as one line* Q2 **20** his] Qq; your *Collier*

8 circumstance 1) circumlocutions, 2) ceremony (*OED* sv 6 and 7).

14 Catilines Catiline, a noble dissatisfied with his role in the state, conspired against the Roman Republic in 62 BC. He was considered the type of the political malcontent (see 13).

15 gape are eager (*OED* sv *vb* 4).

16 changing Capell's emendation ('change') for metrical reasons is unnecessary: 'alteration' was treated as a trisyllable.

19–21 Compare 1.2.18–34.

20 his There is no need to emend to 'your': in replying to Prince Charles, Lorraine speaks of King John in the third person.

25–7 those . . . come Dutchmen, Flemings, and Germans had a reputation for drunkenness and gluttony ('epicures' = those who indulge in sensual pleasures; compare *Mac.* 5.3.8: 'the English epicures'). Hence the use of 'bibbing' (tippling), 'frothy' (with reference to drinking strong-'double'-beer), and 'swill' (drink greedily; WP quote *R3* 5.2.7–9: 'The . . . usurping boar . . . Swills your warm blood').

29–30 the . . . authority See 2.2.10–11; 'stalls' = 'installs'; compare *R3* 1.3.205: 'Decked in thy rights as thou art stalled in mine'.

31–2 all . . . victory Proverbial (Tilley D35). Compare *3H6* 5.1.70: 'The harder matched, the greater victory'.

Some friends have we, beside domestic power:
The stern Polonian, and the warlike Dane,
The King of Bohemia, and of Sicily,
Are all become confederates with us,
And, as I think, are marching hither apace.
[*Drum within*]
But soft, I hear the music of their drums,
By which I guess that their approach is near.

Enter the King of BOHEMIA *with Danes, and a* POLONIAN CAPTAIN *with other soldiers another way*

BOHEMIA King John of France, as league and neighbourhood
Requires, when friends are any way distressed,
I come to aid thee with my country's force.
POLONIAN CAPTAIN And from great Moscow, fearful to the Turk,
And lofty Poland, nurse of hardy men,
I bring these servitors to fight for thee,
Who willingly will venture in thy cause.
KING JOHN Welcome, Bohemian King, and welcome all;
This your great kindness I will not forget.
Besides your plentiful rewards in crowns
That from our treasury ye shall receive,
There comes a hare-brained nation, decked in pride,
The spoil of whom will be a treble gain.
And now my hope is full, my joy complete:
At sea we are as puissant as the force
Of Agamemnon in the haven of Troy;

33 domestic] *Capell;* drum stricke Q1; drumsticke Q2 35 King] Qq; kings *Collier* 35 Bohemia] Qq; Boheme *Capell, Tyrrell, Collier* 35 Sicily] Cycelie Qq 37 hither apace] Qq; hitherward *Capell* 37 SD] *Capell; not in* Qq 40–2] *As in* Q1; *lines divided at* league / way / force. Q2 43 Moscow] *Capell;* Musco Qq 49 Besides] Qq; Beside *Capell* 51 hare-brained] Q2 (hare-braind); hare braind Q1 52 gain] Q2 (gaine); game Q1

33–6 Poles and Danes served as mercenaries in the French army. John of Luxembourg, King of Bohemia, figures frequently in Frois. as an ally of the French from 1338 till the battle of Crécy in 1346, when he was killed (compare 3.4 below). Robert King of Sicily acted as a peacemaker after the sea-battle of Sluys, see Frois. ch. 51 (Ker, I, 149–50): 'Howe kynge Robert of Cycill dyd all that he might to pacyfie the kynges of Fraunce and Englande.' See Appendix, p. 200.

43 **Moscow . . . Turk** Russia was a threat to the expansion of the Ottoman empire.

45 **servitors** Making it clear that the Polish troops are not a national army but mercenaries ('servitors') hired by warlords, but see 5.1.178n.

51 **decked in pride** Compare 2.1.445–7.

52 **treble gain** The first 'gain' is the French King's gratitude (48), the second the monetary recompense ('rewards in crowns', 49–50), the third the sharing of the enemy spoils.

54–5 **the force . . . Troy** Agamemnon was the supreme commander of the Greek army and navy that conquered Troy.

By land, with Xerxes we compare of strength,
Whose soldiers drank up rivers in their thirst.
Then, Bayard-like, blind, overweening Ned,
To reach at our imperial diadem
Is either to be swallowed of the waves,
Or hacked a-pieces when thou comest ashore.

Enter MARINER

MARINER Near to the coast I have descried, my lord,
As I was busy in my watchful charge,
The proud armado of King Edward's ships,
Which, at the first far off when I did ken,
Seemed as it were a grove of withered pines;
But, drawing near, their glorious bright aspect,
Their streaming ensigns wrought of coloured silk,
Like to a meadow full of sundry flowers
Adorns the naked bosom of the earth.
Majestical the order of their course,
Figuring the hornèd circle of the moon;
And on the top gallant of the admiral,

61 SD] Q2 (Marriner); *Enter.* Q1 **62** descried] Q2 (discride); discribde Q1 73 And] Qq; *not in Capell*

56–7 According to Herodotus, Xerxes' Persian army that invaded Greece in the fifth century BC comprised over two million soldiers and three million auxiliary forces.

58 Bayard-like Bayard was the magic horse Charlemagne gave to Rinaldo; in proverbial phrases (Tilley B112) the name became synonymous with blind recklessness. Whiting (B71), under 'As bold as blind Bayard', records entries since c. 1380.

58 Ned The diminutive is used derogatorily of King Edward. Compare the king's familiar use of it for his son Prince Edward at 1.1.141, 157.

62 descried sighted.

64 armado An early variant form of the Spanish 'armada' to designate a fleet.

65 ken catch sight of (*OED* sv v^1 6).

66 The simile is used by Frois. of the French, not the English, fleet (Metz, p. 60): Edward 'sawe so great a nombre of shippes that their mastes semed to be lyke a gret wood'.

67–70 their . . . earth An ambiguous construction, in which 'Like' (69) means both 'similar to' (the 'ensigns' at 68), and 'in the same way as' (the meadow 'Adorns the . . . earth' at 70); in turn 'Adorns' (70), though grammatically depending on 'aspect' (= appearance) at 67, does duty also as the verb of a relative clause depending on 'meadow' at 69 (flowering meadow that adorns the earth).

72 Possibly a reminiscence of the descriptions of the 'Invencible Armada', the Spanish fleet that attacked England in 1588, proceeding in half-moon formation, before being dispersed by a storm. 'Figuring' = 'Reproducing'. According to Hol. (II, 614) at Sluys 'the nauies on both sides were diuided into three battels'.

73–6 Edward added the arms of France to his own in 1339; see Frois. ch. 43 (Ker, I, 122–4): 'How kyng Edwarde toke on hym to bere the armes of Fraunce, and the name to be called kyng thereof'. The mention of the new ensign was prompted by the remark in Frois. (Metz, p. 60) that the French at Sluys 'sawe well howe the kyng of England was ther personally, by reason of his baners'; see Appendix, p. 201.

73 gallant flag borne on the mast of a ship (*OED* sv *sb* 5).

73 admiral flagship (also at 148 and 149).

And likewise all the handmaids of his train,
The arms of England and of France unite
Are quartered equally by herald's art.
Thus, titely carried with a merry gale,
They plough the ocean hitherward amain.

KING JOHN Dare he already crop the fleur-de-lis?
I hope, the honey being gathered thence,
He, with the spider afterward approached,
Shall suck forth deadly venom from the leaves.
But where's our navy? How are they prepared
To wing themselves against this flight of ravens?

MARINER They, having knowledge brought them by the scouts,
Did break from anchor straight, and, puffed with rage
No otherwise than were their sails with wind,
Made forth as when the empty eagle flies
To satisfy his hungry griping maw.

KING JOHN There's for thy news, return unto thy bark;
And if thou scape the bloody stroke of war
And do survive the conflict, come again,
And let us hear the manner of the fight. *Exit Mariner*
Mean space, my lords, 'tis best we be dispersed
To several places, lest they chance to land.
First you, my lord, with your Bohemian troops
Shall pitch your battles on the lower hand;

75 unite] QQ; united *Delius* 77 titely] QQ; tightly *Smith, WAA, RLA* 79 SH] Q2 (*K. Iohn*); *not in* Q1 79 fleur-de-lis] Flower de Luce QQ (Flewer Q1) 83 our navy?] our Nauie? Q2; out Nauy, Q1 84 flight] Q1; fleete Q2 90 There's] Q2; Thees Q1 93 SD] Q2; *Exit.* Q1 97 hand QQ; land *conj. Lapides*

74 his 'Admiral', though a ship, is treated as masculine.

75 unite united (*OED* sv *ppl.a.*).

76 quartered equally In heraldry, indicating a shield divided into four sections, alternating hereditary and additional arms.

77 titely quickly (*OED* sv *adv*), agreeing with 'amain' (= at full speed) at 78. The reading 'tightly' (meaning 'adroitly' or 'properly'), adopted by Smith and all modern-spelling editions, is misleading.

79 fleur-de-lis lily or iris, the heraldic device borne on the royal arms of France.

80–2 the . . . leaves A variant of the proverbial conceit (Tilley B208) fully developed at 2.1.283–6 (see n.).

84 wing themselves hoist their sails.

84 flight Q2's 'fleete' is a typical miscorrection by the reviser of the text of Q1. The play on the near homophony flight/fleet is deliberate, anticipating the ominous 'flight of ravens' that causes havoc in the French army at Poitiers (see 4.5).

89 griping maw voracious gullet (*OED* Maw *sb* 3).

90 There's Q1 has 'Thees' (= These). Both forms imply that the king is giving money to the Mariner.

90 bark boat, ship (now used poetically to describe a small sailing ship)

94 Mean space In the meantime.

97 battles troops arrayed for combat.

97 on . . . hand on the right side (presumably on lower ground in respect of the 'higher ground' on which the other wing of the army is to be deployed, see 100). There is no need to suppose that 'land' instead of 'hand' was intended.

My eldest son, the Duke of Normandy,
Together with this aid of Muscovites,
Shall climb the higher ground another way;
Here in the middle coast, betwixt you both,
Philip my youngest boy and I will lodge.
So, lords, be gone, and look unto your charge:
You stand for France, an empire fair and large.

Exeunt [*all but King John and Philip*]

Now tell me, Philip, what is thy conceit
Touching the challenge that the English make.

PHILIP I say, my lord, claim Edward what he can,
And bring he ne'er so plain a pedigree,
'Tis you are in possession of the crown,
And that's the surest point of all the law;
But were it not, yet ere he should prevail,
I'll make a conduit of my dearest blood,
Or chase those straggling upstarts home again.

KING JOHN Well said, young Philip! Call for bread and wine,
That we may cheer our stomachs with repast,
To look our foes more sternly in the face.

The battle heard afar off

Now is begun the heavy day at sea.
Fight, Frenchmen, fight, be like the field of bears
When they defend their younglings in their caves.
Steer, angry Nemesis, the happy helm,

104 SD] *This edn after Capell; Exunt / or/ Exeunt (after 103)* Qq **105** thy conceit] Q2; their concept Q1; thy concept *WP, TB, RLA* **106** make.] Qq; make? *Capell and all mod. edns* **111** yet] Q1; *not in* Q2 **114–15**] *Divided as in* Q1; *divided at* bread / Q2 **116** SD] Qq *(in margin of 115–17* Q1, *of 117–19* Q2*); A Table and Provisions brought in; King and his Son set down to it. Ordinance afar off / Capell, WP* **120** Steer] *Capell;* Stir Qq

99 this . . . Muscovites The mercenary forces from Poland; see 'Moscow' in the speech of the Polonian Captain at 43–6.

103 look . . . charge follow your instructions.

105 conceit opinion (*OED* sv *sb* 4).

108 pedigree Compare 1.1.5–27.

109–10 Proverbial: 'Possession is the surest point of the law' (Tilley P487).

112 Compare *Tit.* 2.4.29–30, 'all this loss of blood, / As from a conduit with their issuing spouts', and *Err.* 5.1.314, 'all the conduits of my blood froze up'.

114–16 Call . . . face The French King's call for food in order to face the enemy is an ironical advance comment on his statement, in his speech before Crécy, that the English will not fight unless on a full stomach (3.3.155–62).

118 field of bears Both the ground on which bears fight and the fighting bears themselves. Bear fights were a popular entertainment.

120 Nemesis The goddess of retribution and revenge. She is invoked to guide successfully ('happy') the French fleet.

That with the sulphur battles of your rage
The English fleet may be dispersed and sunk.

Shot

PHILIP O father, how this echoing cannon shot,
Like sweet harmony, disgests my cates!

KING JOHN Now, boy, thou hearest what thund'ring terror 'tis
To buckle for a kingdom's sovereignty.
The earth, with giddy trembling when it shakes,
Or when the exhalations of the air
Breaks in extremity of lightning flash,
Affrights not more than kings when they dispose
To show the rancour of their high-swoll'n hearts.

Retreat

Retreat is sounded: one side hath the worse.
O, if it be the French, sweet Fortune, turn,
And in thy turning change the froward winds,
That, with advantage of a favouring sky,
Our men may vanquish, and th'other fly.

Enter MARINER

My heart misgives. – Say, mirror of pale death,
To whom belongs the honour of this day?
Relate, I pray thee, if thy breath will serve,
The sad discourse of this discomfiture.

MARINER I will, my lord.
My gracious sovereign, France hath ta'en the foil,

121 sulphur] Qq; sulphur'd *Capell* **122** SD] Qq *(at 123); Ordinance again. / Capell* **124** sweet . . . disgests] Qq; sweetest . . . digests *Capell* **125** SH] Q2; *as catchword* (K. *Io.*) *on previous page* Q1 **125–6]** *Divided as in* Q1; *divided at* thundring / Q2 **126** buckle] Qq; battle *conj. Collier* **129** Breaks] Qq (Breakes); Break *Capell* **131** high-swoll'n] *Capell* (high-swoln); high swolne Qq **131** SD] Qq *(at 132); Retreat heard / Capell* **133** it be] Q1; *not in* Q2 **134** froward] Q2; forward Q1 **136** th'other] Q2; thither Q1; the other *Capell* **138** this day] Qq; the day *Collier*

121 sulphur . . . rage hellish forces raised by your fury. 'Sulphur' is always associated with hell (Nemesis is an infernal goddess). For 'battles' see 97n.

124 disgests The old form of 'digests' is retained in the specific meaning 'favours the digestion of'.

124 cates choice viands, delicacies (*OED* Cate *sb*[1] 2).

126 buckle engage [in a fight] at close quarters (*OED* sv *v* 3a).

129 Breaks A singular form for the plural, see 1.2.134n.

130 dispose decide.

133–6 Suggested by Hol. (II, 614), 'both heauen, sea, and the wind, seemed all to haue conspired against the Frenchmen'.

134 froward contrary, perverse.

136 th'other Used as a collective noun = the others.

142 hath . . . foil has been defeated (*OED* Foil *sb*[2] 2).

And boasting Edward triumphs with success.
These iron-hearted navies,
When last I was reporter to your grace,
Both full of angry spleen, of hope and fear,
Hasting to meet each other in the face,
At last conjoined, and by their admiral
Our admiral encountered many shot.
By this, the other, that beheld these twain
Give earnest penny of a further wrack,
Like fiery dragons took their haughty flight,
And, likewise meeting, from their smoky wombs
Sent many grim ambassadors of death.
Then 'gan the day to turn to gloomy night,
And darkness did as well enclose the quick
As those that were but newly reft of life.
No leisure served for friends to bid farewell,
And if it had, the hideous noise was such
As each to other seemèd deaf and dumb.
Purple the sea, whose channel filled as fast
With streaming gore that from the maimèd fell
As did the gushing moisture break into
The crannied cleftures of the through-shot planks.
Here flew a head dissevered from the trunk,
There mangled arms and legs were tossed aloft
As when a whirlwind takes the summer dust

144 iron-hearted] *Capell;* Iron harted Qq **164** crannied] *Capell* (cranny'd)*;* cranny Qq **164** through-shot] *Capell;* through shot Qq

144–84 The description of the naval battle is a set piece based on Hol. and Frois. and possibly other unidentified reports, cast in a form that may have influenced the verse letters 'The Storm' and 'The Calm' by John Donne, written about 1597. In turn, as A. R. Braunmuller convincingly suggests, the description closely imitates a passage in Thomas Kyd's *The Spanish Tragedy* (first published 1592, ed. Ph. Edwards, 1959), the Spanish General's account of a land battle at 1.2.22–84; the two texts, in Braunmuller's words, 'stress the way actions of the contending parties alternate ritually or balletically, the link between light/dark and life/death, the fragmentation of whole bodies into body parts, the purple-colouring of land (sea) by human blood etc.'

146 spleen temper (*OED* sv *sb* 6).

148, 149 admiral flagship, see 73.

149 shot cannonfire.

150 By this By this time.

150 the other Plural, 'the other ships', see 136.

151 earnest penny guarantee (the money given in earnest of future larger payments, see *OED* Earnest *sb*[2] 1b).

152 took . . . flight Compare 84n.

156 quick living.

157 reft bereft, deprived.

161 channel Narrow expanse of water at the entrance of a haven. Compare Hol. (II, 614) 'the French fleet was driuen into the streights of the hauen'.

164 the chink-like fissures caused by cannon-shot in the planks. Compare *MND* 5.1.157–8: 'a wall . . . That had in it a crannied hole or chink'.

And scatters it in middle of the air.
Then might ye see the reeling vessels split
And tottering sink into the ruthless flood,
Until their lofty tops were seen no more.
All shifts were tried, both for defence and hurt,
And now the effect of valour and of force,
Of resolution and of cowardice
Were lively pictured: how the one for fame,
The other by compulsion laid about.
Much did the Nonpareille, that brave ship;
So did the Black Snake of Boulogne, than which
A bonnier vessel never yet spread sail;
But all in vain: both sun, the wind, and tide,
Revolted all unto our foemen's side,
That we perforce were fain to give them way,
And they are landed. Thus my tale is done:
We have untimely lost, and they have won.

KING JOHN Then rests there nothing but with present speed
To join our several forces all in one,
And bid them battle ere they range too far.
Come, gentle Philip, let us hence depart:
This soldier's words have pierced thy father's heart.

Exeunt

173 effect] Qq; effects *Capell* **173** force] Qq; fear *Capell* **174** cowardice] Q2 (cowardize); a cowardize Q1 **175** Were] *Capell;* We Qq **177** Nonpareille] *Capell; Nom per illa* Qq; *Nonperillo / Collier* **178** Black . . . Boulogne] *This edn;* blacke snake of Bullen Qq; black-snake of *Boulògne / Capell* **180** wind] Q2 (winde); Wine Q1

172 shifts expedients (*OED* Shift *sb* 3).

172 hurt attack.

173 force Capell suggests 'fear' in opposition to 'valour', by analogy with the contrasts 'hope/fear' at 146 and 'resolution/cowardice' at 174. But 'valour/force' looks forward to 'fame/compulsion' at 175–6.

176 by compulsion forced (to fight). See 173.

176 laid about fought valiantly (*OED* Lay v^1 32e).

177–9 The two French vessels are not mentioned in the chronicles. Hol. (II, 614) describes the night battle to capture 'a mightie great vessell, called the Iames of Deepe [Dieppe, near Boulogne]', in which were found 'aboue four hundred dead bodies'. Frois. (Metz, pp. 60–1) reports the boarding and recapture by the English of 'the great Christofer', that the French 'had won the yer before'; in the hand-to-hand battle, 'all that were within it [were] taken or slayne'. For the name *Nonpareille* see Introduction, p. 28.

180–2 both . . . way From Hol., II.614: 'at length the Englishmen hauing the aduantage, not onlie of the sunne, but also of the wind and tide, so fortunatlie, that the French fleet was driuen into the streights of the hauen [see 161 n.], in such wise that neither the souldiers nor mariners could helpe themselues', and compare the quotation at 133–6n.

182 were fain were obliged.

183 my . . . done The formal close of oral narratives. Compare *R2* 5.3.37: 'no man enter till my tale be done'.

184 untimely unseasonably, at an unsuitable time (*OED* sv *adv* 1).

185 with . . . speed without delay.

3.2. *Enter two* FRENCHMEN; *a* WOMAN *and two little children meet them, and other* CITIZENS

FIRST FRENCHMAN Well met, my masters; how now, what's the news,
And wherefore are ye laden thus with stuff?
What, is it quarter day, that you remove
And carry bag and baggage too?
FIRST CITIZEN Quarter day, ay, and quartering day, I fear.
Have ye not heard the news that flies abroad?
FIRST FRENCHMAN What news?
SECOND CITIZEN How the French navy is destroyed at sea,
And that the English army is arrived.
FIRST FRENCHMAN What then?
FIRST CITIZEN What then, quoth you? Why, is't not time to fly
When envy and destruction is so nigh?
FIRST FRENCHMAN Content thee, man, they are far enough from hence,
And will be met, I warrant ye, to their cost,
Before they break so far into the realm.
FIRST CITIZEN Ay, so the grasshopper doth spend the time

Act 3, Scene 2 **3.2**] *Capell; no scene division in* Qq **0** SD.1 *Enter . . . them,*] Q2*; Enter two French men, a woman and two little Children, meet them* Q1*;* Picardy. *Fields near* Cressi. *Enter a* Frenchman, *meeting certain Others, a* Woman, *and two Children, laden with Houshold-stuff, as removing. / Capell* **0** SD.1–2 *and . . .* CITIZENS] Q2*; another Citizens* Q1*; not in Capell* **1, 7, 10, 13, 27, 30** SH] *This edn after WAA (1 Fr.); One* Qq*; 1.F. / Capell* **2** ye] Q1*;* you Q2 **5, 11, 16, 32** SH] *This edn after WAA (1 cit.); Two* Qq*; 2.F. / Capell* **5** quartering day] Q2*;* quartering pay Q1 **6** ye] Q2*;* we Q1 **8, 29** SH] *This edn after WAA (2 cit.); Three* Qq*; 3.F. / Capell* **11** is't not] Qq (ist not)*;* is not *Collier* **12** envy] enuie Qq*;* the en'my *Delius, conj. Capell* **12** is] Qq*;* are *Collier* **14** ye] Q1*;* you Q2

Act 3, Scene 2

3.2 Located in the countryside near Crécy, the scene is an invention of the dramatist in preparation for the battle fought on 26 August 1346, and it echoes Froissart's account of the invasion of Normandy in July (ch. 123, Metz, p. 71): 'It was no marveyle though they of the countrey were afrayed, for before that tyme they had neuer sene men of warre, nor they wyst nat what warre or batayle meant. They fledde away as ferr as they might here spekyng of thenglysshmen, and left their houses well stuffed, and graunges full of corne, they wyst nat howe to saue and kepe it.'

0 SD It appears from the context that the two 'Frenchmen' (as well as a third entering at 45) arrive from other parts of the country, while the 'woman' and the 'citizens' are local townspeople. The second Frenchman is a mute, and only two of the 'citizens' and the woman speak. The synthetic speech headings of Qq, 'One' for the Frenchman, 'Two' and 'Three' for the citizens, have been changed to conform to modern usage.

3 quarter day moving day. Quarter days marked the beginning of each quarter, when land and house leases began or expired, and removals took place.

5 quartering day A grim pun on 'quarter day', with reference to the practice of hanging, drawing, and quartering (= dismembering) offenders sentenced to death. Q1's 'quartering pay' is due to the accidental setting of the letter 'd' upside-down.

6 ye Q1's 'we' is acceptable if the Citizen includes the newcomer among those aware of the news that is spreading around ('abroad').

8 Anachronistic, referring to the sea battle of Sluys (15 June 1340), described in 3.1. Six years elapsed between this and the landing in Normandy (July 1346), mentioned in the next line.

12 envy harm, mischief (*OED* sv *sb* 2). There is no evidence that it is a misreading of 'en'my', as conjectured by Capell.

12 is A singular form for the plural, see 1.2.134n.

16–19 Referring to the traditional moral tale of the ant and the grasshopper.

In mirthful jollity till winter come,
And then too late he would redeem his time,
When frozen cold hath nipped his careless head.
He that no sooner will provide a cloak
Than when he sees it doth begin to rain,
May peradventure, for his negligence,
Be throughly washed when he suspects it not.
We that have charge and such a train as this
Must look in time to look for them and us,
Lest when we would, we cannot be relieved.

FIRST FRENCHMAN Belike you then despair of ill success,
And think your country will be subjugate.

SECOND CITIZEN We cannot tell: 'tis good to fear the worst.

FIRST FRENCHMAN Yet rather fight than, like unnatural sons,
Forsake your loving parents in distress.

FIRST CITIZEN Tush, they that have already taken arms
Are many fearful millions, in respect
Of that small handful of our enemies;
But 'tis a rightful quarrel must prevail:
Edward is son unto our late king's sister,
Where John Valois is three degrees removed.

WOMAN Besides, there goes a prophecy abroad,
Published by one that was a friar once,

23 throughly] Qq; thoroughly *Tyrrell, Collier* 27 ill] Qq; all *Capell* 37 Where] Qq; When *Collier*

18 **redeem . . . time** compensate for time lost. Compare *1H4* 1.2.217: 'Redeeming time when men think least I will'.

19 **careless** improvident.

20–3 Proverbial, 'Have not thy cloak to make when it begins to rain', Tilley C418, quoting this as the first example.

23 **throughly** A common disyllabic form of 'thoroughly'.

24 **charge . . . this** so many dependants in our charge.

25 **look . . . look for** take timely measures to protect.

27 **despair . . . success** A false double negative: 'despair of' = 'fear', 'success' = 'results'. There is no need to suppose that 'ill' is a mistake for 'all'.

28 **subjugate** subjugated: a participial form, like 'unite' for 'united' at 3.1.75.

29 **'tis . . . worst** A common proverb, Tilley W912.

32 **Tush** An exclamation of impatience or contempt, compare *Oth.* (Q1) 1.1.1 (not in F).

33 **fearful** inspiring dread. The strength of the French ('many millions') is expressed in terms of total population rather than of actual fighting forces.

35–7 The argument that Edward's claim to the throne of France was a 'rightful quarrel' recalls 1.1.5–27 and repeats the same mistake: not John, but Philip VI of Valois, succeeded Charles IV of France. He, as the son of Charles IV's uncle, was in fact 'three degrees removed' from the main line of succession, see 1.1.21n.

37 **Where** Whereas (Abbott 134).

38–43 No trace of this prophecy is found in the known sources of the play. It is probably an invention of the dramatist by analogy with those of the spirit in *2H6* 1.4, evoked through the agency of the false priest John Hume. A lion rampant ('roused lion') figures in the crest of England, and for the 'fleur-de-lis' see 3.1.79n.

Whose oracles have many times proved true;
And now he says, the time will shortly come
Whenas a lion rousèd in the West
Shall carry hence the fleur-de-lis of France.
These, I can tell ye, and such like surmises
Strike many Frenchmen cold unto the heart.

Enter a FRENCHMAN

THIRD FRENCHMAN Fly, countrymen and citizens of France!
Sweet flow'ring peace, the root of happy life,
Is quite abandoned and expulsed the land;
Instead of whom, ransack-constraining war
Sits like to ravens upon your houses' tops,
Slaughter and mischief walk within your streets
And unrestrained make havoc as they pass;
The form whereof even now myself beheld,
Upon this fair mountain whence I came.
For so far off as I direct'd mine eyes,
I might perceive five cities all on fire,
Cornfields and vineyards burning like an oven;
And as the leaking vapour in the wind
Turned but aside, I likewise might discern
The poor inhabitants, escaped the flame,
Fall numberless upon the soldiers' pikes.

41–3 the time . . . France] Qq; *as quotation / Capell, WP etc.* **43** fleur-de-lis] fluerdeluce Q1; Flower de Luce Q2 **45** SD] Qq; *Enter another* Frenchman, *hastily. / Capell* **46** SH] *This edn after WAA (3 Fr.); not in* Qq; *4.F. / Capell; Four / WP* **49** whom] Qq; which *conj. Capell* **49** ransack-constraining] *Capell;* ransackt constraining Qq **50** like . . . upon] Qq; raven-like upon *Delius, conj. Capell* **50** upon] Qq; on *Capell, Tyrrell, Collier* **54** Upon] Qq; Now, upon *Capell, Tyrrell, Delius* **55** far . . . direct'd] Qq (directed); far as I did direct *Capell* **58** leaking] Qq; reeking *Delius, conj. Capell, Collier* **59**] *Delius, Collier, WP, RLA;* I tourned (turned Q2) but aside I likewise might disserne. (discerne Q2) Qq; Turned aside, I likewise might discern *Capell, Tyrrell;* Ay turned but aside, I might discern *conj. Capell*

44 surmises ideas or expectations (*OED* Surmise *sb* 4b). Compare *2H4* 1.3.23–4: 'Conjecture, expectation, and surmise / Of aids incertain, should not be admitted.'

46 SH Since two 'Frenchmen' are already on stage (see 0 SD n.) 'Third Frenchman' is the appropriate form for the speech heading missing in Qq.

49 ransack-constraining war war that leads inevitably to looting. Qq's 'ransackt' is a misreading of the copy.

50 Emendation of this line (see Collation) to avoid an extra syllable is unnecessary: 'ravens' is pronounced as a monosyllable (WP).

51 Slaughter and mischief are personifications. Possibly reminiscent of *Tit.* 5.2, where Titus incites Rapine and Murther (presented as the 'ministers' of Revenge – see 'ministers of wrath' at 62) to 'Look about the wicked streets of Rome.'

54 fair Treated as a disyllable (WP).

55 direct'd The elision mark is used to indicate that Qq's 'directed' is pronounced as a disyllable.

58 leaking vapour smoke issuing from the fires. There is no authority for emending 'leaking' into 'reeking'.

59 The hypermetrical 'I' at the beginning of the line in Qq is a printer's misinterpretation of the copy.

Three ways these dreadful ministers of wrath
Do tread the measures of their tragic march:
Upon the right hand comes the conquering king,
Upon the left his hot unbridled son,
And in the midst their nation's glittering host;
All which, though distant, yet conspire in one
To leave a desolation where they come.
Fly therefore, citizens, if you be wise,
Seek out some habitation further off.
Here if you stay, your wives will be abused,
Your treasure shared before your weeping eyes;
Shelter yourselves, for now the storm doth rise.
Away, away! Methinks I hear their drums.
Ah, wretched France, I greatly fear thy fall:
Thy glory shaketh like a tottering wall.

[*Exeunt*]

3.3. *Enter* KING EDWARD *and the Earl of* DERBY, *with Soldiers and* GOBIN *de Grace*

KING EDWARD Where's the Frenchman by whose cunning guide

65 his] Q2; is Q1 **66** their] *this edn, conj. Lapides;* our Qq **73** yourselves] *Capell;* you your selues Qq **76** SD] Q2; *not in* Q1 Act 3, Scene 3 **3.3**] *Capell; no scene division in* Qq **0** SD *Enter*] Qq; *The same. Drums. Enter/ Capell* **0** SD *Grace*] *This edn;* Graie Q1 *and most mod. edns;* Gray Q2; Grey *Capell, Smith, WAA* **1** Where's] Qq; Where is *Capell* **1** guide] Qq; guidance *Delius, conj. Capell*

62–6 This description comes directly from Frois., ch. 128 (Metz, p. 76; reported nearly verbatim by Hol. II, 637, see Appendix, pp. 202–3): 'Of the order of the Englysshmen at Cressy, and how they made thre batayls a fote'. The English were deployed in three 'battles' (62, 'Three ways'), the first led by 'the yonge prince of Wales' (sixteen years old at the time – see 65, 'his hot unbridled son'), and the third by the king himself (see 64). The strongest posse, in a central position, was the second 'battle' comprising the flower of English nobility, described in the play as a 'glittering host' (66). Some confusion is caused by the use in Qq of 'our' for 'their' at 66, giving the impression that the speaker refers to the French instead of the English forces. This is surely an error due to inadvertence by author or printer, since the 'dreadful ministers of wrath' at 62 are the English, and the French army is not yet in sight.

63 tread the measures An image from dancing (*OED* Measure *sb* 20: 'a grave or stately dance, esp. in phr. *tread a measure*') to convey the powerful rhythm of the marching armies.

Act 3, Scene 3

3.3 The location is in Picardy somewhere beyond the Somme not far from 'Crécy plains' (42), on the eve or in the morning of 26 August 1346. The episode of Gobin de Grace (1–12) and the report of the English progress in France (19–26) are based on Hol., II, 634–6, as well as Frois., chs. 122–7 (see Appendix, pp. 203–4), whereas the rest of the scene (the meeting of the two kings, the arming of the Black Prince) freely elaborates hints from the chronicles.

0 SD. 1–2 GOBIN *de Grace* The name is given once in this form and twice as Gobin Agace in Hol. (Gobyn a Grace in Frois.). The printer of Q1 misread 'Graie' for 'Grace', and Q2 'improved' it to 'Gray'.

1–10 The account of how a French prisoner revealed to the English the tidal ford across the River Somme at Blanchetaque is taken directly from Hol., II, 636, which summarises the more extended report in Frois., chs. 126–7 (Metz, pp. 73–5).

1 This line lacks one syllable. 'Where is' is a better emendation than 'guidance' for 'guide'.

We found the shallow of this River Somme,
And had direction how to pass the sea?
GOBIN Here, my good lord.
KING EDWARD How art thou called? Tell me thy name.
GOBIN Gobin de Grace, if please your excellence.
KING EDWARD Then, Gobin, for the service thou hast done,
We here enlarge and give thee liberty;
And for recompense beside this good,
Thou shalt receive five hundred marks in gold. –
I know not how we should have met our son,
Whom now in heart I wish I might behold.

Enter ARTOIS

ARTOIS Good news, my lord: the prince is hard at hand,
And with him comes Lord Audley and the rest,
Whom since our landing we could never meet.

Enter PRINCE *Edward, Lord* AUDLEY, *and Soldiers*

KING EDWARD Welcome, fair prince; how hast thou sped, my son,
Since thy arrival on the coast of France?
PRINCE Successfully, I thank the gracious heavens.
Some of their strongest cities we have won,
As Barfleur, Lô, Crotoy, and Carentan,

2 Somme] *Capell;* Sone QQ **5** Tell me] QQ*; not in Capell* **6** Grace] *This edn (see Collation* 0 SD*)* **6** if please] QQ*;* if it please *Collier* **9** for] QQ*;* for a *WP* **13** SH] Q2 *(Art.); not in* Q1 **16**] *So* Q1*; as two lines divided at* /Prince,/ Q2 **20** Barfleur . . . Carentan] *This edn;* Harslen, Lie, Crotag, and Carentigne QQ*; Harfleur, Lo, Crotage*, and *Carentan* / *Capell;* Harfleur, Loo, Crotage and Charenton *Collier;* Harflew, Lo, Crotaie, and Carentine *WP after Hol., TB (*Crotay . . . Carentigne*)*

2 Somme 'Sone' in QQ is a n/m confusion for the spelling 'Some' in the sources.

3 sea The broad estuary of the river.

4–5 Capell, taking 'Tell me' for a non-authorial interpolation, considered the two speeches a single line.

7–10 Compare Hol., II, 636: 'he acquitted Gobin Agace, and all his companie of their ransomes, and gaue the same Gobin an hundred nobles, and a good horsse' (from Frois., ch. 127, Metz, p. 175).

14 with . . . Audley At 2.2.202–3 Edward had coupled Audley with the Prince, and he does so again before Crécy (220–5), to 'temper' the young man's 'lusty spirit' with 'Audley's gravity', courage with experience. Audley is presented throughout as 'aged' (see 124), though, as RLA remarks, 'at Crécy he was actually not much more than thirty'.

15 Historically incorrect: King and Prince were not separated after landing in Normandy in July 1346. According to Frois. (ch. 123, Ker I, 281–2) the English 'went in thre batayls; the marshalles on the right hande and on the lyft, the kyng and the prince of Wales, his sonne, in the myddes'.

17–26 From the spelling of French place-names, it appears that the report on the progress of the English forces is based on Hol. (II, 634–6) rather than on its source in Frois., chs. 122 and 127 (Metz, pp. 68–70, 74–5).

20 Barfleur A double mistake is involved in the naming of this coast town, the first conquered by the English after landing in Normandy. QQ's 'Harslen' is an obvious printer's misreading [long 's' for 'f' and reversed 'u'] of 'Harflew', an alternative spelling of 'Harfleur', that figures in the reports both of Hol. (II, 634, also in a marginal note) and of

And others wasted, leaving at our heels
A wide apparent field and beaten path
For solitariness to progress in.
Yet those that would submit we kindly pardoned,
For who in scorn refused our proffered peace
Endured the penalty of sharp revenge.

KING EDWARD Ah, France, why shouldst thou be this obstinate
Against the kind embracement of thy friends?
How gently had we thought to touch thy breast,
And set our foot upon thy tender mould,
But that in froward and disdainful pride
Thou, like a skittish and untamèd colt,
Dost start aside, and strike us with thy heels!
But tell me, Ned, in all thy warlike course
Has thou not seen the usurping King of France?

PRINCE Yes, my good lord, and not two hours ago,
With full a hundred thousand fighting men

25 For] Qq; But *Delius, WP, conj. Capell* **27** this] Q1; thus Q2 **29** gently] Q1; gentle Q2 **33** heels!] Q2 (heeles?); heeles, Q1 **36** hours] Q2 (houres); owers Q1 **37** a] Q1; an Q2

the English Frois. (ch. 122, Metz, p. 69). But the original French Frois. has 'Barfleur', and 'Harflew' is an error of the translator Lord Berners, who was influenced by the fame achieved in England by Henry V's siege and conquest of Harfleur (now a suburb of Le Havre, on the Seine estuary) in October 1415 (see *H5* 3.1–3).

20 Lô Saint Lô, seventeen miles south of Carentan and forty-seven from Barfleur, is mentioned by Hol. (II, 634) as 'a great towne called saint Lo, a rich towne of draperie . . . it was soone taken and robbed by the English vpon their first approch'. Qq's 'Lie', though probably a printer's misreading of 'Lo', could refer to 'S. Germans in Laie' (now St-Germain-en-Laye, fifteen miles north-east of Paris), mentioned in Hol. (II, 635, evidenced in the margin) as a town burnt by the 'English marshals' in their progress to the interior.

20 Crotoy Qq's 'Crotag' is the printer's misreading of 'Crotay', now Le Crotoy, a port north of the Somme estuary, mentioned in Hol. (II, 636, in the margin 'Crotay burnt') after the report of the crossing of the Somme (see 1–10n.): 'His [Edward's] marshals road to Crotaie by the sea side, and burnt the towne.'

20 Carentan Near the Normandy coast between Barfleur and Saint Lô, see note on Lô and Hol., II, 634 (in margin 'Carentine'): 'The town of Carentine was deliuered vnto them [the English] against the will of the soldiers that were within it.'

21–6 Both Frois. and Hol. describe the scorched-earth policy adopted by the advancing English, and the destruction of the towns that resisted them (see Appendix, pp. 202–3).

22 wide . . . field extensive wasteland.

23 solitariness desolation, absence of life (*OED* sv *sb* 2).

25 For who Whereas those who. 'For' acts both as disjunctive (= instead, see Abbott 148), and in the sense of 'as regards' (Abbott 149). Some emend to 'But' assuming that 'For' is a printer's eyeslip from 23.

27 this obstinate so obstinate. Q2's 'improvement' ('thus') is unnecessary.

30 mould (1) earth (*OED* sv *sb*[1] 1), (2) body (*OED* sv *sb*[3] 10b).

31 froward ungovernable (*OED* sv *adj* 1).

37 hundred . . . men The figure is given in Hol., II, 636 (from Frois.), in a passage quoted in the Appendix, p. 204.

Upon the one side of the river's bank
And on the other, both his multitudes.
I feared he would have cropped our smaller power,
But happily, perceiving your approach,
He hath withdrawn himself to Crécy plains,
Where, as it seemeth by his good array,
He means to bid us battle presently.

KING EDWARD He shall be welcome: that's the thing we crave.

Enter KING JOHN, [*Prince* CHARLES] *Duke of Normandy*, [*Duke of*] LORRAINE, *King of* BOHEMIA, *young* [*Prince*] PHILIP, *and Soldiers*

KING JOHN Edward, know that John, the true King of France,
Musing thou shouldst encroach upon his land
And, in thy tyrannous proceeding, slay
His faithful subjects, and subvert his towns,
Spits in thy face, and in this manner following
Upbraids thee with thine arrogant intrusion:
First, I condemn thee for a fugitive,
A thievish pirate, and a needy mate –
One that hath either no abiding place,
Or else, inhabiting some barren soil
Where neither herb nor fruitful grain is had,
Dost altogether live by pilfering;
Next, insomuch thou hast infringed thy faith,
Broke league and solemn covenant made with me,

38 of] *Capell* (o'); with QQ **39**] *RLA*; . . . other . . . multitudes, QQ; I on the other; with his multitudes *Capell, Collier* (And I . . .), *WP*; And on the other both, his multitudes. *TB* **40** cropped] QQ (cropt); coped *conj. Collier* **42** Crécy] *Mod. edns*; Cressey Q1; Cressy Q2 **45** SD.1–2 *Prince* CHARLES . . . *Soldiers*] *This edn after* QQ (*Dukes of Normanndy* [Normandie Q2] *and Lorraine, King of Boheme* [Bohemia Q2], *yong Phillip and Souldiers*); CHARLES, *and* PHILIP, *his sons;* Bohemia, Lorrain, *etc. and Forces.* / *Capell* **46** Edward . . . John, the true] QQ (*subst.*); Now, *Edward* . . . *John*, true / *Capell* **56** fruitful] Q2 (fruitfull); fiutfull Q1

38–40 The misleading punctuation of QQ obscures the basic meaning: the French 'multitudes' were sighted on both banks of the Somme, and the Prince's fear is expressed in a new sentence. Most editors adopted Capell's emendations implying that all the French were on the north bank of the river and the Prince on the south, and that a new sentence expressing the Prince's fears began in the middle of 39.

41 happily (1) haply, as it chanced, (2) fortunately.

46–167 Historically there was no meeting between the two kings and no negotiations before the battle.

46 The extra syllable in this line disappears if 'the' is elided (= th') before 'true'.

47 Musing Complaining, deploring (*OED* Muse *v* 6).

52 fugitive vagabond (*OED* sv. *sb* 2).

53 needy mate (1) unworthy fellow, see *2H4* 2.4.124–5: 'you poor, base, rascally, cheating, lack-linen mate', (2) common sailor (in a pirate ship).

57 altogether exclusively.

I hold thee for a false pernicious wretch;
And last of all, although I scorn to cope
With one so much inferior to myself,
Yet, in respect thy thirst is all for gold,
Thy labour rather to be feared than loved,
To satisfy thy lust in either part
Here am I come, and with me have I brought
Exceeding store of treasure, pearl, and coin.
Leave therefore now to persecute the weak,
And armèd ent'ring conflict with the armed:
Let it be seen, 'mongst other petty thefts,
How thou canst win this pillage manfully.

KING EDWARD If gall or wormwood have a pleasant taste,
Then is thy salutation honey-sweet;
But as the one hath no such property,
So is the other most satirical.
Yet wot how I regard thy worthless taunts:
If thou have uttered them to foil my fame,
Or dim the reputation of my birth,
Know that thy wolvish barking cannot hurt;
If slyly to insinuate with the world

60 false] Q1; most Q2 **60** pernicious] Qq; perfidious *conj. Elze apud WP* **62** so much] *Capell;* such Qq; such an *Delius;* such, so *Collier* **64** Thy] Q2; They Q1 **66** have I] Q1; I haue Q2 **77** have] Qq; hast *conj. Capell* **77** foil] Qq; soil *Delius, conj. Capell*

60 false Q1's reading, an added insult, is more effective than Q2's 'most'.

62 so much Qq's 'such' implies some kind of omission. Capell's emendation is the most likely among those suggested.

64 rather . . . loved Proverbial (Dent, *PLED*, F131.11).

65 either part Referring to greed ('thirst . . . for gold', 63) on the one hand, and to military action ('labour', 64) on the other.

66–71 The insistence on the looting of France by the English may have been prompted by Frois., ch. 123 (Metz, p. 71): 'They [the English] . . . founde the countrey so fruteful, that they neded nat to make no provisyon for their hoost . . . Thus as ye haue harde, the kyng rode forth, wastynge and brennyng [burning] the countrey.' Compare 3.2n.

69 armèd . . . armed Depending on 'Leave' at 68, meaning: you, with your arms, [refrain from] entering into conflict with armed men.

72 Gall and wormwood (= absinthe) were proverbial for their bitter taste.

74–5 In the same way as gall ('the one') is not sweet, your speech ('the other') is no friendly greeting but merely sarcastic ('satirical', compare 2.1.112n.).

76 wot learn, be informed of (imperative). A form of the archaic verb 'to wit', meaning 'to know'; compare 'Know' at 79.

77 foil dishonour (*OED* sv *v*[1] 7). There is no need to suppose a long s/f confusion and emend to 'soil' (= stain).

79 thy . . . hurt Alluding to such old proverbs as 'the dog barks in vain to the moon' (Tilley D449) or 'the moon does not heed the barking dog' (Tilley M1119).

80–2 The infinitives at 80 and 82 depend on 'If thou have uttered them' [thy taunts] at 77.

80 to . . . world to spread public defamation.

And with a strumpet's artificial line
To paint thy vicious and deformèd cause,
Be well assured the counterfeit will fade
And in the end thy foul defects be seen.
But if thou didst it to provoke me on,
As who should say I were but timorous,
Or, coldly negligent, did need a spur,
Bethink thyself how slack I was at sea,
How since my landing I have won no towns,
Entered no further but upon thy coast,
And there have ever since securely slept;
But if I have been otherwise employed,
Imagine, Valois, whether I intend
To skirmish not for pillage, but for the crown
Which thou dost wear, and that I vow to have –
Or one of us shall fall into his grave.

PRINCE Look not for cross invectives at our hands,
Or railing execrations of despite:
Let creeping serpents hid in hollow banks
Sting with their tongues; we have remorseless swords
And they shall plead for us and our affairs.
Yet thus much briefly, by my father's leave:
As all the immodest poison of thy throat
Is scandalous and most notorious lies,
And our pretended quarrel is truly just,
So end the battle when we meet today –
May either of us prosper and prevail,

81 line] Qq; hue *conj. Collier;* lime *conj. Elze apud WP* **89** How] *Capell;* Now, Qq **90** thy] Q2; the Q1 **92** otherwise] Q1; otherwayes Q2 **94** for the] Qq; the *Capell* **96** his] Q2; this Q1 **99** hid] Q2; hide Q1 **105** is] Qq; *not in Capell*

81 line painting (compare *OED* sv *sb*[2] 7d). There is no reason to suspect an n/m confusion: 'lime' mixes the metaphor based on cosmetic painting developed consistently from 81 to 84. See *Ham.* 3.1.142–4: 'I have heard of your paintings, well enough. God hath given you one face, and you make yourselves another.'

85–96 Edward's sarcastic speech conterbalances what he considered King John's 'satirical' salutation, see 74–5n.

89 How Qq's 'Now' is an obvious printer's misreading.

93–6 A double construction: Edward begins by asking ironically John to guess ('Imagine') whether he is fighting for booty or the crown, but at 94 he makes his intention clear by denying the first alternative, so that 'Or' at 96 refers only to the fight for the crown.

96 his Q1's misreading 'this' is corrected in Q2.

97 cross (1) furious, (2) in reply to yours.

98 railing . . . despite bombastic insults.

103 immodest shameless.

105 pretended quarrel purposed claim (*OED* Pretended *ppl.a* 4).

Or, luckless cursed, receive eternal shame.
KING EDWARD That needs no further question, and I know
His conscience witnesseth it is my right.
Therefore, Valois, say, wilt thou yet resign
Before the sickle's thrust into the corn
Or that enkindled fury turn to flame?
KING JOHN Edward, I know what right thou hast in France,
And ere I basely will resign my crown
This champion field shall be a pool of blood,
And all our prospect as a slaughterhouse.
PRINCE Ay, that approves thee, tyrant, what thou art:
No father, king, or shepherd of thy realm,
But one that tears her entrails with thy hands
And, like a thirsty tiger, suckst her blood.
AUDLEY You peers of France, why do you follow him
That is so prodigal to spend your lives?
CHARLES Whom should they follow, agèd impotent,
But he that is their true-born sovereign?
KING EDWARD Upbraidst thou him, because within his face
Time hath engraved deep characters of age?
Know that these grave scholars of experience,
Like stiff-grown oaks, will stand immovable
When whirlwind quickly turns up younger trees.
DERBY Was ever any of thy father's house
King, but thyself, before this present time?
Edward's great lineage, by the mother's side,

108 cursed] QQ (curst); crost *conj. Collier* **113** turn] Q1 (turne); turned Q2, *Capell* **116** champion] QQ; champain *Collier* **120** tears] QQ (teares); tear'st *conj. Capell* **125** he] QQ; him *Collier* **125** true-born] *Capell;* true borne QQ **128** Know that] QQ; Know, *Capell, WP, TB* **130** whirlwind . . . turns] QQ (whirlewind . . . turnes); whirlwinds . . . turn *Delius, conj. Capell* **131–2**] *As in Capell and all mod. edns; divided after* king QQ

108 luckless cursed damned by ill fortune.

113 Another case of double construction: 'that' supplies the place of 'Before' at 112 (WP), i.e. 'Resign before the conflagration begins', but it is also consecutive to an implicit question, 'Do you want . . .?', as suggested by the use of the subjunctive 'turn', i.e. 'that the destructive action already begun should reach its climax'.

116 champion An adjectival use, see *OED*, Champian, -ion *sb* 5, 'the level open country as the chief scene of military operations'.

117 prospect (1) extensive vista, (2) outlook.

118 approves proves, demonstrates.

126–30 Audley is consistently presented as an aged man (124), the incarnation of gravity and experience, see 14n. There is a pun on 'grave' (sedate and wise, 128) and the wrinkles 'engraved' on his face (127) as the inscriptions ('characters') of old age.

129–30 A deliberate reversal of the old saying (Tilley O3) 'Oaks may fall when reeds stand the storm.'

131–4 The usual argument for Edward's right to the French throne, though 'Five hundred years' is an exaggeration: Edward claimed direct descent from William the Conqueror, who became king in 1066, some three hundred years before the time of the action of the play.

Five hundred years has held the sceptre up.
Judge then, conspirators, by this descent,
Which is the true-born sovereign, this, or that.

PHILIP Father, range your battles, prate no more.
These English fain would spend the time in words,
That, night approaching, they might escape unfought.

KING JOHN Lords and my loving subjects, now's the time
That your intended force must bide the touch.
Therefore, my friends, consider this in brief:
He that you fight for is your natural king,
He against whom you fight, a foreigner;
He that you fight for rules in clemency,
And reins you with a mild and gentle bit;
He against whom you fight, if he prevail,
Will straight enthrone himself in tyranny,
Make slaves of you, and with a heavy hand
Curtail and curb your sweetest liberty.
Then, to protect your country and your king,
Let but the haughty courage of your hearts
Answer the number of your able hands,
And we shall quickly chase these fugitives.
For what's this Edward, but a belly-god,
A tender and lascivious wantonness,
That th'other day was almost dead for love?
And what, I pray you, is his goodly guard?

134 held] Q1 (helde); kept Q2 **137** SH] Q2; *Pri.* Q1 **137** Father] Qq; Good father *Capell, Tyrrell, Delius* **139** escape] Qq; scape *Capell* **140** now's] *Capell, WP* (nowes) *and mod. edns;* knowes Qq **144** you] Q1; ye Q2 **157** th'other] thother Q1; tho'ther Q2

137 SH Q1's *Pri.* (Prince) for Philip is an erroneous expansion of an abbreviated heading, corrected in Q2.

138 fain would would prefer to.

139 unfought without having been engaged in battle.

140–64 The king's speech before a battle is a regular convention in history plays, see for instance Richmond's 'oration to his soldiers' and Richard's 'oration to his army' in *R3* 5.3.237–70 and 314–41.

140 now's Q1's 'knowes' is a printer's aural mistake undetected by the reviser of the play for Q2.

141 intended extended, strained (*OED* sv *ppl.a* 2).

141 bide . . . touch stand the trial (as the metal the touchstone). *OED* Touch *sb* 7 quotes *R3* 4.2.8–9.

154 fugitives Compare 52n.

155–7 The allusion here and at 3.4.113–14 to Edward's infatuation for the Countess of Salisbury suggests that either these scenes are by the same author as 1.2 and 2.1–2, or that different dramatists worked in close collaboration (see Introduction, p. 24, n. 6).

155 belly-god One who makes a god of his belly (*OED* sv *sb* 1). Compare 'epicures', used for the Dutch at 3.1.25.

156 wantonness wanton (also at 3.4.113).

Such as, but scant them of their chines of beef,
And take away their downy featherbeds,
And presently they are as resty-stiff
As 'twere a many overridden jades.
Then, Frenchmen, scorn that such should be your lords,
And rather bind ye them in captive bands.

ALL FRENCH *Vive le roi!* God save King John of France!

KING JOHN Now on this plain of Crécy spread yourselves,
And, Edward, when thou darest, begin the fight.

[*Exeunt King John, King of Bohemia, and all the French*]

KING EDWARD We presently will meet thee, John of France. –
And, English lords, let us resolve the day,
Either to clear us of that scandalous crime,
Or be entombèd in our innocency.
And, Ned, because this battle is the first
That ever yet thou fought'st in pitchèd field,
As ancient custom is of martialists,
To dub thee with the type of chivalry,
In solemn manner we will give thee arms.
Come, therefore, heralds: orderly bring forth
A strong attirement for the prince my son.

Enter four Heralds bringing in a coat of armour, a helmet, a lance, and a shield

Edward Plantagenet, in the name of God,
As with this armour I impall thy breast,

161 resty-stiff] *Capell;* resty stiffe Q1*;* restie stiffe Q2 **165** SH] Qq (*All Fra.*) **166** Crécy] Qq (Cressie) **167** SD] *Capell, subst.; not in* Qq **169** the] Qq*;* this *Capell and mod. edns* **171** innocency] Q2 (innocencie)*;* innocence Q1 **178** SD *Enter*] Qq*; Flourish. Enter / Capell* **178** SD *shield*] Qq*; Shield: First Herald delivers the Armour to King* Edward*; who, putting it on his son, / Capell* **179** Edward] *Capell and mod. edns; Kin:* Edward Q1*; K.Ed.* Edward Q2

159 scant deprive.

159 chines joints (*OED* Chine sb^2 5). An allusion to the reputation of the English as 'bursten bellyed Gluttons' (Nashe, *Pierce Pennilesse*, 1592, sig. F4v), insisted upon in *The Description of England* (Bk 2, ch. 6, 'Of the Food and Diet of the English') added to the 1587 edition of Hol.

161 resty-stiff stiff with too much rest, disinclined for action (*OED* Resty a^1 2).

162 overridden jades worthless horses worn out by too much riding.

164 captive bands prisoners' shackles.

169 resolve . . . day face the battle ('day' = 'day of battle', see *OED* Day *sb* 10). Capell's emendation of 'the' to 'this' reduces the meaning to 'decide today'.

170 scandalous crime libellous accusation (contained in King John's speech at 155–62).

172–218 The whole episode of the arming of the Prince, deferring until after the battle the ceremony of dubbing him as a knight, is the dramatist's invention based on a hint in Frois. (ch. 130, Metz, p. 80), when King Edward replies to a messenger sent by some nobles to ask for reinforcements for the Prince (see 3.4.23–67): 'say to them that they suffre hym this day to wynne his spurres'. Historically the Black Prince was knighted shortly after landing in Normandy in July 1346.

174 martialists warriors (lit.: 'those born under Mars').

175 type badge, distinction.

178 strong attirement suit of armour.

180 impall enfold.

So be thy noble unrelenting heart
Walled in with flint and matchless fortitude,
That never base affections enter there.
Fight and be valiant, conquer where thou com'st. –
Now follow, lords, and do him honour too.

DERBY Edward Plantagenet, Prince of Wales,
As I do set this helmet on thy head,
Wherewith the chamber of thy brain is fenced,
So may thy temples with Bellona's hand
Be still adorned with laurel victory.
Fight and be valiant, conquer where thou com'st.

AUDLEY Edward Plantagenet, Prince of Wales,
Receive this lance into thy manly hand,
Use it in fashion of a brazen pen
To draw forth bloody stratagems in France
And print thy valiant deeds in honour's book.
Fight and be valiant, conquer where thou com'st.

ARTOIS Edward Plantagenet, Prince of Wales,
Hold, take this target, wear it on thy arm,
And may the view thereof, like Perseus' shield,
Astonish and transform thy gazing foes
To senseless images of meagre death.
Fight and be valiant, conquer where thou com'st.

KING EDWARD Now wants there nought but knighthood, which deferred
We leave till thou hast won it in the field.

PRINCE My gracious father, and ye forward peers,
This honour you have done me animates
And cheers my green, yet scarce appearing, strength
With comfortable good-presaging signs,

186 SH] *Capell adds* SD: *receiving the Helmet from the second Herald* **188** thy] *Capell;* this QQ **189** with] QQ*;* by *conj. Capell* **192** SH] *Capell adds* SD: *receiving the Lance from the third Herald* **193** manly] Q1*;* manlike Q2 **197** conquer] Q2*;* vanquish Q1 **198** SH] *Capell adds* SD: *receiving the Shield from the fourth Herald* **204**] Q1*; as two lines, divided after* 'nought' Q2 **206** SH] Q2 (*P.Ed.*)*; not in* Q1 **209** good-presaging] *Capell after* Q2 (*no hyphen*)*;* good persaging Q1

183 base affections unworthy feelings.

189 Bellona The Roman goddess of war.

190 laurel victory laurel as token of victory. Compare *Ant.* 1.3.99–100: 'Upon your sword / Sit laurel victory.'

195 stratagems Used in a positive sense: 'acts of generalship' (*OED* Stratagem *sb* 1).

199 target round shield.

200 Perseus' shield Perseus succeeded in killing Medusa, whose sight transformed people into stone, by not looking at her directly but at her image reflected in a polished shield given him by Athena. Here (201–2) the paralysing effect of Medusa is transferred to the shield.

202 meagre lean.

204–5 See 172–218n.

206 forward (1) chief, foremost, (2) eager for action.

No otherwise than did old Jacob's words,
Whenas he breathed his blessings on his sons:
These hallowed gifts of yours when I profane,
Or use them not to glory of my God,
To patronage the fatherless and poor,
Or for the benefit of England's peace,
Be numb, my joints, wax feeble, both mine arms,
Wither, my heart, that like a sapless tree
I may remain the map of infamy.

KING EDWARD Then, thus our steelèd battles shall be ranged:
The leading of the vaward, Ned, is thine,
To dignify whose lusty spirit the more
We temper it with Audley's gravity,
That, courage and experience joined in one,
Your manage may be second unto none;
For the main battles I will guide myself,
And Derby in the rearward march behind.
That orderly disposed, and set in 'ray,
Let us to horse, and God grant us the day.

Exeunt

3.4. *Alarum. Enter a many Frenchmen flying. After them* PRINCE *Edward running. Then enter* KING JOHN *and the Duke of* LORRAINE

KING JOHN Oh, Lorraine, say, what mean our men to fly?

216 Be numb,] Be numbe Qq; Benumb *Tyrrell* **219** thus] Q2; this Q1 **219** battles] Qq (battailes); battle *Collier* Act 3, Scene 4 **3.4**] *Capell; no scene division in* Qq **0 SD.1** *Alarum*] Qq; *The same. Alarums / Capell* **0 SD.1–2** *After . . . running*] Qq; *Prince, and* English, *pursuing; and Exeunt / Capell*

210–11 See Gen. 48–9. Before dying in Egypt, Jacob blessed his three sons and prophesied their return to the land of their fathers.

214 patronage protect. Used as verb also by Shakespeare, *1H6* 3.1.48, 3.4.32.

218 map true picture, emblem.

219–28 The dramatist departs deliberately from the description of the deployment of the English forces at Crécy in the sources (see 3.2.62–6n.) in order to emphasise once again the union of the Prince's courage with Audley's experience (14n.) and to give the king the command of the main body of the army.

219 steelèd battles troops (see 3.1.97n.) in steel armour.

220 vaward vanguard.

224 manage conduct.

225 battles battalions, bodies of soldiers, as at 219; not, as Lapides suggests, 'engagements, encounters'.

227 set in 'ray deployed ('ray = array).

Act 3, Scene 4

3.4 The account of the battle of Crécy is a selective rendering of chs. 130–2 of Frois. (Metz, pp. 78–83), which are reproduced with slight variants in Hol., II, 637–40.

0 SD. 1–2 ***Alarum . . . running*** Alarums (loud noises, see *OED* Alarm *sb* 10) and the 'crossing of the stage' were the conventional signal to the audience of a battle in progress.

0 SD. 2 ***Duke of* LORRAINE** This character makes his last appearance here, though the play does not mention the fact, reported by Frois. and Hol., that he was one of the 'Eleven princes of esteem' (109) slain at Crécy.

Our number is far greater than our foes'.
LORRAINE The garrison of Genoese, my lord,
That came from Paris, weary of their march,
Grudging to be suddenly employed,
No sooner in the forefront took their place
But straight retiring, so dismayed the rest
As likewise they betook themselves to flight.
In which, for haste to make a safe escape,
More in the clustering throng are pressed to death
Than by the enemy, a thousandfold.
KING JOHN O hapless fortune! Let us yet assay
If we can counsel some of them to stay. [*Exeunt*]

Enter KING EDWARD *and* AUDLEY

KING EDWARD Lord Audley, whiles our son is in the chase,
Withdraw our powers unto this little hill,
And here a season let us breathe ourselves.
AUDLEY I will, my lord. *Exit.*

Sound retreat

KING EDWARD Just-dooming heaven, whose secret providence
To our gross judgement is inscrutable,
How are we bound to praise thy wondrous works,
That hast this day given way unto the right,

3 Genoese] *Capell* (*Genoeses*)*;* Genoaes Qq 5 suddenly] Qq*;* so suddenly *Capell, WP, TB* **10** clustering throng] Q1*;* clustring through Q2 13 SD.1] Q2*; not in* Q1 13 SD.2 *Enter*] Qq*;* SCENE V. *The same. Drums. Enter / Capell and all mod. edns, subst.* 15 our] Q1*;* your Q2, *Capell, WP* 17 SD.2 *Sound*] Q1*; not in* Q2 18 Just-dooming] *Capell;* Iust dooming Qq

3–11 The dramatist follows closely the account in Frois. (Metz, pp. 78–9), but the wording is that of Hol. (II, 638): the 'Genowaies crosbowes . . . were commanded to go on before, and with their shot to begin the battell; but they were so werie with going on foot that morning six leagues armed with their crosbowes' that they at first refused to fight, and later, attacked by the English archers, 'cast downe their crosbowes, and cut the strings, and returned discomfited'. See Appendix, p. 205.

5 suddenly so soon. The line lacks one syllable, and editors supply 'so' before 'suddenly'.

10 throng Q2's 'through' is a miscorrection discussed in the Textual Analysis, p. 176. Compare Hol., II, 638: 'manie fell horsse and man amongst the Genowayes . . . and when they were once downe they could not recouer againe. The throng was such that one ouerthrew another.' Frois. uses 'preace' (= press) for 'throng'.

13 SD.2 All modern editions, except Smith and WAA, begin a new scene at this point. In fact the brief exchange between King John and Lorraine (1–13) is not a separate scene, but part of the description of the battle represented in dumb show in the opening stage direction (0 SD. 1–2 n.).

13 SD.2 AUDLEY According to the battle plan (3.3.220–4), Audley should not be with the king but with Prince Edward. Historically he was not present at Crécy.

15 our Q2's 'your' is a misunderstanding by the reviser of the copy.

15 little hill All historians report that Edward took position for the day on a 'little windmill hill' overlooking the battlefield. The place is now known as 'Moulin Edouard III'.

16 breathe ourselves take breath, pause.

And made the wicked stumble at themselves.

Enter ARTOIS

ARTOIS Rescue, King Edward, rescue for thy son!
KING EDWARD Rescue, Artois? What, is he prisoner?
Or by violence fell beside his horse?
ARTOIS Neither, my lord, but narrowly beset
With turning Frenchmen, whom he did pursue,
As 'tis impossible that he should scape,
Except your highness presently descend.
KING EDWARD Tut, let him fight; we gave him arms today,
And he is labouring for a knighthood, man.

Enter DERBY

DERBY The prince, my lord, the prince! Oh, succour him!
He's close encompassed with a world of odds.
KING EDWARD Then will he win a world of honour too,
If he by valour can redeem him thence.
If not, what remedy? We have more sons
Than one, to comfort our declining age.

Enter AUDLEY

AUDLEY Renownèd Edward, give me leave, I pray,
To lead my soldiers where I may relieve
Your grace's son, in danger to be slain.
The snares of French, like emmets on a bank,
Muster about him, whilst he, lion-like,

22 SD, 31 SD, 37 SD] *Capell adds* / *hastily* / *to each* SD 23 SH] Q2 (*Art.*)*;* *not in* Q1 25 Or] Qq*;* Or, else, *Capell* 25 fell] Qq*;* fell'd *anon. conj. apud Collier* 28 As] Qq*;* And *conj. Melchiori* 28 'tis] Q1*;* it is Q2 37 declining] Q1*;* declying Q2 42 lion-like] *Capell;* Lion like Qq

23–69 According to the chronicles not three knights, but a single messenger was sent to ask for the king's intervention, see Appendix, p. 206.

25 fell felled. Compare Frois. (Metz, p. 80): 'Is my sonne deed or hurt, or on the yerthe felled?'

27 turning facing about.

28 As So that. Possibly 'As' is a printer's misreading of 'And'.

28 scape Not an elided form, but a current alternative of 'escape'.

31 labouring . . . knighthood The hint at the knighting of the Prince is clearer in Frois. ('this day to wynne his spurres', see 3.3.172–218n.) than in Hol., who puts the whole sentence in the plural. Compare the passage reproduced in the Appendix, p. 206.

33 a . . . odds adverse circumstances.

34 Compare Frois. (Metz, p. 80): 'for if god be pleased, I woll this iourney [= day] be his, and the honoure therof'.

35 redeem him free himself.

36–7 more . . . one At the time of Crécy, Lionel of Clarence was eight, John of Gaunt (the future Lancaster) six, and Edmund Langley (the future York) five. Thomas of Woodstock was born ten years later.

41 emmets . . . bank ants on an ant-hill.

Entangled in the net of their assaults,
Franticly rends and bites the woven toil.
But all in vain, he cannot free himself.

KING EDWARD Audley, content. I will not have a man,
On pain of death, sent forth to succour him.
This is the day, ordained by destiny,
To season his courage with those grievous thoughts
That, if he breaketh out, Nestor's years on earth
Will make him savour still of this exploit.

DERBY Ah, but he shall not live to see those days.

KING EDWARD Why, then his epitaph is lasting praise.

AUDLEY Yet, good my lord, 'tis too much wilfulness
To let his blood be spilt, that may be saved.

KING EDWARD Exclaim no more, for none of you can tell
Whether a borrowed aid will serve or no.
Perhaps he is already slain or ta'en;
And, dare a falcon when she's in her flight,
And ever after she'll be haggard-like.
Let Edward be delivered by our hands,
And still, in danger, he'll expect the like;
But if himself, himself redeem from thence
He will have vanquished, cheerful, death and fear,
And ever after dread their force no more
Than if they were but babes or captive slaves.

AUDLEY O cruel father! Farewell Edward, then.

DERBY Farewell, sweet prince, the hope of chivalry.

ARTOIS Oh, would my life might ransom him from death!

KING EDWARD But soft, methinks I hear

44 rends] Qq (wrends) **44** bites] Q2 (bytes); byts Q1 **49** his . . . thoughts] Qq; his green courage with those thoughts *Capell, Tyrrell, Collier* **50** breaketh out,] Qq; breathe out *Delius, Collier, conj. Capell* **50** earth] Q2; earth, Q1, *Capell, Delius, Collier* **53** epitaph] *Capell and mod. edns;* Epitaph, Qq **54** SH] Q2 (*Aud.*); *An.* Q1 **54** good my] Qq; my good *Collier* **60** haggard] Q2; huggard Q1 **64** vanquished, cheerful,] *Capell;* vanquisht cheerefull Qq **69**] Qq; *not in Collier* **70** But] Qq; Forbear, my lords, – But *Capell* **70** hear] Qq; hear [*Retreat sounded* / *Capell*

44 woven toil A net set as a snare to capture wild animals (*OED* Toil *sb*[2] 1–2).

48 This . . . day See Frois. quoted in 34n.

49 season temper.

49 those . . . thoughts such grave responsibilities.

50 if . . . out if he forces his way out (WP).

50–1 Nestor's . . . exploit He will still take pleasure in the memory of this exploit even if he lives as long as Nestor, proverbial among the Greeks at the siege of Troy for his age and wisdom (Dent, *PLED*, N126.11).

53 his . . . praise he will have eternal glory for an epitaph.

59–60 dare . . . haggard-like If a falcon is intercepted ('dare' = 'interfere with') in her flight to catch a prey, she becomes useless for future employment. 'Haggard', in falconry a wild female hawk, was synonymous with 'untrained, intractable' (*OED* Haggard *sb*[2] 2, for the compound 'haggard-like').

64 cheerful Used adverbially.

The dismal charge of trumpets' loud retreat:
All are not slain, I hope, that went with him –
Some will return with tidings, good or bad.

Enter PRINCE *Edward in triumph, bearing in his hand his shivered lance, and [the body of] the King of* BOHEMIA *borne before, wrapped in the colours. They run and embrace him*

AUDLEY O joyful sight, victorious Edward lives!
DERBY Welcome, brave prince.
KING EDWARD Welcome, Plantagenet.
PRINCE (*Kneels and kisses his father's hand*) First having done my duty as beseemed,
Lords, I regreet you all with hearty thanks.
And now, behold, after my winter's toil,
My painful voyage on the boist'rous sea
Of war's devouring gulfs and steely rocks,
I bring my fraught unto the wishèd port,
My summer's hope, my travel's sweet reward,
And here with humble duty I present
This sacrifice, this first fruit of my sword,
Cropped and cut down even at the gate of death:
The King of Boheme, father, whom I slew,
Whose thousands had entrenched me round about,
And lay as thick upon my battered crest

73 SD.1 *Enter*] QQ; *Flourish. Enter* / *Capell* 73 SD.1 *lance,*] QQ; *Lance; his Sword, and batter'd Armour, born before him* / *Capell* 73 SD.2 *the body of*] *Capell (omitting* / *borne before*/); *not in* QQ 76 SD] QQ (*kneele . . . kisse*), *in right margin opposits 75–7* 84 this first] QQ; the first *Collier* 86 Boheme] Q1; Bohemia Q2 87 Whose thousands] *Capell and most mod. edns;* Whom you said QQ; Who you said *Collier;* Who you saw *anon. conj. apud Collier*

71 **charge** injunction (*OED* sv *sb* 15). The trumpets sound the order of retreat.

73 SD.1 ***shivered*** shattered in combat.

73 SD.2 ***the colours*** the Bohemian flag. See 86n.

73 SD.2–3 ***They . . . him*** Compare Frois., ch. 131 (Metz, p. 81): 'Than he went with all his batayle to his sonne the prince and enbraced hym in his armes and kyst hym.'

76 SD Compare Frois. (Metz, p. 82): 'the prince inclyned himselfe to the yearthe, honouryng the kyng his father'.

76 **done . . . beseemed** paid homage in the proper form ('as beseemed').

77 **regreet** greet again.

78–85 The battle is compared to a winter sea-journey.

81 **fraught** freight.

86 The form 'Boheme' (Q1) is adopted for metrical reasons. Hol. (II, 638, based on Frois.) reports that the King of Bohemia 'went so far forward, that ioining with his enimies he fought right valiantlie, and so did all his companie: but finallie being entred within the prease of their enimies, they were of them inclosed and slaine, togither with the king their master, and the next daie founde dead lieng about him'. The dramatist reverses the situation, presenting (87–98) the Prince surrounded by the Bohemians. In fact the Prince never encountered the King of Bohemia, but fought with the Earls of Alençon and of Flanders.

87 **Whose thousands** Editors accept Capell's palaeographically sound emendation, but Lapides defends QQ's 'Whom you said' as referring to the king's speeches at 30–1, 34–7, 46–51, and remarks: 'the author has forgotten that the king's words could not have been heard by his son'.

88 **lay . . . upon** belaboured (*OED* Lie v^1 6).

As on an anvil with their ponderous glaives.
Yet marble courage still did underprop,
And when my weary arms, with often blows,
Like the continual labouring woodman's axe
That is enjoined to fell a load of oaks,
Began to falter, straight I would recover
My gifts you gave me and my zealous vow –
And then new courage made me fresh again,
That, in despite, I carved my passage forth,
And put the multitude to speedy flight.
Lo, thus hath Edward's hand filled your request,
And done, I hope, the duty of a knight.

KING EDWARD Ay, well thou hast deserved a knighthood, Ned,
And therefore with thy sword, yet reeking warm

His sword borne by a soldier

With blood of those that fought to be thy bane,
Arise, Prince Edward, trusty knight at arms.
This day thou hast confounded me with joy,
And proved thyself fit heir unto a king.

PRINCE Here is a note, my gracious lord, of those
That in this conflict of our foes were slain:
Eleven princes of esteem, fourscore barons,

94 recover] Qq, *RLA;* remember *Capell, Delius, WP;* record *TB* **97** carved] caru'd Q2*;* craud Q1 **99** thus] Q2*;* this Q1 **102** reeking] reaking Q1*;* wreaking Q2 **102** SD] *As in* Q2 *and all mod. edns; in margin of 98–100* Q1*; receiving it from the Soldier who bore it, and laying it on the kneeling Prince / Capell* **103** that fought] Qq*;* who sought *Collier* **109–11**] *So divided* Qq, *TB, RLA; as four lines, divided at* score / knights; / soldiers; / *Capell, WP, Smith, WAA* **109–10** barons . . . knights] Qq*;* Barons, and earls; a hundred twenty knights *Capell, Tyrrell (subst.), Collier*

89 glaives spears, consisting of blades fastened to long handles.

90 marble enduring; an attributive usage, see *OED* sv *sb* 7c.

90 underprop support me. A rare intransitive usage.

91 often Used as adjective: frequent, continuous.

94 recover recall, bring back to memory (*OED* sv *v*[1] 8b). The emendations suggested (see Collation), though plausible, are unnecessary.

95 zealous earnest.

97 carved This, a revision appearing in Q2, is an improvement on Q1's 'craud' (= craved).

102–4 Knighthood was conferred by imposing (dubbing) a sword on the shoulders of the kneeling figure of the recipient.

102 reeking Q2's 'wreaking' is a wrong correction by the reviser, noted in the Textual Analysis, p. 177.

103 fought Collier's suggestion, 'sought', though a plausible long s/f confusion, is unnecessary.

103 bane murderer, destroyer (*OED* sv sb[1] 1); compare *Tit.*5.3.73: 'Let Rome herself be bane unto herself.'

105–6 Compare Frois. (Metz, p. 80): 'fayre sonne, god gyue you good perseuerance, ye ar my good son, thus ye haue aquyted you nobly, ye ar worthy to kepe a realme'. Hol. (II, 639) elaborates the last sentence.

107–11 The list of the enemy losses is reproduced verbatim from the sources (Frois., ch. 132, Hol., II, 640) with a single mistake: the knights killed were not a hundred and twenty but twelve hundred (xii.C in Frois., 12 hundred in Hol.).

A hundred and twenty knights, and thirty thousand
Common soldiers; and of our men, a thousand.

KING EDWARD Our God be praised. Now, John of France, I hope
Thou knowest King Edward for no wantonness,
No love-sick cockney, nor his soldiers jades.
But which way is the fearful king escaped?

PRINCE Towards Poitiers, noble father – and his sons.

KING EDWARD Ned, thou and Audley shall pursue them still;
Myself and Derby will to Calais straight,
And there begirt that haven town with siege.
Now lies it on an upshot, therefore strike
And wistly follow whiles the game's on foot. –
What picture's this?

PRINCE A pelican, my lord,
Wounding her bosom with her crooked beak,
That so her nest of young ones might be fed
With drops of blood that issue from her heart.
The motto *Sic et vos*: 'And so should you'.

Exeunt

111 Common] Q1; Priuate Q2, *Capell etc.* **112** SH] Q2 (*K.Ed.*); *not in* Q1 **112–13**] *So divided* Q1; *lines divided after* France, / Q2 **114** love-sick] *Capell;* loue sicke Qq **116** Poitiers] Poyctiers Qq **118** Calais] Calice Qq *(throughout play, but* / Callis / *at times* Q1*)* **122** What] Q2; *Ki.* What Q1 **122** picture's this?] Q1 (Pictures this.); picture is this? Q2; picture's this? [*pointing to the Colours* / *Capell* **124** might] Q1; may Q2 **126** SD] Q1; *not in* Q2

111 Common soldiers Q2's 'Private' is a curious refinement on Q1's 'Common' to designate the French casualties listed in Hol. as 'other of the meaner sort' and in Frois. simply as 'other'.

112 Our . . . praised Frois. (Metz, p. 80): 'the kynge wolde that no manne shulde be proude, or make boost, but euery man humbly to thanke god.' Hol. (II, 639) amplifies this statement.

112–14 Now . . . jades Edward's retort to King John's speech at 3.3.155–62, with a further allusion to the Countess of Salisbury episode. For 'wantonness' = 'wanton' see 3.3.156n., and for 'jades' 3.3.162n.

114 cockney milksop (*OED* sv *sb* 2). Compare *TN* 4.2.15.

116 Poitiers Historically incorrect. The mention of the town (the capital of Poitou, over three hundred miles away) signals the author's intention to drastically compress the acting time, by making the battle (presented in Act 4) which took place on 19 September 1356 at Poitiers, follow closely upon that of Crécy (26 August 1346).

118–19 will . . . Calais will proceed to Calais. Substantially correct: Edward moved directly from Crécy through Montreuil and Boulogne to Calais, and began the siege of the harbour town on 30 August 1346 (Hol., II, 640, Frois., chs. 132–3).

120 lies . . . upshot depends on the final stroke. 'Upshot' was the last shot in an archery competition, determining its result (*OED* Upshot *sb* 1).

121 wistly attentively, intently, see 2.2.88n.

121 the . . . foot A common hunting expression: the prey is roused (and must be pursued). See *H5* 3.1.32–3: 'The game's afoot! Follow your spirits.'

122–6 The scene is obviously concluded at 121. The presence of these additional five lines is puzzling. The pelican feeding its young with its own heart-blood, blasoned as 'a pelican at its piety', was an emblem of self-sacrifice, and the Latin motto implies that all should be ready to follow its example, i.e. to give their lives for their kin, their king or their God, a meaning discussed in the Appendix, p. 207. 'Azure, three pelicans argent, vulning [wounding] themselves proper', were the arms of the Pelham family, quartered with two belts, an addition reputedly granted Sir William Pelham in 1356 for having captured King John of France at Poitiers. The latter is an unfounded tradition unrecorded by

4.1. *Enter Lord* MOUNTFORD *with a coronet in his hand, with him the Earl of* SALISBURY

MOUNTFORD My lord of Salisbury, since by your aid
Mine enemy, Sir Charles of Blois, is slain,
And I again am quietly possessed
In Bretagne's dukedom, know that I resolve,
For this kind furtherance of your king and you,
To swear allegiance to his majesty.
In sign whereof receive this coronet,
Bear it unto him, and withal my oath
Never to be but Edward's faithful friend.
SALISBURY I take it, Mountford. Thus I hope ere long
The whole dominion of the realm of France

Act 4, Scene 1 4.1] *Capell; no act or scene division in* Qq 0 SD *Enter*] Q1*; Enter the* Q2*;* Bretagne. *Camp of the* English *Forces under the Earl of* Salisbury; Salisbury's *Tent. Enter/ Capell; Bretagne. Camp of the English. Enter / WP, TB etc.; Brittany. Camp of Mountford and Salisbury. Enter / RLA* 1 your] Q2*;* our Q1 4 Bretagne's] *RLA;* Btittaines Q1*;* Brytanes Q2*;* Britain's *Smith* 8 withal my] Q2*;* with all mine Q1 10 Mountford] Q2*;* Mountfort Q1

either Frois. or Hol., but the dramatist may have learnt it from other sources, and, having decided to transfer the honour of the capture to the Black Prince, he wrote this passage on a separate slip of paper for insertion at the conclusion of 4.7, but later changed his mind, and the lines were erroneously added at this point during the printing; see Textual Analysis, p. 173.

Act 4, Scene 1

4.1 This scene, as well as 4.3.1–56 and 4.5.56–126 (with further references in 5.1.97–156), dramatises an episode found only in Frois., immediately after the account of the battle of Crécy and of the beginning of the siege of Calais: ch. 135 (Metz, pp. 84–5) 'Howe sir Gaultier de Manny rode through all Fraunce by save conduct to Calys'. The persons and places figuring in the episode have been replaced by others in order to fit into the plot of the play, see Appendix, p. 208. The location has therefore been transferred from Aiguillon (Frois., ch. 134, Ker, I, 306) to Brittany, in order to establish a link with events hinted at in 1.1.132–5.

0 SD.1–2 ***Earl of*** **SALISBURY** The introduction of the Earl of Salisbury (the sources report his death upon his return from imprisonment in France in 1341 – Painter – or during a tournament at Windsor in 1344 – Holinshed) follows a hint in 1.1.133–4, where his absence from the siege of Roxborough is attributed to his being in Brittany, helping to establish Lord Mountford. The English commander in Brittany had been in fact Walter de Manny, who had earlier accompanied Salisbury in the Scottish campaign of 1332, and, after defeating Charles of Blois in Brittany in 1341–2, was engaged in 1346 against the Duke of Normandy in Gascony, see Appendix, p. 202.

1 SH Historically, Lord Mountford (Jean IV de Montfort) died in captivity in the Louvre, where he had been imprisoned in 1341 (Frois., ch. 72, Ker, I, 184–5). Brittany was saved by the heroic resistance of his wife, Jeanne of Flanders, for whom see Appendix, with reference to 1.1 (pp. 182 and 185) and 1.2 (pp. 187–8).

2 Sir . . . slain Charles of Blois was not killed but taken prisoner by the English during a new attempt to conquer Brittany in 1347 (battle of Roche-Derrien, Frois., chs. 142–3, Ker, I, 321–4). He was ransomed and survived till 1364. For the confusion here see Appendix, n. 23.

4–9 know . . . friend The sequence of events is transposed. Mountford declared his allegiance to King Edward in 1341, in order to obtain England's support against Charles of Blois's claim to the dukedom of Brittany (Frois., ch. 68, Metz, pp. 62–3: 'Howe the erle Mountfort dyd homage to the kyng of England for the duchy of Bretayne'). See Appendix, pp. 185 and 209.

Will be surrendered to his conquering hand.

Exit [*Mountford*]

Now, if I knew but safely how to pass,
I would at Calais gladly meet his grace,
Whither I am by letters certified
That he intends to have his host removed.
It shall be so, this policy will serve. –
Ho, who's within? – Bring Villiers to me.

Enter VILLIERS

Villiers, thou knowest thou art my prisoner,
And that I might for ransom, if I would,
Require of thee a hundred thousand francs,
Or else retain and keep thee captive still.
But so it is, that for a smaller charge
Thou mayst be quit, and if thou wilt thyself.
And this it is: procure me but a passport
Of Charles the Duke of Normandy, that I
Without restraint may have recourse to Calais
Through all the countries where he hath to do –
Which thou mayst easily obtain, I think,
By reason I have often heard thee say
He and thou were students once together –
And then thou shalt be set at liberty.
How sayest thou? Wilt thou undertake to do it?

VILLIERS I will, my lord, but I must speak with him.

12 SD] *Capell, subst.; Exit* Q1; *not in* Q2 14 at] *Capell;* to Qq 15 Whither] Q2; Whether Q1 16 That] *Capell;* Yet Qq 21 a] Q1; an Q2 31 thou] Qq; thyself *Capell* 31 were] Q1; wert Q2 32 thou] Qq; thyself *Collier*

14 at Calais Qq's 'to Calais' echoes 3.4.118, 'Myself . . . will to Calais straight', omitting the verb of motion after an auxiliary and before 'to' (compare Abbott 405). The author meant 'I would [go] to Calais [and there] meet his grace', but the awkward ellipsis forces the change from 'to' to 'at', introduced by Capell.

16 That Qq's 'Yet' is a wrong expansion of the common abbreviation 'y[t]' for 'that', but WP prefer 'yet' in the sense 'now, by this time (German jetzt)'.

18 Villiers An invention of the dramatist. Frois. (ch. 135, Metz, p. 84) does not name the 'knyght of Normandy' held prisoner for ransom by Walter de Manny (= Salisbury), see Appendix, p. 209, for its possible origin.

19–32 These lines, except for the identity of the speakers, echo closely and at times verbatim Frois., ch. 135 (Metz, p. 84), quoted in the Appendix, p. 208.

24 and . . . thyself if you are so disposed; 'and if' = if indeed (Abbott 105).

26 Charles . . . Normandy The Duke of Normandy referred to by Frois. at this point was not Prince Charles, but his father John, who became King of France in 1350 and transferred that title to his firstborn.

27 have . . . to have the possibility of going to (*OED* Recourse *sb*[1] 5).

28 through all the territories under his (the Duke of Normandy's) control.

SALISBURY Why, so thou shalt: take horse and post from hence.
Only, before thou goest, swear by thy faith
That, if thou canst not compass my desire,
Thou wilt return my prisoner back again,
And that shall be sufficient warrant for me.
VILLIERS To that condition I agree, my lord,
And will unfeignedly perform the same. *Exit*
SALISBURY Farewell, Villiers.
Thus once I mean to try a Frenchman's faith. *Exit*

4.2. *Enter* KING EDWARD *and* DERBY, *with Soldiers*

KING EDWARD Since they refuse our proffered league, my lord,
And will not ope their gates and let us in,
We will entrench ourselves on every side,
That neither victuals, nor supply of men
May come to succour this accursed town:
Famine shall combat where our swords are stopped.

Enter six POOR *Frenchmen*

DERBY The promised aid that made them stand aloof
Is now retired and gone another way:
It will repent them of their stubborn will. –
But what are these poor ragged slaves, my lord?
KING EDWARD Ask what they are; it seems they come from Calais.

39 me] Qq; thee *Capell, WP* **43** Thus] Qq; This *Delius, conj. Capell* Act 4, Scene 2 **4.2**] *Capell; no scene division in* Qq **0 SD** *Enter*] Qq; Picardy. *The* English *Camp before* Calais. *Enter*/ *Capell* **2** their] Q1; the Q2 **6 SD**] *As in* Qq; *after 9 / Capell* **6 SD** *six*] Qq (*sixe*); *some / Capell* **11**] *One line* Q1; *as two lines, divided after* 'seemes' Q2

36–9 Frois. (Metz, p. 84): 'if ye can nat do this [procure the safe-conduct], retourne agayn hyder within a moneth, and yelde yourself styll as my prisoner'.

Act 4, Scene 2

4.2 The location is outside the walls of Calais. The episode of the poor citizens is from Frois., ch. 133 (Metz, pp. 83–4), and the report on the Scottish campaign of 1346 from chs. 138–9 (Metz, pp. 85–8). Compare Hol., II, 642–3 and 644–5.

0 SD DERBY At the time of the siege of Calais the Earl of Derby was engaged in Gascony and Poitou, see Frois., ch. 136 (Ker, I, 308–11), discussed in Appendix, pp. 206 and 208.

1–9 Frois. (Metz, p. 83) 'The kyng wolde nat assayle the towne of Calys, for he thought it but a lost labour; he spared his peple and his artillery, and sayd, howe he wolde famysshe them in the towne with a long siege, without the French kyng come and reyse his siege perforce.'

6 SD *six* According to Frois. (Metz, pp. 83–4) 'on a Wednysday ther yssued out of men, women, and chyldren, mo than xvii. C. [seventeen hundred]'. The dramatist reduces them to six by analogy with the episode of the six burghers presented in 5.1.7–59, and anticipated here at 73–8. There is no need to move the SD (see Collation): the poor people enter quietly while Derby is speaking and are noticed only at 9.

DERBY You wretched patterns of despair and woe,
What are you, living men or gliding ghosts,
Crept from your graves to walk upon the earth?
FIRST POOR MAN No ghosts, my lord, but men that breathe a life
Far worse than is the quiet sleep of death.
We are distressèd poor inhabitants
That long have been diseasèd, sick, and lame;
And now, because we are not fit to serve,
The captain of the town hath thrust us forth,
That so expense of victuals may be saved.
KING EDWARD A charitable deed, no doubt, and worthy praise!
But how do you imagine then to speed?
We are your enemies, in such a case
We can no less but put you to the sword,
Since, when we proffered truce, it was refused.
FIRST POOR MAN And if your grace no otherwise vouchsafe,
As welcome death is unto us as life.
KING EDWARD Poor silly men, much wronged, and more distressed!
Go, Derby, go, and see they be relieved,
Command that victuals be appointed them
And give to everyone five crowns apiece.
[*Exeunt Derby and the poor Frenchmen*]
The lion scorns to touch the yielding prey,
And Edward's sword must flesh itself in such
As wilful stubborness hath made perverse.

Enter Lord PERCY

12 patterns] Q1; partners Q2 13 What are you] Q1; What, are ye Q2 15 SH] *This edn after* Qq (*Poore*); *I. F. / Capell; First Fr. / Smith* 15 breathe] Q2; breath Q1 22 no doubt] Qq; *not in Capell, Tyrrell, Delius* 25 you] Q2; ye Q1 27 SH] *This edn after* Q2 (*Poore*); *So:/* Q1 30 Go, Derby] Qq; Good Derby *conj. Capell* 32 SD] *Capell* (*subst.*); *not in* Qq 34 flesh] *Collier, conj. Delius, TB;* fresh Qq

12 patterns pictures; more effective than the reviser's improvement, 'partners', found in Q2.

17–21 Frois. (Metz, pp. 83–4): 'Whan the capten of Calys sawe the manner and thorder of thenglysshmen, than he constrayned all poore and meane peple to yssue out of the towne . . . as they passed through the hoost they were demaunded why they departed, and they answered and sayd, bycause they had nothyng to lyue on.'

22 no doubt Hypermetrical for emphasis.

23 speed survive.

27 no . . . vouchsafe allows no alternative.

29 silly helpless, see 1.1.137n.

30–2 Frois. (Metz, p. 84): 'Than the kyng dyd them that grace, that he suffred them to passe through his host without danger, and gaue them mete and drinke to dyner, and euery person ii.d. [2 pence] sterlyng in almes.'

33 Proverbial (Tilley L316), based on a belief mentioned by Warwick in one of his 'virtuous sentences' at 2.1.397–8, see n.

34–5 flesh . . . As plunge into the flesh of those whom (*OED* Flesh *v* 3). Compare *1H6* 4.7.36: 'did flesh his puny sword in Frenchmen's blood'.

35 perverse stubborn in their error (*OED* sv *a* 2).

35 SD *Lord* PERCY Lord Percy is mentioned by Frois. (ch. 138, Metz, p. 86) as a leader of those peers (see 43) who defeated King David of Scotland in the 1346 campaign.

Lord Percy, welcome. What's the news in England?
PERCY The queen, my lord, comes here to your grace,
And from her highness, and the lord vicegerent,
I bring this happy tidings of success:
David of Scotland, lately up in arms,
Thinking belike he soonest should prevail,
Your highness being absent from the realm,
Is, by the fruitful service of your peers
And painful travail of the queen herself,
That, big with child, was every day in arms,
Vanquished, subdued, and taken prisoner.
KING EDWARD Thanks, Percy, for thy news, with all my heart.
What was he took him prisoner in the field?
PERCY A squire, my lord; John Copland is his name,
Who since, entreated by her majesty,
Denies to make surrender of his prize
To any but unto your grace alone,
Whereat the queen is grievously displeased.
KING EDWARD Well, then we'll have a pursuivant dispatched
To summon Copland hither out of hand,
And with him he shall bring his prisoner king.

36 Lord Percy] *Mod. edns; Ki:* Lord Persie Q1; *K. E.* Lord Percie Q2 **37** comes here] Qq; commends her *Capell, WP, RLA* **43** fruitful] Q1; faithfull Q2 **44** travail] trauell Qq **49** squire] Q2; Esquire Q1 **54** dispatched] dispatcht Q2; dispatch Q1

36–56 Closely modelled on Frois., chs. 138–9 (Metz, pp. 85–7).

37 comes here Capell's emendation 'commends her[self]', the usual form in messages, is very attractive and mends the metre, but Percy may be anticipating here the announcement at 57–9.

38 lord vicegerent When he left England for France in July 1346, Edward 'stablysshed the lorde Persy and the lorde Neuyll [Neville] to be wardyns of his realme' (Frois., ch. 121, Ker, I, 276).

43 fruitful Q2's 'faithful' seems to be another 'improvement' by the reviser replacing the significant with the obvious.

44 painful travail painstaking efforts, with an allusion to the travail of childbirth (45), as well as to the risks of Channel crossing (37 and see 5.1.160–1). Qq's wording is deliberately ambiguous, since 'trauell' was a current alternative spelling of 'travail'.

45 big . . . child Queen Philippa's pregnancy is mentioned by Frois. (ch. 146, Metz, p. 91) only when she pleads for the life of the burghers of Calais (see 5.1.39–59) a year later. She was delivered of a daughter, Margaret, in Calais in September 1347.

50–2 entreated . . . alone Compare Frois., ch. 139 (Metz, p. 87): 'Whan the quenes letter [commanding to deliver to her King David] was brought to Johan Coplande, he answered and sayd, that as for the kyng of Scottes his prisoner, he wolde nat delyuer hym to no man nor woman lyueng, but all onely to the kynge of Englande his souerayne lorde.'

54–5 See Frois., ch. 139 (Metz, p. 87): 'Than the kyng sende incontynent to Johan Copland, that he shulde come ouer to see hym to the siege before Calays'; 'pursuivant' = state messenger; 'out of hand' = at once.

56 History is altered for dramatic reasons: Copland did not take King David with him to Calais. Upon his return to England he surrendered the prisoner to Queen Philippa, who sent him to the Tower of London.

PERCY The queen's, my lord, herself by this at sea,
And purposeth, as soon as wind will serve,
To land at Calais, and to visit you.
KING EDWARD She shall be welcome, and to wait her coming
I'll pitch my tent near to the sandy shore.

Enter a [French] CAPTAIN

CAPTAIN The burgesses of Calais, mighty prince,
Have by a council willingly decreed
To yield the town and castle to your hands,
Upon condition it will please your grace
To grant them benefit of life and goods.
KING EDWARD They will so? Then, belike, they may command,
Dispose, elect, and govern as they list!
No, sirrah, tell them, since they did refuse
Our princely clemency at first proclaimed,
They shall not have it now, although they would.
I will accept of nought but fire and sword,
Except, within these two days, six of them,
That are the wealthiest merchants in the town,
Come naked, all but for their linen shirts,
With each a halter hanged about his neck,
And prostrate yield themselves upon their knees,
To be afflicted, hanged, or what I please;
And so you may inform their masterships.
Exeunt [all but Captain]

57 queen's . . . herself] Q2; Queene . . . her selfe Q1; queen . . . herself's *conj. Capell* **61** SD *French*] *Capell; not in* Qq **62** SH] Q2; *not in* Q1 **67** so?] *RLA;* so: Qq; so! *Capell, WP, TB* **72** I will] Q2; Will Q1 *(but* /I will/ *as catchword)* **73** these] Q1; this Q2 **79** SD *all . . . Captain*] *This edn; not in* Qq; *Edward and Derby* / *Capell and mod. edns, subst.*

57–61 Compare Frois., ch. 139 (Metz, p. 88): 'she went to Douer and there tooke the see, and had so good wynde, that in a shorte space she arryued before Calays, thre dayes before the feest of Al Sayntes [28 October 1346], for whose commyng the kyng made a great feest and dyner, to all the lordes and ladyes that were ther'.

62–79 The report of the conditions for the surrender of Calais is faithful to Frois., ch. 146 (Metz, pp. 88–9), though the negotiations with the Captain of the town, Jean de Vienne, were not conducted personally by the king but through Sir Walter de Manny, see Appendix, p. 210.

67 belike perhaps (ironical).

68 list please.

73 Except Unless.

73–8 six . . . please Compare Frois., ch. 146 (Metz, p. 89): 'say to the capytayne that all the grace that he shall finde nowe in me is that they lette sixe of the chiefe burgesses of the towne come out bare heeded, bare foted and bare legged, and in their shertes, with haulters about their neckes, with the kayes of the towne and castell in their handes and lette theym sixe yelde themselfe purely to my wyll'.

79 their masterships those gentlemen (ironical).

CAPTAIN Why, this it is to trust a broken staff.
Had we not been persuaded John our king
Would with his army have relieved the town,
We had not stood upon defiance so.
But now 'tis past that no man can recall,
And better some do go to wrack, than all. *Exit*

4.3. *Enter* [*Prince*] CHARLES [*Duke*] *of Normandy and* VILLIERS

CHARLES I wonder, Villiers, thou shouldst importune me
For one that is our deadly enemy.
VILLIERS Not for his sake, my gracious lord, so much
Am I become an earnest advocate,
As that thereby my ransom will be quit.
CHARLES Thy ransom, man? Why needst thou talk of that?
Art thou not free? And are not all occasions
That happen for advantage of our foes
To be accepted of and stood upon?
VILLIERS No, good my lord, except the same be just;
For profit must with honour be commixed,
Or else our actions are but scandalous.
But, letting pass these intricate objections,
Will't please your highness to subscribe, or no?
CHARLES Villiers, I will not nor I cannot do it;
Salisbury shall not have his will so much

Act 4, Scene 3 4.3] *Capell; no scene division in* QQ 0 SD *Enter*] QQ; Poitou. *Fields near* Poitiers. *The* French *Camp; Tent of the Duke of* Normandy. *Enter*/ *Capell* 6 man? Why needst] *TB, RLA;* man: why needest Q1; man, why, needst Q2; man! why, need'st *Capell;* man? why, needest *WP;* man! why need'st *Smith* 8 of our] QQ; on our *Delius, conj. Capell;* over *conj. Collier* 9 and stood] QQ; unstood *conj. Capell* 14 Will't] *Smith, WAA;* Wilt QQ *and most mod. edns*

80 **trust . . . staff** Proverbial, Tilley S805, ultimately from Isaiah 36.6. The Captain seeks comfort in popular wisdom, see 84, 85.

83 **stood . . . defiance** resisted.

84 **'tis . . . recall** Compare 'Things past cannot be recalled' Tilley T203.

85 **better . . . all** Another proverb, 'Better one die than all' (Tilley O42), from John 11.50.

Act 4, Scene 3

4.3 The first part of the scene (1–56) develops the safe-conduct episode (see 4.1), turning into a debate on the rules of chivalry a single sentence in Frois., ch. 135 (Metz, p. 84), reported in the Appendix, p. 210. The date (1346) is moved forward by ten years and the location changed from Paris to the Poitou region, connecting the episode to the battle of Poitiers (19 September 1356), the subject of the second part of the scene (57–85).

8 **for . . . foes** to give us advantage over our enemies.

9 **stood upon** made the most of (*OED* Stand *v* 78i).

To claim a passport how it pleaseth himself.
VILLIERS Why, then I know the extremity, my lord:
I must return to prison whence I came.
CHARLES Return! I hope thou wilt not.
What bird that hath escaped the fowler's gin
Will not beware how she's ensnared again?
Or what is he so senseless and secure
That, having hardly passed a dangerous gulf,
Will put himself in peril there again?
VILLIERS Ah, but it is mine oath, my gracious lord,
Which I in conscience may not violate,
Or else a kingdom should not draw me hence.
CHARLES Thine oath! Why, that doth bind thee to abide.
Hast thou not sworn obedience to thy prince?
VILLIERS In all things that uprightly he commands.
But either to persuade or threaten me
Not to perform the covenant of my word
Is lawless, and I need not to obey.
CHARLES Why, is it lawful for a man to kill,
And not to break a promise with his foe?
VILLIERS To kill, my lord, when war is once proclaimed,
So that our quarrel be for wrongs received,
No doubt is lawfully permitted us;
But in an oath we must be well advised
How we do swear, and, when we once have sworn,
Not to infringe it, though we die therefor.
Therefore, my lord, as willing I return
As if I were to fly to paradise.
CHARLES Stay, my Villiers, thine honourable mind
Deserves to be eternally admired.
Thy suit shall be no longer thus deferred:
Give me the paper, I'll subscribe to it,
And wheretofore I loved thee as Villiers,

17 pleaseth] Qq; please *Delius, conj. Capell* 20 not] Qq; not, Villiers *Capell* 26 mine] Q1; my Q2 42 therefor] *RLA;* therefore Qq 44 paradise.] Qq; paradise. *going. / Capell* 45 thine] Q1; thy Q2 48 it,] Qq; it: *signs, and gives it back. / Capell*

17 pleaseth Pronounced as a monosyllable.
18 extremity conclusion. Compare 3.1.129: 'in extremity of lightning flash'.
21 gin snare.
23 senseless . . . secure foolish and over-confident.
24 hardly at great risk.
38 So that Provided that.
40 in . . . oath in taking an oath.
49 wheretofore while until now.

Hereafter I'll embrace thee as myself.
Stay, and be still in favour with thy lord.

VILLIERS I humbly thank your grace. I must dispatch
And send this passport first unto the earl,
And then I will attend your highness' pleasure.

CHARLES Do so, Villiers, and, Charles, when he hath need,
Be such his soldiers, howsoever he speed. *Exit Villiers*

Enter KING JOHN

KING JOHN Come, Charles, and arm thee. Edward is entrapped,
The Prince of Wales is fall'n into our hands,
And we have compassed him – he cannot scape.

CHARLES But will your highness fight today?

KING JOHN What else, my son? He's scarce eight thousand strong,
And we are threescore thousand at the least.

CHARLES I have a prophecy, my gracious lord,
Wherein is written what success is like
To happen us in this outrageous war.
It was delivered me at Crécy's field
By one that is an aged hermit there:
[*Reads*] 'When feathered fowl shall make thine army tremble,
And flintstones rise and break the battle 'ray,
Then think on him that doth not now dissemble,
For that shall be the hapless dreadful day.
Yet in the end thy foot thou shalt advance

58 is] Qq; has *Collier* 61] *As in* Q1; *two lines divided at* sonne?/ strong, Q2 66 Crécy's] Q2 (Cressyes); Cresses Q1 68 SD] *Capell; not in* Qq

51 still always, forever (the usual meaning of the adverb at the time).

55–6 and . . . speed Charles addresses himself in the third person.

56 May his soldiers be like this, however he may fare.

57–9 Edward . . . scape Unhistorical: the Black Prince's forces were never trapped or surrounded ('compassed') at Poitiers, see 4.4n. 'Scape' is not an elided form, but a current alternative of 'escape'.

61–2 He's . . . least The figures provided are suggested by Hol. (II, 664–5), who puts the Prince's forces at about seven thousand five hundred, and the French as divided into three 'battles' of sixteen thousand men each, for a total of about fifty (not sixty) thousand. But the numbers vary considerably according to the different historians.

63–73 Prophecies, and premonitory dreams, are the most common dramatic devices to create suspense, compare 3.2.38–43n. above. The sextet at 68–73 suggests three separate prophecies, to be fulfilled at 4.5.1–55, 4.6.4–52 and 5.1.210–15 respectively. Their origin is discussed in the Appendix, pp. 210–11.

64 success outcome.

65 outrageous excessively fierce (*OED* sv *a* 2).

66 Crécy's field The episode of the ravens frightening the French army, prophesied at 68, is reported by both Frois. and Hol. not of the battle of Poitiers but of that of Crécy. See Appendix, p. 210 and 4.5 headnote.

69, 76 'ray array.

71 hapless unfortunate.

72–3 The deceptive nature of the third prophecy is acknowledged by King John at 5.1.214–15.

As far in England as thy foe in France.'
KING JOHN By this it seems we shall be fortunate:
For as it is impossible that stones
Should ever rise and break the battle 'ray,
Or airy fowl make men in arms to quake,
So is it like we shall not be subdued.
Or say this might be true: yet in the end,
Since he doth promise we shall drive him hence
And forage their country as they have done ours,
By this revenge that loss will seem the less.
But all are frivolous fancies, toys, and dreams:
Once we are sure we have ensnared the son,
Catch we the father after as we can.
Exeunt

4.4. *Enter* PRINCE *Edward*, AUDLEY, *and others*

PRINCE Audley, the arms of death embrace us round,
And comfort have we none, save that to die
We pay sour earnest for a sweeter life.
At Crécy field our clouds of warlike smoke
Choked up those French mouths, and dissevered them,
But now their multitudes of millions hide,
Masking, as 'twere, the beauteous burning sun,
Leaving no hope to us but sullen dark
And eyeless terror of all-ending night.

Act 4, Scene 4 4.4] *Capell; no scene division in* Qq 0 SD *Enter*] Qq; *The same. The* English *Camp. Enter*/ *Capell* 3 We pay] Qq; To pay *Capell, Tyrrell* 5 mouths] Q1, Q2 (mouthes); moths *conj. WP*

78 like likely, probable.

81 forage plunder.

Act 4, Scene 4

4.4 The account of the battle is deliberately distorted to create suspense (see 4.3.57–9n.). The French attacked the Prince frontally in successive waves, but met with constant resistance. Frois. (ch. 162, Metz, pp. 96–100) places strong emphasis on the bravery of Lord Audley, who, though being 'of a great season', asked and obtained from the Prince the privilege of being 'one of the first setters on', fulfilling a vow he had made a long time before.

2–3 Our only comfort is that our death is a bitter pledge of a sweeter life to come. 'To die' = 'by dying' or 'in dying', an indefinite use of the infinitive discussed in Abbott 356.

5 mouths WP suggest that 'mouths' stands for 'moths', meaning 'motes', to describe the 'multitudes of millions' of the French. But 'mouths' is metonymically appropriate to the French in connection with the 'choking' image.

7 Masking Pleonastic; the French multitudes hide the sun by masking it.

9 eyeless blind, sightless (*OED* sv *a*[3], with earliest citation from 1627).

9 all-ending night death and doom. In *R3* 3.1.78, doomsday is described as 'the general all ending day'.

AUDLEY This sudden, mighty, and expedient head
That they have made, fair prince, is wonderful.
Before us in the valley lies the king
Vantaged with all that heaven and earth can yield,
His party stronger battled than our whole.
His son, the braving Duke of Normandy,
Hath trimmed the mountain on our right hand up
In shining plate, that now the aspiring hill
Shows like a silver quarry, or an orb
Aloft the which the banners, bannerets,
And new-replenished pendants cuff the air
And beat the winds, that for their gaudiness
Struggles to kiss them. On our left hand lies
Philip, the younger issue of the king,
Coting the other hill in such array
That all his gilded upright pikes do seem
Straight trees of gold, the pendants, leaves,
And their device of antique heraldry,
Quartered in colours seeming sundry fruits,
Makes it the orchard of the Hesperides.

22 Struggles] Qq; Struggle *Collier* **24** Coting] Qq; Coating *Capell* **26** the pendants,] *WP and later edns;* the pendant Qq; the pendant streamers, *Capell, Tyrrell, Delius;* with pendant *Collier* **28** sundry] Q2; sundy Q1

10 expedient head rapid headway.

12–39 The description of the deployment of the French army is the dramatist's invention, paralleling that of the sea battle at 3.1.62–78 and 144–84. According to Hol. (II, 664) 'the French king caused his host to be diuided into three battels or wards . . . The first battell was gouerned by the duke of Orleance, wherein were six and thirtie banners, and twise as manie penons. The second was led by the duke of Normandie and his brethren, the lord Lewes & the lord Iohn. The third the French king himselfe conducted.'

14 stronger . . . whole deploying more fighting men than our whole army. According to Hol. each French 'battle' included sixteen thousand armed men.

15–32 Words and imagery in these lines echo closely the description of the English fleet at 3.1.64–76.

15 braving (1) defiant, (2) stately.

16 trimmed decorated, arrayed.

17 plate armour.

18 an orb a ring.

19 bannerets The ensigns of knights entitled to lead their own companies into the field.

20 new . . . pendants pennons (streamers attached to the head of lances or pikes) blown in the wind.

22 Struggles A singular form for the plural.

23 Philip, the future Duke of Burgundy, only fifteen at the time, did not lead a 'battle' at Poitiers but was in that led by King John and was taken prisoner with him.

24 Coting Coating, covering as with coats of paint.

25–9 Compare 3.1.68–70.

26 pendants WP's emendation of Qq's unpunctuated 'pendant' is the most likely among those suggested to make sense of this passage.

27 device . . . heraldry The heraldic emblems painted on the pennons ('antique' = ennobled by antiquity).

28 Quartered See 3.1.76n.

29 orchard . . . Hesperides The mythical garden from which Hercules stole the golden apples.

Behind us too the hill doth bear his height,
For, like a half-moon opening but one way,
It rounds us in: there at our back are lodged
The fatal crossbows, and the battle there
Is governed by the rough Chatillon.
Then thus it stands: the valley for our flight
The king binds in, the hills on either hand
Are proudly royalisèd by his sons,
And on the hill behind stands certain death
In pay and service with Chatillon.

PRINCE Death's name is much more mighty than his deeds:
Thy parcelling this power hath made it more.
As many sands as these my hands can hold
Are but my handful of so many sands:
Then, all the world – and call it but a power –
Easily ta'en up, and quickly thrown away.
But if I stand to count them sand by sand
The number would confound my memory
And make a thousand millions of a task
Which briefly is no more indeed than one.
These quarters, squadrons, and these regiments,
Before, behind us, and on either hand,
Are but a power. When we name a man,
His hand, his foot, his head, hath several strengths,
And, being all but one self instant strength,

30 too] *Capell and mod. edns;* two QQ **30** bear] beare QQ; rear *conj. Collier* **35–7**] *As in* Q1*; two lines divided at* binds in,/ sonnes, Q2 **35** flight] QQ; fight *Collier* **44** Then,] QQ (*no punct.*); They're *conj. Melchiori* **44** but a] QQ; but one *Collier* **45** Easily] QQ; Is easily *Capell* **50** quarters, squadrons] QQ; quarter'd squadrons *Capell, Tyrrell* **53** hath] QQ; have *Capell*

30 doth . . . height rises (the hill is personified in the masculine).

31 half-moon Compare the formation of the English fleet at 3.1.72 and n.

33 battle body of soldiers, see 3.3.219 and 225n.

34 Chatillon A Lord Châtillon figures as the French ambassador in *The Troublesome Reign of King John* (1591) and in *John* 1.1 and 2.1. The dramatist must have decided to use this name, already familiar to English audiences, rather than that of the Duke of Orleans, the leader of the first battle at Poitiers (see 12–39n.), when he found 'the lord Chatellon' listed by Froissart (not by Holinshed) among the 'great barownes of France' consulted by King John before the battle, in ch. 160, 'Of the order of the Frenchemen before the batayle of Poycters' (Ker, I, 364).

44–5 'Is' must be understood before 'Easily' at 45, an ellipsis frequent in Shakespeare (Abbott 403). The only possible, but unlikely, alternative, is to take 'Then' as a printer's misreading of 'Theyr' (= They are), where 'they' refers to 'sands'.

44, 52 a power one single power (see 41).

46–7 count . . . memory Compare 2.1.136–8, 'tell . . . the massy earth by sands / And sand by sand print them in memory', a proverbial expression.

48 task (1) the act of counting, (2) the forces (power) involved.

50 quarters army divisions (*OED* Quarter *sb* 14c, giving as examples this and *1H6* 2.1.63).

53 hath A singular form for the plural.

54 self instant self-contained.

Why, all this many, Audley, is but one,
And we can call it all but one man's strength.
He that hath far to go, tells it by miles:
If he should tell by steps, it kills his heart;
The drops are infinite that make a flood,
And yet thou knowest we call it but a rain.
There is but one France, one King of France:
That France hath no more kings, and that same king
Hath but the puissant legion of one king;
And we have one. Then apprehend no odds,
For one to one is fair equality.

Enter a HERALD *from King John*

PRINCE What tidings, messenger? Be plain and brief.
HERALD The King of France, my sovereign lord and master,
Greets by me his foe, the Prince of Wales.
If thou call forth a hundred men of name,
Of lords, knights, esquires, and English gentlemen,
And with thyself and those kneel at his feet,
He straight will fold his bloody colours up,
And ransom shall redeem lives forfeited;
If not, this day shall drink more English blood
Than e'er was buried in our British earth.
What is the answer to this proffered mercy?
PRINCE This heaven that covers France contains the mercy
That draws from me submissive orisons:

61 France, one] Qq; France and one *Capell, WP* **68** Greets by] Qq; Greets thus by *Capell, Tyrrell, Delius;* Greeteth by *Collier* **69** call] Qq; cull *Collier* **69** a hundred] Q1; an hundreth Q2 **70** esquires] Q1; Squires Q2 **75** our] Qq; your *conj. Collier, Smith, WAA*

57 tells counts, compare 2.1.136.

63 legion army, fighting power.

64 apprehend . . . odds be not afraid of numerical inequality.

66–123 The taunting of the Prince is the dramatist's invention, suggested by the peace-making efforts of the Cardinal of Périgord, that failed because of the excessive demands of the French. See Frois. ch. 161: 'Howe the cardynall of Pyergourt treated to make agrement bytwene the Frenche kyng and the prince before the batell of Poycters' (Metz, pp. 93–6), and Hol., II, 665 (Metz, pp. 129–31).

69–73 Compare Hol. (Metz, p. 130): 'the vttermost that he [the French king] would agree vnto, was this, that the prince and an hundred of his knights should yeeld themselues as prisoners vnto him, otherwise he would not haue the matter taken vp . . . But the prince in no wise cold be brought to any such vnreasonable conditions.'

75 British Breton (Brittany is the English name for Bretagne), with reference to the bloody English campaigns against Charles of Blois, first alluded to in 1.1.133–4, and again in 4.1, see notes 0 SD. 1–2 and 2. to the latter. The emendation of 'our' to 'your' is wrong, since here a Frenchman is speaking of Bretagne as French soil.

77–8 The Prince intends to address his prayers ('orisons') for mercy only to God in heaven, not to the King of France, a mere man (80).

That such base breath should vanish from my lips
To urge the plea of mercy to a man
The Lord forbid. Return and tell thy king
My tongue is made of steel, and it shall beg
My mercy on his coward burgonet.
Tell him my colours are as red as his,
My men as bold, our English arms as strong:
Return him my defiance in his face.

HERALD I go. [*Exit*]

Enter another [HERALD]

PRINCE What news with thee?

SECOND HERALD The Duke of Normandy, my lord and master,
Pitying thy youth is so engirt with peril,
By me hath sent a nimble-jointed jennet,
As swift as ever yet thou didst bestride,
And therewithal he counsels thee to fly,
Else death himself hath sworn that thou shalt die.

PRINCE Back with the beast unto the beast that sent him!
Tell him I cannot sit a coward's horse,
Bid him today bestride the jade himself,
For I will stain my horse quite o'er with blood
And double gild my spurs, but I will catch him.
So tell the cap'ring boy, and get thee gone. [*Exit Herald*]

Enter another [HERALD]

THIRD HERALD Edward of Wales, Philip, the second son
To the most mighty Christian King of France,
Seeing thy body's living date expired,

81 thy] Q2*; the* Q1 **87** SD.1] Q2*; not in* Q1 **87** SD.2 HERALD] *Capell; not in* Qq **89** SH SECOND] *This edn; not in* Qq **91** nimble-jointed] *Capell;* nimble ioynted Qq **100** cap'ring] Q1 (capring)*;* carping Q2 **100** SD.1] *Capell, subst.; not in* Qq **100** SD.2 HERALD] *Capell; not in* Qq **101** SH,123 SH THIRD] *This edn; not in* Qq

79 vanish from be exhaled by.

83 burgonet close-fitting helmet. WP notice that the word is found in Shakespeare only three times in *2H6* 5.1 and once in *Ant.*

89–100 This exchange anticipates the episode of the tennis balls sent by the Dauphin to Henry V in *H5* 1.2 (RLA). The common source for both *E3* and *H5* is *The Famous Victories of Henry the Fifth*, a much earlier play printed only in 1598.

90 engirt surrounded.

91 jennet A small Spanish horse.

97 jade Horse of inferior breed, see 3.3.162 n.

99 double gild cover twice over (with blood as if it were gold).

100 cap'ring frolicsome (lit.: 'turning capers'), used in a derogatory sense; compare *1H4* 3.2.63, 'cap'ring fools'. Q2's 'carping' (= prating) is a reviser's misguided improvement.

All full of charity and Christian love,
Commends this book full fraught with prayers
To thy fair hand, and, for thy hour of life,
Entreats thee that thou meditate therein,
And arm thy soul for her long journey towards.
Thus have I done his bidding, and return.

PRINCE Herald of Philip, greet thy lord from me.
All good that he can send I can receive,
But thinkst thou not the unadvisèd boy
Hath wronged himself in thus far tend'ring me?
Haply he cannot pray without the book:
I think him no divine extemporal.
Then render back this commonplace of prayer
To do himself good in adversity.
Besides, he knows not my sins' quality,
And therefore knows no prayers for my avail.
Ere night his prayer may be to pray to God
To put it in my heart to hear his prayer.
So tell the courtly wanton, and be gone.

THIRD HERALD I go. [*Exit*]

PRINCE How confident their strength and number makes them!
Now, Audley, sound those silver wings of thine
And let those milk-white messengers of time
Show thy time's learning in this dangerous time.
Thyself are busy and bit with many broils,
And stratagems forepast with iron pens

105 prayers] QQ; holy prayers *Capell, Tyrrell, WP* **113** thus] Q2; this Q1 **114** Haply] Q2; Happily Q1 **118** sins'] Q1 (sinnes); sin's *Capell* **123** SD] Q2; *not in* Q1 **125** wings] QQ; strings *Delius* **126** milk-white] *Capell;* milke white QQ **128** busy and bit] QQ (busie,); bruis'd and bent *Capell*

105 fraught loaded. Capell introduces 'holy' before 'prayers' to mend the metre.

108 towards Used as adverb: at hand, imminent. Compare *Rom.* 1.5.122: 'We have a trifling foolish banquet towards.'

112 unadvisèd rash, inconsiderate (Lapides).

113 tend'ring caring for (*OED* Tender v^2 3).

114 Haply Perhaps.

115 divine extemporal improvised parson.

116 render . . . prayer return this prayer-book ('commonplace' = commonplace-book, handbook; *OED* sv *sb* 4).

122 courtly wanton roguish young courtier; compare *John* 5.1.69–70: 'a beardless boy, / A cock'red silken wanton'.

124 makes A singular form for the plural.

125–7 sound . . . dangerous time Audley as an old man is invited, in a time of danger, to show the ancient wisdom (time's learning) resulting from his experience. But the imagery is confused. WP take 'silver wings' to refer to his 'winged words', and Delius replaces 'wings' with 'strings'; the 'milk-white messengers of time' are his white locks; as Lapides puts it, 'the white-haired Audley is the Nestor-like combination of age, experience and eloquence'.

128 busy . . . broils engaged in and marked by many battles. Capell's reading 'bruis'd and bent' for 'busy and bit' is palaeographically unwarranted.

129 stratagems forepast past military actions. Not a complement parallel with 'broils' at 128, but the subject of a new sentence.

Are texted in thine honourable face.
Thou art a married man in this distress,
But danger woos me as a blushing maid:
Teach me an answer to this perilous time.

AUDLEY To die is all as common as to live:
The one in choice, the other holds in chase,
For from the instant we begin to live
We do pursue and hunt the time to die.
First bud we, then we blow, and after seed,
Then presently we fall, and, as a shade
Follows the body, so we follow death.
If then we hunt for death, why do we fear it?
If we fear it, why do we follow it?
If we do fear, how can we shun it?
If we do fear, with fear we do but aid
The thing we fear, to seize on us the sooner.
If we fear not, then no resolvèd proffer
Can overthrow the limit of our fate,
For, whether ripe or rotten, drop we shall,
As we do draw the lottery of our doom.

PRINCE Ah, good old man, a thousand thousand armours
These words of thine have buckled on my back.
Ah, what an idiot hast thou made of life,
To seek the thing it fears! And how disgraced
The imperial victory of murd'ring death,
Since all the lives his conquering arrows strike

130 texted] Q1; texed Q2, *Capell, Tyrrell* **135** in choice] Qq; inch-wise *TB* **142** If] Qq; Or, if *Capell, Tyrrell* **143**] Qq; *line omitted by Capell and early edns*

130 texted inscribed (*OED* Text *v* 1), referring to the scars of the wounds received in battle.

131 Audley's familiarity with the perils of war is presented metaphorically as a marriage.

134 Proverbial, 'Death is common to all' (Tilley D142).

135 No fully satisfactory interpretation has been offered for this line, which anticipates the prince's words at 159–60: 'to live is but to seek to die / And dying but beginning of new life'. Life and death, whichever we prefer (hold in choice), pursue (hold in chase) each other. Replacing 'in choice' with 'inch-wise' (inch by inch, TB) does not clarify the meaning.

136–7 from . . . die Modelled on the saying 'we die from birth' or 'from day to day' (Dent, *PLED*, D108.11).

138–9 Braunmuller compares John Bodenham, *Bel-vedere* (1600), sig. Q2 ('Of Life'): 'First doe we bud, then blow; next seed, last fall.'

141–5 The argument, based on the proverb that fear doubles danger (Tilley F138), is developed in *JC* 2.2.32–7. Capell omits line 143 as repetitive.

146–7 no . . . fate no determined effort on our part can change our destiny.

153 To seek A consecutive infinitive: in that it seeks.

153 how disgraced how hast thou (see 152) disgraced.

Seek him, and he not them, to shame his glory.
I will not give a penny for a life,
Nor half a half-penny to shun grim death,
Since for to live is but to seek to die,
And dying but beginning of new life.
Let come the hour when he that rules it will:
To live or die I hold indifferent.

Exeunt

4.5. *Enter* KING JOHN *and* CHARLES

KING JOHN A sudden darkness hath defaced the sky,
The winds are crept into their caves for fear,
The leaves move not, the world is hushed and still,
The birds cease singing, and the wandering brooks
Murmur no wonted greeting to their shores;
Silence attends some wonder, and expecteth
That heaven should pronounce some prophecy.
Where or from whom proceeds this silence, Charles?
CHARLES Our men with open mouths and staring eyes
Look on each other, as they did attend
Each other's words, and yet no creature speaks:
A tongue-tied fear hath made a midnight hour,
And speeches sleep through all the waking regions.
KING JOHN But now the pompous sun in all his pride
Looked through his golden coach upon the world,

Act 4, Scene 5 4.5] *Capell; no scene division in* Qq 0 SD *Enter*] Qq; *The same. The* French *Camp. Enter/ Capell* 3 world] Qq; wood *Delius, conj. Capell* 8 Where] Qq; Whence *Delius, conj. Capell*

159 Since for An emphatic form of 'since'.

161 when . . . will when God, that rules time (the hour), wills.

Act 4, Scene 5

4.5 The first part of the scene (1–55) elaborates a few lines at the beginning both of Froissart's (ch. 130, Metz, pp. 78–9) and of Holinshed's (II, 638) report of the battle not of Poitiers but of Crécy ten years earlier, while the rest (56–126) is the continuation of the safe-conduct episode (see 4.1 and 4.3.1–56), based on Frois. ch. 135 (Metz, p. 84).

1–55 Compare Frois. (Metz, p. 78): 'Also the same season there fell a great rayne and a clyps [an eclipse] with a terryble thonder, and before the rayne ther came fleyng ouer bothe batayls a great nombre of crowes, for feare of the tempest commynge. Then anone the eyre beganne to waxe clere, and the sonne to shyne fayre and bright.' Actually the disruption in the French army was not caused by the the sight of the crows but by the failure of the Genoese archers, see 3.4.3–11 n.

6 attends awaits.

7 some prophecy Compare 4.3.63–73.

10 as . . . attend as if listening for (*OED* Attend *v* 1).

14 But now Even now, a moment ago.

14 pompous splendid.

And on a sudden hath he hid himself,
That now the under earth is as a grave,
Dark, deadly, silent, and uncomfortable.
A clamour of ravens
Hark, what a deadly outcry do I hear?

[*Enter* PHILIP]

CHARLES Here comes my brother Philip.
KING JOHN All dismayed.
What fearful words are those thy looks presage?
PHILIP A flight, a flight!
KING JOHN Coward, what flight? Thou liest, there needs no flight.
PHILIP A flight –
KING JOHN Awake thy craven powers, and tell on
The substance of that very fear indeed
Which is so ghastly printed in thy face.
What is the matter?
PHILIP A flight of ugly ravens
Do croak and hover o'er our soldiers' heads,
And keep in triangles and cornered squares,
Right as our forces are embattled;
With their approach there came this sudden fog
Which now hath hid the airy floor of heaven
And made at noon a night unnatural
Upon the quaking and dismayèd world.
In brief, our soldiers have let fall their arms
And stand like metamorphosed images,
Bloodless and pale, one gazing on another.
KING JOHN Ay, now I call to mind the prophecy,
But I must give no entrance to a fear. –

18 SD] *Capell (subst.); in right margin after* 'uncomfortable' Qq **19** a] Q1*; not in* Q2 **19** SD] *Capell and mod. edns (after 20); not in* Qq **20–1**] *As in WP, TB subst.; lines divided at* Phillip./ presage? Q1*; at* Philip./ words/ presage? Q2 **22** SH PHILIP] Q2*; Pr.* Q1 (*and so throughout scene*) **26** substance . . . fear] Qq*;* very substance of that fear *Delius, conj. Capell* **33** floor] Qq (flower), *Capell, WP, TB;* flower *RLA*

18 uncomfortable comfortless.

22–4 flight Equivocating on (1) running away, (2) flight of birds.

25 Awake . . . powers Pull yourself together ('craven' = cowardly).

26 The proposed rearrangement of this line (see Collation) is unnecessary: 'fear', not 'substance', is the word emphasised by 'very'.

27 ghastly Used adverbially.

31 as . . . embattled reproducing the battle formations of our forces ('embattled' is pronounced as a quadrisyllable).

33 floor Qq's 'flower' is found elsewhere as an alternative spelling of 'floor'. The sky is called 'the floor of heaven' in *MV* 5.1.58.

37 metamorphosed transformed into stone, petrified.

39 See 7 and 4.3.68–71.

Return, and hearten up those yielding souls,
Tell them the ravens, seeing them in arms,
So many fair against a famished few,
Come but to dine upon their handiwork
And prey upon the carrion that they kill;
For when we see a horse laid down to die,
Although not dead, the ravenous birds
Sit watching the departure of his life:
Even so these ravens for the carcases
Of those poor English that are marked to die
Hover about, and if they cry to us
'Tis but for meat that we must kill for them.
Away, and comfort up my soldiers,
And sound the trumpets, and at once dispatch
This little business of a silly fraud.
Exit [*Philip*]

Another noise. SALISBURY *brought in by a French* CAPTAIN

CAPTAIN Behold, my liege, this knight and forty more,
Of whom the better part are slain and fled,
With all endeavour sought to break our ranks
And make their way to the encompassed prince.
Dispose of him as please your majesty.
KING JOHN Go, and the next bough, soldier, that thou seest,
Disgrace it with his body presently,
For I do hold a tree in France too good
To be the gallows of an English thief.
SALISBURY My lord of Normandy, I have your pass
And warrant for my safety through this land.
CHARLES Villiers procured it for thee, did he not?
SALISBURY He did.
CHARLES And it is current: thou shalt freely pass.

41 those] Q2; these Q1 **47** Although not] Qq; Although he be not *Capell, Tyrrell, Delius, WP* **50** those] Q1; these Q2 **55** SD.1] Q2; *Exit Pr.* Q1 **56** more] *Capell;* mo Qq

43 fair in fair array.

47 The line lacks a foot, compensated by a pause for emphasis after 'dead'. There is no need to suppose an omission (see Collation).

55 silly fraud stupid deception.

56–102 Developing, in the same vein as 4.3, the safe-conduct episode in Frois., ch. 135 (Metz, pp. 84–5), as reported in the Appendix, p. 212.

56 forty more According to Frois., Manny was allowed to take with him not forty but twenty knights, and on their way from Aiguillon to Calais they never engaged in military operations.

59 encompassed prince Compare 4.3.58–9.

KING JOHN Ay, freely to the gallows to be hanged,
Without denial or impediment.
Away with him.
CHARLES I hope your highness will not so disgrace me
And dash the virtue of my seal at arms.
He hath my never broken name to show,
Charact'red with this princely hand of mine,
And rather let me leave to be a prince
Than break the stable verdict of a prince:
I do beseech you let him pass in quiet.
KING JOHN Thou and thy word lie both in my command.
What canst thou promise that I cannot break?
Which of these twain is greater infamy:
To disobey thy father or thy self?
Thy word, nor no man's, may exceed his power,
Nor that same man doth never break his word
That keeps it to the utmost of his power.
The breach of faith dwells in the soul's consent,
Which, if thyself without consent do break,
Thou art not chargèd with the breach of faith.
Go, hang him; for thy licence lies in me,
And my constraint stands the excuse for thee.
CHARLES What, am I not a soldier in my word?
Then, arms, adieu, and let them fight that list.
Shall I not give my girdle from my waist,
But with a guardian I shall be controlled
To say I may not give my things away?
Upon my soul, had Edward Prince of Wales
Engaged his word, writ down his noble hand,

70 SH] Q2 (*K. Iohn.*); *En. Io*: Q1 **73** SH] Q2; *Vil.* Q1

73 SH The speech heading *Vil.* (*Villiers*, see 67) instead of *Charles* in Q1 looks like an authorial slip, if this was written immediately after 4.3 by the same person responsible for that scene.

74 dash . . . seal at arms infringe the power of the seal bearing my arms (appended to the safe-conduct).

75 never . . . name signature as a pledge never broken before.

76 Charact'red Written.

77 leave cease.

78 stable verdict firm pledge.

85 Nor . . . never An emphatic double negative (Abbott 406).

88 Which Referring to 'faith'.

90 licence freedom of action.

91 my . . . thee my power of coercion exonerates you from responsibility.

93 list please.

97–102 The hypothetical behaviour of the King of England in a similar situation was suggested by the actual behaviour of the French King towards Manny, as reported in Frois. (Metz, p. 85), see Appendix, p. 212.

For all your knights to pass his father's land,
The royal king, to grace his warlike son,
Would not alone safe-conduct give to them,
But with all bounty feasted them and theirs.

KING JOHN Dwellst thou on precedents? Then be it so.
Say, Englishman, of what degree thou art.

SALISBURY An earl in England, though a prisoner here,
And those that know me call me Salisbury.

KING JOHN Then, Salisbury, say whither thou art bound.

SALISBURY To Calais, where my liege King Edward is.

KING JOHN To Calais, Salisbury? Then to Calais pack,
And bid the king prepare a noble grave
To put his princely son black Edward in.
And as thou travelst westward from this place,
Some two leagues hence, there is a lofty hill
Whose top seems topless, for the embracing sky
Doth hide his high head in her azure bosom,
Upon whose tall top when thy foot attains,
Look back upon the humble vale beneath –
Humble of late, but now made proud with arms –
And thence behold the wretched Prince of Wales
Hooped with a bond of iron round about.
After which sight, to Calais spur amain
And say the prince was smothered, and not slain,
And tell the king this is not all his ill,
For I will greet him ere he thinks I will.
Away, be gone, the smoke but of our shot
Will choke our foes, though bullets hit them not.

[*Exeunt*]

101 safe-conduct] *Capell; unhyphenated* Qq **103** precedents] Qq (presidents); precedence *conj. Lapides* **108, 109, 121** Calais] Callice Q1; Calice Q2 **116** Upon] Qq; Unto *Delius, conj. Capell* **117** beneath] Qq; below *Capell* **120** bond] Q1; band Q2 **126** SD] *Exit* Q1; *not in* Q2

103 Dwellst . . . precedents Do you insist on applying the rules (of chivalry)?

109–26 The French King's speech is intended to fit the safe-conduct episode (historically ten years earlier) into the context of the battle of Poitiers, as presented in 4.3.57–9, 4.4, and hinted at 56–9 above.

111 black Edward The attribute by which Edward Prince of Wales was universally known – the Black Prince – is given, when first mentioned in the play by King John, a negative ring.

112–20 This description, couched in the most conventional language, has no historical foundation.

120 bond Q1's 'bond', though merely a spelling variant of 'band' (Q2), seems more appropriate as suggesting 'boundary' as well as 'chain'; the reviser responsible for the change may have thought of 'band' = 'troop' (of iron-clad men).

122 smothered suffocated by the number of the enemy, compare 'choke' at 126.

123 all . . . ill his only trouble.

125–6 the . . . choke the smoke of our shot will be enough to choke. For this use of 'but' see Abbott 128.

4.6. *Alarum. Enter* PRINCE *Edward and* ARTOIS

ARTOIS How fares your grace? Are you not shot, my lord?
PRINCE No, dear Artois, but choked with dust and smoke,
And stepped aside for breath and fresher air.
ARTOIS Breathe, then, and to it again. The amazèd French
Are quite distract with gazing on the crows,
And, were our quivers full of shafts again,
Your grace should see a glorious day of this.
O for more arrows, Lord! That's our want.
PRINCE Courage, Artois, a fig for feathered shafts
When feathered fowls do bandy on our side!
What need we fight and sweat and keep a coil,
When railing crows outscold our adversaries?
Up, up, Artois, the ground itself is armed
With fire-containing flint: command our bows
To hurl away their pretty-coloured yew,
And to it with stones! Away, Artois, away!
My soul doth prophesy we win the day.
Exeunt

Alarum. Enter KING JOHN

KING JOHN Our multitudes are in themselves confounded,
Dismayèd, and distraught; swift-starting fear
Hath buzzed a cold dismay through all our army,
And every petty disadvantage prompts
The fear-possessèd abject soul to fly.

Act 4, Scene 6 4.6] *Capell; no scene division in* Qq 0 SD *Alarum. Enter*] Qq (Allarum)*; The same. A Part of the Field of Battle. Alarums, as of a Battle join'd; Skirmishings. Enter/ Capell* 4, to it] Qq; to't *Capell* 14 With fire-containing] *Capell;* Fire containing Qq 15 pretty-coloured] *Capell* (*subst.*)*;* pretie colored (coloured Q2) Qq 17 SD *Alarum. Enter*] Qq (Allarum)*; Alarums, and Parties skirmishing. Enter/ Capell;* Scene VII. *The same. Another Part of the Field of Battle. Alarum. Enter/ WP and all subs. edns* 18 SH] Q2 (*K. Iohn*)*; not in* Q1 19 swift-starting] *Capell; unhyphenated* Qq 22 fear-possessèd] *Capell* (*subst.*)*;* feare possessed Qq

Act 4, Scene 6

4.6 The location is the battlefield at Poitiers. 1–52 develop, independently of the historical sources, the prophecy of the flying flintstones suggested by the words of the Cardinal of Périgord (see 4.3.63–73n. and Appendix, pp. 210–11); 53–62 are based on Frois., ch. 163 (Metz, p. 100).

8 our want what we need.

10 feathered fowls The Prince, though unaware of the prophecy, echoes its words, see 4.3.68, playing on the 'feathered shafts' (9) of the arrows.

10 bandy (a) play (as at tennis); (b) band together (*OED* sv *v* 1 and 7, respectively).

11 keep . . . coil make much ado (*OED* Coil *sb*[2] 4a).

13–17 Compare the words of the prophecy at 4.3.69: 'flintstones rise and break the battle 'ray'.

14 bows bowmen, archers.

15 pretty-coloured yew Long bows were made out of yew-tree wood, polished in orange, red, or brown finish (Lapides).

17 SD.2 Editors since WP begin a new scene here, but, in spite of a short time-lapse, the location is unchanged and the action uninterrupted.

19 swift-starting spreading rapidly.

Myself, whose spirit is steel to their dull lead,
What with recalling of the prophecy,
And that our native stones from English arms
Rebel against us, find myself attainted
With strong surprise of weak and yielding fear.

Enter CHARLES

CHARLES Fly, father, fly! The French do kill the French:
Some that would stand let drive at some that fly,
Our drums strike nothing but discouragement,
Our trumpets sound dishonour and retire;
The spirit of fear, that feareth nought but death,
Cowardly works confusion on itself.

Enter PHILIP

PHILIP Pluck out your eyes and see not this day's shame!
An arm hath beat an army: one poor David
Hath with a stone foiled twenty stout Goliaths.
Some twenty naked starvelings with small flints
Hath driven back a puissant host of men
Arrayed and fenced in all accomplements.
KING JOHN *Mort Dieu*! They quoit at us and kill us up.
No less than forty thousand wicked elders
Have forty lean slaves this day stoned to death.
CHARLES O that I were some other countryman!
This day hath set derision on the French,
And all the world will blurt and scorn at us.
KING JOHN What, is there no hope left?

28 SH] Q2*; not in* Q1 34 SH] Q2 (*Phil.*)*; not in* Q1 38 **Hath**] Q1*;* **Haue** Q2 39 **accomplements**] Qq*;* **accoutrements** *WP* 40 *Mort Dieu*] *This edn;* **Mordiu** Q1*;* **Mordieu** Q2 *and mod. edns* 45 **will**] Q2*;* **wilt** Q1

26–7 attainted . . . of quite unexpectedly affected by.

28–39 Reminiscent of Froissart's description (ch. 130, Metz, p. 79) of the havoc caused by the English crossbows among the Genoese forces at Crécy, see Appendix, pp. 205–6.

29 let drive at shoot against.

32 nought . . . death nothing more than death.

33 Cowardly Used adverbially.

38 Hath A singular form for the plural.

39 fenced . . . accomplements fully equipped (protected by all the appropriate equipment).

40 ***Mort Dieu*** ''Sdeath!' A blasphemous French oath, also in *2H6* 1.1. 123.

40 quoit throw, from the game of quoits, consisting in throwing a flat disk or a ring against a pin.

41–2 The subject is 'forty lean slaves'; the French are 'elders' as senior in age and rank in respect of the English 'slaves', and 'wicked' because of their cowardice.

43 some . . . countryman citizen of some other country.

45 blurt puff contemptuously (*OED* sv *v* 2).

PHILIP No hope but death, to bury up our shame.
KING JOHN Make up once more with me. The twentieth part
Of those that live are men enow to quail
The feeble handful on the adverse part.
CHARLES Then charge again. If heaven be not opposed,
We cannot lose the day.
KING JOHN On, away!
Exeunt

Enter AUDLEY *wounded, and rescued by two* [ESQUIRES]

ESQUIRES How fares my lord?
AUDLEY Even as a man may do
That dines at such a bloody feast as this.
ONE ESQUIRE I hope, my lord, that is no mortal scar.
AUDLEY No matter if it be, the count is cast,
And, in the worst, ends but a mortal man.
Good friends, convey me to the princely Edward,
That in the crimson bravery of my blood
I may become him with saluting him.
I'll smile and tell him that this open scar
Doth end the harvest of his Audley's war.
[*Exeunt*]

4.7. *Enter* PRINCE *Edward*, KING JOHN, CHARLES, *and all, with ensigns spread. Retreat sounded*

PRINCE Now John in France, and lately John of France,

47 SH] Q2 (*Phil.*); *Pr.* Q1 52 On, away] Qq *subst.*; On, on; Away *Capell* 52 SD. 2 *Enter*] Qq; *Alarums* &c. *Enter/ Capell*; Scene VIII. *The same. Another Part of the Field of Battle. Enter/ WP and all subs. edns* 52 SD *and . . .* ESQUIRES] Q2 (*subst.*); & rescued by two squirs. Q1; *and two* Esquires, *his rescuers. / Capell* 53 SH] Q2; *Esq.* Q1; 1. *Esq./ Capell* 55 SH] *This edn; Esq.* Q1; *Esquir.* Q2; 2.*Esq./ Capell* 62 SD] Q2; *Ex.* Q1 Act 4, Scene 7 4.7] *Capell; no scene division in* Qq; Scene IX *WP and all subs. edns* 0 SD *Enter*] Qq; *The same. The* English *Camp. Flourish. Enter/ Capell*

48 **Make up** Fill up the gaps (in our forces) (*OED* Make *v* 96b).

49 **enow** An alternative spelling and pronunciation of 'enough'.

49 **quail** dishearten (*OED* sv v^1 5).

50 **adverse part** other side.

52 SD.2 Editors since WP unnecessarily begin a new scene here.

53–62 The passage is modelled on Frois., ch. 162 (Metz, p. 100), quoted in the Appendix, p. 212.

55, 61 **scar** wound.

56 **the . . . cast** the account is closed.

59 **bravery** finery, rich dress.

60 **become** grace.

Act 4, Scene 7

4.7 The scene, in the same location as 4.6, is freely based on Hol., II, 667–9, and Frois., chs. 164–5 (Metz, pp. 100–3).

1 **lately . . . France** formerly ruler of France.

Thy bloody ensigns are my captive colours,
And you, high-vaunting Charles of Normandy,
That once today sent me a horse to fly,
Are now the subjects of my clemency.
Fie, lords, is't not a shame that English boys,
Whose early days are yet not worth a beard,
Should in the bosom of your kingdom thus,
One against twenty, beat you up together?

KING JOHN Thy fortune, not thy force, hath conquered us.

PRINCE An argument that heaven aids the right.

[*Enter* ARTOIS *with* PHILIP]

See, see, Artois doth bring with him along
The late good counsel-giver to my soul.
Welcome, Artois, and welcome Philip too.
Who now, or you or I, have need to pray?
Now is the proverb verified in you:
Too bright a morning brings a louring day.
Sound trumpets

Enter AUDLEY

But say, what grim discouragement comes here?
Alas, what thousand armèd men of France
Have writ that note of death in Audley's face?
Speak thou, that wooest death with thy careless smile
And lookst so merrily upon thy grave
As if thou wert enamoured on thine end,
What hungry sword hath so bereaved thy face

6 is't] Q2, *Capell and mod. edns;* is it Q1   11 SD] *Capell; not in* Qq   12 with . . . along] Qq*;* along with him *Capell*   13 good counsel-giver] *Capell;* good counsell giuer Qq   15 or you] *This edn;* of you Qq   17 SD.1 *Sound trumpets*] Qq *on same line as /* Enter Audley   17 SD.2] Qq*; Enter* AUDLEY, *led by the two Esquires./ Capell*   23 thine] thyne Q1*;* thy Q2   24 bereaved] Qq (bereaud)*;* bewreath'd *Collier*

3 high-vaunting boastful, with reference to the message sent at 4.4.89–94, recalled in line 4.

3 Charles . . . Normandy Historically, Charles Duke of Normandy was not captured with King John at Poitiers; see Appendix, p. 212.

9 beat . . . together beat both of you.

11 An argument A demonstration.

11 SD Though kept alive in the play, Artois had died in 1343, before the battle of Crécy (see Appendix, p. 204). The confusion arises from Froissart's mention, as the captor of young Prince Philip as well as of King John at Poitiers, of a 'Denyce of Morbecke, a knyght of Arthoys' (Metz, pp. 101–2).

13–15 Referring to the message sent by Philip to the Prince at 4.4.101–8.

16–17 An old proverb (Tilley M1175), echoed also in Shakespeare, *Ven.* 453–6 and *1H4* 5.1.1–6.

20 writ . . . face Compare 4.4.128–30, and Frois. quoted in the Appendix, p. 212: 'he was soore hurte in the body and in the vysage'.

21 careless smile Compare 4.6.61.

23 enamoured on in love with.

And lopped a true friend from my loving soul?
AUDLEY O prince, thy sweet bemoaning speech to me
Is as a mournful knell to one dead sick.
PRINCE Dear Audley, if my tongue ring out thy end,
My arms shall be thy grave. What may I do
To win thy life or to revenge thy death?
If thou wilt drink the blood of captive kings,
Or that it were restorative, command
A health of king's blood, and I'll drink to thee.
If honour may dispense for thee with death,
The never-dying honour of this day
Share wholly, Audley, to thyself, and live.
AUDLEY Victorious prince – that thou art so, behold
A Caesar's fame in kings' captivity –
If I could hold dim death but at a bay
Till I did see my liege thy royal father,
My soul should yield this castle of my flesh,
This mangled tribute, with all willingness,
To darkness, consummation, dust, and worms.
PRINCE Cheerily, bold man, thy soul is all too proud
To yield her city for one little breach,
Should be divorcèd from her earthly spouse
By the soft temper of a Frenchman's sword.
Lo, to repair thy life I give to thee
Three thousand marks a year in English land.

29 thy] Q2; the Q1 **33** health] *Capell;* Heath Qq **35** never-dying] *Capell;* unhyphenated Qq **40** royal] *Capell;* loyall Qq **46** Should] Qq; She'ld *Delius* **47** sword.] *Smith, RLA;* sword: Qq, *Capell;* sword? *WP, TB*

25 lopped cut away, like a branch from a tree.

28–59 The exchange between the Prince and Audley is closer in wording and for some additional details to the report in Hol., II, 668–9 than to its source in Frois., chs. 165 and 167 (Metz, pp. 103 and 104–5).

28 if . . . end if I must speak of your death.

32 Or that As if. Compare 2.1.298n. for a similar construction.

34–6 Another confused contruction: since death is not a requirement to secure honour, the Prince wishes Audley both to live and to have to himself the honour of the day of victory.

37–8 that . . . captivity the proof that you are a victorious prince is in your having captured kings, deserving Caesar's fame.

41 this . . . flesh Traditionally the body was represented as the palace or castle of flesh housing the soul, see 2.1.238–43n.

44–7 The imagery of this passage, fusing together the ideas of the body as city (equivalent to the castle at 41) and as spouse of the soul (46), is curiously similar to that of John Donne's *Holy Sonnet* XIV.

46 Should be Elliptical, depending on 'too proud' at 44: Audley's soul is too proud to let herself be divorced from the body. The soul is personified in the feminine and the body ('spouse') in the masculine.

47 soft temper Said of steel not properly tempered, suggesting the yielding (soft) nature of the French.

48–59 Frois. and Hol. mention four esquires and a larger gift. See Appendix, pp. 212–13.

AUDLEY I take thy gift to pay the debts I owe.
These two poor 'squires redeemed me from the French
With lusty and dear hazard of their lives:
What thou hast given me I give to them,
And, as thou lovest me, prince, lay thy consent
To this bequeath in my last testament.
PRINCE Renownèd Audley, live, and have from me
This gift twice doubled to these esquires and thee;
But, live or die, what thou hast given away
To these and theirs shall lasting freedom stay.
Come, gentlemen, I'll see my friend bestowed
Within an easy litter. Then we'll march
Proudly toward Calais with triumphant pace,
Unto my royal father, and there bring
The tribute of my wars, fair France his king.
[*Exeunt*]

5.1. *Enter* KING EDWARD, QUEEN *Philippa*, DERBY, *Soldiers*

KING EDWARD No more, Queen Philippe, pacify yourself:
Copland, except he can excuse his fault,
Shall find displeasure written in our looks.

51 'squires] *Capell, WP subst.*; Esquires QQ 53 me] QQ; to me *Capell* 60 I'll] Ile Q2; I will Q1 62 Calais] Callis Q1; Calice Q2 64 France his] QQ; France's *Capell* 64 SD] Q2; *Ex.* Q1 Act 5, Scene 1 5.1] *Capell; no act or scene division in* QQ 0 SD *Enter*] QQ; Picardy. *The* English *Camp before* Calais. *Enter/ Capell* 0 SD *Philippa*, DERBY] *Phillip, Derby* Q1; *Philip, Darby* Q2 1, 53, 88, 162, 185 Philippe] *Capell;* Phillip Q1; Philip Q2

51 'squires Capell's metrical emendation is justified by Q1's spelling 'squirs' at 4.6.52 SD.2.

55 bequeath bequest.

55 in . . . testament Suggested by Frois. (Metz, pp. 104–5): 'I clerely disheryte [disinherit] me therof [of the prince's gift] and inheryte them [the esquires]'.

56–9 The doubling of the prince's gift is mentioned only in Hol., see Appendix, p. 213.

59 shall . . . stay will be freely granted in perpetuity.

61 easy comfortable.

61–4 In fact at the time of Poitiers King Edward was not at Calais but in London; see 5.1.186 SD n. and 241–3n.

64 France his France's. An emphatic form of the genitive, Abbott 217.

Act 5, Scene 1

5.1 The last scene reverts to the Calais location of 4.2, used as a frame for events distant in space and time. The episode of the burghers and the surrender of the town in 1347 (4–62) is based on Frois., ch. 146 (Metz, pp. 89–91), that of Copland refusing to surrender King David to the Queen in 1346 (1–3 and 64–96) on ch. 139 (Metz, pp. 87–8), and that of the Black Prince's triumph at Poitiers in 1356 (176–235) on chs. 168 and 173 (Metz, pp. 105–7).

0 SD *Philippa* The name of Edward's queen was Philippa of Hainault (see 1.1.148n.), spelt in the play 'Phillip' or 'Philip' and treated as a bisyllable; hence Capell's adoption, followed here in speeches, of the French bisyllabic form 'Philippe'.

1–3 Compare 4.2.37–61, especially lines 49–53.

And now unto this proud resisting town:
Soldiers, assault! I will no longer stay
To be deluded by their false delays.
Put all to sword, and make the spoil your own.

Enter six CITIZENS *in their shirts, barefoot, with halters about their necks*

ALL CITIZENS Mercy, King Edward, mercy, gracious lord!
KING EDWARD Contemptuous villains, call ye now for truce?
Mine ears are stopped against your bootless cries.
Sound drums' alarum, draw threat'ning swords!
FIRST CITIZEN Ah, noble prince, take pity on this town,
And hear us, mighty king.
We claim the promise that your highness made:
The two days' respite is not yet expired,
And we are come with willingness to bear
What torturing death or punishment you please,
So that the trembling multitude be saved.
KING EDWARD My promise? Well, I do confess as much;
But I require the chiefest citizens
And men of most account that should submit.
You, peradventure, are but servile grooms,
Or some felonious robbers on the sea,
Whom, apprehended, law would execute,
Albeit severity lay dead in us.
No, no, you cannot overreach us thus.

7 SD] *As in* Q2*; before* 0 SD Q1 8 SH] *All* Qq*; 1.Cit./Capell, WP, TB; Cit./Smith, WAA* 11 drums' alarum,] *TB, Smith, WAA (subst.)*; drummes allarum, Qq*;* drums; [*Alarum*] *Capell, WP*; drums, alarum! *RLA* 12 SH] *Capell and all edns; All.* Qq 12–13] *So divided* Qq*; divided at* prince,/ king/ *Capell* 20 require] Qq*;* requir'd *Delius, conj. Capell*

7 SD In Q1 the entrance of the six Citizens is placed at the beginning of the scene, before that of Edward and his train. It may reflect particular stage requirements, discussed in the Introduction, pp. 8–9.

10 bootless useless.

11 An elliptical exclamatory sentence. Edward is not calling on his drummers to sound the alarum, but reproaching the citizens for having refused surrender by rallying to the sound of their drums and threatening the English with their swords. There is no reason to treat 'alarum' as a stage direction (see Collation).

12 SH Qq's heading *All* indicates that the speaker acts as mouthpiece for all the citizens; *Two*, a conventional abbreviation for 'second speaker', at 27 confirms that 'first citizen' must be understood here.

13 A short line for greater emphasis.

14 promise See 4.2.72–8.

21 that Transposed for metrical reasons from after 'require' at 20.

22 grooms fellows, expressing contempt (*OED* Groom *sb*[1] 2).

24–5 subject to capital punishment when apprehended, even if we were disposed to clemency.

26 overreach outwit (*OED* sv *v* 6).

SECOND CITIZEN The sun, dread lord, that in the western fall
Beholds us now low brought through misery,
Did in the orient purple of the morn
Salute our coming forth when we were known,
Or may our portion be with damnèd fiends.

KING EDWARD If it be so, then let our covenant stand –
We take possession of the town in peace;
But for yourselves look you for no remorse,
But, as imperial justice hath decreed,
Your bodies shall be dragged about these walls
And, after, feel the stroke of quartering steel.
This is your doom. Go, soldiers, see it done.

QUEEN Ah, be more mild unto these yielding men!
It is a glorious thing to stablish peace,
And kings approach the nearest unto God
By giving life and safety unto men:
As thou intendest to be king of France,
So let her people live to call thee king,
For what the sword cuts down or fire hath spoiled
Is held in reputation none of ours.

KING EDWARD Although experience teach us this is true,
That a peaceful quietness brings most delight
When most of all abuses are controlled,
Yet, insomuch it shall be known that we
As well can master our affections
As conquer other by the dint of sword,

27 SH] QQ (*Two*) **30** known,] Q2; knowne Q1; known / To be the chiefest men of all our town: / Of this, my sovereign lord, be well assured. *conj. Elze apud WP* **31** fiends] QQ; friends *Capell* **33** the] QQ; this *Collier* **44** her] Q1; thy Q2

27–30 A similar elaboration of the proverbial 'In the morning the heights, in the evening the depths' (Tilley M1174) is found in Senecan plays, notably *Thyestes* (trans. J. Heywood, 1560): 'Whom dawne of day hath seene in pryde to raygne, / Hym ouerthrowne hath seene the euening late.'

31 may we be damned in hell (if what we say is untrue).

34 remorse remission (*OED* sv *sb* 3 lists 'compassion, mitigation').

37 quartering steel The blades with which the bodies of capital offenders were dismembered, see 3.2.5n.

39–46 Compare Frois., ch. 146 (Metz, p. 91), quoted in the Appendix, pp. 213–14.

41–2 kings . . . men Proverbial, 'It is in their mercy that kings come closest to Gods' (Tilley M898). Compare Tamora's appeal for mercy in *Tit.* 1.1.117–18, and *MV* 4.1.196–7: 'earthly power doth then show likest God's / When mercy seasons justice'.

46 held . . . reputation considered, reputed.

49 abuses . . . controlled offences are punished.

50 insomuch . . . be in order to make it.

50–2 we . . . sword Referring to the proverb, 'He is not fit to command other that cannot command himself' (Tilley C552).

51 affections passions (*OED* Affection *sb* 3).

52 other others, a collective plural, see 3.1.136.

Philippe, prevail: we yield to thy request;
These men shall live to boast of clemency,
And, Tyranny, strike terror to thyself.

CITIZENS Long live your highness, happy be your reign!

KING EDWARD Go get you hence, return unto the town,
And if this kindness hath deserved your love,
Learn then to reverence Edward as your king.
[*Exeunt Citizens*]
Now might we hear of our affairs abroad.
We would, till gloomy winter were o'erspent,
Dispose our men in garrison a while –
But who comes here?

Enter COPLAND *and* KING DAVID

DERBY Copland, my lord, and David King of Scots.

KING EDWARD Is this the proud presumptuous esquire of the North
That would not yield his prisoner to my queen?

COPLAND I am, my liege, a northern esquire indeed,
But neither proud nor insolent, I trust.

KING EDWARD What moved thee then to be so obstinate
To contradict our royal queen's desire?

COPLAND No wilful disobedience, mighty lord,
But my desert, and public law of arms.
I took the king myself in single fight
And, like a soldier, would be loath to lose
The least pre-eminence that I had won.
And Copland, straight upon your highness' charge,
Is come to France, and with a lowly mind

56 SH] *Capell, Smith, WAA; Two* Qq; *2.Cit. / WP, RLA (subst.)* 59 SD] *Capell and mod. edns; Ex.* Q1; *Exit.* Q2 62–3] *As in* Q1; *one line* Q2 64 Scots] Q1; Sots Q2 65, 67 esquire] Qq; 'squire *Capell;* Squire *WP* 69 SH] Q1 (*Ki:*); *not in* Q2 72 of] Q2; at Q1

53 Compare Frois., ch. 146 (Metz, p. 91) 'The kyng behelde the quene and stode styll in a study a space, and than sayd, A dame . . . ye make suche request to me that I can nat deny you.'

56 SH Qq repeat here the heading *Two* used at 27, as if the line were spoken by the second citizen. But the reaction is common to all of them, like the plea for mercy at 8.

61–2 Hol. (II, 648) gives 3 August 1347 as the date of the surrender of Calais, and Frois. devotes ch. 147 (Ker, I, 332–4) to 'Howe the kyng of Englande repeopled the towne of Calys with Englysshmen'.

64 **David** John Copland (or Copeland) did go to Calais in reply to the royal summons, but did not take King David with him; see 4.2.56n.

65–96 Closely modelled on Frois., ch. 139 (Metz, pp. 86–8), except for the fact that at the time Queen Philippa had not reached Calais.

65, 67 **esquire** Pronounced as a monosyllable.

72 **public . . . arms** accepted code of warfare.

Doth vail the bonnet of his victory.
Receive, dread lord, the custom of my fraught,
The wealthy tribute of my labouring hands,
Which should long since have been surrendered up,
Had but your gracious self been there in place.

QUEEN But, Copland, thou didst scorn the king's command,
Neglecting our commission in his name.

COPLAND His name I reverence, but his person more.
His name shall keep me in allegiance still,
But to his person I will bend my knee.

KING EDWARD I pray thee, Philippe, let displeasure pass:
This man doth please me, and I like his words;
For what is he that will attempt great deeds
And lose the glory that ensues the same?
All rivers have recourse unto the sea,
And Copland's faith, relation to his king.
Kneel therefore down. – Now rise, King Edward's knight,
And, to maintain thy state, I freely give
Five hundred marks a year to thee and thine.

Enter SALISBURY

Welcome, Lord Salisbury, what news from Bretagne?

SALISBURY This, mighty king: the country we have won,
And Charles de Mountford, regent of that place,
Presents your highness with this coronet,

90 great] Qq; high *Capell* **94** King] Q1; K. Q2 **96** SD *As in* Q2; *after 97* Q1 **97** Bretagne] Brittaine Q1; Britaine Q2 **99** Charles] Qq; John *Capell and most edns*

78 doth . . . bonnet A current phrase (*OED* Bonnet *sb* 1): makes a show of submission.

79 custom tribute (owed by a tenant to his lord: *OED* sv *sb* 3).

79 fraught freight, cargo – with reference to King David, taken to Calais in Copland's ship.

82 in place present (*OED* Place *sb*[1] 19b).

84 Ignoring that I represented the king; 'our' is a 'royal plural'.

92 Proverbial (Tilley R140).

93 Copland's allegiance (faith) bears the same relation to his king as that of rivers to the sea.

94–6 Compare Frois. (Metz, pp. 87–8), but closer to Hol. (II, 645): 'the king did not onelie pardon him, but also gaue to him fiue hundred pounds sterling of yearelie rent, to him & to his heires for euer . . . and made him esquire for his bodie'.

97–175 All this section of the scene is the dramatist's original invention, imagining the aftermath of the safe-conduct episode (see 4.1, 4.3.1–56, and 4.5.56–126) to bridge over the siege of Calais and the victory at Poitiers, in preparation for the *coup de théâtre* at 176. Frois. (ch. 135, Metz, p. 85) reports that Sir Walter de Manny (Salisbury in the play) 'went to Cales, and was welcome to the kynge [Edward]', who asked him to return the gifts received from the King of France, see 4.5.97–102n.

99–101 See 4.1.4–9n. for this episode, which dates from 1341. The name of the historical Lord Montfort was John, not Charles, and many editors alter it accordingly.

Protesting true allegiance to your grace.
KING EDWARD We thank thee for thy service, valiant earl.
Challenge our favour, for we owe it thee.
SALISBURY But now, my lord, as this is joyful news,
So must my voice be tragical again,
And I must sing of doleful accidents.
KING EDWARD What, have our men the overthrow at Poitiers,
Or is our son beset with too much odds?
SALISBURY He was, my lord, and as my worthless self
With forty other serviceable knights,
Under safe-conduct of the Dauphin's seal,
Did travel that way, finding him distressed,
A troop of lances met us on the way,
Surprised, and brought us prisoners to the king,
Who, proud of this and eager of revenge,
Commanded straight to cut off all our heads,
And surely we had died, but that the duke,
More full of honour than his angry sire,
Procured our quick deliverance from thence.
But ere we went, 'Salute your king', quoth he,
'Bid him provide a funeral for his son:
Today our sword shall cut his thread of life,
And sooner than he thinks we'll be with him
To quittance those displeasures he hath done.'
This said, we passed, not daring to reply;
Our hearts were dead, our looks diffused and wan.
Wandering, at last we climbed unto a hill
From whence, although our grief were much before,
Yet now, to see the occasion with our eyes
Did thrice so much increase our heaviness.

108 our] Qq; my *Capell* **114** prisoners] Qq ; prisoner *Collier* **117** we had] Qq ; had we *Collier*

108 is . . . odds Compare 3.4.33: 'He's close encompassed with a world of odds'; 'much' = 'many', as frequently at the time.

109–26 Recalling the scene with King John at 4.5.56–126.

110 serviceable faithful.

113 lances lancers (horse soldiers armed with lances; see *OED* Lance *sb*[1] 4a, first example 1602).

118 sire father.

122 cut . . . life A current commonplace referring to the thread believed to be spun and cut off by the Fates, see *OED* Thread *sb* 6, and compare *1H6* 1.1.33 and *2H6* 4.2.31.

124 quittance Used verbally: repay (*OED* sv *v* 3). So in *1H6* 2.1.14, 'to quittance their deceit'.

124 displeasures injuries (*OED* Displeasure *sb* 3); at 3 and 88 the word is used in its current meaning.

126 diffused confused, distracted (*OED* sv. *ppl. a* 1).

129 occasion event, happening (*OED* sv. *sb.*[1] 7a).

130 heaviness sadness.

For there, my lord, oh, there we did descry
Down in a valley how both armies lay:
The French had cast their trenches like a ring
And every barricado's open front
Was thick embossed with brazen ordinance.
Here stood a battle of ten thousand horse,
There twice as many pikes in quadrant wise,
Here crossbows and deadly wounding darts,
And in the midst, like to a slender point
Within the compass of the horizon,
As 'twere a rising bubble in the sea,
A hazel wand amidst a wood of pines,
Or as a bear fast chained unto a stake,
Stood famous Edward, still expecting when
Those dogs of France would fasten on his flesh.
Anon the death-procuring knell begins,
Off go the cannons that with trembling noise
Did shake the very mountain where they stood.
Then sound the trumpets' clangor in the air,
The battles join, and, when we could no more
Discern the difference 'twixt the friend and foe,
So intricate the dark confusion was,
Away we turned our wat'ry eyes with sighs
As black as powder fuming into smoke.
And thus, I fear, unhappy, have I told
The most untimely tale of Edward's fall.

QUEEN Ah me, is this my welcome into France?

138 crossbows and] Qq; crossbows, arm'd with *Capell, WP conj. Capell* 146 death-procuring] Q2; *unhyphenated* Q1 148 they] Qq; we *Capell* 149 clangor] Qq; clangors *Capell*

131–54 Another conventional 'battlescape' similar to those at 3.1.144–84 and 4.4.12–39.

134 barricado protective barrier.

135 embossed . . . ordinance The cannons dotting the French entrenchment are compared to the metal bosses decorating the straps and belts of the armour. 'Embossed' = covered with ornamental bosses or studs (*OED* sv *ppl. a* 2); 'ordinance' = battle array (*OED* sv *sb* 1), but also a trisyllabic form of 'ordnance' = artillery.

136 battle military array, see 3.3.219 and 225n.

137 in . . . wise in the manner of a quadrant, i.e. a quarter of a circle (Lapides).

143 bear . . . stake The image is from the popular entertainment of bear-baiting, consisting in unleashing dogs (145) against a bear tied to a stake at the centre of the arena. Compare 3.1.118–19.

146 death-procuring fatal.

148 they Capell suggests 'we', identifying the 'mountain' with the 'hill' (127) from which Salisbury and his knights were watching the battle.

149 sound Depending on 'clangor'; the plural form is due to the attraction of 'trumpets'.

153–4 sighs . . . smoke WP compare with several Shakespearean passages, notably *Rom.* 1.1.190, 'a smoke made with the fume of sighs'.

156 untimely premature, unseasonable (qualifying 'fall' rather than 'tale'); see 3.1.184.

Is this the comfort that I looked to have,
When I should meet with my belovèd son?
Sweet Ned, I would thy mother in the sea
Had been prevented of this mortal grief.

KING EDWARD Content thee, Philippe: 'tis not tears will serve
To call him back, if he be taken hence.
Comfort thyself, as I do, gentle queen,
With hope of sharp, unheard of, dire revenge.
He bids me to provide his funeral!
And so I will; but all the peers in France
Shall mourners be, and weep out bloody tears
Until their empty veins be dry and sere.
The pillars of his hearse shall be their bones,
The mould that covers him, their city ashes,
His knell, the groaning cries of dying men,
And in the stead of tapers on his tomb
A hundred fifty towers shall burning blaze,
While we bewail our valiant son's decease.

After a flourish sounded within, enter a HERALD

HERALD Rejoice, my lord, ascend the imperial throne:
The mighty and redoubted Prince of Wales,
Great servitor to bloody Mars in arms,
The Frenchman's terror and his country's fame,
Triumphant rideth like a Roman peer,
And, lowly at his stirrup, comes afoot

170 their] *Delius, WP;* his QQ **171** city] QQ*;* city' *Capell;* city's *Collier;* cities' *Delius, WP (subst.)* **174** A hundred] *This edn;* An hundred QQ **174** fifty] QQ*;* lofty *Collier* **175** SD] *As* SD Q2*; as a line of verse* Q1 (an herald)

161 prevented of spared (by dying at sea).

162–3 'tis . . . back Proverbial, Dent, *PLED*, T82.12, quoting Brooke's *History of Romeus and Juliet*, 1797, 'You can not call him back with tears', and *Locrine* 5.1.20, 'Teares cannot raise him from the dead againe.'

166 He . . . his 'He' refers to the King of France, 'his' to Prince Edward.

167–75 A tirade echoing closely in words and imagery Tamburlaine bewailing Zenocrate in Marlowe, *2 Tamburlaine* 3.2.

169 sere Literally 'withered', reinforcing 'dry'.

170 their QQ's 'his' is a slip due to the attraction of 'his hearse'.

171 mould earth.

171 their . . . ashes An adjectival use of 'city': the ashes of their cities.

174 A hundred fifty 'Hundred and fifty' is a favourite number with Shakespeare, recurring three times in *1H4*, in *AYLI* 5.1.56–7 ('I will kill thee in a hundred and fifty ways'), *Wiv.* 3.4.48, and *AWW* 4.3.161–2. But perhaps Capell was right in thinking 'fifty' a printer's misreading of 'lofty', see e.g. Marlowe, *1 Tamburlaine* 4.2.102, 'Damascus' lofty towers'.

177 redoubted (1) dreaded, (2) reverenced.

178 servitor attendant, soldier (*OED* sv *sb* 1 and 3, and compare 3.1.45 above) of the god of war.

181–3 lowly . . . bonds Compare *JC* 1.1.33–4, 'What tributaries follow him to Rome / To grace in captive bonds his chariot wheels?', recalling in turn *1H6* 1.1.20–2, 'death's dishonourable victory / We with our stately presence glorify,/ Like captives bound to a triumphal car'.

King John of France together with his son
In captive bonds, whose diadem he brings
To crown thee with, and to proclaim thee king.
KING EDWARD Away with mourning, Philippe, wipe thine eyes!
Sound, trumpets, welcome in, Plantagenet!

Enter PRINCE *Edward*, KING JOHN, PHILIP, AUDLEY [*and*] ARTOIS

As things long lost when they are found again,
So doth my son rejoice his father's heart,
For whom even now my soul was much perplexed.
QUEEN Be this a token to express my joy,
Kiss him
For inward passions will not let me speak.
PRINCE My gracious father, here receive the gift,
This wreath of conquest and reward of war,
Got with as mickle peril of our lives
As e'er was thing of price before this day.
Install your highness in your proper right,
And herewithal I render to your hands
These prisoners, chief occasion of our strife.
KING EDWARD So, John of France, I see you keep your word:
You promised to be sooner with ourself
Than we did think for, and 'tis so indeed.
But had you done at first as now you do,
How many civil towns had stood untouched
That now are turned to ragged heaps of stones?
How many people's lives mightst thou have saved
That are untimely sunk into their graves?

186 SD *and*] Q2; *not in* Q1 **187** As] Q2; *Ki*: As Q1 **189** perplexed.] Qq (perplext); perplexed! *running to the Prince, and embracing him. / Capell* **190** SD] Qq *in right margin opposite 190; kissing him / Capell* **192** gift,] Qq; gift, *presenting him with King* John*'s crown. / Capell, WP* **202** you . . . you] Q1; ye . . . ye Q2 **205** mightst thou] Q1; might you Q2

182 his son In the play two sons are captured with King John at Poitiers, but here the author recalls Frois., ch. 173 (Metz, p. 106): 'the prince of Wales . . . ordayned for shyppes, to conuey the Frenche kyng and his sonne . . . into England'. Compare 186 SD n.

186 SD Historically, at the time of Poitiers King Edward was in London, and only in the following winter 'the prince conueyed the Frenche kyng fro Bordeux into Englande' (Frois., ch. 173, Metz, pp. 106–7).

188 rejoice A transitive use: gladden.

189 perplexed troubled.

193 wreath The crown of France, called 'diadem' at 183.

194 mickle great.

198 occasion cause.

200–1 See 123 above and 4.5.124.

204 ragged broken, jagged. Compare *2H4* Ind.35: 'worm-eaten hole of ragged stone'.

206 untimely Used adverbially: 'prematurely', see 156 above.

KING JOHN Edward, recount not things irrevocable.
Tell me what ransom thou requirest to have.
KING EDWARD Thy ransom, John, hereafter shall be known.
But first to England thou must cross the seas,
To see what entertainment it affords –
Howe'er it falls, it cannot be so bad
As ours hath been since we arrived in France.
KING JOHN Accursed man! Of this I was foretold,
But did misconster what the prophet told.
PRINCE Now, father, this petition Edward makes
To thee, whose grace hath been his strongest shield:
That as thy pleasure chose me for the man
To be the instrument to show thy power,
So thou wilt grant that many princes more,
Bred and brought up within that little isle,
May still be famous for like victories;
And for my part, the bloody scars I bear,
The weary nights that I have watched in field,
The dangerous conflicts I have often had,
The fearful menaces were proffered me,
The heat and cold, and what else might displease,
I wish were now redoubled twentyfold,
So that hereafter ages, when they read
The painful traffic of my tender youth,
Might thereby be inflamed with such resolve
As not the territories of France alone,
But likewise Spain, Turkey, and what countries else
That justly would provoke fair England's ire,
Might at their presence tremble and retire.
KING EDWARD Here, English lords, we do proclaim a rest,

221 that] Qq; this *Collier* **232** territories] Qq; territory *conj. Capell*

210–13 According to Frois. (ch. 173, Metz, p. 107), once in England 'the French kyng was remoued fro the Sauoy to the castell of Wyndsore, and all his householde, and went a huntyng and a haukyng ther about at his pleasur'.

212 falls falls out.

215 misconster An alternative form of 'misconstrue': misinterpret.

215 what . . . told See 4.3.72–3 and n.

226 fearful menaces Alluding to the heralds' taunts at 4.4.67–76, 89–94, 101–9.

227 displease harm, compare 'displeasures' at 124.

229 hereafter Used as adjective: future.

230 traffic employment.

235 their Referring to 'many princes' (220).

An intercession of our painful arms:
Sheathe up your swords, refresh your weary limbs,
Peruse your spoils, and after we have breathed
A day or two within this haven town,
God willing, then for England we'll be shipped,
Where in a happy hour I trust we shall
Arrive, three kings, two princes, and a queen.

[*Exeunt*]

FINIS.

237 An] QQ; And *Delius* 237 intercession] Q1; interceasing Q2 243 SD] *Capell* (*Flourish. Exeunt omnes*); *not in* QQ

237 intercession intermission, suspension (*OED* sv *sb* 5).

237 painful (1) harmful, (2) painstaking (compare 230).

241–3 for England . . . queen Historically, King Edward and Queen Philippa were in England at the time of the battle of Poitiers (see 186 SD n.), though they had been at Calais in 1347; King David of Scotland was never in Calais; he remained a prisoner in London from late 1346 till 1357. Prince Charles Duke of Normandy escaped capture and remained in France. The dramatist seems suddenly aware of this when he mentions 'two princes', i.e. Edward Prince of Wales and Prince Philip, the youngest son of the French King. In fact those taking ship for England were only Prince Edward with King John and Prince Philip (see 182 n.), one king (not three), two princes and no queen.

TEXTUAL ANALYSIS

Only two early editions of *The Reign of King Edward the third* are extant, the quartos dated 1596 and 1599, both published by Cuthbert Burby, who had entered 'A book Intitled Edward the Third and the blacke prince their warres wth kinge Iohn of Fraunce' in the Stationers' Register on 1 December 1595. Though after Burby's death in 1609 the rights to this, as well as to a number of other books belonging to him, were transferred repeatedly from publisher to publisher (W. Welby in 1609, T. Snodham in 1618, W. Stansby in 1626, R. Bishop in 1639), there is no reason to believe that the play was ever reissued in the seventeenth century. The first quarto of 1596 remains therefore the only authoritative copy-text for modern editions of the play, though some of the variants introduced in the second quarto of 1599 must be taken into account for reasons that will appear later.

The title-page of the first edition is uncommonly concise: THE RAIGNE OF KING EDVVARD the third: *As it hath bin sundrie times plaied about the Citie of London.* LONDON, *Printed for Cuthbert Burby.* 1596. There is no mention of the author or of a London company that performed the play. The formula used in this case is the same appearing on the title-page of 'a pleasant conceited comedy' published the same year by Burby after having registered it not long before *Edward III* (26 November 1595): *A Knack to Know an Honest Man.* In both cases the printer is not indicated, but it is clear from certain repeated features and peculiarities, for instance the uncommon practice of not indenting speech headings, and the way of 'signing' each quarto gathering, omitting the signature letters on the second and third leaf,[1] that both plays came from the same shop. Fred Lapides, in his exhaustive study of the printing of the quarto prefixed to his critical edition of the play,[2] has incontrovertibly established that the work was done in the shop of the little-known printer Thomas Scarlet, who died in August or September 1596, and who, two years earlier, had printed for Burby the first quarto of John Lyly's *Mother Bombie*.[3]

[1] The fourth leaf is unsigned. R. A Sayce, 'Compositorial practices and the localization of printed books 1530–1800', *Library* 5 series 21 (1966), 1–45, confirms (pp. 26–30) that this practice was very unusual in the whole of Europe: in England, up to 1665, at least the first three leaves of each quarto quire were generally signed with letters as well as numbers. In Q1 of *Edward III* only C3 is signed with the letter as well as the number.

[2] Fred Lapides, *The Raigne of King Edward the Third. A Critical Old-Spelling Edition*, 1980, pp. 56–72. The edition was prepared as a doctoral dissertation in 1966.

[3] Greg, *BEPD*, I, 225–6, remarks: 'The reappearance of an ornament and the common peculiarities of the signatures and speakers' names suggest that this book [Q1 of *Edward III*] came from the same press as *A Knack to Know an Honest Man.*' And about the latter: 'The printer appears from the device to have been either Thomas Scarlet, who died Aug.–Sept. 1596, or Robert Robinson, who seems to have used it in the following year; but the ornament at the end points rather to Adam Islip.' Lapides (p. 58) remarks that neither Robinson nor Islip ever used Scarlet's type of signature.

The varying number of lines per page, irregular spacing, erratic catchwords,[1] and the use of extra-large type for the directions on two occasions (signatures E1ᵛ and E2), suggest that the text was not set continuously but by formes – in other words, the compositors[2] had to work out in advance how many lines of the manuscript would fill each page so as to be able to set them irrespective of the sequential order in the manuscript. This accounts for a number of irregularities and omissions, especially in stage directions and speech headings, while numerous errors in the latter are certainly due to the compositors' misdirected attempt at expanding headings which in the manuscript copy were indicated, if at all, by single initials or by a couple of letters.[3] One omission of a speech heading, on the very first page of the text (A3 – 1.1.28) is discussed in the Commentary, but headings are frequently omitted not only for speeches following immediately upon the speaker's entrance direction ('Countess' at 1.2.1 (B1ᵛ), 'Frenchman' at 3.2.46 (F1), 'Artois' at 3.3.13 (F1ᵛ) and 3.4.23 (G1), 'Captain' at 4.2.62 (G4), 'King John', 'Charles', 'Philip' at 4.6.18, 28, 34 (all I2)), but also in the main body of scenes.[4]

One such case is worth discussing since it may throw light on the copy that went to the printers. After the general *Exeunt* on sig. B3ᵛ, which in modern editions marks the end of the first act, there is no extra space or entrance direction for the next scene (2.1), but the text continues with a new speech prefixed by the heading *Lor*:. This was the speech heading used throughout the first act for the character of the French messenger or ambassador Lorraine; only forty-eight lines later, from the words of King Edward who has entered at 24, we learn that the speaker at the opening of the scene is called 'Lodwicke'. *Lor:* is an unwarranted expansion of what must have been the prefix *Lo.* in the margin of the manuscript at this point. And in fact, the three speech headings on B4ᵛ (at 49, 52, 60) are simply *Lo:*. But on the next page, C1, we find again *Lor:* or

[1] Here is a list of anomalous catchwords: 'Per-' at A3, which refers to the *second* line of A3ᵛ, where 'Perhaps' is preceded by the heading *Art*:; other catchwords that ignore speech headings preceding them in the text are: 'Ignoble' at A4ᵛ, 'Read' at C1ᵛ, 'All' at C2ᵛ, 'Lets' at D2ᵛ, 'Make' at I2. Instead at E3 'K.*Io.* Now' compensates for a missing speech heading in the text, and at G4 'I will' supplies a missing pronoun in the text. At C3ᵛ 'O' refers to the the last line on the same page instead of the first on the next. There are several other odd mistakes, such as 'Ch:' for 'Cry' at B1ᵛ, 'A' for 'As' at B3ᵛ, 'N' for 'Nor' at B4, 'An' for 'And' at H1.

[2] In his thorough discussion of the printing history of the quarto, Lapides (pp. 67–72) reaches the tentative conclusion that one compositor was responsible for gatherings A–G (up to 4.2.71 in the present edition) and another for H–K; see below.

[3] Mistaken speech headings are found, apart from the case of the character of Lodowick, which is treated later, at: 2.1.348 (C3ᵛ), *King* for *Warwick*; 2.2.8 (D2ᵛ), *King* for *Derby*; 2.2.22 (D2ᵛ), *Ar.[tois]* for *Audley*; 3.3.137 (F3ᵛ) and 4.5.22, 24, 28, 55 (exit direction) (H4–H4ᵛ), *Pr.* or *Pri.[nce]* for *Philip*; 4.5.70 (I1), *En:Io:* for *Ki[ng] Io[hn]*; 4.5.73 (I1), *Vil.[liers]* for *Charles*; 4.6.47 (I2), again *Pr.* for *Philip*. These errors are rectified in the 1599 quarto, where also Q1's mistaken heading *Da.* at 1.2.45 (B2), that could be taken to refer to *King David*, is correctly expanded to *Douglas*.

[4] Apart from 1.1.28, discussed in the Commentary, the speech heading *King (Edward)* is missing at 1.2.117 (B3), 2.1.235 (C3), 2.1.323 (C4ᵛ, at the beginning of the page), 2.2.150 (D4ᵛ), and 3.4.112 (G2ᵛ). *King John* is missing at 3.1.79 (E2ᵛ) and 3.1.125 (E3ᵛ, top of the page, but the catchword at the bottom of E3 is *K.Io.*). *Prince (Edward)* is missing at 3.3.206 (F4ᵛ). All these omissions are made good in the second quarto. Lapides (pp. 60–1), though correctly attributing the faults listed here and in the previous note to the state of the copy, does not make allowances for mistaken expansions or omissions due exclusively to the compositors.

Lor, at 80, 95, 99. On C1^v^ and C2 Lodwick is correctly designated seven times *Lo:* (at 130, 142, 150, 151, 168, 170, 174), while on his last appearance in this scene, on C2^v^ (194) the heading is once again *Lor:*.[1] In other words, the noncommittal prefix *Lo:* is used in the outer forme of gathering B and in the inner forme of gathering C (C1^v^, C2), while the wrong prefix *Lor:* appears in the inner forme of B and in the outer of C (C1, C2^v^). It can be hypothesised, then, that, contrary to Lapides's belief, not one, but two compositors worked also on the gatherings A–G of the book, alternating in the setting of the inner and outer formes of each gathering. Neither of them was particularly expert, and both had difficulties in reading the handwriting(s) of the copy, but while one was unimaginative and reproduced as best he could what he read, the other was more adventurous, and attempted repeatedly to expand the scanty indications of the speakers' names (in a number of cases, on F3^v^, H4, H4^v^, I2, the initial 'P' for 'Philip' has apparently been mistakenly expanded to *Pri.* or *Pr.* for 'Prince').

These and several other confusions especially in speech headings and stage directions confirm Lapides's finding that the manuscript that went to the printers was neither a prompt-book prepared by a competent book-keeper for use in performance, nor a scribe's fair copy of the text. He concludes that the available evidence points to an 'author's manuscript'. All the same, the text, apart from the possible omission of a line (at 2.1.106, sig. C1) and a number of misreadings and misprints, all imputable to the compositors' inadvertence or incompetence, does not present any of those hopeless muddles which characterise plays set from an author's foul papers, where corrections, deletions, interlineations and marginal additions can mislead quite competent printers. Here, instead, even line divisions appear on the whole exceptionally correct. Only in one case a line seems to have been misplaced (at 4.4.42–4, sig. H2, but it may well be a printing-house accident),[2] while the lines on the emblem of the pelican at the close of 3.4 (122–6, sig. G2^v^) look like a misplaced insertion possibly from a slip of paper added to the manuscript.

The contrast between the slovenliness in the treatment of directions and headings, and the comparative accuracy in the layout of the verse, can be explained if we assume that the copy for the quarto was neither authorial foul papers, nor prompt-book or scribal fair copy, but an intermediate document, such as would be required if the play were not the work of a single author. In such cases it generally happened that one of the collaborators in the work, possibly the 'plotter' of the play, would take it upon himself to assemble the materials provided by the playwrights engaged in the communal enterprise, preparing a rough transcript that would be passed on to a professional book-keeper with a view to the compilation of a proper prompt-book.[3] It was a normal

[1] Lodowick makes only another brief appearance in the play, in 2.2, and his three speeches there, at 44 (D3), 73 and 101 (D3^v^) are all headed *Lo:*.

[2] Noted by MacD. P. Jackson, 'A note on the text of "Edward III"', *N&Q*, 216 (1971), 453.

[3] A similar procedure can be exemplified by the best-known theatrical manuscript written at about the same time (1592–3), *The Booke of Sir Thomas Moore*, but in that case the 'plotter' of the play, Anthony Munday, produced neither a rough assemblage of the work of the collaborators, nor a proper prompt-book, but a fair copy of the finished text, presumably with a view to submitting it to literate readers as well as to a company of players. See *Sir Thomas More*, ed. V. Gabrieli and G. Melchiori (Revels Plays), 1990, Introduction, pp. 3, 11–14, 28.

practice, at this early stage, to transcribe first all the speeches one after the other, adding marginally, after completion of each page or leaf, essential indications of the speakers, as well as centred head directions at the beginning of new scenes. It was easy, therefore, when a new scene began on a new page, to forget to add the initial entry direction at the top. I suspect that this is what happened at the beginning of 2.1, where there should have been some indication of the scene change.[1] The omission of the direction 'Enter Lodwick' at this point caused the subsequent confusion in the speech headings for this character. It was also customary to separate each speech from the next by a half-line rule. The accidental omission of such rules in the manuscript would cause the compiler, who added marginal indications of the speakers after completion of each page, to leave out some of them. This accounts for the missing speech headings in the text.

The conclusion to be drawn from an analysis of the first quarto is that it is based on a manuscript which can be called authorial only in so much as it represents the first assemblage of the scenes of the play contributed by different authors. Most playscripts for the public theatre in the Elizabethan age were the result of the collaboration of several writers, as Henslowe's comparatively late records, registering payments to a number of different authors for the same play, amply testify.[2] Since companies were loath to entrust printers with a prompt-book which existed in a single copy, they submitted the nearest thing to it: authorial foul papers in the case of plays by single authors, or the rough copy on which the prompt-book was based when several hands had contributed to the script. The copy for the 1596 quarto of *The Reign of King Edward the third* seems therefore to be in the nature of a final rough copy of the whole play compiled by one of the collaborators, before a professional book-keeper transcribed it as a prompt-book for use in the theatre. At all events, the writing habits attested by the printed text show that the 'assembler' of this rough copy was certainly not Shakespeare. On the other hand, some of the manuscript leaves may have been inserted in it directly as they came from their respective authors.

As I argued discussing the 'Countess scenes' in the Introduction, pp. 36–9, the latter may have been the case of at least part of the presumptive Shakespearean contribution to the play, and more precisely of the leaves containing the text of Act 2. Apart from the already noted lack of the initial stage direction, there are two further reasons for suspecting Shakespeare's hand here. One is the spelling 'emured' for 'immured' at 2.1.178, a spelling testified in no other author except twice in *Love's Labour's Lost* 3.1.124 and 4.3.325 (Q1 (1598) sigs. D1, F3, a text based on authorial foul papers).[3] That this is a typical Shakespearean spelling is confirmed by the use of the nonce word 'emures' as a noun (walls) both in the quarto (1609) and in the Folio text of *Troilus and Cressida*, Prologue 9. The other, less cogent, reason to suspect Shake-

[1] It should be noted that this is one of the scenes generally attributed to Shakespeare, and the evidence of the addition in Hand D in *Sir Thomas More* confirms that he, even more than the other collaborators in that play, left the task of adding stage directions and regularising speech headings to the book-keeper in charge of assembling the script. See Melchiori, 'Hand D'.

[2] See G. E. Bentley, *The Profession of Dramatist in Shakespeare's Time*, 1971, *passim*.

[3] But 'immured' is found in *Sonn.* 84.3 and 'immur'd' elsewhere. *Ven.* 1194 (last line) has 'immure'.

speare's hand is the survival in the first quarto of the play (sig. D4^v) of the use of capital instead of lower case C for 'Cannot' at 2.2.148. This may reflect the author's habit, noted in the three pages in Hand D in the manuscript of *The Booke of Sir Thomas Moore*, of nearly always capitalising initial C not only in nouns or adjectives but also in verbal forms, a feature absent from the rest of that manuscript or in fact from any other manuscript of the time.[1] It can be surmised therefore that the printer of the first quarto of *Edward III* was setting from copy in the same hand responsible for Addition II in Hand D to *Sir Thomas More*, a hand generally recognised as Shakespeare's.

The second quarto of 1599, coming from the press of the more reputable printer Simon Stafford, is, as Lapides remarks, a much better job of printing. The text is completely reset, with a much neater typographical layout, uniform type-setting, spacing, spelling, and punctuation. But it has no independent authority, since it is clear that the copy used was no new manuscript but the earlier edition, subjected to a fairly thorough and competent revision. In other words, while the changes in layout, spelling, and punctuation may be imputed to the house style or rules of the new printers, there is no doubt that somebody undertook the task of going over a copy of Q1 in order to disentangle and clarify as best he could the confusions in stage directions and speech headings – in most cases spelling out the latter in full, so as to leave no doubt as to the identity of the speakers – and to detect and correct the original printers' most obvious misreadings of the manuscript.

It appears that the reviser had no access to the original manuscript from which Q1 had been set. He was certainly not one of the collaborators in the writing of the play, and it is unlikely that he was a mere compositor in the printing-house. In fact, he did not confine himself to correcting by guesswork those words and passages which are undoubted misreadings of the copy, but at times he tried to 'improve' or 'regularise' the text. His interventions are particularly helpful in correctly expanding or replacing the erratic speech headings of the first quarto.[2] In the case of Lodowick in 2.1, the second quarto prints, instead of the misleading *Lor.* of Q1, the name in full, *Lodowicke.* as a heading for his first speech (though the reviser does not supply an entrance stage direction for him), and throughout the scene the unequivocal abbreviation *Lodo.* is used, except at 49 and 80, where the heading is the full *Lodowicke.* The reviser generally took care to supply new speech headings when they were omitted in Q1 because the speaker's name was indicated immediately before in his entrance stage direction, and to omit the unnecessary ones, when in Q1 the heading is repeated after an interruption (such as the entrance of a new character) but the speaker has not changed. This type of regularisation has its drawbacks, when the reasons for the earlier, apparently supererogatory repetition of a heading is imperfectly understood.

[1] Here are, with line references to Addition II in *Sir Thomas More*, ed. W. W.Greg (MSR, 1911), the verbal forms beginning with C capitalised in the manuscript in Hand D: 126 Come; 136 Coms; 150 I Charg; 177 Cannot; 179 Cannot; 184 Cry; 196 hath Chidd; 261 Charterd.

[2] See the lists of mistaken or omitted speech headings on p. 172, nn. 3 and 4. Only in one case, at 5.1.69, a SH present in Q1 is omitted in Q2. Of the four speech headings misplaced in Q1 (*Moun.* at 1.1.121 and 1.2.81 (*Mo.*), *King* at 2.1.203 and 317) the first and third are corrected in Q2, while *Countess* at 1.2.68 is omitted in both editions.

In 1.1 Artois begins a lengthy speech at line 11, and Q1 repeats the speech heading *Art.* at 30, though no other speaker has intervened. The reviser abolished the apparently superfluous second heading: he did not realise that in this case the first printer's sin had not been one of supererogation but of omission. The two previous lines, 28–29, were not spoken by Artois, but were a comment by King Edward, whose speech heading before them had been accidentally left out. Here therefore instead of omitting the Artois prefix at 30, a *King* heading should be prefixed at 28.

The case of another apparently superfluous heading in Q1, at 3.4.122, omitted by the reviser, is different. After the English triumph at Crécy, King Edward gives orders for the pursuit of the French and for the siege of Calais. At the conclusion of what sounds like the closing speech of the scene, he suddenly asks: 'What Pictures this', and the Black Prince replies 'A Pellican my Lord', and proceeds to illustrate the significance and the motto of the Pelican emblem. In Q1 the King's question bears the prefix *Ki.*, suggesting that these lines did not follow immediately upon the previous speech, but belonged somewhere else and were inserted at this point by mistake. But since it is impossible to establish where exactly they should have been placed, the reviser can be forgiven for regularising the text by omitting the repeated speech heading in Q2.

As for other 'improvements', one example is particularly significant. In the 1596 quarto, sig. D4^{v} (2.2.154–5) King Edward compares himself to the mythical Leander:

> But I will throng a hellie spout of bloud,
> To arryue at Cestus where my Hero lyes.

The reviser saw that 'throng' could not be right, and knew that a u/n misreading is very common, and 'through' can easily be read as 'throng', so in the 1599 quarto, sig. D2^{v}, we find:

> But I will through a helly spoute of blood,
> To arriue at Cestus where my Hero lyes.

But his classical knowledge was insufficient to make him realise that a similar misreading had occurred immediately after: the printer of Q1 had taken for a 'u' the 'n' in what in the copy must have looked like 'hellispont' for 'Hellespont'. The reviser at this point simply 'improved' the spelling of 'hellie spout' (which was in fact closer to the original) to what he thought a less equivocal form: 'helly spoute'.

The single-mindedness of the reviser is shown by another intervention in some way connected with the one just quoted. Having noticed the earlier misreading by the printer of Q1 of 'throng' for 'through', when, in the description by Lorraine of the French rout at Crécy, he found at the top of signature G1 in the same text the lines (3.4.10–11),

> More in the clustering throng are prest to death,
> Then by the ennimie a thousand fold.

he felt it was his duty to 'correct' them (Q2, sig. F2^{v}) as:

> More in the clustring through are prest to death,
> Then by the enemie a thousand folde.

introducing an unnecessary and misleading emendation.

Several other miscorrections of the same kind could be quoted, as for instance when at 3.4.102 (sig. G2) the Black Prince's sword is described as 'yet reaking warme, / With blood of those that fought', and the reviser, more mindful of the spelling than of the sense, emends 'reaking' to 'wreaking' (Q2, sig. F4) instead of 'reeking'. The same is true of his replacing 'babble' with 'rabble' at 1.2.17, and 'perfumes' with 'presumes'[1] at 1.2.153, while a whole sentence is wrongly restructured by substituting 'which' for 'with' at 1.2.96.[2] Other false improvements of the text are a matter of taste, such as 'foolish' instead of 'childish' at 1.1.71. But it must be acknowledged that most of the reviser's guesses at the earlier printer's misreadings of the copy are sound.

The only authoritative text of the play remains that of the first quarto of 1596, though it cannot be considered authorial, since it is probably based on a manuscript representing an intermediate stage between the first drafts by those who collaborated in the writing of the play and the final prompt-book prepared with a view to performance. The second quarto of 1599 has no independent authority, being a revision of Q1 done by what we would call now a copy-editor with no access to the manuscript used as copy by the original printers or to any other earlier or later version of the play. The revision is fairly thorough and conscientious, especially for what concerns the placing and expansion of speech headings and the correction of misreadings of the copy by the type-setters of Q1; but it is in all cases the result of mere guesswork on the part of the reviser, and it must therefore be approached with extreme caution.

[1] In this case the reviser may have suspected that the Q1 compositor had confused the common abbreviation of barred 'p' followed by 'e' that could be read either 'pre' or 'per', and taken an 'f' for a long 's'.

[2] Here the reviser presumably assumed that the compositor misread abbreviated 'w^{ch}' as 'wth'.

APPENDIX: THE USE OF SOURCES

The technique used by the author(s) of *Edward III* in 'plotting' the play, briefly outlined in the Introduction, deserves a detailed study, for it illustrates the practices employed by many other devisers of English histories. Such a study was undertaken by G. Harold Metz, *Sources of Four Plays Ascribed to Shakespeare*, 1989, modelled on Geoffrey Bullough's *Narrative and Dramatic Sources of Shakespeare*, 1957–75. For *Edward III* Metz reproduces in full William Painter's novel 46 from *The Palace of Pleasure* (pp. 107–29), gives very ample extracts from Lord Berners's translation of Froissart (pp. 43–107), and two short excerpts from Holinshed's *Chronicles of England* (pp. 129–31) and Scotland (p. 131). He provides also (p. 40) a very useful table identifying the sources for each act and scene.

The present Appendix is meant to complete and in several cases to modify the picture outlined by Metz, thanks to a scene-by-scene account of the way in which the play's scaffolding as well as its whole structure was erected, substantiating Metz's contention (p. 39) that 'The manner in which the sources of *Edward III* are adapted in structure, character, and theme to dramatic uses exhibits an ingenuity and sophistication only intermittently glimpsed in earlier plays and virtually not at all in those based on chronicle materials.'

Page references to Metz's text take the place of full quotations from Painter's novel here and in Commentary notes, except for passages illustrating particular points. The same applies to the passages from Froissart reproduced in Metz, while those overlooked by him are quoted from W. P. Ker's edition, *The Chronicle of Froissart Translated out of French by Sir John Bourchier Lord Berners, Annis 1523–25* (The Tudor Translations, vols. XXVII–XXXII, 1901–3). References to and quotations from Holinshed are from *The Chronicles of England Scotland and Ireland*, edited by Sir Henry Ellis, 1807–8, reprinting the 1587 edition. Those from Froissart's French text are from the copy of the *Premier volume de Froissart de Croniques de France* [etc.], 1513, with marginal notes by Henry Carey, Lord Hunsdon.

Act 1

STAGE ONE – THE GROUNDWORK OF THE PLOT

Edward III was first conceived as a play on the most notable events of that king's reign, as related in the chronicles of Holinshed and Froissart, from the declaration of war against France in 1337 to the triumph of Poitiers in 1356, highlighting as well the legendary figure of Edward the Black Prince. It was modelled on the 'Famous Victories' pattern, which had celebrated in a very successful earlier play the other conqueror of France, Henry V.[1]

That such was the initial plan is proved by the omission, in the quartos' first stage direction, of the name of the Earl of Warwick, though he speaks at 98–100 and very briefly at 135. Possibly his speech at 98–100 belonged originally to Audley; it was reassigned to him (and his words at 135 were added) in the *third* phase of plotting, when the dramatist(s) became familiar with novel 46 of Painter's *Palace of Pleasure* (see below, pp. 184–5).

1.1.0 SD

The opening stage direction of 1.1 lists only five characters: King Edward, Derby, Prince Edward, Audley, and Artois. The reason for the presence of king and prince (though the latter in 1337 was only seven years old) is obvious; that of the other three results from their role in the sources, Holinshed and Froissart.

Derby represents the higher ranks of English nobility: Henry of Lancaster, Earl of Derby, created in 1351 Duke of Lancaster, father-in-law of John of Gaunt who inherited his title, is a leading figure in the chronicles; he accompanied young Edward in France in 1329 to pay homage for the duchy of Guienne (Frois. ch. 24; Metz, p. 45), and led the Gascony expedition of 1345, which opened the way to the conquest of much of France (Hol. II, 630, and Frois. chs. 102–13, not in Metz). But there may be also a practical reason for the prominent role given him in the play: about 1593 Lord Strange, the patron of a leading acting company in London (most of whose members joined the Chamberlain's Men in 1594), was created Earl of Derby, and the players were renamed Derby's Men. If the play was written for that company, the noble part given to an earlier holder of the title may be seen as a homage paid to their patron.[2]

Sir James Audley is named for the first time by Froissart (ch. 121; Ker, I, 277), but not by Holinshed, together with his brother Sir Peter, among the 'bachelars' that accompanied Edward III in the expedition in Normandy in 1346. Like the Earl of Derby, Sir James was one of the Knights Founders of the Order of the Garter. The decision to give him from the beginning the role of the wise old counsellor must have coincided with that of making the battle of Poitiers the culminating scene of the play: both in Holinshed (II, 666–9) and in Froissart (chs. 162, 165–7; Metz, pp. 96–100, 103–5) the account of that battle begins with Audley requesting Prince Edward to let him fight in the forefront and ends with the Prince's recompense and Audley's decision to pass on the reward to the squires who had accompanied him. The fact that the play (4.7.56–9) emphasises a detail (the Prince doubles his gift, learning of Audley's generosity) found only in Holinshed (II, 669) is evidence that Holinshed rather than Froissart was the first source consulted by the 'plotters'.

Artois is indispensable to establishing the initial situation, as the main instigator of the war against France. Though Froissart devotes one chapter (25; Metz, pp. 48–9) to

[1] *The Famous Victories of Henry the fifth*, a Queen's Men's play, possibly in two parts, first performed before 1588, was printed in a very bad and reduced form only in 1598.

[2] The same justification holds also for the key role given to Lord Stanley Earl of Derby in *Richard III*, if Shakespeare planned it before 1594 as a play for the Lord Strange's/Derby's Men.

his banishment from France, and another (28, 'Howe kyng Edwarde was counselled to make warre agaynst the French king'; Metz, pp. 53–6) to the way he influenced Edward, the opening lines of the play (1–4) seem indebted to the neater account in Holinshed (II, 605), based not on Froissart but on Polydore Vergil, Fabian, and others:

This yeare [1337] was the warre proclamed betwixt England and France, cheefelie by the procurement of the lord Robert Dartois, a Frenchman, as then banished out of France, vpon occasion of a claime by him made vnto the earledome of Artois. This lord Robert after he was banished France, fled ouer vnto king Edward, who gladlie receiued him and made him earle of Richmond.[1]

1.1.1–50

Another decision made from the start, for reasons of theatrical expediency (see 1.1.21 n.), was that of ignoring the existence of King Philip VI of Valois in the recital (5–37) of the genealogy of the French royal family, readily available both in Holinshed (II, 611–12, from Polydore Vergil) and in Froissart (ch. 5; Metz, p. 43). It should be noted that the key sentence stating the reason for the exclusion of Edward III from the line of succession (compare 1.1.22–5 n.), is not in Holinshed, while Froissart not only uses it in chapter 5 (Metz, p. 43), but repeats it nearly verbatim in chapter 21 (Ker, I, 72):

[they] sayed and mayntayned, that the realme of Fraunce was of so great nobles, that it ought nat by successyon to fall into a womans hande.

The first outline of the plot, then, was drawn from Holinshed, but the devisers of the story very soon took into account the richer and more lively narrative of Froissart.

STAGE TWO – THE '*CASUS BELLI*'

1.1.52–120

Having established the main lines of the plot, the dramatist(s) had to explain the formal outbreak of hostilities, apart from the dynastic claim (which should have been put forward a long time before, when Philip VI ascended the French throne in 1328). The chronicles are vague about the matter, but an episode in Froissart is suggestive. His chapter 29 (Metz, pp. 44–8) 'Of thomage that kyng Edwarde of Englande, dydde to the kynge of Fraunce, for the duchye of Guyen', relates how young King Edward, at the request of the new French King Philip of Valois, went to Amiens in 1329 to pay homage for the duchy of Guienne, but he did it 'all onely by worde, and nat puttyng his handes bytwene the kynge of Fraunce handes'. After his return to England, he received a French embassage asking him to repeat the homage in the proper form, to

[1] In giving the claim to the earldom of Artois as the reason for the French nobleman's banishment, Holinshed avoids the trap into which Lord Berners had fallen when translating Froissart's original '*dont la conté d'Artois estoit cause, que li dis Messires Robers voloit avoir gaagnié*' (caused by the earldom of Artois, which Sir Robert wanted to obtain) as (Metz, p. 48) 'wherofe the Erle of Artoyse was cause: for he wold haue wonne his entent'. Robert Artois's 'intent' is by no means clear if at the time he was already earl of the County.

which he replied with letters patent, in which he recognised that the homage paid in Amiens had been inadequate, and set down minutely, as a 'promyse for vs and our successours', the form that the ceremony should take. The chapter ends rather ambiguously:

These letters the lordes of Fraunce brought to the kyng their lorde, and the kyng caused them to be kept in his chauncery.

but there is no indication that they were ever acted upon. It is exactly upon this ambiguity that the dramatist played, by turning a homage informally paid and formally promised (which was an implicit recognition of the legitimacy of the accession of Philip of Valois to the crown of France) into a firm refusal of it.

More suggestions came from the same chapter of Froissart. The four earls who accompanied young King Edward in France are listed as

the lorde Henry erle of Derby, his cosyn germayne, sonne to sir Thomas erle of Lancastre, with the wrie necke, therle of Salisbury, therle of Warwyke, and the erle of Hereforde,

while among the French noblemen who received him in Amiens were 'the duke of Lurren, and syr John [not Robert] of Artoyes'. The list is patently incorrect (William Montague was created *first* Earl of Salisbury not earlier than in 1333[1]), but the names are suggestive: Salisbury and Warwick were to be found associated again in Painter's story of the countess of Salisbury, and the mention of the Duke of Lorraine (a powerful lord who figures repeatedly with the French king up to the battle of Crécy) alongside an Artois (albeit not the one presented in the play) may have been instrumental in naming Lorraine as the French envoy sent to ask for the King of England's homage (1.1.51 SD).

The next move of the play plotter(s) was the chronological transposition of a historical fact. The only military event of major note on record between the declaration of war in 1337 and King Edward's landing in Normandy in 1346 was the attempted interception by the French fleet, in June 1340, of the English ships taking Edward to Flanders. In the naval battle fought before the Flemish harbour of Sluys (L'Ecluse), as Holinshed proudly stated (II, 615), 'the Englishmen got a famous victorie'. Following the model provided by *The Famous Victories of Henry the fifth* (the second half of which is a celebration of Henry's triumphs in France, while the first is concerned essentially with the moral character of the future victorious sovereign) the author(s) of *Edward III* reserved Sluys for the second half of their play, as the earliest in the uninterrupted sequence of Edward's 'famous victories', culminating in the siege of Calais and in the battle of Poitiers.

Leaving out for the time being the naval battle, the dramatist culled from the remaining pages of the chronicles covering the years 1337 to 1345 only episodes that could be used as illustrations of the character of the English king. In those pages Holinshed (see Introduction, pp. 21–2) devotes some space to the circumstances of the founding of the Order of the Garter in 1344 (II, 628–9), with the tantalising marginal note on the countess of Salisbury as the lady whose garter, lost in a dance, suggested

[1] See Frois., ch. 26 (Metz, pp. 52–3), quoted below, p. 183 and n. 1.

the emblem and the motto of the Order; but she is never mentioned before or after, and the numerous Scottish campaigns in the period between 1332 and 1346 are dealt with very briefly, because the historian reserved them for his fifth volume, the *Chronicles of Scotland.* The wars in Brittany in 1341–2 receive an ampler treatment (II, 621–6), and the repeated mention of the Earl of Salisbury among the Englishmen sent in 1342 to aid the Countess of Mountford (historically Montfort) besieged in her castle at Hennebont (Hol. II, 623) may have suggested the idea of replacing, in 1.1 and later in the play (4.1, 4.3, 4.5), the name of Salisbury for those of the historical commanders of the Brittany expeditions, Sir Walter de Manny in 1341 and Robert of Artois in 1342.

Scotland and the Countess of Salisbury. 1.1.121–31, 136–69

Apart from these details, the last section of 1.1 relies completely on Froissart, who deals at great length with the various Scottish campaigns. Significantly, Froissart twice interrupts his extremely detailed account of the wars in Brittany in 1341–2 (chs. 64–98) by inserting accounts of the wars in Scotland and of the episode of the Countess of Salisbury (chs. 73–7 and 89). The dramatist combined episodes and characters belonging to different campaigns, from the truce with England broken in 1332 by King David Bruce of Scotland when he took the border town of Berwick, to the third war in Scotland in 1341. The first few lines after the entrance of Montague at 120 SD are a deliberate contamination of historical times and events in order to introduce the 'moral' episode of Edward's 'amours' with the Countess of Salisbury – fundamental in establishing the character of the king – of which there is no trace in Holinshed.

The name Montague for the messenger who brings the news of the siege of the countess's castle is suggested by ch. 76, 'How the Scottes besieged a castell of therle of Salysburies' (Metz, pp. 63–5), which precedes the one relating the King of England's infatuation (ch. 77). According to Froissart, in 1341 'sir Wyllyam Montagu, son to therle of Salysburis suster' was captain of the castle, and

Ther was within present the noble countesse of Salysbury, who was as than reputed for the most sagest and fayrest lady of all England: the castell parteyned to her husbande therle of Salisbury, who was taken prisoner, with the erle of Suffolke, before Lyle in Flanders, as ye haue harde before [ch. 46; Ker, I, 132–3], and was in prison as than in the chatelot of Parys.[1] The kyng of Englande gaue the same castel to the sayd erle, whan he maryed first the sayd lady, for the prowes and gode seruyce that he had done before, whan he was called but sir Wyllyam Montagu. (Metz, p. 64)

This makes it clear that, in spite of the identical name, the captain of the castle was not the earl himself. Fearing they would not be able to resist much longer the forces of King David,

they of the castell . . . toke counsell amonge them, to sende to kyng Edward, who lay at Yorke.

[1] The capture of the earl in 1339 and his release in 1341 (Frois., chs. 46 and 78; Ker, I, 132–3 and 196) are never mentioned in the play, where his absence from the siege of Roxborough is justified by his service in Brittany at the time. Lord Hunsdon instead had duly recorded in the margin of his copy (Frois. 1513), fol. XXXr, 'The Erles of Sal[sb]ery and Suffol[ke] taken prisone[rs]', and fol. LVv, '[Th]e erle of Salsbery [ra]msomid home'.

The captain undertook the dangerous mission (Metz, pp. 64–5):

Thus at mydnight, sir Wyllyam Montagu passed through thoost, and was nat sene, and so rode forth tyll it was day; than he met ii. Scottes, half a leage fro thost, driuyng before them two oxen and a cowe towarde thoost. Syr Wyllyam knewe wel they wer Scottes and set on them, and wounded them bothe, and slewe the catell, to thyntent that they of thost shuld haue none ease by them: than he sayd to the two hurt Scottes, Go your wayes, and say to your kyng, that Wyllyam of Montague hath thus passed through his hoost, and is goyng to fetch ayde of the kyng of Englande.

But the question asked by Edward at line 122, and Montague's reply, hark back to an earlier chapter of Froissart (26; Metz, pp. 49–53), dealing with the Scottish campaign of 1332. The king refers to a truce established with Scotland when King David married Edward's sister Jane, and Montague's answer alludes to the breaking of the truce when (Metz, p. 49)

kyng Edward of Ingland was enformed, that the yong kyng Dauid, of Scotland, who had wedded his suster, was seaced of the towne of Berwyke, the whiche ought to apperteyn to the realme of Ingland.

Froissart's report of the English reaction concludes (Metz, pp. 52–3):

Thus in this season, the kyng of Ingland wanne the most parte of the realme of Scotland, who had many expert knyghtis about hym, among other was sir Wylliam Montague, and syr Walter of Manny; they were hardy knyghtis, and dyd many dedis of armes ageynst the Scottis. And the better to haue their entre into Scotland, they fortified the bastyde of Rosebourge, and made it a strong castel; and syr Wylliam Montague dyd so well in all his entreprises, that the kyng made hym erle of Salysbury, and maried hym nobly.[1]

The mention of Newcastle together with Berwick at line 128 comes from Froissart, chapter 74 (Ker, I, 187–9), when in 1341 King David, bypassing 'Rousburge' and Berwick, 'came with a great hoost to Newcastell vpon Tyne'. Later (ch. 75; Ker, I, 189–90), having 'distroyed the cytie of Dyrrame [Durham]', David, on his way back (ch. 76; Metz, p. 63), 'besieged a castell of therle of Salysburies'. The name of the castle is not given, but the context leaves no doubt that it is Roxborough.[2]

Edward's reaction to Montague's report is recorded at 136–8, and the rest of his speech, on the preparations for the war in France, while he will march against the Scots, concentrates in a few lines information drawn from different chapters in Froissart. The task entrusted to Audley (139–40) is unhistorical, and so is that delegated at 141–6 to Ned, the first born of Edward, seven years old in 1337 and created Prince of Wales in 1342. But the words addressed to him by the king (157–9) and the

[1] In fact, according to Hol. (II, 605), 'William Montacute' was created Earl of Salisbury not in 1333 but 'on the second Sunday in Lent, 1337', at the same time as 'Henry, son of the earl of Lancaster' was created Earl of Derby.

[2] Qq's spelling 'Rocksborough' at 130 is closer to that in Holinshed's report (II, 602) of a Scottish campaign in 1334, with no mention of the Earl or the Countess of Salisbury: 'The king of England . . . about Alhallontide came to Newcastell vpon Tine, with his armie . . . and then entring Scotland, came to Rockesburgh, where he repared the castell which had beene aforetime destroied.' But it may have been modified when the dramatist became acquainted with Painter's version in novel 46 of *The Palace of Pleasure*.

prince's answer (160–9) anticipate, with the telescoping of time usual in history plays, the role he played in the Normandy campaign of 1346.

Lines 147–52 refer to the mission sent by Edward to Valenciennes in 1337 to secure the alliance of William Earl of Hainault (whose daughter Philippa Edward had married in 1328), and his good offices 'to treat with the lordes of thempyre, such as therle of Heynalt had named', reported in Froissart, chapter 28 (Metz, pp. 51–3). The English envoys are not named: the dramatist mentions Derby in view of the ample space given by Froissart (chs. 102–13; Ker, I, 235–60) to the later mission of the earl, when, in 1345, he was sent to wage war in Gascony.[1]

STAGE THREE – PAINTER'S NOVEL

1.1.132–5

The first draft of 1.1 did not include, I think, the two speeches by Edward and Warwick at 132–5. In fact, they mark a turning-point in the use of sources, and the first line (132) is curiously echoed at 1.2.94. Originally the dramatist knew of Edward's infatuation for the countess of Salisbury only through Froissart, chapters 77 and 89 (Metz, pp. 65–8). Later he found the much fuller version of the episode in William Painter's novel 46 of *The Palace of Pleasure*, which offered a richer scope for the presentation of the characters of both king and countess. This discovery determined the insertion of the exchange at 132–5, together with the introduction into the scene of the character of Warwick and the transfer to him of the already discussed speech at 98–100, perhaps originally assigned to Audley. In Froissart the countess is described as 'noble', but there is no mention of her lineage. The Italian Matteo Bandello (in Novella 37 in *Seconda Parte delle Novelle*) invented a father for her and gave him an important role in the story. He called him 'Ricciardo conte di Varuccia' (which Painter, ignoring the Christian name, translated as 'Earle of Warwike'[2]) and presented the countess besieged in the castle not as a 'silly [helpless] lady' (137), but as a strong and determined woman:

> la contessa non si portò mica da giovinetta delicata e timida donna, ma si dimostrò esser una Camilla o una Pentesilea.[3]

[1] For the results of the mission see Froissart, chs. 32 and 34. It is significant that a large majority of Lord Hunsdon's marginal notes and underlinings in his copy of Froissart (Frois. 1513) concern the conquests of Robert d'Artois in Brittany ('De la guerre de bretaigne' fols. XLVIIv–LXVIIIv) and of Lord Derby in Gascony ('De la guerre de gascongne', LXIXr–LXXXIIr), events which are practically ignored in the play. This weakens Prior's argument ('Compliment', *passim*) that the dramatist wanted to reflect in his work Hunsdon's major historical interests.

[2] Bandello had borrowed the name of a historical figure well known in his time, Richard Neville Earl of Warwick, the King-maker (see *2* and *3H6*), but Painter did not dare to suggest so anachronistic an identification. The Earl of Warwick in Edward III's time was Thomas de Beauchamp, repeatedly mentioned in Froissart, chs. 24, 39, 41, 63, 121, 161 (Ker, I, 77, 112, 119, 170, 276 ff., 369), but never in connection with the countess. In fact the historical Catherine Countess of Salisbury was the daughter of Sir William Grandisson (*Chroniques de J. Froissart*, ed. Siméon Luce, 1872, III, i: 'elle s'appellait Catherine, et elle était fille de Guillaume de Grandisson').

[3] 'The countess was no helpless girl or timid woman, but rather proved herself a Camilla or a Penthesilea.' This sentence is not in Painter; while for Bandello she 'con tanta prudenza, animosità e fortezza governò

Lines 133–4, though, mark a departure from both Froissart and Painter, who agree in attributing the earl's absence to his having been taken prisoner in Flanders (Metz, p. 64 for Froissart, ch. 76; Metz, p. 110 for Painter).[1] In contrast with the sources, Edward says that Salisbury was serving in Brittany, 'about the planting of Lord Mountford there'. These lines can have been written only after the dramatist had decided to 'revive' Salisbury in the second half of the play (4.1, 4.3, 4.5), by involving him in the 1341–2 campaign in Brittany, reported in Holinshed (II, 621–6), and more extensively in Froissart (chs. 64–72, 78–88, 90–8). 'The occasion of the wars of Britaine' is neatly summarised by Holinshed (II, 621):

For whereas contention arose betwixt one Charles de Blois, and Iohn earle of Mountfort, about the right to the duchie of Britaine . . . the earle of Mountfort, thinking that he had wrong offered him at the French kings hands, who fauoured his aduersarie Charles de Blois, alied himselfe with the king of England. And (as some write) after he had woone diuerse cities and townes within Britaine, he came ouer into England, and by doing homage to king Edward, acknowledged to hold it of him, as of the souereigne lord thereof, so that he would promise to defend him and that duchie against his aduersaries: which the king promised him to doo.[2]

This situation is referred to at 133–4. Holinshed goes on:

After this, the French king made such warres against this earle of Mountfort, that he was at length taken prisoner in the towne of Naunts, and committed to safe keeping within the castell of Loure at Paris.[3] But his wife being a stout woman, and of a manlie courage, stood vp in the quarrell of hir husband . . .

From this point on Holinshed summarises Froissart's much more extended relation of how valiantly the countess of Mountford resisted Charles of Blois's siege of the castle of Hennebont (ch. 80; Ker, I, 198–202), and of her delivery at the hands of the English under the conduct of Walter de Manny (ch. 81; Ker, I, 202–4). These chapters follow closely upon those describing the siege and delivery of the countess of Salisbury's castle and Edward's infatuation with her (chs. 76–7). In view of the analogous situations (both countesses, in the absence of their respective husbands, courageously resist the sieges of their castles, and both are rescued by the English) the dramatist fused the two episodes.

i suoi soldati, e di modo i nemici offese, che furono astretti . . . levarsi dall'assedio', Painter attributes the successful resistance to the fact that 'the Earle of Sarisburie before his departure, had giuen so good order, that . . . they were constrayned to go further of' (Metz, p. 110).

[1] Frois. and Bandello/Painter differ on another point: according to the first (ch. 78; Ker, I, 196) in June 1341 'therle of Salysbury and therle Moret were delyuerd out of prison by exchaunge', and went on serving their king, while Painter writes (Metz, p. 114) that 'the Earle her husband, being out of pryson, consumed with griefe and sicknes, died by the way homewards'. Hol., who omits the countess episode, correctly states (II, 629): 'William de Montacute earle of Salisburie . . . was so brused at the iusts holden here at Windsore [in 1344] that he departed this life, the more was the pitie, within eight daies after.' William de Montacute, Earl of Salisbury, who figures among the Knights Founders of the Garter, was in fact the first earl's son, and died in 1397.

[2] For Mountford's homage to the King of England see 4.1.1–12.

[3] According to Frois. (ch. 72; Ker, I, 184–5), Mountford died in captivity. This may have suggested to Bandello/Painter the report of the death of the Earl of Salisbury (see n. 1 above).

THE COUNTESS'S IDENTITY

With the addition of Painter's novel to Holinshed and Froissart, the third and last phase of the basic plotting of *Edward III* was complete: the dramatist was to interweave freely his three sources, smoothing out the obvious contradictions among them.

The main stumbling-block was the identity of the countess, whom Bandello had presented as the future wife of the king. The embarassment caused by this is reflected in the fact that in the play her name is never revealed. Bandello called her 'Aelips', from the original French text of Froissart, who spells the name 'Aelis', when speaking of the feasts in her honour in London (Luce, ed., III, 1, 3); this is rendered in Berners's translation 'Alys' (ch. 89; Metz, p. 68). Pointing out the 'errours' of the author in the introduction to his translation of Bandello, Painter says that Froissart's 'Alice' is a more likely name than Aelips, but insists on the fact that Bandello confused (Metz, p. 109)

> Edward the third for his eldest sonne Edward the Prince of Wales (who as I read in Fabian) maried the Countesse of Salesburie, which before was Countesse of Kent, and wife vnto sir Thomas Holland: and whose name (as Polidore sayth) was Iane, daughter to Edmond Earle of Kent, of whom the same Prince Edward begat Edward that died in his childish yeres, and Richard that afterwards was king of England the second of that name.

So, by transferring the 'amours' from father to son, from Edward III to the Black Prince, the countess, identified as Joan, the Fair Maid of Kent, enters English history as no less than the mother of Richard II – a solution adopted by Michael Drayton in his *Englands Heroicall Epistles* (1596–9), but found unacceptable by the dramatist, in view of the hint at the garter in Holinshed, and of Froissart's account.

A recent study, based on existing records, of the confusion (derived by Painter from Froissart, who took it from Le Bel) over the name and identity of the countess, explains it in these terms:[1] (a) the lady in the Earl of Salisbury's castle of Wark (*not* Roxborough) besieged by the Scots in November 1341 was Alice, daughter of the Earl of Norfolk and wife of the captain or governor of the castle during the absence of the earl and his wife Catherine; (b) the captain of the castle was *not* William Montague, but Edward Montague, the earl's youngest brother; (c) he went to the king at Newcastle to ask for help; (d) the king reached Wark, causing the Scots to withdraw, and tried, unsuccessfully, to seduce Alice; (e) still determined to win her, he summoned Montague to the Great Council at Westminster on Easter Monday 1342, ordering him to take his wife there, but once again the lady escaped his attentions. In other words, Le Bel mistook Alice Montague, wife of the governor of the Earl of Salisbury's castle, for her sister-in-law, countess Catherine, the earl's wife. As for Le Bel's story of the rape (Introduction, pp. 22–4), the historian surmises that 'the king had his way with her (though that is not to say that he resorted to brutality)', when visiting her castle at Bungay, in Suffolk, later in 1342, while her husband was in Brittany.[2]

[1] Michael Packe, *King Edward III*, ed. L.C.B. Seaman (1983), pp. 105–30, 170–8.

[2] *Ibid.*, p. 122. Nine years later (Packe, pp. 175–8) Alice was battered to death by her husband, but the king left the crime unpunished.

1.2 THE SIEGE AND DELIVERY OF THE COUNTESS'S CASTLE

The first of the three Countess of Salisbury scenes relies mainly on Painter's novel, but, more than the other two, is also dependent on Froissart.

1.2.1–17

The complaint of the besieged countess is based on Froissart, chapter 76 (Metz, pp. 63–5), already quoted for the mission of Sir William Montague, captain of the castle, but is also reminiscent, in the description of the behaviour of the Scots, of the report of Edward's first campaign against Scotland in 1327, in chapter 17 (Ker, I, 48–50), 'Of the maner of the Scottes, and howe they make their warre'. The stress put by Froissart on their reliance on horses and on their meanness is echoed repeatedly in the first part of the scene (see lines 26–34, 40–7, 57–9, 69–70, and especially 45n.).

1.2.18–39

The alliance concluded in 1338 between France and Scotland is recorded by Froissart (ch. 33, Metz, pp. 58–9), though the names of the French envoys are not given (the Duke of Lorraine was certainly not one of them). The relevant passage is quoted at 18–34n.

1.2.40–80

Both Froissart (ch. 76; Metz, p. 65) and Painter (Metz, p. 110) report that, before the arrival of the English army, the Scots left the siege of Roxborough, in Painter's words,

> hauing intelligence by certaine spies, that the king of England was departed from London, with a great armie, to come to succour the Countesse.

But neither of them mentions the countess's ironical defiance of the Scots. Warnke and Proescholdt in their edition (p. xii) and Metz (p. 131) quote a parallel from Holinshed's *Chronicle of Scotland* (v, 378), where the countess of March, besieged by the English in Dunbar castle, 'vsed manie pleasant words in iesting and tawnting at the enimies dooings'; but the situation is reversed, since there the besieged lady is a Scot while the English besiegers are led by 'sir William Montacute earle of Salisburie'! Surely the dramatist was recalling at this point the valiant behaviour of the countess of Mountford besieged by the French in her castle at Hennebont in 1342, to which Froissart devotes two chapters (80 and 81; Ker, I, 198–204), only a few pages after those (76 and 77) devoted to the Countess of Salisbury episode. According to Froissart (ch. 80; Ker, I, 199)

> This lady [the Countess of Mountford] dyd ther an hardy enterprise; she mounted vp to the heyght of a towre, to se how the Frenchmen were orderd without; she sawe howe that all the lordes, and all other people of thoost, were all gone out of ther felde to thassaut; than she toke agayne her courser, armed as she was, and caused thre hundred men a horsbacke to be redy, and she went with theym to another gate, wher as there was non assaut. She yssued out and her company, and dasshed into the Frenche lodgynges, and cutte downe tentes, and set fyre in their lodgynges: she founde no defence ther, but a certayne of varlettes and boyes, who ran away. Whan the lordes of France loked behynde them, and sawe their lodgynges a fyre, and harde the

cry and noyse ther, they retourned to the felde, cryeng, Treason, treason, so that all thassaut was left.

1.2.81–5

The countess's relief at the approach of the English is derived from the same chapter in Froissart (Ker, I, 202):

Than the countesse [of Mountford] loked downe along the see, out at a wyndo in the castell, and began to smyle for great ioy that she had, to se the socours commyng, the which she had so long desyred. Than she cryed out aloude, and sayd twyse, I se the socours of Englande commyng.

1.2.86–114

The meeting of king and countess, and his first expressions of admiration, closely echo Painter's novel (Metz, pp. 110–11), which is in turn indebted to Froissart, chapter 77 (Metz, pp. 65–6); and it is directly from the latter that the dramatist took the detail of the countess kneeling in front of the king (see 107–12 n.). But the story of the Countess of Mountford was still present in his mind: Froissart (ch. 81; Ker, I, 203–4) tells how, at the approach of the English forces under the conduct of Sir Walter de Manny to the castle of Hennebont, the French besiegers withdrew,

Than the countess discendyd down fro the castell with a gladde chere, and came and kyst sir Gaultier of Manny, and his companyons one after another, two or thre tymes, lyke a valyant lady.

1.2.115–66

The rest of the scene elaborates the next page of Painter's novel (Metz, p. 111), showing the king's admiration not only for the lady's beauty, but also for her wisdom:

The king astonned with so sage and wise aunswere, chaunging his minde, went towarde the castell: where after interteignement and accustomed welcome, he began by litle and litle, to feele himselfe attached wyth a newe fier. Which the more he laboured to resist, the more it inflamed: and feelinge this new mutacion in himselfe, there came into his mind, an infinite nomber of matters, balancing betwene hope and feare, somtimes determining to yeld vnto his passions, and somtimes thinking clerely to cut them of, for feare least by committinge himselfe to his affections, the vrgent affayres of the warres, wherewith he was inuolued, should haue ill successe. But in the ende vanquished wyth Loue . . . he toke her by the hande, and prayed her to shewe him the commodities of the fortresse.

Act 2

KING EDWARD'S 'AMOURS'

The whole of the second act elaborates the contents of Painter's novel 46, which in turn, following Bandello, considerably extended and altered Froissart's chapters 77 and 89 (Metz, pp. 65–8). Froissart's report is brief. In chapter 77 (Metz, pp. 66–7) the king, being a guest in the lady's castle, before leaving solicits her love, but when she replies

Noble prince, . . . God the father glorious be your conduct, and put you out of all vylayne thoughtes,

the king 'departed all abasshed'. Chapter 89 (Metz, pp. 67–8) is devoted to 'the feest and justyinge made at London by the kyng of England for the loue of the countesse of Salisbury', at a time (mid-August 1342) when the Earl of Salisbury, no longer a prisoner in France, 'was one of the priuyest of his counsell'.[1] The names opening the list of the participants in the fifteen-day festivities are significant:

At this feest was sir Henry with the wrye necke, erle of Lancastre, and sir Henry his sonne, erle of Derby; sir Robert Dartoyes, erle of Rychmount; the erle of Northampton and of Glocetter, the erle of Warwyke, the erle of Salisbury . . .

There is no indication that the last two were related to each other as father and husband respectively of the countess. At all events, though 'the gode lady durst nat say nay' to the invitation to the feast, her behaviour was utterly discouraging:

All ladyes and damoselles were fresshely besene accordyng to their degrees, except Alys countesse of Salisbury, for she went as simply as she myght, to the intent that the kyng shulde nat sette his regarde on her, for she was fully determyned to do no maner of thynge that shulde tourne to her dyshonour nor to her husbandes.

There is no new assault against the lady's chastity in London and no further mention of the countess in the rest of the *Cronycles*.

The two basic themes of the first half of the play – that of the intrepid behaviour of the heroine, and that of the education of the prince, shown through Edward's pursuit of illicit love and his reformation – are found only in Painter's novel. The one divergence from Painter is that, after Edward's infatuation with the countess during his visit to her castle, the scene of the novel shifts to London for the rest of the narrative, while in the play the whole action, for obvious dramatic reasons, takes place in a couple of days in Roxborough castle.

2.1.1–184 LODOWICK, THE SECRETARY

Lodowick's soliloquy at the beginning of Act 2 amplifies the description in Painter's novel of the king's behaviour after the first rejection of his love by the countess at Roxborough (Metz, p. 113):

the king well fedde with Loue, dined for that time very soberly, and not able to eate but vppon amorous dishes, did caste his lokes inconstantly here and there, and still his eyes threw the last loke vppon that part of the table where the Countesse sate, meaninge thereby to extinguish the boiling flames, which incessantly did burne him, howbeit by thinking to coole them, he further plonged himselfe therein.

Lodowick, in the traditional role of the confidant, is a creation of the dramatist, suggested by the mention in Painter's novel of a secretary to whom the king entrusts a love-letter for the countess after her retirement to her father's house in London. The

[1] Painter (Metz, p. 114), maintaining that the Earl of Salisbury died on his way back from France, transfers the distinction of being 'one of the king's priuie Counsel' to the Countess's father, the Earl of Warwick.

secretary is presented as a discreet and wise counsellor; when asked by the king, after hearing of the countess's firm rejection of the letter, 'Do you thinke it expedient that I make request to her father, whose counsell I want in other thinges?'

> the Secretarie boldly aunswered, that he thought it vnreasonable to seeke ayde at a father's handes to corrupt the doughter; faithfully telling to the king, the reproche and infamie that would followe thereof, as well for the olde seruice, that her father hadde done to his auncestours, as for his great prowesse in armes for which he was so greatly commended. But loue, the mortall enemie of all good counsell, so blinded the eyes of the kyng, that without anye further delibera-tion, he commaunded the Secretarie to go seke the father, to demande his counsell for matters of importance, (Metz, p. 115).

Later (Metz, pp. 124–6) the secretary takes a message to the countess's mother, to pressure her into forcing her daughter to satisfy the king (an episode not in the play), and he acts as escort to the countess on her visit to the king. Finally, when she threatens suicide rather than yielding, the repentant king

> caused the Countesse to come in with the Secretarie and the gentlewomen, and same time hee called also the Courtiers and Piers of the Realme (Metz, p. 128)

to announce to them all his intention of marrying the lady.

As for the numerous parallels with Shakespeare's Sonnets in this whole scene, the question to be asked is whether those sonnets were written before or after the play. The debate on this point is still open and is neatly summarised by Metz in his Introduction to his treatment of *Edward III*.[1] I have argued elsewhere that the lines and expressions shared by the sonnets and by the play in this and in the next scene (recorded in the Commentary), are so appropriate to the situations presented by *Edward III*, that the borrowings are more likely to go in the direction of the sonnets rather than the other way round.[2] Thus, while the analogies with *Venus and Adonis* and *Lucrece* may be in the nature of echoes from previously written poems, those with some of the sonnets are suggestions for as yet unwritten poems.

2.1.185–277 EDWARD AND THE COUNTESS

This part of the scene is closer to Froissart's report than to Painter's more elaborate narrative of Edward's declaration of love to the countess on the evening of his arrival at her castle. In 2.1.195–204 the playwright first follows Froissart (Metz, p. 66):

> [the king] went to a wyndo to rest hym and so fell in gret study: the lady went about to make chere to the lordes and knyghtes that were ther, and commaunded to dresse the hall for dyner . . . thane she came to the kyng with a mery chere, who was in gret study, and she sayd Dere syr, why do ye study so? . . . Than the kyng sayd, A, dere lady, knowe for trouthe, that syth I entred into the castell, ther is a study come to my mynde, so that I can nat chuse but to muse, nor I can nat tell what shall fall therof; put it out of my herte I can nat.

But the final key question on the 'remedy' for the king's melancholy comes from the much ampler version in Painter's novel (Metz, pp. 111–12):

[1] Metz, pp. 25–9.
[2] Melchiori, *Meditations*, pp. 42–7, 57–9. This view is firmly rejected by Slater, pp. 10–11.

the Countesse seing him so pensife, without any apparaunt occasion, sayde vnto him: 'Sir, I doe not a litle maruell to see you reduced into these alterations: For (me thincke) your grace is maruelously chaunged within these two or thre houres . . . I cannot tell nor yet deuise, what should bee the cause that your highnesse is so pensife and sorowful, sith without great losse on your parte, your enemies vnderstandinge of your stoute approche, be retired, which ought, as I suppose, to driue awaye the Melancholie from your Stomacke. . .' The king hearing this angel's voyce [see 241] . . . thinking that of her owne accord shee came to make him mery, determined to let her vnderstand his griefe . . . with a trembling voice he said vnto her: 'Ah Madame, how farre be my thoughtes farre different from those which you do thincke me to haue: I feele my hart so opprest with care, as it is impossible to tell you what it is . . . since my comminge hether, which troubleth me so sore . . .' The Countesse seing the king thus moued . . . was vncertaine what aunswere to make. Which the king perceyuing, said vnto her, fetching a deepe sighe from the bottome of his stomacke: 'And what say you Madame thereunto, can you giue me no remedie?'

In neither narrative, though, does Edward induce the countess to swear that she will provide the remedy (see 2.1.205–11).

The exchange between king and countess (2.1.212–77) is reported briefly in Froissart (Metz, p. 66), and from it the play borrows three main points: the countess's incredulous reaction, the reference to her husband, and her brusque departure from the room. In Froissart's narrative, when the lady tries to cheer Edward ('sir, leaue your musyng and come into the hall, if it please you, your dyner is all ready'),

A, fayre lady, quoth the Kyng: other thynges lyeth at my hert that ye knowe nat of: but surely the sweete behauyng, the perfyt wysedom, the good grace, noblenes, and exellent beauty that I se in you, hath so sore surprised my hert, that I can nat but loue you, and without your loue I am but deed [see 209]. Then the lady sayde, A, ryght noble prince, for Goddes sake mocke nor tempt me nat: I can nat byleue that it is true that ye say [see 272–5], nor that so noble a prince as ye be, wold thynke to dyshonour me and my lorde, my husbande, who is so valyant a knyght, and hath done your grace so gode seruyce [see 273], and as yet lyethe in prison for your quarell; certenly sir, you shulde in this case haue but a small prayse, and nothyng the better thereby: I had neuer as yet such a thought in my hert, nor I trust in God neuer shall haue, for no man lyveng; if I had any suche intencyon, your grace ought nat all onely to blame me, but also to punysshe my body, ye and by true iustice to be dismembred. Therwith the lady departed fro the kyng, and went into the hall to hast the dyner [see 276–7].

The much ampler treatment of the dialogue in the play contains echoes from Painter (Metz, pp. 112–13):

'Madame . . . my wounde resteth in the inwarde parte of my harte, which pricketh mee so soore, as if I desire from henceforth to prolonge my life, I muste open the same vnto you . . . I must now then confesse vnto you, that in comminge to your Castell, and castinge downe my head to behold your celestiall face . . . I haue felt (vnhappie man as I am) such a sodaine alteration, in al the most sensible partes of my body, as . . . I cannot tel to whom to make complaint . . . but onely to you, that like a faithfull keeper and onely treasurer of my hart [see 185 n.], you may by some shining beame of pitie bring againe to his former mirth and ioye, that which you desire in me: and by the contrarie, you may procure me a life more painefull and greeuous than a thousand deathes together.' When he had ended these woordes, hee helde his peace, to let her speake, attendinge none other thing by her aunswere, but the last decree either of death or life. But the Countesse with a grauitie conformable to her honestie and honour, without other mouing, said vnto him: 'If any other besides your grace had been so forgetful of himself to enter in these termes, or to vse such talke vnto me, I knowe what should be mine aunswere, that he shoulde haue occasion not to be well contented, but knowing this your attempt to proceede rather from the pleasantnes of your hart, than for other affection [see 134n.], I wil beleue from henceforth, and perswade my selfe, that a Prince so renowmed and gentle as you be doth not thincke, and much lesse meane, to attempt any thing against mine honour, which is a thousand times dearer vnto mee than life. And I am perswaded, that you do not so litle esteeme my father and my husband, who is for your seruice prisoner in the hands of the Frenchmen, our mortal enemies, as in their absence to procure vnto them such defamation and slaunder. And by making this request your grace doth swarue from the bounds of honestie very farre, and you do greate iniury to your fame, if men should know what termes you do vse vnto me. In like maner, I purpose not to violate the faith, which I haue giuen to my husband, but I intend to keepe the same vnspotted, so long as my soule shalbe caried in the Chariot of this mortall body [see 238–43n.]. And if I should so far forget my self, as willingly to commit a thing so dishonest, your grace oughte for the loyal seruice of my father and husband toward you, sharpely to rebuke me, and to punish me according to my desert. For this cause (most dradde soueraigne Lord [see 218]) you which are accustomed to vanquishe and subdue other, bee nowe a conqueror ouer your selfe, and throughly bridle that concupiscence (if there be any) vnder the raynes of reason, that being quenched and ouercome, they may no more reuiue in you, and hauing liuely resisted the first assaultes, the victorie is but easie, which shalbe a thousande times more glorious and gaineful for you, than if you had conquered a kingdome.'

In the novel the countess does not leave of her own accord, as in Froissart and in the play, but the dialogue is interrupted by the announcement of dinner, and the king decides to return to London the next morning.

2.1.278–93 EDWARD'S SOLILOQUY

The king's soliloquy after the departure of the countess finds a counterpart in Edward's musings not before but after his interview with Warwick in Painter's narrative (Metz, pp. 120.38–121.11),[1] when he at first deplores in the name of reason his 'vnshamefull and disordinate appetites' and tells himself:

Resist with al thy power this wanton will which doth enuiron thee. Suffer not this tyraunt loue to bewitch or deceiue thee.

But then

Sodainly after he had spoken those wordes, the beautie of the Countesse representing it self before his eyes, made him to alter his minde again, and to reiect that which he before allowed, saying thus: 'I feele in minde the cause of my offence, and thereby doe acknowledge the wrong, but what shall I doe? sithe I am not able any longer to withstande beautie, that cruell murderer, whiche doth force and maister me so much? Let fortune then and loue doe what they list, the faire Countesse shalbe myne, whatsoeuer come of it . . .' [Compare esp. 2.1.292–3].

The transposition of the speech in the play not only serves an immediate dramatic purpose, but also compensates structurally for a break in the original action of the narrative. Both in Froissart and in Painter, after his rejection by the countess, the king

[1] In this section line as well as page numbers are provided from Metz's edition of the novel, to indicate the relative length of speeches.

leaves Scotland. Froissart returns to the subject only in chapter 89 (Metz, pp. 67–8), describing the ineffectual attempt made by Edward in London to conquer the lady by inviting her to 'a great feest' held there. Also Painter moves the action to London, and the lengthy narrative of the events taking place in the capital is the only source for the rest of Act 2 of the play. But the unhistorical conclusion of the novel with the king's marriage to the countess made it imperative for the dramatist to ignore the very reason given by Painter for transferring the action to London (Metz, p. 114):

Certaine dayes after that king Edward was arriued at London, which was the place of his ordinarie abode, the Countesse of Sarisburie was aduertised, that the Earle her husband, being out of pryson, consumed with griefe and sicknes, died by the way homewards . . . And after she had lamented the death of her husband the space of many dayes, shee returned to her father's house, which was Earle of Warwike. And for so much as he was one of the king's priuie Counsel, and the most part of the affayres of the Realme passed by his aduise and counsell, he continued at London, that hee might be more neare vnto the kinge's person. The king aduertised of the comming of the Countesse, thoughte that fortune had opened a way to bring his enterprise to desired effect, specially for that the death of her husband, and the witnesse of his earnest good will, woulde make her more tractable.

By suppressing this section of the story, the playwright ensured: (a) the continuity of the action of the play in the North of England; (b) the impossibility for the countess to become Edward's queen (as the novel suggested against the evidence of history); (c) the availability of her husband Salisbury as a character in the later part of the play. The last point (that the earl did not die in France) was supported by Froissart's chronicle, whose chapter 78 (following immediately upon that devoted to Edward's 'amours') tells 'Howe therle of Salysbury and therle Moret were delyverd out of prison by exchaunge' (Ker, I, 196), while chapter 89 relates that the king 'commaunded expresly the erle of salisbury that the lady his wyfe shulde be ther [at the great feast 'to be holden in the cyti of London']' (Metz, pp. 67–8).

2.1.294–347 EDWARD AND WARWICK

In Painter the king turns to Warwick, the countess's father, after a love-letter of his (the equivalent of the abortive love-sonnet in the play) is answered with the message

tell the kyng, that I doe besech him most humbly, to sende me no more letters or messages touching the matters whereof he hath written (Metz, p. 115).

The novel presents the dialogue between the king and Warwick as a sequence of four lengthy speeches alternating between the two. In the first (Metz, pp. 115.42–117.19) the king, without mentioning the countess, begins by confessing:

I am so vexed with my passions, as being ouercome by them, I haue none other refuge, but to a most unhappie death that euer man can suffer, if presently I bee not holpen.

After discoursing on the necessity of being governed by reason and acknowledging that his 'disordinate affections' are a fault 'both vnprofitable and voyde of reason' (Metz, p. 116.6–42), the king appeals to Warwick:

I haue no place for rest, but in thy mercy, who in my father's dayes diddest liberally spende thy bloud, in manye notable enterprises in his seruice, whiche afterwardes thou haste so well continued, that in many dangerous affaires, I haue diuers times proued the fidelitie of thy counsell, whereby I haue brought to passe thinges of great importaunce, and therein hitherto neuer founde thee slacke and vnfaythfull. Whiche when I remember doe prouoke me to be bolde to declare vnto you mine entent, whiche by youre onely worde you may procure, the fruite whereof being gotten, you shall winne the heart of a king, to be vsed as you liste for euer. And the more the thing shal seeme harde, difficult or painefull, the greater shall your merite be, and the more firmely shall he be bounde, whiche doth receiue it.

Edward concludes by offering rewards and advancement for Warwick's sons.

The earl, moved by the 'sobbes and sighes' interrupting the king's speech, 'made a liberall and very sodayne offer to the king of his life, his children, and of all that he was able to doe' (see 2.1.296–9), in his reply (Metz, p. 117.25–33):

Commaunde, my soueraigne Lorde (quod he with weaping teares) what it shall please you to haue me doe, if it be, euen to bestowe my life for your sake [see 2.1.312–14]. For by the faithe and fealtie that I do owe to God and to your grace, I sweare, that many dayes and yeares paste, I haue bound my selfe inuiolably, and all mine abilitie without exception, so long as this tongue is able to sturre, and breathe shall remaine within this bodye, faithfully and truely to serue your maiestie, not onely for that dutie bindeth me, but if it were for your sake, to transgresse and exceede the bondes of mine honour [see 2.1.323–6].

The playwright has run together the two speeches, breaking them up into a much more dramatically effective exchange of short sentences (2.1. 296–340), that replace Edward's pathetic moralising with a series of ambiguous moral invectives, when he claims to know in advance that Warwick will not fulfil his protestations of complete allegiance to his sovereign (2.1.302–8, 315–20). The stress is placed squarely on the question of allegiance rather than on the king's plight, so that Warwick, instead of spontaneously offering his life out of pity and love for his master, as in the novel, is forced to bind himself more and more tightly to his oath.

The third speech in the novel (Metz, pp. 117.37–118.15), the revelation of the king's love for the countess, is in terms of a plea for his own life:

Your doughter the Countesse of Sarisburie, (my Lorde) is the onely medicine of my trauayles, whome I doe loue better than mine owne life, and I doe feele my selfe so inflamed with her heauenly beautie, as without her grace and fauour I am not able hereafter to liue: for this consideration, sith you desire to do me seruice, and to preserue my life, I praye you to deale with her, that she with compassion may looke vpon me.

The rest of the speech has an even more apologetic ring:

I am prouoked to make this request, and not able to expel the mortall poyson out of my hart, which hath . . . depriued my minde from all good counsell . . . my onely and last refuge and assured port of all my miseries, resteth in you, either by death to ende my life, or by force to obtayne my desire.

Though odd echoes are inevitable, there could be no sharper contrast in tone than between the king's speech in the novel and its equivalent in the play (2.1.338–45), eight lines of imperious command, with no apology, ending with a couplet announcing Edward's abrupt exit (346–7): 'I will not stand to hear thee make reply: / Thy oath break hers, or let thy sovereign die.'

In the novel the king instead remains to listen patiently to Warwick's heart-felt arguments in the longest speech of all (Metz, pp. 118.19–120.26), and at the end it is Warwick who 'without tarying for other replie of the kyng, went his way' (Metz, p. 120.26–7), so that the king is left to soliloquise about his troubled mind (Metz, pp. 120.38–121.11). In the play this, as already noted, is echoed in the king's speech (2.1.278–93) before his meeting with Warwick.

2.1.348–67 WARWICK'S SOLILOQUY

Warwick's solitary meditation in the play is based essentially on his lengthy reply to the king's request in the novel (Metz, pp. 118.19–120.26), the main point of which is (p. 118.22–9):

But to resolue vpon that which is most expedient, hauing geuen vnto you my faithe in pledge, to succour and helpe you euen to the abandoning of honor and life, I will not be contrarie to my woordes [see 2.1.355]. And touching my daughter, for whom you make request, I will reueale vnto her the effecte of your demaunde [2.1.356–65]: yet of one thing I must tell you, sir, power I haue to entreate her, but none at all to force her [2.1.366–7]. Inough it is that she vnderstand of me what hart and affection you beare vnto her.

The final couplet of Warwick's speech (2.1.368–9) echoes his words to his daughter in the novel (Metz, p. 122.3–6):

O immortall God, what man of any discretion would haue thought that a king could be so impudent and vnshamefast, as to committe to a father a charge so dishonest towardes his own daughter?

2.1.368–460 WARWICK AND THE COUNTESS

The last part of the scene is the closest to Painter's narrative. Warwick's speech to his daughter (2.1.380–412) is modelled on that in the novel (Metz, pp. 121.20–122.16), amplified by very effective rhetorical devices, such as the sequence of 'virtuous sentences' (see 386–409 n.) representing worldly wisdom in contrast with true ethical principles. The countess's reply (2.1.413–30) reproduces more pithily that in Painter (Metz, pp. 122.21–123.32). The most significant verbal as well as conceptual analogies between the novel and the play in these two speeches are recorded in the Commentary (see especially notes to lines 385, 413, 417, 418, 428–30).

There is instead a departure from the novel in the conclusion of the scene. In Painter the countess ends her speech with an italicised *sententia*: *That honest death doth honor and beautifie for forepassed life*, after which (Metz, p. 123.32–5)

The father hearing the wise aunswere of his daughter, gaue her his blessing, in his hart praysing her godly minde, beseching God to helpe her and to kepe her vnder his protection, and to confirme her in that holy and vertuous determination [compare 2.1.455–8].

At this point Painter introduces another development (Metz, pp. 123.35–126) that the play ignores completely, as an unnecessary complication slowing down the stage action. In the novel, after hearing of the countess's refusal and after Warwick's retirement to the country, the king, mad with love and encouraged by his courtiers, sends his secretary to the mother of the countess with a threatening message (Metz, p. 125):

he hath determined whether you will or no, to fetch her out openly by force, to the great dishonour, slaunder and infamie of al your kinne.

The distressed old lady pleads with her daughter, who finally decides (Metz, p. 126):

nowe am I ready to goe with you to the kinge, where if it shall please you, wee two withoute other company will do our owne errande [compare 2.1.374] and attempt the beginning of our enterprise.

And the ladies are ushered by the secretary into the king's presence.

All this is replaced in the play by Warwick's final speech (2.1.431–58), in which only the last four lines echo a sentence in Painter (Metz, p. 123.32–5, quoted above), while the rest is constructed as a sustained rhetorical discourse that counterbalances his previous speech (see 386–40 n., 433–54 n.). It is exactly here that the new emphasis placed by the dramatist on the ethics of power comes to the fore: the close parallelism with one Shakespearean sonnet in particular (no. 94), already hinted at before in the scene (see 342 n., 386–7 n.), is fully developed (435–6 n., 444–5), culminating in line 452, which is identical with the last line of that sonnet.

2.2.1–115 EDWARD'S PERPLEXITIES

The first part of this scene effectively replaces Painter's narrative of the king's further attempts at conquering the countess through the agency of her mother, with a return to the pseudo-historical context, in order to illustrate Painter's point that, after the countess's repulse, the king (Metz, p. 124)

fell in suche dispaire of his loue, as he was like to haue runne out of his wittes for sorrowe.

The reappearance first of Derby and Audley (2.2.0 SD) and then of Prince Edward (2.2.74 SD), returning from the missions assigned to them in 1.1.139–52, entails a second look at the sources used on that occasion, and more precisely at two chapters in Froissart relating events of the year 1338: 32 'Howe kyng Edwarde of England made great alyaunces in the empyre', and 34 'Howe kyng Edwarde was made vycare generall of thempyre of Almaygne'. According to the first of them (Metz, pp. 56–8), in August Edward, unsatisfied with the result of the mission sent the year before to the Earl of Hainault (see 1.1.147–52 and Appendix p. 184), personally attended a meeting in Flanders with the German lords, where it was decided to send a deputation led by the Marquis of Juliers to the German Emperor asking him to challenge the King of France. Though the chapter ends with the announcement that (Metz, p. 58)

themperour gaue commyssion . . . to make kyng Edwarde of Englande, his vycarre generall throughout all the empyre,

a much fuller relation is found in chapter 34 (Ker, I, 104):

about the feest of all sayntes, the marques of Jullers, and his company, sent worde to the kyng [of England] how they had sped.

Then, 'about the feest of saynt Martyne' (11 November) Edward called all his allies to a solemn parliament at Arques:

And so the hall of the towne was apparelled and hanged, as though it had ben the kynges chamber; and there the kyng satte crowned with gold, v. fote hygher than any other: and there openly was redde the letters of themperour, by which the kyng was made vycare generall, and lieftenaunt, for the emperour, and had power gyuen hym to make lawes, and to mynistre iustyce to euery person, in themperours name, and to make money of golde and syluer. The emperour also there commaunded by his letters, that all persons of his empyre, and all other his subgiettes, shulde obey to the kyng of England, his vycare, as to hymselfe, and to do hym homage.

The main preoccupation of the dramatist, though, is that of presenting the king's infatuation through his confused replies to Derby and Audley (2.2.23–37), and especially through his changes of mind (2.2.75–118), a feature of his passion emphasised in the novel especially after the relation of his interview with Warwick (Metz, pp. 120.29–121.16), when at first he feels 'his conscience touched at the quicke' for the infamous charge given to Warwick, and therefore 'he determined to chaunge his opinion'; but then he tells himself that 'the faire Countesse shalbe myne' at all costs, and then again

This talke ended, he deluded himself, and thinking vpon the contrary, he accused himself again, and then from this he altered again to the other. And being in this perplexitie, he passed daye and night.

In the novel Edward is a young man, unmarried and childless. The playwright, more appropriately, attributes the emergence of his perplexity to the sight of his son, which evokes as well the memory of his wife. On the other hand, the last part of the king's extended aside in the presence of the prince (2.2.93–8) is modelled on Edward's first confession of his passion to Warwick, before revealing that the object is the countess (Metz, p. 116.31–5):

Haue not I good cause to complaine my Lorde, that after so manye famous victories achieued by Sea and Lande, wherewith I haue re-nowmed the memorie of my name in all places, am now bound and daunted with an appetite so outragious, as I can not helpe my selfe.

2.2.116–209 EDWARD'S TRIAL AND REFORMATION

With the entrance of the countess, the play reverts to Painter's narrative. In the novel the countess is also ushered into the king's presence by the secretary, though she is escorted by two gentlewomen, while her mother is left at the door, and shortly after the king 'commands' to be left alone with the countess (Metz, pp. 126–7):

they [the countess and her mother] sente worde to the Secretary . . . who conducted them to the kinge's chamber, and presenting them before him, sayde: 'Syr, beholde the companye which you haue so long time desired: who are come to do your grace humble reuerence' [2.2.101–2]. The king greatly astonied, went forth to meete them, and with iouful countinaunce . . . approching neer her, toke her by the hande, and kissing her, sayd: 'Welcome, my life and soule' [2.2.119] . . . The kinge . . . commaunded the Gentlewomen, that were in her company, to departe the chamber [2.2.116–18].

The following dialogue (2.2.122–87) is closely patterned on that in Painter's novel, with the all-important variant that in the latter both king and countess are unmarried. All the same, in the novel as in the play, the countess begins by binding Edward to an oath as a test of his love (Metz, p. 127.13–27):

Gracious and redoubted Prince, sithe my heauy fortune hath broughte mee hither . . . and that my parents amazed through your furie [compare 'awe', 132], are become rauishers of me against my will . . . I humbly beseech your maiestie . . . before you passe any further to satisfy your desire, to let me proue and vnderstande by effecte, if your loue be such, as . . . you haue declared vnto me . . . And if my sute shall seeme reasonable, and grounded vppon equitie, before I doe open and declare the same more at large, assure the performaunce thereof vnto me by oth [compare 127–36].

The king's oath that 'I will not refuse any thing, that is in my power and abilitie' (compare 137) is made in a much more solemn and extended form in the novel (Metz, p. 127.30–41), but of course the countess's request to eliminate both the queen and her husband (138–65) is the playwright's original contribution to the situation, that allows for a much subtler formulation of the suicide threat (167–76), followed by a second plea (177–87) that confronts the king with an alternative closer to that expressed in the novel in these terms (Metz, p. 128.1–12):

Then plucking out a sharpe knife, which was hidden vnder her kirtle [compare 171] . . . she said vnto him: 'Sir, the gift that I require, and wherfore your faith is bound, is this. I most humblie desire you, that rather then to dispoile me of mine honour, with the sworde girded by your side, you do vouchsafe to ende my life, or to suffer me presently, with this sharpe pointed knife in my hand to thrust it to my hart, that mine innocent bloud, doing the funerall honour, may beare witnesse before God of my vndefiled chastity, as being vtterly resolued [compare 166–7] honourablie to die. And that rather then to lose mine honoure, I may murther my selfe before you wyth this blade and knife in present hand.'

This passage is closely echoed in the countess's speech in the play, and the insistence in the last lines on her 'vndefiled chastity' prompted the reference to Roman Lucrece in the king's reply (see 192–5 n.). The half-ironical allusion to the many writers who had celebrated Lucrece (194–5) make it unnecessary to think that the dramatist was recalling specifically Shakespeare's *The Rape of Lucrece* (1594), in the same way as the earlier allusion to the story of Hero and Leander was not necessarily suggested by Marlowe's poem, unfinished and unpublished at the time (see 151–5 n.).

The speech of the reformed king at 188–98 is the last to be modelled on Painter's novel (Metz, p. 128.12–27):

The king . . . consideringe the inuincible constancie and chastitie of the Countesse, vanquished by remorse of conscience . . . taking her by the hand, said: 'Rise vp Lady, and liue from henceforth assured: for I will not ne yet pretende all the dayes of my life, to commit any thing in you against your will.' And plucking the knife out of her hand, exclaimed: 'This knife hereafter shall bee the pursiuant before God and men of this thine inexpugnable chastitie, the force whereof wanton loue was not able to endure, rather yelding place to vertue, which being not alienated from me, hath made me at one instant victorious ouer my selfe . . .' [And] hee opened the doore . . . and same time hee called also the Courtiers and Piers of the Realme, which were then in the base Court of the Palace, among whom was the Archbishop of Yorke . . . to whom with the knife in his hand he recited particulerly the discourse of his loue.

In the play the king at the close of the scene (206–7) says that he will have hardly time to 'discover' the story of his 'siege' of the countess's chastity. Besides, the purpose of his call on the peers is different: in the novel it was to announce his decision to marry the countess, and the rest of the story was a description of the royal nuptials; aware of the unhistorical character of that conclusion, the dramatist instead makes the king recognise his 'folly', and impart orders for future military action, in view of the naval battle off Sluys reported in the next scene. The preparations and the battle itself, which took place in 1340, are described by Holinshed (II, 614–15) and in greater detail by Froissart in chapter 50 (Metz, pp. 60–2), several chapters before the relation of the countess episode (chs. 76–7 and 89), which is supposed to have taken place in 1341–2. The dramatist reverses historical chronology for dramatic purposes.

Act 3

The last three acts are completely devoted to Edward III's French conquests, culling from the chronicles of Froissart and Holinshed the salient episodes of the wars – the naval battle off Sluys (L'Ecluse) in 1340, the battle of Crécy in 1346, the siege and conquest of Calais in 1346–7, and the battle of Poitiers in 1356 – interweaving them together by means of further marginal episodes derived from the same sources (Lord Mountford's allegiance to Edward III, 1341, the help received from a Frenchman in crossing the River Somme, 1346, the grant by the Duke of Normandy of a safe-conduct to an English noble, 1346, the flight of ravens before a battle, 1346, the prophecy of flying stones, 1356, Audley and his squires, 1356) in order to achieve that telescoping of time (and space) which characterises all history plays of the Elizabethan and Jacobean period.

Essential to the latter purpose was the already noted authorial decision to eliminate King Philip VI of Valois, who reigned from 1328 to 1350, from the line of descent of the French dynasty, replacing him with his son John (Jean II le Bon) who, before ascending the throne in 1350, held the title of Duke of Normandy. This entailed a further play on the latter title: historically the Duke of Normandy, firstborn of the King of France, appearing in Act 3 was not Charles, son of John (the future Charles V) but John himself, the future king (Charles at the time was only nine), while in Act 4 he is at one and the same time both John (in respect of the episode of the safe-conduct at 4.1, 4.3.1–56, and 4.5.56–126) *and* Charles, John's firstborn (in respect of his role in the battle of Poitiers at 4.3.57–85, 4.4, 4.5.1–55, and the last two scenes).

3.1 SLUYS AND THE FRENCH PREPARATION FOR CRÉCY

The scene, substantially intended as a celebration of Edward's 'famous victory' (Hol. II, 615) in the naval battle of Sluys (L'Ecluse), on midsummer eve 1340, is an example of the playwright's technique of dovetailing historical events six years distant from each other. The opening gambit consists of presenting the battle not from the English but from the French point of view, so as to 'create' for the audience the characters of Edward's antagonists, who had not appeared before on the stage. The French royal trio in the entrance stage direction is the first application of the already mentioned suppression of King Philip VI of Valois from French history and of its immediate consequences. Not only at this time was the King of France not John II but Philip VI and the Duke of Normandy not Charles but John himself, but also the latter's brother was not Philip (John's youngest son, the future Duke of Burgundy, born in 1341, a year after Sluys) but another Philip: John's brother, Philip Duke of Orléans, who played a leading role not in the battle of Crécy (in 1346 he was only thirteen) but in that of Poitiers ten years later. The fourth character in the direction, the Duke of Lorraine, is introduced as a reminder of the Scottish–French alliance of 1338 already referred to at 1.2.18–39, as well as in anticipation of King David's new invasion of England in 1346, shortly after the French defeat at Crécy. King John's comment that the commitment of the Scot is 'the anch'rage of some better hope' (22) may have been suggested by Hol. II, 643–4 (from Polydore Vergil):

the French king amongst other deuises which he imagined how to raise the K. of England from it [the invasion of France], procured the Scots to make warre into England, insomuch that Dauid king of Scotland . . . vpon hope now to doo some great exploit, by reason of the absence of king Edward . . . assembled the whole puissance of his realme, to the number of fortie or threescore thousand fighting men (as some write) and with them entered into England, burning, spoiling, and wasting the countrie.

The next move (23–30) is to evoke once again what had been hinted at 2.2.1–12 (see p. 196) i.e. 'Howe kyng Edwarde of England made great alyances in the empyre' (Frois., ch. 32, Metz, pp. 56–8) and 'Howe kyng Edwarde was made vycare generall of thempyre of Almaygne' (Frois. ch. 34, Ker, I, 103–5), in fact a throw-back to the years 1337–8. In presenting (33–7) French alliances to counterbalance the English, the playwright must have met with some difficulty because he is content with the mention in the first place of 'The stern Polonian, and the warlike Dane' (34) – not formal allies but professional mercenary troops known to be employed on all sides during the Hundred Years War. The King of Sicily – Robert the Wise, King of Naples and Sicily 1309–43, a descendant of the Anjou branch of the French royal family – is listed, though significantly not presented with the others on the stage at 39 SD, in view of what Froissart reports in the short chapter 51 devoted to him (Ker, I, 149–50), immediately after the relation of the battle of Sluys:

In this season ther raygned a kyng in Cicyll called Robert, who was reputed to be a great astronomyer, and alwayes he warned the Frenche kyng and his counsell, that in no wyse he shulde fight agaynst the king of Englande to be right fortunate in all his dedes. This kyng Robert wold gladly haue sene these two kynges at a good acorde, for he loued so moch the crowne of Fraunce.

The one constant foreign ally of the French was Jean (John) of Luxembourg, King of Bohemia, and his mention here and his speech at 40–2 are based on Froissart's report (ch. 123, Metz, pp. 70–2) 'Of the great assemble that the Frenche kynge made to resyst the kyng of Englande' after the invasion of Normandy in 1346:

[The French king] had sent letters to his frendes in thempyre, to suche as wer farthest of, and also to the gentyll kyng of Behayne, and to the lorde Charles his son[1] . . . the Frenche kyng desyred them to come to hym with all their powers, to thyntent to fyght with the kynge of Englande, who brent and wasted his countrey. These princes and lordes made them redy with great nombre of men of armes, of Almaynes, Behaynoes, and Luxambroses, and so came to the Frenche kyng.

The rest of the scene (62–184) reverts from the preparations for Crécy to a description of the sea-battle off Sluys, to which Froissart devotes the chapter (50, Metz, pp. 60–2) immediately before that mentioning the King of Sicily reported above. From this point on the playwright uses details drawn not only from Froissart's but also from Holinshed's account derived from other sources, as imaginative stimuli to construct in the Mariner's speeches (62–78, 85–9, 144–84) an ample verbal fresco of the phases of the battle, to be placed side by side with those presenting the situation at Poitiers at 4.4.12–39 and the battle itself at 5.1.131–54. The recourse to Holinshed as well as to Froissart is clear from the beginning of the first speech of the Mariner (62: 'I have descried', compare Hol. II, 614 'when the king of England approched, either part descried other, & therewith prepared them to battell'). The elaboration into four lines (73–6, see n.) of a passing remark faithfully translated by Berners from Froissart ('Bien veoïent entre eulx normans par les bannieres que le rois dangleterre y estoit personnellement': Frois. 1513, fol. XXXIXV) is more surprising: the dramatist seems to echo the original earlier version of this passage, preserved in the Rome manuscript (Luce, ed., 'Variantes', par. 114, II (1870), 220):

Che estoit biautés et grant plaisance au veoir ces banières et ces estramières [compare 68: 'streaming ensigns'] armoiies des armes des signeurs.

The armorial streamers or banners are mentioned neither by Holinshed nor by Jean Le Bel, Froissart's chief source. Either the dramatist had access to sources closer to the Rome draft of Froissart (rather than, as Roger Prior ('Compliment', *passim*) suspects, to the 1513 Paris edition annotated by Lord Hunsdon), or, more probably, he remembered the gold noble minted by Edward III in 1344, where, in memory of the Sluys victory, the king is shown on board ship bearing a shield with the quartered arms of England and France.[2]

As noted in the Introduction, p. 28, some reports of the defeat of the Spanish Armada in 1588 contributed to the description of the naval battle. The Mariner's second speech (141–84) appears modelled on a passage in Kyd's *The Spanish Tragedy* (see note to 144–84). Other verbal echoes from the chroniclers are recorded in the notes to lines 66, 72, 161, 177–9, 180–2. The orders for a possible land battle at 94–104 are an invention echoing the many descriptions of battle plans, where the opposing

[1] In his previous references to the King of Bohemia (Ker, I, 77, 89, 94) Froissart had called him Charles instead of John, mistaking him for the son that succeeded him after his death at Crécy.

[2] Reproduced in M. Prestwich, *The Three Edwards*, 1980, pp. 176–7. The nineteenth-century editor of Froissart, Siméon Luce, summarising chapter 37 of the *Chroniques* (II, xvii), writes, without mentioning his authority for the additional information, 'Edouard III monte un grand vaisseau construit à Sandwich, sur lequel flotte une bannière mi-partie aux armes de France et d'Angleterre.' Was the eminent scholar, who surely knew about the gold noble, also familiar with the play of *Edward III*?

forces are nearly always ordered in three 'battles'. The following semi-serious conversation between King John and his (historically as yet unborn) younger son (105–31) is the parodic counterpart of Edward's and the Prince's speeches at the close of 1.1.157–69.

3.2 THE DISASTERS OF WAR

The scene is an example of dramatic sleight of hand intended to fill in a yawning time-gap. After the battle of Sluys, 'on the next day, the which was mydsomer day [1340], the kyng and all his toke lande' not in France but on the friendly territory of Flanders, 'and than toke his horse and rode to Gaunt, where the quene recyued hym with great joye' (Frois., ch. 50; Metz, p. 61). Dramatic foreshortening transformed this peaceful reunion into the warlike landing in Normandy six years later. Froissart presents the invasion of Normandy as the result of a last-minute change of mind: Edward's initial plan had been to go to the rescue of Sir Walter de Manny, besieged by the Duke of Normandy at Aiguillon, in Gascony. As Froissart relates in ch. 121 (Ker, I, 276–8) 'Howe the kyng of Englande came ouer the see agayne to rescue them in Aguyllone', the English fleet was

> well onwarde on their way towarde Gascone, but on the thirde day ther rose a contrary wynde and draue them on the marches of Cornewall, and ther they lay at ancre vi. dayes.

A member of the expedition, Godefroi d'Harcourt, a Norman baron who, like Robert d'Artois, had joined forces with the English, when the Valois had dispossessed him of his properties in Cotentin, made a suggestion:

> he counselled the kyng nat to go into Gascoyne, but rather to set a lande in Normandy, and sayde to the kyng, Sir, the countre of Normandy is one of the plentyous countreis of the worlde: sir, on jeopardy on my heed, if ye woll lande ther, ther is none that shall resyst you: the people of Normandy haue nat ben vsed to the warr, and all the knyghtes and squyers of the contrey ar nowe at the siege before Aguyllon with the duke: and sir, ther ye shall fynde great townes that be nat walled, wherby your men shall haue such wynning, that they shall be the better therby xx. yere after.

The dramatist builds this 'link-scene' between Sluys and Crécy on the reactions of country people who 'had neuer sene men of warre' (see 3.2 headnote). Though justifying the invasion by repeating at 35–7 the dynastic argument and by introducing at 38–43 the first of the many invented prophecies intended to give supernatural sanctions to bloody events, both in the opening direction and in the speeches of the First Frenchman at 1–4 and of the Third at 46–68, he provides a word-picture of Edward's plunder and scorched-earth tactics in his progress through Normandy, repeatedly underlined in the chronicles,[1] concluding by borrowing from them the 'order of the English' at Crécy. Here is Holinshed's version (II, 637):

> Then he ordeined three battels, in the first was the prince of Wales, and with him the earle of Warwike [and numerous other noblemen]. They were eight hundred men of armes, and two

[1] There is no reason to believe, with Roger Prior ('Compliment', pp. 245–7), that the wording of the opening stage direction and of the first few lines of the scene was suggested by Lord Hunsdon's marginal comment *not* on the English invasion of Normandy, but on the destruction of Durham by the Scots in 1341 (Frois. 1513, fol. LIIIv): '[y]e towne of duram [ta]ken and burnt [a]nd man woman chylde kylde'.

thousand archers, and a thousand of other with the Welsh men. In the second battell was the earle of Northhampton, the earle of Arundell, the lords Ros and Willowbie, Basset, S. Albine, Multon, and others. The third battell the king led himselfe, hauing with him seauen hundred men of armes, and two thousand archers, and in the other battell were to the number of eight hundred men of armes, and twelue hundred archers.

3.3.1–47 GOBIN DE GRACE AND THE PROGRESS IN FRANCE

The first part of the scene illustrates a typical device common to all chronicle plays: the temporary inversion of the narrative. 3.2.46–68 presented a detailed account of the deployment of the English army in the Crécy plains; 3.3 reverts to events preceding the armed encounter. In this case the author, as can be seen from the spelling of proper names of persons and places, though familiar with Froissart's account, took advantage of Holinshed's more concise report. The episode of the crossing of the Somme (1–12) is presented by Holinshed (II, 636) in these words:

The King of England . . . marched forward through the countries of Pontiew and Vimew [the Counties of Ponthieu and Eu], approching vnto the good towne of Abuile [Abbeville], and at length by one of the prisoners named Gobin de Grace, he was told where he might passe with his armie ouer the riuer of Some, at a foord in the same riuer, being hard in the bottome, and verie shallow at an eb water.

. . . When the K. of England had thus passed the riuer, he acquitted Gobin Agace, and all his companie of their ransomes, and gaue the same Gobin an hundred nobles, and a good horsse, and so the king rode foorth as he did before. His marshals road to Crotaie by the sea side, and burnt the towne, and tooke all such wines and goods as were in the ships and barks which laie there in the hauen.

The mention of Crotaie (le Crotoy) in this context is significant, since a few lines later in the play (20) the name of the town (indicated in a marginal note in the chronicle) is included in Prince Edward's rather arbitrary list of places 'won' and 'wasted' by the English in their progress from the Normandy landing to the Somme, in spite of the fact that the haven-town is beyond the river estuary. The other names in that list (discussed in the n. to 20) are among those noted in the margin in an earlier page of Holinshed (II, 634): Harflew (for Barfleur, see 20 n.), Carentine (Carentan) and Saint Lo (no circumflex 'Lô' in Holinshed). Of the first Holinshed says that it 'was giuen vp, yet neuerthelesse it was robbed, and much goods found in it'; of the second that the defenders after two days' resistance

yeelded it vp into the Englishmens hands, who burned the same, and caused the burgesses to enter into their ships. All this was doone by the battell that went by the sea side, and by them on the sea together.

Holinshed had begun this paragraph with the words:

After that the whole armie was landed, the king appointed two marshals, the lord Godfrey of Harecourt, and the earle of Warwike, and the earle of Arundel was made constable. There were ordeined three battels, one to go on his right hand, following by the coast of the sea; and the other to march on his left hand, vnder the conduct of the marshals; so that he himselfe went in the middest with the maine armie.

Since, unlike Froissart (see 15 n.), Holinshed does not specify that the Prince of Wales was in the king's battle, the dramatist(s) felt at liberty to consider the Prince (together with the inseparable Lord Audley) as the leader of the expeditionary force on the right hand of the king's army, so that it could be said (15) that 'since our landing we could never meet'. These words are attributed in the play to Artois – another liberty taken by the playwright: Robert of Artois had died in England three years before, in 1343, of the wounds received when leading the second English expedition in Brittany, to which Froissart devoted two whole chapters, 92 ('Howe sir Robert Dartoys toke the cytie of Vannes, in Bretayne'), and 93 ('Howe sir Robert Dartoys dyed, and where he was buried' – Ker, I, 221–5). These were certainly known to the dramatist, who deliberately ignored them in order to keep this representative character alive to the end of the play.

The English 'battle' to which Artois seems to be alluding at this point had in fact taken the road to Paris, through Louviers, Gisors and Vernon (all noted in the margin in Holinshed), to within some fifteen miles from the capital; as Holinshed put it (II, 635),

> The English marshals ran abroad iust to Paris, and burnt S. Germans in Laie.

Since the other town mentioned in the prince's speech (20) is spelt 'Lie' in the quartos, the general assumption that this is a printer's misreading of 'Lo' (for 'Saint Lo', Hol., II, 634) can be questioned (see Lô, 20 n.): what if the dramatist was thinking of 'Laie', which he found in the next page of Holinshed?

34–44 are also suggested by Holinshed: first from a passage before the report of the crossing of the Somme (II, 636):

> At the same instant was the French king come to Amiens, with more than a hundred thousand men [37], and thought to inclose the king of England, that he should no waie escape, but be constreined to receiue battell in some place greatlie to his disaduantage.

Then from another, after the description of the deployment of the English forces (II, 637):

> The French king before he approched neere to his enimies, sent forth foure skilful knights to view the demeanor of his enimies, the which returning againe, made report as they had seene . . . Here was the French king counselled to stay and not giue battell that day, but to aduise all things with good deliberation and regard, to consider well how and what way he may best assaile them.

After the backward glance that makes this first part of 3.3 overlap with the last part of 3.2, inducing the author to consult his sources in reverse order, the time sequence is re-established.

3.3.46–228 THE KINGS' PARLEY AND THE ARMING OF PRINCE EDWARD

The rest of the scene is the dramatist's invention, apart from occasional hints from the chronicles, structured according to what was to become a well-established pattern in the stage presentation of the preliminaries to a major battle. First the direct verbal confrontation between the two opposed parties (46–139 – no counterpart in the chronicles), then the 'orations' of the leaders to their respective armies. It is at this point that the author breaks with tradition: while King John's speech (140–64) is a perfect example of martial rhetoric, King Edward's is replaced by a brilliant dramatic variant, based on the vaguest hint in Froissart (see 172–218 n.), and serving admirably the ideological purposes of the play (compare Introduction, pp. 36–45) and providing a visual element of chivalric pageantry. It is the ceremonial arming of Prince Edward before the battle, which has the further advantage of bringing to the fore once for all the legendary figure of the Black Prince.

3.4 THE BATTLE OF CRÉCY

The stage presentation of the battle of Crécy varies the traditional pattern consisting in alternating brief scenes in the two opposing camps, insomuch as only thirteen lines are devoted to the French side, while all the rest of the action is seen through English eyes. Those thirteen lines entrusted to King John and the Duke of Lorraine (surprisingly the author omits to mention that Lorraine was to be one of the major French casualties in the battle[1]) are based on the chroniclers' report of how, as a marginal note in Holinshed (II, 638) states, 'the battell is begun':

> There were of Genowaies crosbowes to the number of twelue or fifteene thousand, the which were commanded to go on before, and with their shot to begin the battell; but they were so werie with going on foot that morning six leagues armed with their crosbowes, that they said to their constables; 'We be not well vsed, in that we are commanded to fight this daie, for be we not in case to doo any great feat of armes, we haue more need of rest.' These words came to the hearing of the earle of Alanson, who said; 'A man is well at ease to be charged with such sort of rascals, that faint and faile now at most need.'

All the same, the Genoese began the battle, by advancing with great leaps and cries:

> The third time againe the Genowaies leapt, and yelled, and went foorth till they came within shot, and fiercelie therwith discharged their crossbowes. Then the English archers stept foorth one pase, and let flie their arrowes so wholie and so thicke togither, that it seemed to snowe. When the Genowaies felt the arrowes persing their heads, armes and breasts, manie of them cast downe their crosbowes, and cut the strings, and returned discomfited. When the French king saw them flee awaie, he said: 'Slea these rascals, for they will let and trouble vs without reason.'
>
> Then ye might haue seene the men of armes haue dasht in amongst them, and killed a great number of them, and euer the Englishmen shot where they saw the thickest prease: the sharpe arrowes ran into the men of armes, and into their horsses, and manie fell horsse and man amongst the Genowaies, and still the Englishmen shot . . . The throng was such that one ouerthrew another; & also among the Englishmen, there were certeine of the footmen with great kniues, that went in among the men of armes, and killed manie of them as they laie on the ground, both earles, barons, knights, and esquires.

[1] Frois., ch. 130 (Metz, p. 81) reports: 'Also therle Lewes of Bloyes, nephue to the Frenche kyng, and the duke of Lorayne fought vnder their baners, but at last they were closed in among a company of Englysshemen and Walsshemen, and there were slayne, for all their prowes.' Hol. (II, 639) has instead: 'Among other which died that daie, these I find registred by name as cheefest, Iohn king of Boheme, Rafe duke of Lorraine, Charles of Alanso brother germane to king Philip, Charles earle of Blois, Lewes earle of Flanders . . .'. The mistaken mention of 'Charles' instead of 'Louis' of Blois in Hol. induced the dramatist to give in the next scene (4.1.2, see n.) the false information that 'Sir Charles of Blois is slain', while in reality he died only in 1364.

Practically all the rest of the scene is a dramatisation with ample additions of the chroniclers' reports, making the most of the central episode, Prince Edward's initiation into feats of arms. The playwright treasures and develops very effectively in the first place (14–69) the hints contained in a single pregnant paragraph in Holinshed, based on Froissart (Hol., II, 639):

Certaine Frenchmen and Almaines perforce opened the archers of the princes battell, and came to fight with the men of armes hand to hand. Then the second battell of the Englishmen came to succor the princes battell, and not before it was time, for they of the battell had as then inough to doo, in somuch that some which were about him, as the earle of Northampton, and others sent to the king, where he stood aloft on a windmill hill [see 15], requiring him to aduance forward, and come to their aid, they being as then sore laid to of their enimies [see 26–9]. The king herevpon demanded if his sonne were slaine, hurt or felled to the earth? [compare Frois. in 25 n.] 'No (said the knight that brought the message) but he is sore matched.' 'Well' (said the king) 'returne to him and them that sent you, and saie to them that they send no more to me for any aduenture that falleth, so long as my son is aliue, for I will that this iourneie be his, with the honor thereof [see 34 n.].' With this answer the knight returned, which greatlie incouraged them to doo their best to win the spurs [compare 31 n.], being half abashed that they had sent to the king for aid.

The playwright makes dramatic capital out of this (23–64), by trebling the number of the messengers, two of whom were not at Crécy:[1] Artois, as noted at p. 204, was dead, while the Earl of Derby was at the time engaged in Gascony and Poitou. In fact Froissart's relation of his campaign in ch. 136, 'Howe therle of Derby the same seson [1346] toke in Poyctou dyuers townes and castels, and also the cyte of Poycters' (Ker, I, 308–11) may well have suggested to the dramatist the notion of making the battle of Poitiers, fought ten years later, follow immediately upon that of Crécy; hence the mention towards the end of this scene (116) of Poitiers as the place to which 'the fearful [French] king escaped'.

After the suspense, the inevitable *coup de théâtre*: the triumphal return of Prince Edward, who is given the honour of the death of the most illustrious and noble victim of the battle, the King of Bohemia, at the cost of reversing the course of events presented in the chronicles (see 86 n.), and finally the pageantry of the knighting of the prince (74–114). All this is a far cry from the economical report in Holinshed (II, 639):

When the Frenchmen were clearelie ouercome, and those that were left aliue fled and gone, so that the Englishmen heard no more noise of them, king Edward came downe from the hill (on the which he stood all that day with his helmet still on his head) and going to the prince, imbraced him in his armes, and kissed him, saieng; 'Faire sonne, God send you good perseuerence in this your prosperous beginning, you haue noblie acquit your selfe, you are well worthie to haue the gouernance of a realme committed to your hands for your valiant dooings [see 104–5 n.].' The prince inclined himselfe to the earth in honouring his father, as he best could [see 73 SD n. and 76 SD n.]. This done, they thanked God togither with their souldiers for their good aduenture [see 112]. For so the king commanded, and willed no man to make anie boast of his owne power, but to ascribe all the praise to almightie God for such a noble victorie.

[1] Neither was there, on the French side, the Duke of Normandy, engaged at the time in the siege of Aiguillon, see p. 202.

Lines 107–11 listing the French losses and 118–19 announcing the siege of Calais are in perfect line with the chronicles: the description of the battle and of its aftermath in Froissart is followed by two consecutive chapters (132 and 133) entitled respectively 'How the next day after the batayle of Cressey they that were deed were nombred by thenglysshmen' (Metz, pp. 82–3), and 'Howe the kyng of Englande layd siege to Calys, and howe all the poore people were put out of the towne' (Metz, pp. 83–4).

The heraldic emblem of the pelican at the close of the scene (see 122–6n.) is misplaced, but its origin and implications are worth discussing. It first appears in an English context in Geoffrey Whitney, *A Choice of Emblemes, and other devises . . . Englished and Moralized*, published at Leyden in 1586 with a dedication to Robert Earl of Leicester.[1] The emblem (at p. 87), reproducing number 7 in *Hadriani Junii Emblemata* (Antwerp, 1575), loses, in Whitney's treatment, its strictly religious meaning (the pelican was interpreted as an emblem of the Eucharist, and as such figures in the arms of the Colleges of Corpus Christi both in Oxford and in Cambridge): Whitney adopts the motto *Quod in te est, prome* (What is in thee, draw forth), addressing it to a member of the Leicester circle, Alexander Nowell, Dean of St Paul's, with an epigram saying in part: 'The Pellican, for to reuiue her younge, / Doth peirce her breste, and geue them of her blood: / Then searche your breste, and as yow haue with tonge, / With penne proceede to doe our countrie good.' In *Edward III* the same exhortation to 'do our country good' (a secularisation of the original symbolism) is transferred from the use of learning to that of arms, in accordance with King Edward's words to his son at 1.1.157–9: 'and, Ned, thou must begin / Now to forget thy study and thy books, / And ure thy shoulders to an armour's weight'. By the time Shakespeare wrote *King Lear* the pelican emblem had undergone a further transformation, from parental and patriotic dedication to filial ingratitude (*Lear*, 3.4.74–5: ''twas this flesh begot / Those pelican daughters'). The motto '*Sic et vos*: "And so should you"' (126) echoes one that figures in several heraldic crests, *Sic vos non vobis*: 'So you not for yourselves'. According to C.N. Elvin (*Handbook of Mottoes*, 1860, revised 1971, p. 184), it 'underlines altruistic feelings' and is taken from four lines attributed to Virgil, each of them beginning with the same words, implying that neither birds build nests, nor sheep grow fleece, nor bees make honey, nor oxen draw ploughs for their own use.

Acts 4 and 5

The technique of dovetailing historical events finds its fullest application in Acts 4 and 5, in which at least four major narrative strands are closely intertwined in a way paralleled only in the most sophisticated multiple plot comedies produced in the period. The first strand, based on the episode of the safe-conduct granted in 1346 by John Duke of Normandy to Sir Walter de Manny, is woven through 4.1, 4.3.1–56, 4.5.56–126, with a further twist in 5.1.97–156, and manages to pick up on its way two

[1] Facsimile reprint, Introduction by John Manning, 1989. Information from Huston Diehl, *An Index of Icons in English Emblem Books 1500–1700*, 1986, s.v. Pelican. For the pelican symbolism and the crest of the Pelham family (see 122–6n.) *Boutell's Heraldry*, revised by J. P. Brooke-Little, 1978, pp. 77 and 126.

previous side events: the war in Brittany and the countess of Salisbury episode (both 1341). The second major strand is the siege of Calais (30 August 1346 to 3 August 1347): it occupies most of 4.2, and it crops up again occasionally in the following scenes, till its conclusion in 5.1. The third strand is the invasion of England by the Scots in September 1346, which resulted in the capture of King David of Scotland in the battle of Neville's Cross. The events are related in 4.2.36–61, but the conclusion comes only at 5.1.64–96. The fourth strand, meant to join together all the rest, is the battle of Poitiers, on 19 September 1356, the different phases of which, either historical or imaginary, take up 4.3.57–85, 4.4, 4.5.1–55 and most of the rest of the act, with an impressive *coda* at 5.1.176–243. But the presentation is fragmented into a number of recurring subsidiary themes, such as the prophecies (4.3.63–82, 4.5.1–40, 4.6.18–52, 5.1.214–15), the dire plight of Prince Edward (4.3.57–62, 4.4.1–65 and 124–62, 4.6.1–17), Audley and his esquires (4.6.53–62, 4.7.18–59). It is perhaps significant that while in Act 3 the play-text mainly echoes Holinshed's wording, from this point on it relies mostly on Froissart.

4.1 THE SAFE-CONDUCT: MOUNTFORD AND SALISBURY

After describing 'Howe the kyng of Englande layd siege to Calys' (ch. 133; Metz, pp. 83–4), the subject of 4.2, Froissart devotes three chapters (134–6) to the events taking place at the same time in Gascony, where another English force under Sir Walter de Manny was besieged in Aiguillon by John Duke of Normandy. Chapter 134 (Ker, I, 305–6) relates how the Duke of Normandy, sent for by his father after the defeat at Crécy to help him 'to defende his herytage fro thenglysshmen', 'brake vp his siege before Aguyllon'. Chapter 136 (Ker, I, 308–11), already referred to at p. 206, tells how, taking advantage of the withdrawal of the Duke of Normandy's forces, the Earl of Derby made an extended incursion from Bordeaux into Gascony and beyond as far as Poitiers, which was ransacked to the point that the English 'at their departyng [to return to Bordeaux] had so moche rychesse, that they wyst natte what to do therwith'. But the dramatist was not so much interested in these as in the middle chapter, 135 (Metz, pp. 84–5), hardly more than an anecdote overlooked by other historians, which, in contrast with the lurid account of the 'many yuell dedes' done by the English in Gascony and Poitou, stood out as an example of the true spirit of chivalry both on the English and on the French side. Froissart's narrative is straightforward:

> It was nat long after [the lifting of the siege of Aiguillon], but that sir Gaultier of Manny fell in communycation with a knyght of Normandy, who was his prisoner, and demanded of hym what money he wolde pay for his raunsome. The knyght answered and sayde he wolde gladly pay thre M. crownes. Well, quoth the lorde Gaultyer, I knowe well ye be kynne to the duke of Normandy and wel beloued with hym, that I am sure, and if I wolde sore oppresse you, I am sure ye wolde gladly pay x. thousand crownes, but I shall deale otherwyse with you. I woll trust you on your faythe and promyse; ye shall go to the duke your lorde, and by your meanes gette a saue conduct for me and xx. other of my company to ryde through Fraunce to Calys, payeng curtesly for all our expenses. And if ye can get this of the duke or of the kyng, I shall clerely quyte you your ransome with moche thanke, for I greatly desyre to se the kynge my maister, nor I wyll lye but one nyght in a place, tyll I come there; and if ye can nat do this, retourne agayn hyder within a moneth, and yelde yourself styll as my prisoner.

This passage was to provide the substance of lines 13–43. In fact, the dramatist's first move was to change the identity of the protagonists of this episode. The name of Walter de Manny – historically Walter or Gualtier Mauny, an esquire from Hainault who came to England among the followers of Philippa of Hainault when she married Edward III in 1327 – had been closely associated with that of the Earl of Salisbury in the Scottish campaign of 1332–3, as reported by Froissart in chapter 26 (see the passage quoted at p. 183 above). Walter de Manny was the rescuer of the Countess of Mountford, besieged in 1342 in her castle at Hennebont in Brittany (Frois., ch. 81, quoted at p. 188 above), and Holinshed (II, 623) mentions the Earl of Salisbury among the members of the English expedition led by Robert d'Artois in Brittany to protect the countess from further attacks. So the playwright made no scruple in substituting the name of Salisbury (who in fact by 1346 was dead, and succeeded by his son) for that of Manny in reporting the safe-conduct episode. He had also to invent a plausible name for Manny's prisoner, the knight of Normandy 'kynne to the duke'. Leafing through Holinshed, he found 'grand Villiers' as the name not of a person but of a place mentioned by Edward's confessor in a letter 'describing the kings voiage into France' before Crécy (Hol., II, 641). As for the Duke of Normandy himself, it little mattered that at the time he was, as we have seen (p. 199 above) John, and not Charles as in the play.

The second move was to create a background for the episode, in order to justify its transfer from one character to the other, and from Gascony to Brittany. For this purpose the dramatist had to revive a person who by 1346 had been dead five years, and to 'kill' one who at the time was still alive. So, in the first part of the scene (1–12) he presented the formal act of allegiance of the Lord Mountford (Montfort) to King Edward for the dukedom of Brittany, which historically had taken place in 1341 and which cost Mountford his life in the same year (see Frois., ch. 68, Metz, pp. 62–3, and for Mountford's death Frois., ch. 72 and 1 SH n.). At the same time he decided to get rid once for all of Charles of Blois, who had been the cause of the war in Brittany, and announced his death on the basis of a mistaken mention in Holinshed (see p. 205, n. 1 above).

With these manipulations of names and facts, the episode fits perfectly into the play.

4.2 THE SIEGE OF CALAIS AND THE WAR WITH SCOTLAND

The scene relies completely on Froissart, chapter 133 (Metz, pp. 83–4) for 1–35, chapters 138–9 (Metz, pp. 85–8) for 36–61, and chapter 146 (Metz, p. 89) for 62–85; relevant parallels are quoted in the nn. to lines 1–9, 17–21, 30–2, 73–8. The most significant departures from the source are: (a) Edward did not offer a 'league' (line 1) to the people of Calais, but determined from the beginning to take the place by famine, and to that purpose had a whole 'lyttel towne' built in wood for his men 'bytwene the towne and the ryuer' (compare 61, 'I'll pitch my tent near to the sandy shore'); (b) The Earl of Derby did not take part in the siege (see pp. 206 and 208 above); (c) The captain of Calais, Jean de Vienne, did not force only six 'poor Frenchmen' to leave the town, but seventeen hundred 'poore and meane people' (see 6 SD n. and 17–21 n.).

Froissart's two chapters (138–9) on the defeat of the Scottish invaders are drastically summarised in the report of Lord Percy, who had been one of the English commanders in that war (see 35 SD n. and 38 n.), and the stress placed on the refusal of John Copland (or Copeland) to surrender to Queen Philippa the King of Scotland, whom he had taken prisoner, is justified by Froissart's devoting his chapter 139 (Metz, pp. 87–8) to the event, under the title 'How John Copland had the kyng of Scottes prisoner, and what profet he gatte therby'. The journey of Queen Philippa to Calais is mentioned at the end of this chapter (see 57–61 n.).

The intervention of the Captain (62–6, 80–5) is based on the speech addressed to King Edward's envoys, whose leader was Sir Walter de Manny, by 'sir John of Vyen', captain of Calais, at the beginning of Froissart's chapter 146 (Metz, p. 88):

Sirs, ye be right valyant knyghtes in dedes of armes, and ye knowe well howe the kynge my maister hath sende me and other to this towne, and commaunded vs to kepe it to his behofe, in suche wyse that we take no blame nor to hym no dammage; and we haue done all that lyeth in oure power. Nowe our socours hath fayled vs [80–3], and we be so sore strayned that we haue nat to lyue withall, but that we must all dye or els enrage for famyn, without [unless] the noble and gentyll kyng of yours woll take mercy on vs: the which to do we requyre you to desyre hym, to haue pyte on vs and to let vs go and depart as we be, and lette hym take the towne and castell and all the goodes that be therin [62–6], the whiche is great habundaunce.

The conditions imposed by Edward summarise the negotiations related at length by Froissart (Metz, p. 89, see 73–8 n.).

4.3 THE SAFE-CONDUCT AND THE PROPHECIES

The scene is divided into two distinct parts. The first (1–56), in order to reveal the ideological implications of the safe-conduct episode broached in 4.1, extends and embroiders upon a sentence in Froissart's report immediately following the passage quoted at p. 208 above (ch. 135, Metz, p. 84):

The knyght [Villiers in the play] was content and so went to Parys to the duke [of Normandy] his lorde, and he obtayned this pasport for sir Gaultier of Manny [Salisbury in the play], and xx. horses with hym all onely: this knyght retourned to Aguyllon, and brought it to sir Gaultier, and ther he quyted the knyght Norman of his raunsome.

In the second part (57–85) the dramatist presents the battle in his own way, reporting, against all historical evidence, that Prince Edward was overpowered (57–9), with a view to a *coup de théâtre* in 5.1 parallel to that after Crécy in 3.4. At this stage the Duke of Normandy (instantly transmuted from John, who granted the safe-conduct to Manny, into his son Charles, who fought at Poitiers) is used as the vehicle for a typical dramatic device: the deceptive prophecy before a crucial event (63–82). In order to put together what are in fact three prophecies in one the playwright explored the chronicles, not only Froissart in this case, but also Holinshed. He based the prophecy of the 'feathered fowl' frightening the French army (68, to be developed at length in 4.5.1–55) on a sentence in the report not of the battle of Poitiers but of that of Crécy both in Froissart (ch. 130; Metz, p. 78) and in Holinshed (II, 638). The relevant passage in Froissart's version is quoted at 4.5.1–55 n. The prophecy of the flintstones breaking the French battle array (69, developed at 4.6.4–52) was no doubt suggested by a marginal title found only in Holinshed (II, 665, based not on Froissart but on Thomas Walsingham), immediately before the report of the battle of Poitiers: 'A prophesie of a prelate'. The prelate in question was the Cardinal of Périgord, who had vainly endeavoured 'to bring the parties [Prince Edward and the King of France] to some agreement'. In the end, he reported to the Pope (see Metz, pp. 130–1):

Most blessed father (said he) either we will persuade them to peace and quietnesse, either else shall the verie flintstones crie out of it. But this he spake not of himselfe, as it was supposed, but being a prelate in that time, he prophesied what should follow; for when the English archers had bestowed all their arrowes vpon their enimies [compare 4.6.6–8], they toke vp pebles from the place where they stood, being full of those kind of stones [compare 4.6.13–16], and approching to their enimies, they threw the same with such violence on them, that lighting against their helmets, armor, and targets, they made a great ringing noise [compare 4.6.24–42], so that the cardinals prophesie was fulfilled, that he would either persuade a peace, or else the stones should crie out thereof.

The third and most obvious prophecy (72–3) is an authorial invention.

4.4 THE TAUNTING OF PRINCE EDWARD

The fourth scene is the proof of the author(s)' determination to provide an independent version of the battle of Poitiers. Contrary to the version in the play, Prince Edward was never in real danger during the action. Even the description of the French battle array is imaginary (see 12–39 n.), and the few hints taken from the chronicles as well as the most blatant departures from them are noted in the Commentary. The dramatist is most concerned with illustrating Froissart's remark on Sir James Audley (ch. 162; Metz, p. 96):

This lorde James was a right sage and valyant knyght, and by hym was moche of the hoost ordayned and gouerned the day before.

The last section of the scene (124–62) is conceived as a demonstration of his wisdom.

The central part (66–123), taken up with the taunting of Prince Edward by the envoys of the French king and princes, is considered by some to be another Shakespearean contribution to the play (see Introduction, p. 16). It is certainly an original contribution by the authors, though the First Herald's message may well have been suggested by Froissart's (Metz, pp. 93–6) and Holinshed's (Metz, pp. 129–31) reports of the intervention of the Cardinal of Périgord as peacemaker (see 66–123 n. and 69–73 n.), and the Second Herald's by the Dauphin's ironical present of tennis balls to Henry V in *The Famous Victories of Henry the fifth* (sigs. D3-D3^{v} in the 1598 edition), an anonymous play performed before 1588.

4.5 THE PROPHECY OF THE RAVENS AND THE SAFE-CONDUCT AGAIN

Contradicting his previous presentation of the dire plight of the English, the author develops in the first part of the scene (1–55) the prophecy of the ravens based on the report of the battle of Crécy (see p. 210 above and 4.5.1–55 n.). The rest of the scene resumes the safe-conduct episode, elaborating the last part of Froissart's report in his chapter 135 (Metz, pp. 84–5):

When he [Walter de Manny = Salisbury in the play] came to Orleance, for all his letter [passport] he was arested and brought to Parys, and there put in prison in the Chatelet. Whan the duke of Normandy knewe thereof, he went to the kynge his father and shewed him howe sir Gaultier of Manny had his saue conduct, wherfore he requyred the kynge as moche as he might to delyuer hym, or els it shulde be sayde howe he had betrayed hym. The kyng answered and sayd howe he shulde be put to dethe, for he reputed hym for his great ennemy. Than sayd the duke, Sir, if ye do so, surely I shall neuer bere armour agaynst the kynge of Englande, nor all suche as I may let. And at his departyng, he sayd, that he wolde neuer entre agayn into the kynges host: thus the mater stode a certayne tyme . . . Finally, the kyng [of France] was so counselled, that he [Walter de Manny] was delyuered out of prison and all his costes payed: and the kynge sende for hym to his lodgyng of Nesle in Parys, and there he dyned with the kynge, and the kynge presented hym great gyftes and jewels, to the value of a thousand floreyns.

The main variant is in the behaviour of the King of France towards his prisoner after freeing him, which the playwright attributes, in Charles's words, to the King of England (see 97–102 n.).

4.6 THE PROPHECY OF THE FLINTSTONES AND AUDLEY'S RESCUE

Taking advantage of the usual practice of alternating the two opposing camps in the representation of battles, the dramatist constructs 4.6.1–53 as a parallel to 4.5.1–55. There the first prophecy was realised (and we are reminded of it at 6–12), here we find the reasons for (13–17) and the results of (18–42) the English using stones as weapons, as predicted in the second prophecy, 'flintstones rise and break the battle 'ray' (4.3.69).

The last ten lines of the scene (53–62) are directly from Froissart (ch. 162, Metz, p. 100):

On the Englisshe parte the lorde James Awdeley with the ayde of his four squyers fought alwayes in the chyefe of the batayle: he was soore hurte in the body and in the vysage; as longe as his breth serued hym he fought; at laste at the ende of the batayle his four squyers tooke and brought hym oute of the felde, and layed hym under a hedge syde for to refresshe hym, and they unarmed hym, and bounde vp his woundes as well as they coulde.

4.7 THE CAPTURE OF KING JOHN AND AUDLEY'S GIFT

The main achievement of the battle of Poitiers, the capture of the King of France, is treated here cursorily (1–11), as if taken for granted, reserving its celebration for the last act of the play. All the same, liberties are taken with history: Charles Duke of Normandy was not taken prisoner with the king, but went back to Paris with his brothers Louis of Anjou and Jean of Berry, never mentioned in the play. Neither did Artois take part in the battle, because he had been dead thirteen years (see p. 204), but in this case the author had some justification, in view of Froissart's mention of a knight of Artois as the captor of King John and Prince Philip at Poitiers, see 11 SD n.

Most of the scene (12–64) is devoted to an episode emphasised by both Froissart and Holinshed, the recompense given to Audley and his generosity in devolving it to the squires who had rescued him. The author, though aware of Froissart (chs. 165, 167; Metz, pp. 103, 104–5), follows the report in Holinshed (II, 668–9):

The prince gaue to the lord Iames Audelie (who had receiued in the battell manie sore wounds) fiue hundred marks of yearelie reuenues assigned foorth of his lands in England. The which gift the knight granted as freely as he had receiued it vnto foure of his esquiers, which in the battell had beene euer attendant about his person, without whose aid & valiant support he knew well that he had beene slaine sundrie times in the same battell by his enimies, and therefore thought it a dutie of humanitie and gratitude to make them amends with some temporall recompense . . .

When the prince heard that he had so doone, he meruelled what his meaning was, and caused him to be brought before his presence, and demanded of him wherefore he had so lightlie giuen away the reward which he had bestowed vpon him, and whether he thought that gift too meane for him or not. The lorde Audelie so excused himselfe in extolling the good seruice doone to him by his esquiers, through whome he had so manie times escaped the dangers of death, that the prince did not onelie confirme the resignation of the fiue hundred marks giuen to the esquiers, but also rewarded the lord Audelie with six hundred marks more of like yearelie reuenues, in maner and forme as he had receiued the other.

That the doubling of the prince's gift (56–9) is not mentioned in Froissart proves that the dramatist had reverted to Holinshed.

5.1 THE MERGING OF THE STRANDS

The last act draws together the different narrative strands running through the play, with complete disregard for historical chronology. The surrender of Calais is closely modelled on the last part of the very detailed account in Froissart, chapter 146 (Metz, pp. 88–91), leaving out all preliminaries:

Whan sir Gaultier [de Manny] presented these burgesses to the kyng, they kneled downe and helde vp their handes and sayd, Gentyll kyng, beholde here we sixe, who were burgesses of Calays and great marchantes: we haue brought to you the kayes of the towne and of the castell and we submyt oure selfe clerely into your wyll and pleasure, to saue the resydue of the people of Calys, who have suffred great payne. Sir, we beseche your grace to haue mercy and pytie on vs through your hygh nobles [12–18, 27–31]: than all the erles and barownes, and other that were there, wept for pytie. The kyng loked felly on theym, for greatly he hated the people of Calys, for the great damages and dyspleasures [compare 124n.] they had done hym on the see before. Than he commaunded their heedes to be stryken of.

The play adds a new touch: the king, before pronouncing the death sentence (32–8), expresses doubts on the real social status of the men (20–6). In Froissart, Walter de Manny, in charge of negotiating the surrender, is the first to plead at some length for the burgesses:

A noble kyng, for Goddessake, refrayne your courage; ye haue the name of souerayne nobles, therfore nowe do nat a thyng that shulde blemysshe your renome, nor to gyue cause to some to speke of you villany; euery man woll say it is great cruelty to put to deth suche honest persons, who by their owne wylles putte themselfe into your grace to saue their company.

Manny's words suggested the arguments used by the queen to convince Edward in the play (39–46). In Froissart she insists on another point:

Than the quene beynge great with chylde, kneled downe and sore wepyng, sayd, A gentyll sir, syth I passed the see in great parell, I haue desyred nothyng of you; therfore nowe I humbly requyre you, in the honour of the Son of the Virgyn Mary and for the loue of me that ye woll take mercy of these six burgesses.

The dramatist recalled her allusion to the perils of the crossing later in the scene (157–61), when she laments the presumed loss of her son, and wishes she had died at sea. Edward's order at 61–2 to garrison the town for the winter is merely a faint hint at the aftermath of the surrender of Calais, to which Froissart devotes chapter 147 (Ker, I, 332–4), deploring the banishment of all the inhabitants in order to 'repeople agayne the towne with pure Englysshmen'.

Lines 65–96 revert to an earlier chapter in Froissart (139; Metz, pp. 87–8), relating the 'profit' that John Copland got from his capture of King David of Scotland. In reply to the king's summons, 'that he shulde come ouer the see to hym to the siege before Calays', Copland went in the autumn of 1346, at a time when Queen Philippa was still in England, but he did not take King David with him: before leaving, 'the same Johan dyd putte his prisoner in saue kepynge in a stronge castell'. Apart from the absence of both Queen and King David, the exchange between Edward and Copland (65–96) echoes Froissart very closely:

> The squyer kneled downe and sayde, Sir, yf God by his grace suffred me to take the king of Scottes by true conquest of armes, sir, I thynke no man ought to haue any enuy thereat, for as well God may sende by his grace such a fortune to fall to a poore squyer, as to a great lorde [compare 67–8, 73–5]; and sir, I requyre your grace be nat dyscontent with me, though I dyde nat delyuer the kynge of Scottes at the commaundement of the quene. Sir, I holde of you, as myne othe is to you, and nat to her but in all good maner [71–2, 79–82, 85–7]. The kyng sayd, Johan, the good seruyce that ye haue done and your valyantnesse is so moch worthe, that hit must counteruayle your trespasse and be taken for your excuse [88–91] . . . You shall retourne agayne home to your house, and thane my pleasure is that ye delyuer your prisoner to the quene my wyfe.

The announcement of the reward is closer to the more concise report in Holinshed, II, 645 (see 94–6 n.).

The arrival at this point of the Earl of Salisbury with his disastrous news is a dramatic device that differs from that used at 3.4.74 ff. (after Crécy) in so much as in this case the audience knows from 4.6 that the news of defeat is untrue, and enjoys the suspense created for the characters on stage. Perhaps this is the reason for the highly rhetorical Marlovian ring of the royal speeches at 157–75. In history, Sir Walter de Manny, the counterpart of Salisbury, reached Calais long before the end of the siege (see 97–175 n.). A further historical manipulation is the insertion here of the homage paid in 1341 by Mountford to the King of England (99–101 n.).

The last part of the scene (176–243) dispenses altogether with history: it is a celebration of the famous victory at Poitiers, on which the legendary fame of the Black Prince was based. The play is right only in stressing that it was Prince Edward's personal triumph, in so much as he was the sole commander of the 1356 campaign in France. King Edward and Queen Philippa received the news in London, but had to wait till the next winter to see their captives, King John of France and Prince Philip, after a four-day progress from Sandwich through Canterbury and Dartford, ride in the streets of the capital, the king 'on a whyte courser, well aparelled, and the prince on a lytell blacke hobbey by hym' as Froissart reports in chapter 173 (Metz, pp. 106–7). Right at the beginning of this chapter Froissart mentions Charles, when he says that the Duke of Normandy, 'as than was called regent of France', confirming that in fact he was not, as in the play, captured at Poitiers. It is curious to note how the playwright seems at some points (182 n. and 241–3 n.) to forget his decision to have Charles taken prisoner also with his father and brother.

The table on the following page shows how the plotter(s) of the play rearranged the sequence of historical events in order to achieve continuity in the dramatic action.

THE REIGN OF KING EDWARD III REARRANGED ACCORDING TO HISTORICAL CHRONOLOGY AND SHOWING PRINCIPAL SOURCES

1.1.1–50	1329	Robert of Artois expelled from France	Hol. + Frois.
1.1.51–120	1337	Declaration of war against France	Hol. + Frois.
3.1.62–189	1340	June 15 – Naval battle off Sluys	Hol. + Frois.
4.1.1–12	1341	Earl of Mountford pays homage for Brittany	Frois.
1.1.121–69	1341	War with Scotland	Frois. + Hol.
1.2	1341	Edward at Roxborough castle	Frois. (leading to Painter)
2.1 and 2	1341	Countess of Salisbury episode	Painter + Frois.
3.1.1–61	1346	French preparations for war	Hol. + Frois.
3.2	1346	July – Invasion of Normandy	Hol.
3.3.16–45	1346	July – Progress through France	Hol.
3.3.1–15	1346	August – Crossing of the Somme (Gobin de Grace)	Hol. + Frois.
3.3.46–228	1346	August 25 – Preparations for battle	Hol. + Frois.
4.5.1–55	1346	August 26 – Ravens before battle	Hol. + Frois.
3.4	1346	August 26 – Battle of Crécy	Hol. + Frois.
4.2.1–35	1346	August 30 – Beginning of siege of Calais	Frois. + Hol.
4.1.13–43	1346	September – Manny (Salisbury) seeks safe-conduct	Frois.
4.3.1–56	1346	September – Safe-conduct to Calais granted	Frois.
4.5.56–126	1346	September – Manny intercepted	Frois.
5.1.97–175	1346	September – Manny reaches Calais	Frois.
4.2.36–61	1346	September 30 – David of Scotland captured	Hol. + Frois.
5.1.63–96	1346	October – John Copland summoned to Calais	Frois.
4.2.62–85	1347	July – Conditions for surrender of Calais	Frois. + Hol.
5.1.1–62	1347	August 3 – Surrender of Calais	Frois. + Hol.
4.3.57–85	1356	September – King John at Poitiers	Hol. + Frois.
4.4	1356	September – Prince Edward at Poitiers	Hol. (+*FV*)
4.6	1356	September 19 – Battle of Poitiers	Frois. + Hol.
4.7.1–17	1356	September 19 – King John taken prisoner	Hol. + Frois.
4.7.18–64	1356	September 19 – Audley rewarded	Hol.
5.1.176–243	1356	November – Prince takes prisoners to England	Frois. + Hol.

READING LIST

This list includes works relevant to the study of *Edward III* and to the question of Shakespeare's authorship of the Apocrypha (notably the most extensive introductions to earlier editions of the play), as well as some relating to Elizabethan theatrical practice. Books on knighthood, heraldry, and providing the historical background of Edward's reign are marked by an asterisk (*).

*Allmand, Christopher. *The Hundred Years War*, 1988

*Boulton, D'A. J. D. *The Knights of the Crown: The Monarchical Orders of Knighthood in Later Medieval Europe 1325–1520*, 1987

**Bouttell's Heraldry*, revised by J. P. Brooke-Little, 1978

Bradbrook, M. C. *The Living Monument*, 1976

Bradley, David. *From Text to Performance in the Elizabethan Theatre*, 1992

Brooke, C. F. Tucker, ed. *The Shakespeare Apocrypha*, 1908

Capell, Edward. Introductory material to *Prolusions: or, select pieces of Antient Poetry. Part II. Edward the third, an historical Play*. 1760

Chambers, E. K. *The Elizabethan Stage* (4 vols.), 1923

Champion, Larry S. '"Answere in this perillous time": ideological ambivalence in *The Raigne of King Edward III* and the English chronicle plays', *ES* 69 (1988), 117–29

*Elvin, C. N. *Elvin's Handbook of Mottoes* (1860), revised with supplement and index by R. Pinches, 1971

Erickson, Peter. 'The Order of the Garter, the cult of Elizabeth, and class–gender tension in The *Merry Wives of Windsor*'. In *Shakespeare Reproduced*, ed. Jean E. Howard and Marion O'Connor, 1987, pp. 116–40

Everitt, E. B. 'The Young Shakespeare', *Anglistica* 2 (1954)

Everitt, E. B., ed. *Six Early Plays Related to the Shakespeare Canon*, *Anglistica*, 14, (1965)

*Gies, Frances. *The Knight in History*, 1986

Greenblatt, Stephen. 'Invisible bullets'. In *Political Shakespeare*, ed. John Dollimore and Alan Sinfeld, 1985, pp. 18–47

Hart, Alfred. 'The vocabulary of *Edward III*'. In his *Shakespeare and the Homilies*, 1934, pp. 219–41

Stolne and Surreptitious Copies, 1942

*Harvey, John. *The Black Prince and His Age*, 1976

*Hewitt, H. J. *The Organization of War under Edward III 1338–1362*, 1966

Hope, Jonathan. *The Authorship of Shakespeare's Plays*, 1994

Isar, Wolfgang. *Staging Politics*, 1993

Jackson, MacD. P. '*Edward III*, Shakespeare, and Pembroke's Men', *N&Q* 210 (1965), 329–31

Koskenniemi, Inna. 'Themes and imagery in *Edward III*', *NM* 65 (1964), 146–80

Lapides, Fred. Introduction to *The Raigne of King Edward the Third. A Critical, Old-Spelling Edition*, 1980

*McCoy, Richard C. *The Rites of Knighthood: The Literature and Politics of Elizabethan Knighthood*, 1989

McMillin, Scott. *The Elizabethan Theatre and 'The Book of Sir Thomas More'*. 1987

Matthews, Robert A. J. and Thomas V. N. Merriam, 'Neural computation in stylometry II: an application to the works of Shakespeare and Marlowe', *L&LC* 9 (1994), 1–6

Melchiori, Giorgio. *Shakespeare's Dramatic Meditations: An Experiment in Criticism*, 1976

Shakespeare's Garter Plays. 'Edward III' to 'Merry Wives of Windsor', 1994

Shakespeare. Genesi e struttura delle opere, 1994

Merriam, T. V. N. 'Marlowe's hand in *Edward III*', *L&LC* 8 (1993), 59–72

Metz, G. Harold. *Four Plays Ascribed to Shakespeare. An Annotated Bibliography*, 1982

Sources of Four Plays Ascribed to Shakespeare, 1989

Muir, Kenneth. *Shakespeare as Collaborator*, 1960

O'Connor, F. *The Road to Stratford*, 1948

*Ormrod, W. M. *The Reign of Edward III*, 1990

Østerberg, V. 'The "Countess Scenes" of *Edward III*', *Shakespeare Jahrbuch* 65 (1929), 49–91

*Packe, Michael. *King Edward III*, ed. L. C. B. Seaman, 1983

*Perroy, Edouard. *The Hundred Years War*, trans. by W. B. Wells, 1951

Pinciss, G. M. 'Shakespeare, Her Majesty's Players and Pembroke's Men', *S.Sur.* 27 (1974), 129–36

*Prestwich, Michael. *The Three Edwards*. 1980

Prior, Roger. 'The date of *Edward III*', *N&Q* 235 (1990), 178–80

'Was *The Raigne of King Edward III* a compliment to Lord Hunsdon?', *Connotations* 3 (1993/4), 243–64

Proudfoot, Richard. '*The Reign of King Edward the third* (1596) and Shakespeare', *PBA* 71 (1985), 169–85

Rabkin, Norman. *Shakespeare and the Problem of Meaning*, 1981

Riggs, David. *Shakespeare's Heroical Histories: 'Henry VI' and its Literary Tradition*, 1971

Rossiter, A. P. *Angel with Horns and Other Shakespearian Lectures*, 1961

*Rudorff, Raymond. *The Knights and their World*, 1974

Salingar, Leo. 'The "grand design" of Shakespeare's first history plays'. In *Surprised by Scenes*, ed. Yasunari Takada, 1994, pp. 41–53

Sams, Eric. *The Real Shakespeare. Retrieving the Early Years, 1564–1594*, 1995

Slater, Eliot. *The Problem of 'The Reign of King Edward III': A Statistical Approach*, 1988

Smith. M. W. A. 'The authorship of *The Raigne of King Edward the Third*'. *L&LC* 6 (1991), 166–75

Smith, Robert Metcalf. 'Edward III (a study of the authorship of the drama in the light of a new source)', *JEGP* 10 (1911), 90–104

Tillyard, E. M. W. *Shakespeare's History Plays*. 1944

*Vale, Juliet. *Edward III and Chivalry: Chivalric Society and its Context, 1270–1350*, 1982

Warnke, Karl and Ludwig Proescholdt, eds. Introduction to *Pseudo-Shakespearian Plays* (5 vols.), vol. III: *Edward III*, 1886

Wentersdorf, Karl P. 'The date of *Edward III*', *SQ* 16 (1965) 227–31

'The origin and personnel of the Pembroke Company', *TRI* 5 (1989–90), 45–68

Yates, Frances A. *Astraea: The Imperial Theme in the Sixteenth Century*, 1975